Th

12

26.

-2.

2

y

1

14

THE HIDDEN STRUGGLE

The Hidden Struggle

Statutory and voluntary sector responses to violence against black women in the home

Amina Mama

Acknowledgements

The Hidden Struggle owes its existence to the courage and commitment of all the women who participated in the study, and is dedicated to their liberation and that of oppressed women worldwide. Nor would it have been possible without the help of all the dedicated workers and residents in the participating London Refuges, at the London Office and at WAFE's National Office in Bristol. These, and the many other women who cannot be named, worked on the project and helped in ways too numerous to detail.

Ayesha Mangera and Audrey Donegan conducted many of the interviews with emotional strength, compassion and respect for the women who shared their experience with us. Sheila Brown-Peterside transcribed most of the interviews.

The London Race and Housing Research Unit commissioned and conceptualised the research, and went on to support the project long after they had been closed down themselves. I would especially thank Errol Lawrence and Grace Natoolo, but also Neetinder Boparai, Terry Waterman, Beverly Mullings, Sabes Sugunasabesan, Marcia and Sharon. Veronica Hill and Claudia Bernard, members of the project steering group, worked on the manuscript and actively supported the project in a number of ways all the way through.

Chetan Bhatt and Kaushika Amin became good friends in the course of giving their practical and political support to the project. Thanks also to David Rosenberg, Ovais, Joan, Lola, Richard and Anna at Runnymede Trust.

Adotey Bing, Wanjiru Kihoro, the members of Akina Mama Wa Afrika and other close friends gave me personal support and a positive angle on life during the hardest periods of this work.

Amina Mama

Published by the London Race and Housing Research Unit
c/o The Runnymede Trust, 11 Princelet Street, London E1 6QH
December 1989
ISBN 0 9514833 2 3
© Amina Mama
Designed by David Rosenberg
Typeset and printed by the Russell Press, Nottingham

Contents

List of illustrations

Preface

This is the first comprehensive study in Britain that looks specifically at black women's experience of domestic violence. It focuses on women from African, Asian and Caribbean backgrounds, who have experienced domestic violence, whether emotional or physical.

From the beginning of this project we were very much aware of the lack of material which considered black women's specific experience in any depth. Where references to black women were found they were often incidental, relegated to a footnote and more often than not perpetuated stereotypical notions such as the passive Asian woman and the strong matriachal African/Caribbean woman.

The central focus of this study is the manner in which racism and sexism combine to further exacerbate the problems that these women face. Given the cultural background of the women concerned this study places this complex and multi-faceted problem within a historical, international and political context.

Given the traumatic nature of domestic violence, notions of eurocentric and androcentric research practice were discarded in order that the findings would be rich and substantive. This was achieved by a research methodology which was sensitively designed and conducted; all the interviewers were black women and wherever possible they were ethnically matched.

Once again this study highlights the common experience of black researchers, investigating the black experience — the pressure on them to conduct in-depth examination covering all issues vis-a-vis black people — something that a lack of resources does not facilitate. This was the experience of this project, where the lack of resources militated against the possibility of examining, for example, the causes of domestic violence, although we are aware of the existence of numerous theoretical explanations which consider this. This lack of resources further influenced the manner in which this project developed. For example, the research was initially supposed to take one year and be informed by a steering group of about ten members whose role it was to collate and disseminate information with a view to developing themes and discussion around black women's experience of domestic violence. However, the project lasted for two years and on its completion only two members of the steering group remained.

This study considers the development of an international perspective of domestic violence as it introduces the cultures and socio-political factors apparent in these women's countries of origin which are important to consider when attempting to analyse this issue. The study also highlights how these factors have some relevance when we examine how statutory agencies respond to black women. For example, we were able to demonstrate how the police's response to domestic violence in the black community, is often as oppressive as their policing of that community in general. We use case studies to demonstrate how requested police intervention in domestic violence incidents resulted in them choosing to focus on matters of immigration rather than investigating the matter they were initially called to deal with.

The study further exposes the manner in which racist assumptions operate to reduce the efficacy of existing policies and practices on domestic violence in both statutory and non-statutory agencies.

In addition the study examines the strategies used by the women to facilitate their attempts to reduce or otherwise cope with violence. This was done so as not to present the women as passive victims, but to recognise that the women were trying to take some control of their lives but more often than not lacked the resources or were given very little support — hence the title, *The Hidden Struggle*.

This study is an important contribution to the growing literature on domestic violence and crimes against women, as it adds a perspective far too often ignored; notably that of black women.

Claudia Bernard
Veronica Hill
October 1989

Summary

The Hidden Struggle is the outcome of a research project commissioned by the London Race and Housing Research Unit, as part of a range of action-research projects carried out in the Greater London area. It is the first ever study of domestic violence in London's black communities and includes the detailed and insightful accounts of women from the African, Asian and Caribbean communities. These describe how they have survived a series of brutalisations at the hands of their menfolk and a range of statutory organisations. Not only do black women, like black men, have their lives circumscribed and limited by widespread racism in British society, but inestimable numbers are also subjected to extremely oppressive and often violent behaviour from the men they live with.

Based on over one hundred depth interviews, *The Hidden Struggle* documents and analyses the prevailing political conditions which force many women to tolerate high levels of abuse both inside their homes and when they leave violent men. In the case of black women, male violence in the home is compounded by general societal racism and state repression, to create a situation of multiple oppression and further punishment for those bravely struggling to establish lives for themselves and their children, away from violent men.

While black women as well as black men are subjected to the physical violence and abuse of race attacks and coercive inner-city policing, black women are also expected to continue to show sympathy and understanding when the men that live with them also turn violent. The prevalence of violence against women in the black communities illustrates the full meaning of triple oppression along the dimensions of race, class and sex.

Many black women are having to abandon their homes to escape life-threatening abuse from men with whom they have been having relationships. Many are seriously injured by both violence and the breakdown of their relationship, as are their children. It is in this state that they are forced to confront the additional traumas of long term homelessness.

The experience of homelessness, damaging to any family at the best of times, is particularly painful where the family have already been traumatised by male violence. For black women, all of this is made worse by the racism and sexism they are subjected to by the various statutory agencies they will be forced to have contact with as they struggle to obtain temporary accommodation, rehousing, financial support and legal assistance. Existing services and provisions are particularly inadequate when it comes to meeting the needs of black women seeking to build lives away from violent partners. The research discovered,for example, that black women and their children are spending between 18 months and three years waiting for rehousing after they have become homeless through fleeing violence. It also exposes the conditions of temporary accommodation and the negative effects of lengthy stays in such accommodation on the physical and mental health of these already vulnerable families. This situation is getting steadily worse with the erosion of all forms of welfare by the Thatcher Government.

The invaluable role that the women's movement has struggled to play through the establishment of a network of refuges is commended in the report and on the basis of consultation with the refuge movement and black women working within it, strategies for development towards meeting the needs of women from the minority communities are outlined.

On the more disturbing side, police responses to domestic violence against black women come in for serious criticism in the report because of the insults and abuses, and in some cases further violence that police inflicted on some of the women in this study. This evidence is timely, and must be of particular concern in view of recent attempts by the Metropolitan Police to develop more sympathetic responses to domestic violence. These have included the recent establishment of domestic violence response units in black communities. Clearly the race implications of these developments have to be addressed before the women's movement can herald them uncritically as positive initiatives. Similarly, the report highlights the need for a critical assessment of the wider political implications of increasing police powers in an area where the main problem has not been the lack of police power. On the contrary, as other studies have shown and as this study confirms, the main problem continues to be the refusal of police officers to enforce the existing law in relation to crimes not thought to be 'proper police work'.

Racist and sexist immigration laws are exposed as compounding the damaging effects of male violence and coercion in the home. The scandalous situation in which British men can call the immigration department to deport wives they have abused, or simply decided that they have no further use for, is condemned. So is the use of the immigration service by some men to further terrorise the women with whom they live. Immigration law currently empowers individual men to torture with impunity, women with uncertain or dependent immigration status, because it enables them to threaten to have the woman deported, perhaps away from her British born children,

The policing of all welfare and health services in the name of immigration is also a means of excluding black women from support. Welfare is being policed with increasing stringency, even as it is being eroded by Central Government. It is black women who are most often asked to 'prove' their eligibility for healthcare and other forms of welfare. Whether or not they are entitled to such provision, black women are met with suspicion and called on to prove their right to resources that their own taxes and national insurance may have paid for. Some escape violence without obtaining their passports from their spouses, and those here as dependent wives would in any case be excluded by the 'no recourse to public funds' clauses.

Social services responses were found to be contingent on whether there are children at risk. For some women, childcare support and temporary fostering are appreciated, but for many, contact with a social worker was forced on women by housing departments 'passing the buck' instead of rehousing the family. In some instances women were cautioned that their children would be removed from them if they did not leave the violent man. However, leaving sometimes resulted in mothers of British born children being threatened with deportation by the Home Office. Thus the women were placed them in a vicious and inhuman dilemma.

The housing outlook is also bad, with privatisation and the more general introduction of 'market forces' undermining the improved access to affordable public sector homes that women have gained through the struggles waged by the women's movement inside and outside public housing bureaucracies. While the policies addressing women's housing have not always addressed race equality in their implementation, there is no doubt that black women have also benefited from women's improved access to council homes. Even these small gains, however, are now being undermined with the decrease in the public housing stock that most women depend upon. Black families are already concentrated in the worst quality accommodation, testimony to long term racism in the allocation of housing. Unless urgent measures are taken, this situation will be going from bad to worse in the context of the more general housing crisis. Housing stress is not only implicated as a cause of domestic violence, but also as a factor forcing many women, and especially black women, to remain in life-threatening situations.

Autonomous women's refuges appear to be the only form of support currently available to women who have been subjected to violence. Yet they have continued to be grossly under-resourced. This means that despite all the commitment and expertise of refuge workers, the refuge movement is unable to keep up with the growing demands on their service. The situation is becoming chronic, since the temporary accommodation that they do offer is being kept fully occupied as a result of the growing lengths of time it is taking for women to be rehoused. Thus the specialist temporary houses organised and managed by autonomous groups of women are forced to become longstay hostels, and the commendable goals and targets of the refuge movement are thereby being undermined. Growing numbers of black women now live and work in refuges, and Women's Aid Federation are committed to anti-racism. There are a small number of refuges specifically for black women, but these are discriminated against by funding bodies so that although they face additional burdens of work, they receive less money per bedspace than other refuges.

The Hidden Struggle throws down a challenge to housing activists, feminists and community workers to take action against the present trends in housing and social policy, and to rally around black women who are at present left to wage a hidden and individualised struggle against huge and often hostile state bureaucracies, simply for the freedom to live free from violent abuse in safe and decent homes. Finally, the report includes a range of recommendations for action to ameliorate the desperate situation currently facing many black women.

PART I: Behind closed doors: violence against black and Third World women

1. Developing an international perspective on violence against women

Violence against women as the enactment of power relations

Over the last decade, violence against women has received some long overdue attention in various parts of the world. This is at least partly due to the continuing growth and development of women's struggles in all corners of the globe both during and since the United Nations Decade for Women. These factors have assisted the international manifestation of the women's movement.

In this chapter we shall briefly look at some of the international material on domestic violence, for the purpose of setting out the wider terrain on which to develop our understanding of the violence inflicted on black women by their sexual and/or emotional partners in Britain, and the responses of various agencies to this. Examples of violence, and of some of the attempts to combat it are presented from a range of different nations, cultures and socio-political contexts.

Western feminists took up the challenge of combating violence against women as perhaps the most central terrain on which to fight the battle for women's liberation. In the West it is sexual violence which has been most publicly addressed, and this has been termed 'male violence'. The vigorous anti-pornography campaigns of the late '70s and early '80s directed women's anger at the multi-million dollar industry which they saw as being underlined by misogyny and feeding into sexual violence by creating and reproducing a culture of contempt for women.

Feminist writings of the period reflect the developing analyses of violence against women (see eg Kanter et al (eds.) 1984, Rhodes and McNeill eds. 1985). While radical feminists for the most part take male violence against women as a 'natural' result of patriarchy, socialist feminists in the West have been more inclined to focus on the role of class divisions and the machinations of international capital. Both schools have fallen short of being able to generate frameworks that incorporate all the basic facts of woman abuse.

Black feminists in the West have demanded that race, religion and culture be incorporated into the analysis of violence against women. In doing so they have begun to articulate an approach which challenges the ethnocentrism and essentialism of the approaches that have been generated by those Western feminists who have focused too narrowly on patriarchy and sexual oppression, and therefore failed to consider class, racial and cultural oppressions. In other words, it has become clear that in order to challenge violence against women it is necessary to develop a feminist praxis that takes the various social divisions more fully into account. Black women and women in Asia, Africa and the Americas have begun to do this.

The assumption that violence against women is necessarily or intrinsically 'male', for example, has been challenged by black women in the West. Davis (1984) is one of several who have pointed out (in reference to the United States of America) that black men have been subjected to violence, including the sexual violence of castration during lynchings, by white men and women. Amin (1987) has drawn attention to the fact that white women as well as men also inflict violence on black women through their participation in race attacks in Britain, while Bhavnani (1988) has raised the pertinent question of whether violence is 'masculine' in her critique of white feminist perspectives on violence.

For the broader international women's movement, north, south, east and west, violence against women has generally been articulated as the crude use of physical force to coerce women into the subordinate position afforded them by patriarchal societies.

The evidence below indicates not only the international prevalence of violence against women, but also the dynamism with which women's organisations across the globe have responded to oppression through violent abuse. The diversity of strategies and organisation adopted by the international women's movement supports the thesis that oppressed groups will find ways of resisting, however crude and extreme their subjugation is. There is not the space or time to do justice to the material here but since our purpose is to develop a general framework for analysing domestic violence against women in any particular context, I have thought it necessary to provide a brief overview of the international situation in order to highlight some general themes that emerge from such a consideration.

This review has also been stimulated by a more general recognition of the inadequacy of existing Western feminist theory (radical, liberal and

4

socialist) for considering the social lives and circumstances of black women in the West. This inadequacy is even more apparent when we come to consider women in the countries of Africa, Asia and the Americas. I have opted to place examples of violence against women alongside a review of the feminist praxis emerging independently in the peripheral capitalist countries that black women living in the West originate from, rather than attempting to reformulate and develop Western feminist theory to 'fit around' black women (African, Asian and Caribbean women in particular).

This is an approach informed by my earlier work and experience in black and African women's organisations which all indicates that the social situation of black women in Britain can best be understood when our analyses incorporate both the history of black people and current international relations between Britain and the capitalist periphery. These international relations manifest at the source, so to speak, in racist immigration laws, popular culture and in the political discourses of contemporary Britain. Imperial social relations are particularly important in considering what happens at the interface between black women and British statutory institutions and voluntary organisations.

The framework developed here will then be applied in the rest of this report, to an analysis of both state and voluntary sector responses to domestic violence in the black communities, in one particular post industrial society — Britain.

Violence against black and Third World women and the struggle against it

Asia

In some parts of Asia, notably India, a strong women's movement has developed, and struggled bitterly against many of the patriarchal practices that are damaging to women. Campaigns have been waged against *suttee* and dowry deaths as well as against the more widespread everyday violence and abuse of wives by husbands, policemen, landowners and in-laws (see the Indian feminist journal *Manushi*, and Mies 1986 for examples). The nature of violence against women was summed up at the end of a meeting on Women and Violence organised by the South Gujerat University and Centre for Women's Development Studies in January 1985:

'The specificity of the gender dimension lies in the fact that while violence against women perceived as a structural phenomenon is indeed

5

part of the general violence against oppressed classes, the forms of control and coercion exercised in the case of women are gender specific and arise out of a hierarchical gender relationship, where men are dominant and women are subordinate. The forms of control exercised over women cover essentially three areas: sexuality, fertility and labour. Secondly, women become instruments through which the social system reproduces itself and through which systemic inequality is maintained. This is achieved through rules of legitimacy of offspring, through controlling sexual access to women (as for example in cast-endogamy rules) and in general through the establishment of possessional rights over women which men have as husbands, or fathers or older male relations. Such possessional rights include promise of protection (whether actually fulfilled or not in reality) in return for submission and exclusive use. This is further strengthened and maintained over time by the socialisation process that embeds women strongly within the familial structure and hierarchic gender relations such that they have little or no independent status, and transgressions outside the family and male authority expose them to swift retributions and confirm their vulnerability' (cited in Kelkar 1987).

Violence against women then, is fundamentally about enforcing power relations between men and women. There is however a strong class-caste component. Kelkar goes on to note that mass rapes of women have traditionally been an instrument for the repression of landless labourers and poor peasants, which is used whenever these social groups get organised or show militancy. In addressing the lack of legal action in cases of woman abuse, she notes that a high proportion of rapes in rural areas are committed by government officials. Violence against women, she concludes, must be understood in terms of broader relations between people and the state, and in terms of the ideologies of subordination geared to maintaining particular forms of exploitation, and the oppression of women in particular.

Both Kelkar and Mies observe that there has been an increase in dowry-deaths in recent years. They relate this to what we can refer to as the increased commoditization of social relationships, pointing out that in this context, women are burned when their own relatives are unable to meet the endless demands of their in-laws for money and domestic goods. Disposing of the bride in this way enables the man's family to arrange another marriage for him, and so open up a new route for their accumulation of goods and cash at a time of economic stress and national

6

indebtedness. Both Kelkar and Mies draw attention to the lack of police action in such cases. Ninety per cent of all deaths of women by burning in Delhi are recorded as 'accidents', only 5 per cent as murders and a further 5 per cent as suicides. Delhi has a shocking death-through-burning rate and in this city alone in 1983 an average of two women died of burns every day, figures which recall the spectre of the great European witch hunts of an earlier epoch, during which an estimated 6-8 million women were tortured, dismembered and burnt alive (Mies 1986).

The historical relations between Asian women and Europe are also relevant to our consideration of violence against women. During the colonial occupation too, the administration refused to act against the perpetrators of woman abuse (Mies 1986). The history of relations between women from the Indian subcontinent and Europe depends very much on which class-caste of women we choose to consider. Documentation indicates that women in India and what is now Pakistan, like those in other colonies, served as domestics and childcarers (Ayahs) for European families during the occupation. Visram (1986) notes that many Indian women came to Britain in earlier centuries when these families returned. Once the long voyage was over, many were discharged and left to fend for themselves. Romantic fiction has dwelt on sexual relations between European men and Indian women, and the fate of the offspring of such relationships, at some length. In such films and literature, 'the Indian woman' is treated as an exotic and mysterious sexual object, beautifully clothed, supremely passive, and fundamentally unintelligent. She has wiles but not brains. The facts, as usual, tell a very different tale. The primary relationship of women from the Indian subcontinent to Europe has been one of exploitation and domestic servitude; endless hours of grinding labour in factories and sweatshops, minding the offspring of the colonisers, scrubbing and cleaning their affluent homes.

In contemporary times, as the literature of the Indian women's movement indicates, we see a growing militancy among Asian women workers and a shattering of imperial-racist stereotypes about passivity and submissiveness, both on the Indian subcontinent and in the metropolis.

In South East Asia, Malaysian, Singaporean, Indonesian and other groups of women are actively analysing and fighting against the derogation of women within oppressive and exploitative social relations. In Thailand, a collective of social activists established the Women's Information Centre (WIC), which initially aimed to improve the situation of Thai women, especially prostitutes working both locally and overseas. There are an estimated 700,000 prostitutes in the country. The Thai prostitution industry is one legacy of the huge American military bases set up to facilitate their operations in South East Asia (Vietnam in particular). It now also services the tourist industry. The staff of the Women's Information Centre soon observed that large numbers (50%) of the women they worked with suffered inordinate amounts of physical violence, either at the hands of their own husbands, or at the hands of their clients and pimps (Skrobanek 1987). They set up the Women's Shelter Programme to offer temporary refuge to women for mental and physical recovery and to offer legal consultation (WIC 1987).

Like Thailand, the Philippines under the Marcos dictatorship saw prostitution developing as a major source of foreign exchange, closely linked to sex tourism and 'hospitality'. In both contexts this often involves young children being sold or kidnapped into sexual slavery in the cities. The sex tourism industry does not only deal in girls and women. In the West, a gay magazine comments that boys can be brought for a packet of cigarettes in the Philippines (Mercer and Julien 1988 p134).

The economic underdevelopment in these nations also forces women to seek employment abroad; as domestic helpers, chambermaids or through commercialised marriage arrangements. Filipinas are openly advertised as 'pliant, submissive and domesticated' yet 'passionate' women; women who, despite being poverty-stricken, 'bestow their friendship for free'. Despite their long history of colonisation and Catholicism, Filipino women are described as possessing 'traditional values', a portrayal which provokes a question about just whose traditions they are alleged to be upholding. Commercial marriage bureaux have grown out of this situation. These hold out the promise, through arranged marriages to European men, of a better life and the possibility of being able to send money home to poor relatives. This situation places many women in extremely vulnerable situations both at home and in the West, where they are isolated and have few civil rights as 'imported wives' on marital visas, and where they can be subjected to extreme forms of abuse (Raquisa 1987, Gabriela 1986 Statement).

The relationship of servitude and sexploitation between women from Asia and the West is a direct product of both colonial and military history and contemporary economic relations. It has direct implications for the treatment and status of Asian women both in those countries and in the West, as this report will go on to demonstrate.

Africa

On the African continent too, the abuse of women is widespread. Since the commercial basis of marriage is quite different from that on the Indian subcontinent, dowry deaths do not occur, and the murder of wives which occurs here, is the result of different types of economic bondage. Generally, tradition has it that the brides family receive money from the husbands, rather than providing money to the family into which their daughter is married. In addition to wife-beating by husbands, violence against young wives by their in-laws however, is also commonplace in Africa, as it is in Asia. It is simply that the local practices and forms it takes have their own cultural content. Where households are polygamous for example, violence and mental torture may be inflicted by co-wives. This is most commonly the persecution of younger wives by senior wives, indicating the role that power relations play even between women in the household. Nowadays inter-wife conflict, may be exacerbated by the fact that later marriages are often to a younger, westernised wife who the traditional first wife finds unacceptable, and by whom she feels degraded. In other words rural-urban, traditional-modern, ethnic and religious divisions may feed into the animosities based on sexual jealousy and competition over resources. This implies that even between wives, woman abuse is rooted in the social relations of the society, and that these favour men and the dominant women (Thiam 1986).

In various parts of Africa, a range of culturally sanctioned mutilations of women occur, often with severely damaging effects. Nawal el Sadaawi (from Egypt) discusses the practice of genital mutilation in the Arab world (including Arabic-speaking parts of Africa) in the context of the status of women in the history and culture of ancient Egypt and Islam (El Sadaawi 1980). Female circumcision and infibulation in Sudan and the Horn of Africa have also received some attention, and have been challenged by health and educational organisations over the years (Asma El Dareer 1982, Raqiya Haji Dualeh Abdalla 1982). These practices have been exposed as crude means for enforcing subordination and control over the sexuality and reproductive capacity of women, regardless of the pain, physical damage and even deaths, caused. Removal of the clitoris, in contrast to male circumcision literally means excising the woman's ability to enjoy sex. Stitching the vagina up after each delivery is the most extreme form of enforcing chastity, causing a build-up of scar tissue and often subsequent delivery complications. In contexts lacking sterilisation facilities infections are common, resulting in sterility, rejection and ostracism, and sometimes, death.

In Subsaharan Africa too, circumcision has come under attack, as have other forms of surgical wounding inflicted on women. Thiam (1986) documents these and other aspects of women's oppression in Black Africa on the basis of research in Guinea, Mali, Ghana, Nigeria and Cote D'Ivoire. According to her, excision and infibulation are practised in Cote D'Ivoire, Burkina Faso, Mali, Guinea, Niger, Senegal, Benin (as well as Somalia, Sudan, Egypt, Ethiopia and Algeria), and amongst Muslims, Christians and Animists alike. Yet neither the Bible nor the Koran advocate genital mutilation. Koso-Thomas (1987) conducted a detailed study of circumcision in Sierra Leone, highlighting the negative consequences on women's health and fertility. In Nigeria, another form of 'genital cutting' also occurs, particularly done to women in labour suspected of having obstruction. Known locally as 'gishiri cutting' ('gishiri' literally means salt in Hausa), the anterior wall of the vagina is cut with a razor, supposedly to make the childbirth easier. In the process, however, the urethra, bladder and other internal organs may be damaged, and infections introduced. This cutting, like childhood pregnancy can result in vesico-vaginal fistula, characterised by urinal incontinence, which in turn leads to social ostracism (Women In Nigeria 1985). The fact that women carry out these practices challenges oversimplistic analyses about 'male violence' and raises important questions about the nature of patriarchy, and women's *active* participation in it. More specifically it suggests that in certain contexts women have vested interests in these forms of mutilation.

The murder of wives has also been observed to often go unchallenged. In some cases this is the result of her lacking any protection from her own family, particularly where her parents are indebted to her spouse. In such cases her removal to her husband's home may well have been a vain attempt to settle accumulated obligations on the part of her family. Marriages contracted on such a basis leave the bride in an unprotected situation. The tragic case of Hauwa Abubakar a 12 year-old girl who died in March 1987 is a case in point. She lost both legs after her husband, one Shehu Kiruwa, took an axe to her after she had repeatedly ran away from him. In this incident, Hauwa's family owed money to the man that they had promised her to three years earlier. Because of their indebtedness, they were not in a position to repay the brideprice and so allow her to remain at home when she ran to them. Nor were they in a position to protest or take legal action when she died after lying for days, refusing to eat, in a local hospital.[1] This case would have passed unnoticed (probably like many others) had it not been taken up by Women In Nigeria (WIN), an autonomous Nigerian women's organisation. It raises important points about the economic conditions under which women are abused with impunity.

Another disturbing feature exacerbating violence against women is the upsurge of various forms of religious fundamentalism, accompanied by scapegoating and derogation of women. In Kano, Northern Nigeria, an underground brotherhood known as 'yan daukar amariya' was revealed when several members of them were arrested for rape and violent abuse of women (West Africa, 4 March 1987). Their professed purpose was to molest and violate women found on the streets alone, on the basis that they should not be there. This would be alarming in any context, but is particularly so in a context where, in 1986, the Kano state government itself saw fit to 'outlaw' single women, delivering an ultimatum of three months for all women to get married or 'be dealt with'. This decree gave license to village heads and all other functionaries to harass and violate women with impunity. In effect their actions were 'law enforcement'. Most of the above examples have been taken up and challenged by WIN.

In Eastern and Southern Africa we have also seen some campaigns and actions against wife-beating and other forms of woman abuse, with varying degrees of governmental support. We have also seen situations in which African governments and other authorities have been exposed as main perpetrators of woman abuse.

In Kenya for example, with its big-game tourist industry and American military bases, relations between Europe and African women have progressed little from the colonial days of hard labour on white farms and domestic and sexual servitude to settler families. Rape and abuse of Kenyan women by bored American soldiers with their inherent disrespect for Third World people is covered up and unchallenged. In a context of economic underdevelopment, where productive employment is not widely available to women, prostitution is an important means of income-generation for many. In a political double standard, prostitution is tolerated (presumably as a sort of 'tourist service' as it is in many parts of South East Asia), but prostitutes are afforded no legal protection against abuse. In an atmosphere like this, it is not therefore surprising to find that members of Parliament were united in opposition to legislative reforms to the laws left (and since abandoned) by the British, where these reforms were designed to combat wife-beating. Ironically the refusal to reform this aspect of the colonial legacy was opposed in the name of 'African tradition' in 1968, just after independence (Nairobi Law Monthly February 1988). As Betty Nafuna Wamalwa (1987) has noted however, traditions, while tolerating some degree of wife-beating, also restricted both its frequency and severity, and wives could appeal to parents or elders, or in some contexts, to traditional women's councils. Clearly the scandalous case of Piah Njoki had little to do with 'traditional' male rights. In 1983, her husband, helped by two other men gouged out both of her eyes as punishment for bearing him only daughters. The fact that as many as 40 per cent of the cases of domestic violence reported in the Kenyan newspaper *Nation* over a nine-year period (1976-1985) were actually killings (and most of the perpetrators were sentenced quite lightly), indicates a high degree of toleration by the authorities, of violence against women at the hands of the men they are in relationships with. The same study indicates that wife maiming and killing occurs in rural as well as urban areas (Wamalwa 1987).

In Zimbabwe the abuse of black women by the authorities has provoked some outcry, even since independence. This is particularly disturbing in the light of women's active participation in the war for liberation, since it would suggest some regression of the status of women since ZANU became the government. During November 1983 several thousand women were arrested and detained, often to the accompaniment of beating and victimisation by government officials and members of youth brigades in an exercise termed 'Operation Clean-up'. This had been intended to rid the streets of 'vagrants' and 'beggars', using the emergency clause of the infamous Vagrancy Act of 1960. On one occasion 200 women workers were picked up at Mutare, on their way to work in the Liebzig factory, and detained in a football stadium. This led their manager to conclude that they had gone on strike (Zimbabwe Women's Action Group 1987). Women here were made the main targets of the furore over 'moral laxity', just as they had been in Kano State, Nigeria.

In South Africa and Namibia, both structural and direct violence against African people are integral to the apartheid system. Women are not exempt from the violence, harassment, detention and torture that the apartheid state inflicts on the African population. Domestic servitude is the main source of employment available to African women, and this in a context in which inter-racial sexual violence can occur with impunity, much as it did during slavery in the Americas.

In the townships, high levels of violence of all kinds prevail. The situation is extreme, and to discuss violence against African women in South Africa or Namibia is to reflect on mass murder; the genocide of women, children and men by the apartheid regime and its supporters in the West (*African Woman*, 2). As we would expect, some African men adopt the values of their oppressors and/or draw on their own patriarchal traditions to abuse African women in this context.

The political character of the African countries mentioned so far is one in which woman abuse in the home is tolerated, as are many other forms of woman-abuse. Indeed the state apparatuses and law enforcers themselves frequently perpetrate acts of violence towards women. However, there are African nations where the governments have actively promoted women's development and involvement in political and productive processes. In Angola, Mozambique and Guinea-Bissau for example, we have seen radical changes in the legal system left by the colonialists (see OMA, 1984 and Urdang, 1979). This has been accompanied by the setting up of mass women's organisations which are autonomous but supported and encouraged by these governments. In all of these contexts sexual exploitation and violence against women are central issues that have been actively taken up and campaigned against, so that while wife-beating and murder have not been eliminated they are being challenged, and the social process can at least be said to be pointing in the right direction.

Unhappily, in the frontline states of Mozambique and Angola, national development efforts including those aiming to curb woman-abuse are being overtaken by the South African regimes destabilisation strategy. African women are suffering the most extreme forms of violence as a result of the constant attacks by the (Mozambique National Resistance) (MNR) in Mozambique and the UNITA forces in Angola, both of which are backed by the apartheid regime. The toll that the war is taking militates against all programmes and plans for both national development, and women's development. This has been the situation since the victorious wars of liberation, which should have allowed these nations to start effecting their own social processes. Instead development efforts have constantly been held back, with resources being poured into defence against regular military incursions and sabotage. Huge numbers of women are raped, mutilated and murdered by terrorists on a daily basis, while the West watches and continues to economically sustain the apartheid regime.[2]

In the context of the long and tragic history of colonial brutalisation of African people, this continuing holocaust can only leave one wondering why the violation, mutilation and murder of African women, men and children (UNICEF 1987) that is occurring in the frontline states is not considered to be a serious slur on humanity.

The Americas

Like Asia and Africa, the Americas have a long history of colonial relations. The majority of the population in the Caribbean, and a significant proportion of the population in North and South America, were imported from Africa and Asia as slaves and indentured labourers respectively. The situation of women during the period of slavery and since has been well-documented in recent years (Lerner (ed) 1973, Davis 1981, Steady 1981, Hull et al (eds) 1982, Aptheker 1982, Ellis 1986). The role of African women as heavy labourers on the plantations, alongside African men has been highlighted. So has the sexual exploitation of black women by the white plantation owners and overseers. In short, black women in the Americas have, along with their sisters in Africa and Asia, suffered extreme forms of violence in the context of their exploitation as slave labour, and later as cheap labour.

In Nicaragua, where the government has introduced more progressive policies on women, the situation is similar to that of the African front line states, with women and men being killed in the American backed war being waged by the Contras. Despite these wider problems, however, women's liberation is still very much on the national political agenda. In Cuba, ideological war and economic isolation from the West have failed to arrest the social processes which have included the liberation of Cuban women and which are encapsulated in the Cuban Family Code. The status of women in that society now sets it ahead of the rest of the Caribbean and Latin America.

Since the nominal independence of some Caribbean countries, the impact of a tourist industry relying on the descendents of slavers and plantation owners, has worked against fundamental changes in the class, race and gender characteristics of those countries' social relations. Black women continue to be marginalised and derogated (often still according to the darkness of their skin), and crimes of violence are commonplace. Kamugisha (1986) observes that crimes of violence against women have been on the increase during the '70s and '80s in the places she examined (Trinidad and Tobago, Barbados and Jamaica):

'crimes of violence against women — rape, incest, sexual harassment — are prevalent throughout the Caribbean. Women are beaten, mentally abused, raped and sexually harassed . . . on the streets, in their workplace and in their homes in practically every Caribbean country'.

She notes that some women's organisations have started to take up the issue: in Jamaica she cites the Committee of Women for Progress, in Trinidad Concerned Women for Progress and the Women's arm of the National Joint Action Committee. In Trinidad the government has set land aside for a women's refuge.

Gordon too, writing of Jamaica (1986) records an increase in rape and wife-battering, and cites women complaining that police refused to offer any assistance to women beaten by their husbands. The deep misogyny in the lyrics of many contemporary reggae artists testifies to the nature of gender relations in contemporary Jamaica, as the macho quality of the earlier 'Rudie' culture did. On the other side of the coin, the survival of Caribbean women, against all odds, is testified in the work of women's groups and organisations. The resistance of rural and working class black women to multiple oppression is celebrated by *Sistren*, the Jamaican women's theatre group, and domestic violence is a recurring theme in their work.

A great deal of social anthropological work has been carried out on 'The West Indian family' and 'kinship patterns' which will not be reviewed here. Suffice to point out that most of it has been Eurocentric and sexist, often depicting Caribbean families as pathological, and attributing this to the fact that many households are headed by women. This type of analysis is of little use to our understanding of the violent abuse of women in the Caribbean. It often overlooks the class relations of the highly stratified societies under examination. The negative impact of European racial oppression on 'West Indian psychology' is overstated, and there is a dearth of serious analyses of the various forms that gender relations take in Caribbean societies (but see Steady 1981, Ellis 1986), or of the socio-economic circumstances under which these particular forms of social relationships have gained ascendance.

For present purposes, as for the other countries above, let us simply take note of the fact that violence against women is commonplace throughout the Caribbean, and that here, as anywhere else it is related to long traditions of patriarchy and social divisions along the lines of class, race and gender. The particular traditions that feed into Caribbean social life are as numerous as the peoples now populating the region. It needs to be remembered in this context that one consequence of England's colonisation of much of the Caribbean, was the extension of the cultural values of Victorian England, including the double-standards of sexual morality and the emphasis on the superiority of the male-headed nuclear family, to what is now the English-speaking Caribbean. As a rigorously stratified class society, the treatment of middle and upper class 'ladies' was very different from that meted out to working class women, many of whom were themselves deported to the colonies. The ladies of the ruling classes in the Caribbean have been predominantly white or light-skinned, and their lives have relied on the domestic labour of black women of African or Asian descent. Black women, even now, long after the abolition of direct slavery, continue to occupy the lower social strata in Caribbean society. In the context of overpopulation (since slavery) and underdevelopment, outward migration in search of employment has always been a feature of Caribbean life (Peach 1972).

The response of international agencies: research and resolutions

The United Nations decade for women generated research into and exposure of the issue of violence against women in both the West and the peripheral capitalist countries of Africa, Asia, Latin America and the Caribbean. Feminists and concerned persons in the large international bureaucracies have had their hand strengthened by the Decade for Women (1975-1985), and are in a position to mobilise resources for women in developing countries. Their efforts can for example, enable the establishment of women's centres and projects, and the holding of seminars and conferences on subjects of concern. At the World Conference in Nairobi 1985, domestic violence featured strongly in the forward-looking strategies adopted.

In response to this, in 1987 an expert group on 'Violence in the Family' was convened in Vienna, by the UN's Branch for the Advancement of Women. (It is notable that many organisations have opted to consider 'violence in the family' rather than give specific attention to 'violence against women')

The UN expert group, not surprisingly, observed that:

'. . . violence has immediate and traumatic effects for the victimised woman and long-term effects on the future of women and children, in the perpetration of further violence in families and in the community at large. It crosses all barriers of class, income, race, culture and religion. It is founded on the unequal treatment of women and men' (1987, United Nations, Vienna).

Violence against women in the family was deemed to have structural roots, and not to be in keeping with the themes of the decade for women: Equality, Development and Peace. They also made a wide-ranging set of recommendations at international and national levels. At the national level the expert group called on governments to improve the operations of criminal justice systems and the police, and to provide resources for battered women (ensuring access to existing welfare and social security provisions, financial support for refuges and educational resources), to improve healthcare practice in relation to battered women and to make commitments in the area of education and improving public awareness on the issue of violence against women in the family:

'in view of the complexity and multidimensional nature and effects of violence against women in the family, concerted, comprehensive social support, social services, legal assistance, counselling and co-ordinated action to protect victims and control perpetrators, as well as actions to prevent such violence should be taken by all governments, their relevant institutions and personnel, intergovernmental organisations, the United Nations system, non-governmental organisations, professional organisations and individuals. In addition to taking the strongest possible protective action to assist victims, as well as undertaking long-term preventive measures, the education of the public and the socialisation of children to promote new forms of gender interaction in the future are a crucial component of any strategy'.

Woman abuse challenged: initiatives in socialist states

Outside the capitalist world and its periphery, socialist states have consistently condemned all forms of woman abuse on a much greater scale, as the history of the changes in the status of women in the Soviet Union, China, Cuba and Vietnam clearly demonstrates (see Croll 1978, Stone 1981, Eisen 1984).

The struggle to abolish colonial and capitalist class relations in these contexts has, to a varying extent, been accompanied by a struggle against the inequities of patriarchy. This struggle has been carried out by strong mass organisations of women which are supported at government level. Radical reforms of divorce laws and marital norms have directly attacked the circumstances that continue to militate against women ending or leaving relationships with men who are physically violent towards them.

The Cuban family code is one of the most advanced in the world in this respect, granting women, for example, the right to divorce their husbands for refusal to share domestic responsibilities in the family home. At the social and cultural level, the battle against sexual oppression and concomitant woman abuse, embodied in the concept of 'machismo', has been taken up and waged by the Federation of Cuban Women (FMC), which was formed in 1960. This is not to say that sexism has been completely eliminated, as is readily acknowledged by Cubans, who view their revolution as a continual process. Meanwhile there is ample evidence of huge strides in the right direction, particularly when we compare the contemporary situation with the widespread prostitution and degradation of women prior to 1959. Havana was then famous as a city of nightclubs and gambling casinos and particularly renowned for her 'mulatto' prostitutes. The 'exotic' erotic qualities of brown-skinned Cuban women were openly advertised to American and European tourists in ways that would make today's companeras shudder.

In Vietnam, wide-ranging educational campaigns and legal reforms have been adopted to tackle the problem they refer to as 'holding women in contempt'. This includes all forms of woman abuse and sexploitation, most of which had flourished under the American military occupation. Most of these reforms were spearheaded by the Vietnam Women's Union but fully supported by the socialist government. The Vietnamese had a very long history of extreme patriarchal and racial oppression, initially with the feudal Chinese Confucianist domination, followed by European and later American colonial occupations.

The situation of women in the socialist states on the southern part of the African continent has been noted above as being dominated by destabilising military attacks, so that attacks on civilian targets damage women far more than domestic violence. It is also noteworthy that women have participated in the armed struggle in all of the above contexts. The extent to which military participation translates into long term gains for women in the post-war society has varied, and to some extent has been contingent on the political character of the regime. Algeria is often cited as an example in which women have lost ground since their participation in the bitter war of liberation against the French, with the introduction of new repressive legislation in recent years. Women's liberation, however, remains on the national political agendas of most regimes that can be said to be working towards socialism, and within that generally progressive sexual politics, the various forms of woman abuse are challenged through women's organisations. (See Urdang 1979 on women in Guinea-Bissau).

Towards a perspective on the abuse of black women in Britain and responses to it

The international material briefly examined here suggests a number of ways in which we can elaborate and develop the definition of domestic violence, so as to get beyond the ethnocentrism and class bias of existing feminist accounts, and the misogyny underlying more traditional individualised ('blaming the victim') views on the 'wife-beating'. This is necessary for the study of domestic violence in general, but most obviously so when working in non-Western contexts, or in black communities in the West. Despite the diversity of the contexts in which women are abused by their partners, a number of themes emerge from the international literature and on the basis of the brief overview presented here, a number of general points can be made:

1. that the physical abuse of women occurs across most if not all cultures and religious groups, although the local forms and dynamics have culturally specific content;
2. that it also occurs across many nations and therefore within a variety of social and political conditions;
3. that the abuse of women occurs across all socio-economic classes, even though its manifestations within different classes may vary;
4. that the degree to which violence against women by their male partners is tolerated by the dominant institutions varies considerably according to the political character of the regime in power;
5. that within a given nation, the 'acceptability' of physical abuse of a woman depends on the class, caste, and in racist contexts, race, of both the perpetrator and his victim(s), in such a way that it is more acceptable for a man dominant along any or several of these dimensions to assault women socially 'inferior' to himself than the converse;
6. that once a woman has engaged in any form of sexual relationship with a man, his social dominance over her is assumed, regardless of the class, caste or religious background of each of them prior to that relationship, and this dominance tacitly or expressly includes the right to abuse her, and may even continue after the relationship has ended.

The implications of these points have guided the rest of this report, and the investigations upon which it is based. There are two main areas to consider in any investigation into domestic violence. Firstly, there are those factors that are implicated in the genesis of violence towards women — in this case black women in Britain — and secondly, there are those factors that reinforce and perpetuate domestic violence in any given community — in this case the African, Asian and Caribbean communities in Britain. These include factors creating a high toleration of violence, and reluctance to 'interfere'.

The first of these two areas includes the difficult question of why black and other men should brutalise the women they have taken as wives or sexual and emotional partners, or women who they have otherwise found themselves living with. Since there are men of all colours and creeds who beat women, racially or culturally deterministic explanations will not be satisfactory. Since all classes of men beat women, simple economically deterministic answers are also not satisfactory.

Racism, colonialism and violence

There is however, evidence to suggest that socially oppressive circumstances produce more intra-communal violence, including wife-beating and other abusive behaviour. Oppressive conditions such as poverty, overcrowding, living in fear of police harassment and racist attack and being subjected to violence from these forces, are all likely to exacerbate relational problems between black people and within couples, so increasing the likelihood of these then degenerating into physical violence. Isolation from family and community networks reduces the likelihood or possibility of intervention and mediation over disputes.

Frantz Fanon put forward a thesis that under extremely oppressive conditions — such as during colonial occupation — intra-communal and fratricidal violence increases. The South African and neo-colonial examples given in this chapter offer support for this view. Staples (1982) has already adapted this thesis to the oppressed situation of black Americans, as a way of explaining the high levels of interpersonal violence, including woman abuse, which occurs in those communities. In relation to abuse of black women by men, this can also be seen as a historically-based demonstration of contempt. It reflects the historical devaluation of black womanhood which has occurred under imperialist domination, and the internalisation of values which subordinate and degrade black women. African, Caribbean and Asian women have all been subjected to the violence of colonialism and conquest, as were the men. In the case of women, however, imperialism also involved sexual exploitation, with black women being raped, abused and taken as prostitutes and concubines on a large scale. I have argued elsewhere that the imperialist project involved subordinating women where they were not already subordinated, and compounding that subordination where they were traditionally subordinated, in a colonising process which forced Victorian forms of patriarchy on the colonised.[3]

There is little doubt that Britain's black communities too, are economically and socially marginalised and racially oppressed. Many of the women who participated in this research had been involved with men who were economically stressed (through unemployment or irregular casual work) or men who had no home of their own and were not likely to ever be wealthy enough to obtain one. Many of the women were also themselves severely stressed by poverty, lack of childcare support and squalid living conditions, long before they were additionally subjected to violence from their partners. It is clear that being trapped in highly oppressive conditions is likely to exacerbate any relational problems that people may be experiencing with their partners.

The appalling conditions in which black people are forced to live are an indictment of British society, indicating clearly that the long term racism in all areas of social policy has kept much of the black population where it is. Black people continue to be concentrated on the least habitable housing estates in deprived inner city areas, disproportionately unemployed, and sometimes unemployable and unskilled. As a result many black people are forced to live in overcrowded conditions, and sometimes with people not of their choosing. It is in this context that many black women become trapped in life-threatening domestic situations.

However, the oppressive circumstances of many black peoples' lives do not explain or in any way excuse the brutality that some men inflict on black women. The majority of poor and extremely oppressed men who have been subjected to violent oppression themselves do not become abusive to women. Racially oppressed men do not *necessarily* become passive victims of their circumstances and mindlessly beat it all out on the woman nearest to them. For those that do, their own oppression must therefore be acting in concert with other factors (for example a misogynistic attitude). Many of the violent men that the women in this study lived with were not unemployed, and some were indeed quite wealthy. Some were white men who did not experience racism themselves, but had decided to discard or force out the black women they lived with or had married.

Even from this brief discussion, it will be clear that the case material does not facilitate simple causal analysis. Rather it exposes the conditions in which the quite extreme violence we uncovered occurred. It became increasingly academic to try and separate factors in the genesis of violence (which will include individual psychological histories of both partners as well as all the broader social and material conditions), from factors in the perpetuation of violent relationships and situations.

Black Women in Britain

Black women[4] from all over the colonised world have often found it necessary to leave their countries of origin or birth to seek better lives for themselves and their children in the metropolis; the heartland of the empire of which they have always been an integral part. Women were often recruited by European governments seeking cheap labour during the post-war economic boom. Others came to join men who had been similarly drawn to the metropolis. People from ex-colonies and other economically weak countries have been used in richer post-industrial societies like Britain to staff the welfare state as workers, fulfilling the roles allocated to black women all over the capitalist world. It is perhaps ironic that these roles have often involved caring for and generally nurturing white British people; as nurses, cleaners and caterers, as well as low-rank administrative workers. Black women have been taken in to large hierarchical structures at the bottom echelons, undertaking the heaviest labour and working the most inhospitable hours as shift-workers (see Mama 1984, Bryant, Dadzie and Scafe 1985).

It has already been pointed out that Britain in particular has always had a contradictory relationship to black and migrant workers here. On the one hand she has sought their labour at exploitatively cheap rates, while on the other seeking as far as possible to restrict their access to human resources. Black workers were treated as 'working hands', as if there were no minds or bodies accompanying them. The fact that when the first shipload of recruits arrived, they had to sleep in an old dungeon-like air raid shelter, has proved to be indicative of what was to come (see chapters 4 and 7-9). The history of immigration legislation from that time on reflects a concern with restricting and selecting, pandering to racist popular sentiment yet acquiring cheap labour (see Peach 1972). This contradiction between needing workers but not wanting to bear the human costs of black workers has underpinned much social administration, and is evidenced in the racial policing of welfare in particular.

22

Black people were at first almost completely denied access to council housing, through residency requirements. Even then there were black British people (ex-servicemen, descendants of sailors etc), some of whom were married to white Englishwomen who were not excluded by the administrative devices that kept most black people out of public housing. The exclusion of black people from housing has become increasingly difficult to administer over the years, particularly since the first Race Relations Act of 1969 (as is discussed in chapters 7-9). More recently, Labour boroughs have tried a number of ways of dealing with race, under the general heading of Equal Opportunities policies.

The treatment of black women by both statutory and voluntary agencies often epitomises the grudging reluctance, sometimes even refusal of British society to meet the basic needs of black people in general. There is a wicked irony here, since the development of health and welfare services have particularly relied on the labour of black women, not to mention the fact that black people, as members of the society, have paid taxes and national insurance for many years for the maintenance of these same services. The often unsympathetic, insensitive and sometimes overtly racist, treatment of black women experiencing domestic violence and the related problems documented in Part I of this report demonstrates, quite unequivocally, the persistence of racist attitudes and the practice of 'petty apartheid' in service delivery. The roots of these responses go far beyond present day sexism and racist hysteria through the politically expedient notions of a 'small and overcrowded' island and the government-orchestrated panic over 'scarce resources', deep into Britain's imperial past and her capitalist economic priorities.

At risk of repeating common knowledge, it needs to be reiterated that the British state has had a history of inhumanity towards women in the colonies. Even today the British State continues to be one of the South African apartheid regime's staunchest allies, in the face of all the evidence on that continuing holocaust. Contempt for African people is evidenced too in present day media portrayals. Here African women are always beggars and victims; starving women with babies on their backs, or (and particularly since Aids), as infective prostitutes with strange sexual prowess. On the other hand, Asian women are seen as passive vehicles of patriarchal religions, conforming to calcified Eastern traditions (which racists assume to necessarily include wife beating, maiming and killing).

In the colonies, British rule often meant the reinforcing of feudal and other oppressive social relations. Some traditions were respected (keeping women in *purdah* for example) while others were undermined (traditional

23

women's organisations and land rights, for example). There is not space to go into the complex and contradictory impact of British rule on the status of women, but contemporary studies have pointed out that far from being a liberating force, colonial occupation often saw the demise of traditional woman-empowering structures and the introduction of the 'housewifization' process (Amadiume 1987, Mies 1986).

In the local British context this history and its texturing of the present, can be seen to affect the way in which local government officials and voluntary agencies treat black women. They are likely to be regarded as desperate or parasitic and to be treated with contempt or suspicion, in accord with the dominant stereotypes and values. It is little wonder that self-respecting African, Asian and Caribbean women are often reluctant to approach agencies for assistance, however dire their need may be (See Chapter 3). This means that many of the very grave problems experienced by black women continue to be hidden from public awareness. This is particularly true for women isolated in more closed communities (refugee women, and wives of refugees, women restricted by religious and cultural traditions, women who have recently arrived in Britain and women with dependent immigration status). For those able to surmount the initial hurdles and approach a housing department or some other agency for what are in most cases, statutory rights, there follows a long ordeal of waiting and humiliation as they are passed around the various state bureaucracies. This project highlighted the fact that this ordeal may continue for several years, during which time women and their children may be homeless and dispossessed, and in some cases, also threatened with deportation. At every stage in the struggle for rehousing, black women may well be encouraged to abandon their hope for a decent home, to accept substandard accommodation, to get used to semi-permanent homelessness or may simply be advised to 'go back to your country'.

Bureaucratic oppression

Oppression and the denial of rights is a shifty phenomenon, often unspecified and insidious in its enactment, often belied by contradictions which manifest themselves in ambiguities, halting speech and rows of teeth fixed into grimaces while files are lost, names forgotten and individuals buried under caseloads and queues.

Power does not move in unitary or monolithic ways, but in contradictory dynamics, through payoffs and betrayals that deny its existence even as it is exercised. Bureaucratic power is exercised by governmental

24

institutions, in ways that enable it to operate as a mask for the practice of white supremacy.

To study what happens to black women at the hands of British institutions involves first and foremost an understanding of the history of these institutions and the discourses running through them; the organisational culture of housing departments, police and law enforcement agencies and so on. It also calls for detailed understanding of the historical and contemporary relations between black women and the British state apparatuses, and between black women and civil society in Britain. The remainder of this report is one more contribution to a wider effort in this direction.

Finally, in the light of the political character of the context in which this report will be published, it is necessary to direct the readers not familiar with domestic violence to material covering the nature and extent of domestic violence in the white communities in Britain (see Dobash and Dobash 1980, Binney, Harkell and Nixon 1981, Wilson 1983, Carew-Jones and Watson 1985, Turner 1984, Pahl 1985, Borkowski, Murch and Walker 1983, Yllo and Bograd 1988). The vast majority of women in women's refuges are white women who have been brutalised, maimed and tortured by white men, as were some of the black women in this study. All previous studies on violence against women by their male partners has covered the experience of white women only. This study aims to redress that imbalance by looking at violence against black women specifically, but it also has much wider political and practical implications for British state and society.

Notes

1. The details of this case history were provided through personal correspondence with WIN.
2. Lina Magaia's book, *Peasant Tales of Tragedy*, documents the atrocities committed by the MNR in rural Mozambique.
3. 'Imperialism and Patriarchy; Developing an International Perspective on Violence Against Women'. Unpublished lecture delivered at the Institute for Social Studies, The Hague, April 1989.
4. International reports and studies often adopt the term 'Third World' to denote people from peripheral capitalist or developing countries. This research focuses on women who have origins in those countries, but who have settled in Britain, or whose parents, grandparent or earlier foreparents settled in Britain. As such they are all British women within the terms of the research ie they are entitled to basic civil rights and welfare provisions. The local contemporary terminology would refer to us as 'black women' or 'ethnic minority' women. For the rest

of this publication both these terms have been abbreviated into 'black women'. Where a particular group is being referred to the terms Asian, Caribbean or African are used accordingly. These terms too refer to parentage or origins, and not to nationality or birthplace.

2. Appropriate paradigm research

Introduction

In the planning stages of this project, a search of the British literature revealed that there was virtually no existing published research on black women and domestic violence, and very little on black women and social policy. There are few publications that can be said to have gone into any detailed analysis of the relationship prevailing between black women as a social group and societal institutions, whether we are considering voluntary organisations, state institutions or the private sector. This lack of material meant that there were no existing studies whose research methods could be consulted. Our methodological aim was to develop a paradigm that would enhance our understanding of the lives of black and ethnic minority women and the forces oppressing them, and remain empirically valid, without degenerating into the 'numbers game' which currently dominates both ethnic research and policy.

A number of considerations, which we may refer to as the politics of the research, influenced the range of methods that were eventually used. Research has a tendency to reproduce the dominant power relations of the society in which that research is being conducted, but to mask this fact with rhetoric.[1] This has provoked extensive criticisms of traditional Western research methods from Third World peoples, black peoples, women and other oppressed groups living in societies, such as Britain, which can be defined analytically as an industrial capitalist social formation. Historically Britain has also been a patriarchal and imperialistic society, with gender and race relationships that are still fundamentally based on power relations that derogate and discriminate against black people, women and other marginalised and exploited social groups (gays and lesbians, disabled and elderly people, migrant workers, travellers, refugees, ex-prisoners etc). Black women living in British society (as in other industrial capitalist societies) have the dubious distinction of falling into a number of the categories of people who are economically and socially oppressed or discriminated against. Hence the assertions by black women worldwide from the 1970s onwards that we are 'triply oppressed'. This understanding demanded and has inspired a burst of activity and organising both at international and local levels.[2] It has also produced an international quest for appropriate methods for researching black and Third World women.[3]

In the analyses which have followed, a major argument has been that conducting social and policy research on oppressed groups — in this instance — black women, requires that the cultural, social and economic position of both the researchers and the target group be taken into account. This applies to all social groups, but in doing research on oppressed groups it becomes vitally necessary if we are to avoid the tendency of research to reinforce and contribute to the plethora of stereotypes and derogatory myths that prevail in the dominant society. The failure of academic and research institutions to develop a critical understanding of the politics of research processes has produced a situation in which unspecified class and ethnocentric assumptions in the research process implicitly reinforce the dominant social order and fail to transcend or challenge the divisions of industrial capitalist society.

The artificial separation between theory and method which underpins this situation, was identified in the 1960s as contributing to the conservatism of research (Glaser and Strauss 1967). In the present study, therefore, care was taken to use an approach which, throughout the research process, integrated a range of methods with the analysis and theorising, in keeping with previously established alternatives to empiricist reductionism and critiques of purely quantitative methods.[4] Readers will therefore find that in addition to this summary and overview, notes on the method are also included in the rest of the text. This approach is based on the assumption that there is no method without an implicit theory (or set of assumptions), and no theory that does not have methodological implications.

Reducing racial inequality in the research process

There are a number of other ways that research can avoid reproducing the dominant power relations of a society. In this project the following precautions were taken:

28

1) Ethnic matching of the researchers with the subject group. In contrast to most research, all the people who worked directly on the project and the project steering group were black women (of Caribbean, Asian and African descent). In this way the normal power balance of research in favour of the dominant social groups was reversed. This will have had specific effects on the type of information generated by the research tools (interview schedules etc). The more detailed effects of this will become apparent in chapter 3 where interviewing techniques are discussed. The research team included the researcher/writer, interviewers, transcribers and an administrative co-ordinator. Translators were employed as necessary. It is also significant that the project was commissioned by an independent body — the London Race and Housing Research Unit — so that even decisions concerning finance and publication were supported and made by black people functioning with a high degree of autonomy, and outside state structures.

2) Black women's accounts of their experience were the major source of information. The subject group was therefore given a space to articulate their experiences in their own terms and from their own frames of reference. Furthermore this material is given status in the analysis and discussion. This meant treating women who are traditionally treated as 'passive victims' (Asian women) or 'aggressive criminals' (women of Caribbean descent women) and who are often blamed for their situation by institutions and services, as credible informants and whose accounts are valid data. In this research their experiences are given credibility, and as research subjects, black women are given the status of citizens who are assumed to be entitled to basic human rights. In particular, the right of women to live their lives with their children in decent accommodation, free from the threat of violence in their homes, was assumed throughout the project. It was also assumed that the people who knew most about what happens to black women who experience domestic violence were those who have had that experience. While this may seem obvious to the lay person, it contradicts most (orthodox) social scientific research practice.

3) The accounts of relevant professionals — for the most part state agents (housing officers, social workers etc.) — were also taken to be credible accounts of what occurs from the perspective of their professional (institutional) roles. This is more in keeping with orthodox research (see eg Borkowski, Murch and Walker 1983) but in this instance has different

implications because in this report, their accounts are not taken to be more credible than the accounts of those they 'process'. In less critical research, professional accounts would generally be given more status than those of the public they service, with the conservative class, gender and race consequences that this implies.

4) The analysis of people's accounts was conducted in the light of their collective histories and cultures. For example, in the case of housing workers, this meant British history and culture, and the organisational culture of large local state bureaucracies. Since black women were the subject of the research, the history of Britain's relations with black people was also taken into consideration. This has been a history with particular power relations prevailing between white and black people; a history of colonial conquests, enslavement and economic exploitation in the Caribbean, Asia and Africa. The particular history of relations between black women and British institutions was, at all stages of the research from its conceptualisation right through to the data analysis, deemed the most relevant of all. It was also assumed that present day international relations affect the treatment of particular national groups and those who apparently look like them. For example, specific changes have been made concerning the treatment of Nigerians and Ghanaians by immigration authorities, and these filter across statutory bodies to affect the the way Nigerians and Ghanaians are treated by all other state agencies (the police, social services etc).

Research design

The research was divided into three main parts:

1) An in-depth survey of black women's experiences of both statutory and voluntary institutions was undertaken. This included housing departments, police and legal agencies, social services, the National Health service on the state side (Part II) and community organisations (particularly ethnic minority and women's organisations and women's refuges) on the voluntary side (Part III).

2) A survey of local authority policies on rehousing women who have been subjected to violence in the home.

3) An investigation of the practices of two local authorities. This examined

how these local authorities actually treat Black women who have approached them for help as a result of domestic violence.

4) An investigation of the service provided by women's refuges to highlight how well this is meeting the needs of Black women. This looked at how successful they are in obtaining local authority housing for Black women who are homeless as a result of domestic violence.

Sources of information
The absence of any research on black women and domestic violence was one of the factors that inspired this project. The existing literature on domestic violence was reviewed. A wider literature search of the history of public housing, and race relations in British society was also conducted to identify the origins of present day relations between black people and public services, particularly housing. This material is referenced, and provided as a backdrop to the research (see chapter 3). It heavily influenced the choice of methods and priorities made in the research design.

In addition to the literature searches, a wide range of people were interviewed or otherwise consulted in the course of the research. These can be placed into three main groups:

1) Black women who have had housing problems that relate to domestic violence. These were selected to fall into three main groups: women of Caribbean, Asian and African descent.

2) A range of voluntary sector workers who come into contact with women abused by their sexual and emotional partners: refuge workers, social workers, law centres, housing advice centres and other researchers in the area of domestic violence.

3) Relevant local authority employees in housing departments, race units and women's units.

Summary of research techniques
Various research techniques were employed to contact and collect information from these different groups of people.

Black women who have experienced housing problems resulting from domestic violence
The researcher set a target sample size of 120, to comprise 50 women of

31

Caribbean descent, 50 women of Asian descent and 20 women of African descent, and then set about contacting them by a number of means:

— Letters and later circulars were sent to all traceable black women's organisations in London. These were followed up by telephone, and several were visited to discuss the project with the workers. Those whose work did bring them into contact with women who experienced domestic violence were asked to assist in contacting them for interviews.

— A number of black community organisations were consulted, but these either did not appear to be aware of the problem, denied that it was a problem, referred us to black women's organisations or simply did not offer support in this area (see chapter 10). This avenue was not therefore pursued.

— Circulars were distributed amongst a range of people whose work did bring them into contact with the subject group, and they were asked to inform the women they knew of about the project and to request interviews. This also did not prove very successful and was not pursued extensively since resources were limited.

— London Women's Aid were approached to assist and support the project. After a meeting and discussion with the workers there, they undertook to support the project and assist in whatever ways they could. In particular they forwarded mail to women's refuges in Greater London, made telephone numbers available and invited the researcher to attend regional meetings with refuge workers. At these meetings, the purposes and importance of the project was put to those in attendance and support lobbied for it.

— With the assistance of the regional office for London refuges, letters were sent to all refuges in the Greater London area, requesting support for the project and summarising its aims and objectives. These were later followed up with telephone calls and circulars, requesting meetings with one or more of the workers. Refuge workers were then met with, interviewed about their work and the refuge itself, and asked if we could approach and interview women of Caribbean, Asian or African origin who were staying at, or had stayed at the refuge. The vast majority of refuges were fully supportive of the project, and many of the workers took it upon themselves to ask the black women they were in contact with if they were willing to be interviewed. As a result of such positive support, this method proved to be the most successful, with the result that the majority of our sample was obtained through the women's aid network.

— The author drew on a number of personal contacts with black women's organisations, and other researchers and activists.

People in the voluntary sector whose work brings them into contact with black women who have experienced domestic violence
— Refuge workers were contacted by telephone, following up letters sent to refuges through WAFE's London Office.

— Housing Advice Centres, law centres, women's organisations and community organisations were contacted by letter and telephone. Workers in these organisations in the two boroughs selected for particular attention (Lambeth and Kensington and Chelsea) were interviewed wherever possible.

Relevant local authority personnel
— Letters were sent to all 33 Directors of Housing, or their equivalents, in the Greater London area. These asked what policies they currently had that related to dealing with women who experienced domestic violence and related housing problems, how these were implemented generally and how they were implemented specifically in the case of black women.

— These were followed up with further letters and by telephone calls to other relevant local authority personnel. In the two boroughs selected for further study, meetings were held with persons identified as being involved with this area of policy and practice. The relevant personnel and structures varied within the different boroughs; some had race units and women's units, while others had a single officer whose tasks included these areas of work (see section II). The information required to identify the relevant personnel in all local authorities's was obtained from the Association of Labour Authorities directory and by making enquiries.

— Housing department officers were identified and approached through their local authority. They were interviewed to identify the constraints within which they operate in implementing the relevant policies in their particular boroughs, and as far as possible, to identify the assumptions influencing their treatment of black and ethnic minority women who have housing problems that result from domestic violence.

The research design ensured that information was gathered from two sides, from the State and from the community. Both black women and housing workers have been interviewed about their contact with each other. In this way, we have aimed to demystify what actually happens when black women, with housing difficulties, seek assistance from a local authority.

The interviews

Interviews with housing department and voluntary sector workers were conducted on the basis of the role they played, but they were particularly asked about the race implications of their working practice regarding women who have experienced domestic violence.

For refuge workers a questionnaire was designed to gather basic information about the refuge such as: sources of funding, ethnic origins of women using the refuge, ethnic breakdowns of the workers, the history of the refuge, refuge workers experiences of various local authority housing departments and any other agencies etc. Interviews with refuge workers also included some open discussion on race and culture in refuge work.

For the interviews with black women, a schedule was designed and developed by the researcher, and then tested out in the preliminary stages of the research. A computing consultant was employed to work with the researcher in designing a database programme, for the recording of data, which covered the main sections of the interview schedule.

The interview covered several areas of experience:
a) demographic details, personal and relational history
b) community and family support
c) contact with statutory agencies, namely healthcare services, social services, housing, police and legal agencies
d) contact with voluntary sector agencies.

At the end of each interview, there were open questions on how women felt provision could be developed and improved, and what plans they had for the future (and that of their children where relevant). The style in which interviews were conducted was particularly important because of the emotive nature of the project (see p.41).

Storing and processing the information

It will by now be clear that the project involved coping with a large body of information from different sources and in various forms which all required appropriate techniques of statistical and theoretical analysis.

i) Published work was collected, read and reviewed and then filed, to be referred to again at the writing up stage.

ii) Interviews with black women were all tape recorded. Interviewers were trained to fill in the schedule, and to summarise each case in the form of a biographical sketch, highlighting the overall situation of that woman, her violent relationship and her housing history in particular. Thirty-eight per cent of the interviews were fully transcribed to provide direct, experiential data for use in the write up. These were selected on the basis of two criteria;

a) where a good rapport had been established so that information was freely given,
b) where women had been in contact with a range of agencies and therefore had more to tell that was relevant to the concerns of the project.

The data was then loaded on to the data base programme for the purposes of statistical analysis and summarising the characteristics of the sample of women interviewed.

iii) Interviews with refuge workers were filled in on the schedule by interviewers, and a smaller proportion of these tape recorded. Files and a smaller database were also kept on all the refuges visited, taking care to note the names of refuge workers and any other details which facilitated liaising with them in seeking out women to be interviewed.

Statistical and other information on all the refuges visited included the following:

iv) Notes were taken of meetings with the wider group of people whose work brought them into contact with black women who have experienced domestic violence.

v) Notes were made of interviews with housing workers, and some of these tape recorded and transcribed for later analysis.

vi) Other information about policy and practice relating to the housing of women who have been subjected to domestic violence was obtained from committee reports and local authority surveys and incorporated into the development of the research as a whole.

Ethnicity in the interviews

All interviewers and interviewees were black women. In this study this meant women of African, Caribbean or Asian origin. All lived in Britain, so that Part I is a study of the experience of black women who have been subjected to domestic violence, statutory and voluntary agencies in Britain. 'African' meant women who had origins on the African continent, but did not include white or Asian women. 'Asian' meant women who had origins in Asia (India, Pakistan, Bangladesh, as well as China, Hong Kong, Malaysia, Vietnam, Iran, Afghanistan and the Philippines). The Asian sample included six Asians born and/or raised on the African continent. In terms of the three research categories (African, Caribbean and Asian descent), again most women were ethnically matched with the interviewers (90/106). The exceptions to this were two Asian and 14 Caribbean interviews conducted by the researcher (who is of mixed African and European parentage).

The three research categories were not internally homogenous, but included women of various class backgrounds, and religious, national and cultural specificities. Translators were used to interview some of the Chinese, Tamil, Bengali and Punjabi-speaking women, and Ayesha the Asian interviewer spoke Urdu, Gujerati and Arabic. Language differences did not emerge in the African or Caribbean samples because the women we identified were comfortable to be interviewed in English, and Audrey (the Caribbean interviewer) was able to understand the two women who communicated in patois.

Women of mixed European and Caribbean, African or Asian origin were included in the sample according to their black ethnic origin.[5]

Notes

1. This argument is more fully developed in other work; see chapter five of my unpublished 1987 Ph.D. thesis *Race and Subjectivity*, or see *Foundation* no. 5 for a brief article on 'Race and Research Processes'.
2. Publications produced by the black women's movement in Britain include *FOWAAD*, the newsletter of the Organisation for Women of African and Asian Descent produced between the late 1970s and early 1980s, *Speak Out*, the

Brixton Black Women's Group magazine produced in the early 1980s, *Outwrite* the international women's newspaper which was finally forced to close down at the end of 1988. In addition *Spare Rib*, the mainstream feminist magazine has covered black and international women's news since the early 1980s, and *Feminist Review* made space for a special issue on and by black women in 1984 (FR 17), and have since increased their coverage of the race and feminism debate.

3. See eg Association of African Women For Research And Development (AAWORD) papers from 1983 seminar *Research on African Women: What Type of Methodology?*

4. Other work in the area of developing critical research has been compiled in Reason and Rowan 1981 (eds.) *Human Enquiry: A Source book of New Paradigm Research* and by Roberts 1981 (ed.) *Doing Feminist Research*. The use of qualitative methods is explored in detail in Filstead (1970) *Qualitative Methodology: First-hand Involvement in the Social World*.

5. Some women of Asian origin, and one of the women of mixed origin did not identify themselves as 'black', but nonetheless the term black women has been used throughout, rather than the other more cumbersome and equally problematic terms available (e.g. 'black and ethnic minority women' 'third world women' or the American 'women of colour' etc.). This reflects the political legacy of black political organising in the 1970s and early 1980s in which the necessity for concerted and united action against racism and oppression in Britain was emphasized. Since that time there has been an orchestrated emphasis on ethnic specificities and religious orthodoxies that has made it more opportune for some groups to lobby for resources on ethnically specific tickets, rather than on the basis of shared experience of racism. The very real cultural and religious differences between people of Asian and African descent have therefore become translated into bureaucratic practice and political lobbying. This is ironic since growing numbers of all these communities are 'home grown' ie born and educated in Britain, and it is racism (whether there is a cultural difference or not) that continues to ensure that black people's access to resources and services is circumscribed.

3. Woman abuse in London's black communities

Introduction

This section of the report examines the form, severity and extent of domestic violence experienced by the black women in this study, and the time over which they are subjected to violence before seeking to escape it. It also looks at the strategies employed by the women in the study in their attempts to survive or otherwise cope with repeated physical assault and/or mental cruelty. The report is based on the results of in-depth interviews with over 100 women, conducted in London over a period of 12 months (November 1987-October 1988). This makes it the first detailed investigation of domestic violence in Britain's black communities. The content of the material is of a highly disturbing nature. This is evidenced by the emotional stress experienced by the interviewers taken on to assist with this aspect of the research. Out of four employed and trained to conduct interviews with the full support of the researcher, only two found themselves emotionally able to cope with the depressing and disturbing nature of the subject group's experiences. The two who remained had substantial experience and training (one as a medical doctor and the other as a social worker who had lived and worked in Women's Aid), which enabled them to cope with the task in a sympathetic and highly skilled manner. The material presented here should be considered in the context of the following methodological considerations.

Method note:

Sample characteristics

The sample was not a random sample, which means that generalisations about the communities included cannot be drawn from the interview findings. The material reported here should *not* be used as a basis for constructing new, or supporting old, stereotypes about the Caribbean, Asian or African communities, about gender relations, or about the treatment of women by men in those communities.

The sample was predominantly obtained through the Women's Aid network. Contacting a range of community and voluntary sector organisations in the preliminary stages did not yield many interviews; only the Chinese and Philipino women were contacted solely through their respective community organisations, and a small number (n = 5) of the Asian and Caribbean women were contacted through social networks (eg through friends or the community, health or social workers who responded to publicity about the project). This will have meant that the vast numbers of women experiencing domestic violence but not contacting Women's Aid were under-represented because of the fact that we ended up relying so heavily on this particular agency.

Many of the sample characteristics may be related to the mode of contact; in particular most of them had left their homes, or were otherwise seeking to terminate their relationships with violent partners. In this sense, the sample must be regarded as a highly select tip of the iceberg. Consultations with community organisations indicated that large numbers of women in all the communities addressed here are forced to tolerate quite high levels of domestic violence without ever contacting Women's Aid or, for that matter, any outside agency. Even within the subject group, many had tolerated violence for quite long periods of time (ranging from months to 30 years) before hearing of and contacting outside agencies. Some, particularly the older women in the sample, had repeatedly sought help and found none. Similar observations were made by the Select Committee's Report to Parliament in 1975 regarding the population in general. It is particularly likely that violence will be hidden in the more isolated and marginalised black communities.

All the women interviewed had been subjected to quite serious degrees of cruelty. As such it should be regarded as an extreme sample, and not representative of connubial relationships in the respective communities. It will become apparent that nearly all the women in the study had experienced high degrees of physical abuse, only two having been subjected to emotional cruelty without physical violence. (In both cases emotional suffering drove them from their marital homes). This rendered the definitional problems around more borderline cases irrelevant. The emphasis on physical abuse is not intended to minimize the suffering of women subjected to mental cruelty without actual bodily assaults, and we did not set out to exclude such women. In all cases the physical violence that women experienced was accompanied by mental and emotional cruelty, as will become apparent in the examples below.

All the women interviewed self-defined their relational experience as that of domestic violence. To reiterate, in the terms of this project this means physical and mental abuse by current or past emotional and sexual partners: husbands, cohabitees or men with visiting relationships.

Whereas much research has focused on violence against wives — 'wife-battering' — it became clear in the course of this research that a significant proportion of the women we interviewed at refuges had not been legally married. Furthermore, a significant proportion had not been cohabiting on a full-time basis with their partners during the period of violence, and some of the women never had. It was therefore decided to include these two last groups in this study, in contrast to existing research on domestic violence because growing numbers of women (and in this study, women of Caribbean descent in particular) had what we refer to as 'visiting relationships' with the men who assaulted them. Their assailants stayed with them on a part-time basis, while also retaining residential rights with their mothers, or with other women. Domestic violence is not restricted to any particular family form or structure. In a study of black women it was definitely necessary to also include relationships not conforming to the monogamous nuclear form generally depicted in publications that have in any case not dealt with the situation of black women.

No black lesbian women were encountered in the process of contacting people to interview. The problems faced by black women in violent lesbian relationships are not therefore addressed in this study, although it is apparent that lesbian relationships are not free from abuse and violence, and may well be treated even less sympathetically.

Interview procedure and recording
The interview schedule was designed and piloted by the researcher, who then started conducting interviews. On the basis of that experience, a training programme was devised, and supporting interviewers recruited and trained on the use of the schedule, the interviewing style and the systematised recording of data.

Style
Interviews were conducted in an empathic and supportive style, centred around building a good rapport with each woman, but avoiding leading questioning. Women were encouraged to articulate their own experience

41

for themselves as much as possible, in a freely-flowing discussion, and to indicate any areas they preferred not to discuss. This required the interviewer to have a thorough knowledge of the schedule so that they were able to allow the natural flow of the discussion rather than rigidly following the order of the schedule, while ensuring that all areas were covered in the course of the interview. The degree of rapport obtained varied widely within the subject group.

All women were assured of complete confidentiality. All names and details likely to reveal individual identities have been altered in this report for the protection and security of the women who participated in the research. Women were paid a flat rate of £10, and interviews lasted for between 45 and 90 minutes.[1]

Training

Interviewers were trained and supported by the researcher. Training consisted of:

a) familiarising themselves thoroughly with the schedule and the purpose of each question;
b) observing the researcher conducting two or more interviews;
c) simulation exercises; trying out the schedule under the researcher's supervision by interviewing each other;
d) conducting their first interviews with the researcher present to give feedback on their development of the desired style;
e) the researcher playing back their first few interviews and discussing these with them in some detail to further develop their skills.

Interviewers were supplied with revisory notes on the style and conduct of interviews, and instructed to ensure ending the interview on a positive note, and to enquire if the interviewee had any questions about the interview, or any other information they felt was important.

Recording

Interviews were recorded in four different ways, and then 40 of these were fully transcribed in English. The discussions were tape-recorded with the permission of the woman.[2] Interview schedules were filled during interviews. As soon as possible afterwards, interviewers also filled in the data sheet for the computer analysis, and wrote a short precis of each case history summarising the central and distinctive features as they had emerged during the interview, or subsequently.

The schedule
This was designed to cover eight areas:
a) background and demographic details — place of birth, age, number of children, age and ethnicity of partner etc;
b) the domestic violence itself — descriptions of severity, use of weapon(s), injuries sustained, periodicity, relation to drug-abuse or other factors, coping strategies adopted by the woman, injuries to children;
c) family and friends support or lack of it;
d) uptake of medical services and social services, experience of these if approached;
e) housing situation during violence and subsequently, attempts to secure alternative accommodation;
f) contact with police and legal agencies and outcome of contact;
g) contact with voluntary sector agencies and women's refuges, experience of these;
h) hopes and plans for the future.

The women who participated in the study

Race and ethnicity
The terms of the research specified the inclusion of women from various ethnic communities — loosely divided into women of Caribbean, Asian and African origin. Out of these, only domestic violence in the South East Asian communities has received any attention in the mainstream and ethnic media and in the black feminist press (see eg Grewal (ed) 1987, back issues of *Outwrite*), and this has not been substantial. With respect to women of African and Caribbean origin in Britain, no literature was found which addressed domestic violence. Regarding violence against African and Caribbean women only police brutality appears to have been mentioned at all (see chapter 9).

Table 3.1 *Ethnic origins of women interviewed*

Ethnic origin	Number
Caribbean	54
Asian	40
African	6
Total	100

Table 3.2 *Birthplace of women*

Birthplace	Number
Afghanistan	1
Bangladesh	2
Barbados	2
Britain	37
China	2
Ghana	3
Guyana	1
Hong Kong	3
Indonesia	1
India	9
Iran	1
Jamaica	17
Kenya	3
Malaysia	1
Nigeria	1
Pakistan	8
Philippines	2
Sierra Leone	1
St Lucia	1
Uganda	2
Vietnam	1
Zimbabwe	1
Total	100

The fact that all were resident in London at the time of interview was the main unifying factor in this ethnicallly diverse sample of abused women. Many had been born in Britain, and most of the remainder had lived here for many years. As such all were assumed to be entitled to protection under British law and to the basic human rights set out in the UN Charter. These include the right to shelter, food and to lead productive lives. It was shocking to find that several women were threatened with deportation at the time of the research, as a direct result of having left their violent spouses. Several were not sure of their status at the time of interview, since their spouses kept their papers. None in our sample had or were applying for refugee status. All were resident by birth, residence and/or (least securely) by marriage to British citizens.

Most interviews were conducted in English, and those that were not were conducted through translators, or in the relevant language and then translated onto tape.

Sample size and modes of contact

The research target was initially set at a total of 120 interviews comprising

50 Caribbean, 50 Asian and 20 African interviews. In the end 106 interviews were completed, comprising 54 Caribbean, 46 Asian and 6 African women. Out of these, 6 were not included in the final analysis because the women had been subjected to abuse by other relatives or their employers, rather than their male partners (as defined in this research). The final sample therefore consisted of 100 women (Table 3.1).

Interviews were scheduled to take 6 months, but in the end took 12 because of the time spent to conduct them in a sensitive manner, and the difficulties encountered in setting them up. The shortfall of African women is most likely a direct result of the small numbers taking up existing provision, as well as the smaller size and character of the community. It is not thought to be because there is less domestic violence in the African communities, but rather that they are less organised around women's issues. It is unlikely to have been due to the non-random nature of the sample because special effort was made to contact black women in all refuges, a bias which should have favoured contact with any in that network.

Contact with Asian women was facilitated by the existence of Asian Women's Resource Centres and the six Asian refuges in London, all of which were full throughout the research period. The network of other Asian women's groups was not in a position to offer much assistance, although several were visited (see chapter 10).

Caribbean women were contacted through mainstream refuges (within which they are very unevenly distributed), and the single black women's refuge. Black women's centres and groups were also contacted, but again did not result in any direct contacts with women for interview.

African women's organisations and hostels in London were contacted, but did not yield interviews, although discussions were held with those that responded positively. There is no African refuge in London, and the few African women's groups were too under-resourced to offer much support to individual cases (eg Akina Mama Wa Afrika, based in Camden), although FOWARD (based at the Africa Centre, also in Camden) does some counselling and has worked on circumcision. Some African women are involved in black women's organisations with Caribbean women of African descent (eg Camden Black Sisters, East London Black Women's Organisation) and Asian women (eg Southall Black Women's Centre).

Marital status, class and ethnicity

It soon became clear that there were a variety of family forms in the sample. The 100 women who were abused by their sexual and emotional partners comprised women who had been married legally and/or according to their cultural tradition, as well as women who had cohabited or had visiting relationships. Some were escaping violent assaults by ex-partners.

Within each of these three relationship categories, numerous variations existed in terms of roles and expectations, duties and responsibilities. It was not possible to go into any finer analysis in this project, but this variation should be borne in mind.

The three relationship categories identified for the research purposes were not independent of ethnic background. In this sample, the women of Asian and African descent were all legal and/or traditional wives, while more than half of the women of Caribbean origin were cohabitees or were engaged in visiting relationships. This may bear some relation to the fact that the Caribbean sample were predominantly born and raised in Britain where a growing proportion of the population cohabit at some stage in their relationship (Barrett and MacIntosh 1982). It may also be strongly related to the material circumstances of the working class Caribbean communities in Britain. The economic and power relations are very different when one is considering domestic violence against a middle class but financially dependent wife, as compared to domestic violence against a single mother of three in a local authority flat, or violence against a professional working woman. Men who were violent to the women in this study also came from all socio-economic classes, ranging from businessmen rich enough to keep several homes (and women), to working class men who had never been afforded the dignity of earning a decent wage. What was most striking is that women across a very diverse range of domestic economic relationships and situations can be forced to flee their homes to escape violence from their partners.

This fact raises a major theoretical question about previous research on domestic violence, which has often tended to regard it as part and parcel of male power and women's economic dependence on the men battering them. While this may be true for 'housewives' in the traditional white middle class nuclear family, it was clearly not the case for a significant proportion of the black women in this study. Many were in fact being beaten by men who were dependent on them, regardless of marital status. This and other issues raised by the research findings are taken up in the discussion at the end of this chapter.

Redefining domestic violence
The case material presented here illustrates the enormous diversity in the manifestation of domestic violence. Culture, material circumstances such

as bad housing and economic stresses, drug abuse, childhood relational experiences, sexual insecurities and jealousies, deep mistrust and suspicion, misogynistic (woman-hating) attitudes, and lack of communication are just some of the recurring themes of the material. These factors are not specific to domestic violence between black people, since very similar themes recurr in European and American literature on the subject (Dobash and Dobash 1980, Yllo and Bograd 1988, WAFE 1981). Orthodox clinical approaches to 'family violence' tend to treat social and economic factors as 'confounding variables' rather than as variables that should be integrated into the analysis of domestic violence (Bolton and Bolton 1987). Yet social and economic factors constantly appear in women's accounts of their partners violence towards them as rationalisations and reasons given, as women struggle to comprehend their partners' behaviour.

On the matter of race, the existing research is contradictory, focusing on the non-issue of whether black and minority families are more or less violent than white ones and producing reasons for each side of the argument (Bolton and Bolton). Staples' work is more interesting on race, and he utilises Frantz Fanon's (1967) thesis on violence in colonial contexts to go into the analysis of black male violence (Staples 1982).

Cultural analysis does not appear to have been part of existing research on domestic violence, although it is another recurring theme in women's accounts. It seems to manifest itself most commonly in terms of husbands invoking 'tradition' or 'religion' to justify their expectations of and demands for subservient or obedient behaviour from their womenfolk. None of the world's major religious texts condone (or actively challenge) the abuse of women. Rather the issue seems to me to be more about men appropriating religion in their own exercise of power over the women with whom they live. There is certainly no justification for tolerating woman-abuse in black communities on the basis of it being 'their culture', as appears to occur in racist and colonial contexts. In Britain, other crimes are depicted as 'black crimes' and are far from tolerated. For example in the case of 'mugging' or robbery with violence, a disproportionate number of victims are black women, but popular representations imply that it is a crime in which most victims are elderly white women attacked by violent black men (see Hall et al 1978 for an extended discussion of this phenomenon).

The subject group were all volunteers and no working definition of domestic violence was imposed on the women by the researcher. In addition to their self-definition, women had also been defined as having experienced domestic violence by the agencies through which we contacted them (women's refuges and community groups), so that some filtering by these agencies had also occurred. Beyond this, the range and extent of violence described below indicates the degrees and forms of violence upon which the research project is based. As was noted above, it turned out that the vast majority had experienced at least some physical injury as well as considerable amounts of emotional anguish.

Although the initial research proposal also included the much broader and harder to define category of 'relationship breakdown', it was decided to focus on domestic violence because of the definitional complexities of the wider area of relationship breakdown and the practical constraints on the project. This was felt to be appropriate because of the central concern with housing policy and practice and because our preliminary research indicated that in the present housing climate, relationship breakdown was seldom grounds for rehousing. Where there were written policies on relationship breakdown, these were not being implemented at a time when only homeless persons are being housed in many boroughs. In any case, in terms of local authority rehousing practices and policies, domestic violence is often treated as an extreme instance of relationship breakdown.

Many women would not have been forced to tolerate violence if there had been any possibility of one or other of the couple securing alternative housing in the earlier stages of relationship breakdown. The high incidence of black male and female homelessness resulted in many couples living together more through lack of options than through choice. Since single black men have no access to public housing at all, black male homelessness can be seen in a number of cases to have been a major factor in determining the decision to cohabit in the first place. In this context the nature of relationships themselves is affected. Sometimes men had simply moved in with black women who had local authority tenancies. Many of these had previously been staying with other women and/or their mothers on a semi-permanent basis and had never had tenancies of their own. As such they would constitute part of the 'hidden homeless' population that has no statutory right to housing. Local authorities (in theory at least) are statutorily obliged to house people who have dependent children living with them, so that parents (who do have their children living with them) have a means of gaining entry to public sector housing that is not open to women or men whose children are not living with them.[3] When relationships deteriorated, men in these living arrangements not only became violent, but quite often also refused to leave, so forcing mothers and children out of their local authority accommodation to join the long queues awaiting housing in hostels, reception centres and refuges.

In terms of the assailants, these fell into a number of categories:

a) husbands;
b) cohabitees;
c) men with whom the woman had a visiting relationship;
d ex-husbands, cohabitees or visiting partners.

A small number of women interviewed had been subjected to violence by other parties. If this was in addition to violence from their sexual partner, cohabitee or husband they were included in the study. Several of the Asian subjects fell into this category, having been multiply abused by in-laws as well as spouses. One older Caribbean woman was assaulted by her son when he grew up, after she had been subjected to years of violence at the hands of her husband.

If however their experience of violence did not include violence from the man they were having or had been in a relationship with, they were excluded from the data analysis. There were six such cases including for example, Lalita a Philipino domestic worker who suffered abuse at the hands of her employer, and Sharon, a 23 year-old woman of European and African parentage who was sexually abused by her stepfather and step-brother and then violently assaulted when she matured and at the age of 16 tried to resist having sexual intercourse with them. The others were Asian women who were assaulted by in-laws, like Neelim, the 34-year old Asian woman who had her nose smashed leaving her face permanently deformed by her sister's husband, or the teenager who went into refuge with her mother, having been beaten by her father for trying to protect her mother.

While certain themes occur frequently in the data, others are more idiosyncratic. This is not the place to attempt a detailed study of the causes of domestic violence, or to go into the detail that an individual psychological understanding of would require. Rather the case material is presented to highlight some of the ways in which violence has manifested, as recounted by women who have been subjected to assaults by their male partners. These highly disturbing accounts are treated and discussed as authentic descriptive data. They are presented to illustrate the circumstances which lead women to approach existing statutory and voluntary agencies, or to desist from, or delay in approaching outside agencies, even when they are being subjected to extreme and often life-threatening behaviour. Within each unhappy tapestry there also lies a rich undercurrent of courage which testifies to the resilience and resistance these women have shown, often without any of the support that one might expect any humane society to offer, in the face of the most extreme degradation and brutality.

The violence

Domestic violence against women of Caribbean descent

SUKIE was staying at a women's refuge with her two young sons (aged six and three) when we spoke. When she was 18 she moved into a council flat with the tenancy in her name. Eugene, a casual painter/decorator came to help with the decorating. They related to each other quite well, and a few weeks later he arrived at Sukie's flat, with his baggage and moved in. Things went well until after the birth of their first son, when Eugene started to feel bitterly jealous of the young infant, and Sukie became pregnant and had their second son. Arguments began and continued, with Eugene forbidding Sukie to have her brother visit, and accusing her of having affairs with other men. When she went to visit her aunt, she would return to find her clothes and pictures hidden and clear evidence that he had entertained other women in their bedroom:

'. . . these things were going on because he used to take the children's toys and hide them in the cupboard; take all my things off the dressing table and put them inside the drawer, and once he pretended that I was his sister . . . when I used to go down to my auntie's he sort of gave this as an excuse for bringing the women there because I wasn't there, which I thought was wrong. If he wanted to do anything I thought he should go outside of the house to do it, not do it inside my house — I've got the children staying there as well. So from there we started fighting every day. One night I had to run out and he came looking for me. While he was looking he got this knife from my cousin's kitchen drawer and slashed me across the face and tore Neville (son) away from me. I've got the scar here (Sukie still bore a number of scars).'

The violence got worse, as did her partner's extreme jealousy, with him waiting outside her workplace and deploying other people to trail her and monitor her movements.

'He was possessive and the fact that I was working and saving my money really got to him because he's self-employed and every time he wants anything he wants me to help, so I was not getting any benefit out of working. He said that I was working and hiding my money from him, and that I bring up my kids too fancy — I shouldn't dress them up like that. Every time I visit my friends he said they were a bad influence on me, and he banned me from walking down that particular road. If I took the kids to my friend's house he would sort of trail me, and he got people to spy on me after work.'

'The thing is he wanted to be the ruler of the house. He said there can't be two kings in one house, and on one occasion he said that I musn't cook for the kids and don't cook for him, that he would buy separate shopping and sort of ban me from using the cooker. When we're fighting I wasn't to sleep on my bed, I wasn't to sleep on the kids' bed and I wasn't to sleep on the settee. One night he locked me in the toilet — sort of nailed it down.'

'When I was pregnant one time he said that he would see that Neville was born crippled.'

Sukie's workmates observed what was happening through the heavy bruising to her face and arms, and she saw the doctor on several occasions with her injuries. She suffered from frequent nose bleeds, headaches, developed as a result of frequent blows to the head, and high blood pressure. She also called the police on several occasions and obtained ouster injunctions from the courts. Her reason for not leaving before this stage:

'I've always said because of the kids — because of the kids I'll stay with him, so the kids can have a father'.

She had left after Eugene had wrapped a cord round her throat in a strangle grip until she almost blacked out. She still bore the scars of that assault on her neck at the time of interview. After that episode, Eugene was convicted for grievous bodily harm and bound over for a year, but it was not safe for her to go near her flat, so she fled. Her local authority acknowledged she was homeless as a result of domestic violence and placed her in a Bayswater bed and breakfast hotel where she bore filth, cockroaches and no cooking facilities for 8 months in one room with her two sons, who repeatedly became ill. Eventually she moved into the women's refuge. A year later I met her again at a different refuge, still awaiting rehousing, thinner and even more worn looking.

ROWEENA is 26 years old. She and her three children were staying in one room at a women's refuge at the time of interview. She moved away from him into her own council tenancy in 1983 after he began to drink heavily and subject her to violent attacks, but friends told him where she was. She has been fleeing from one place to another trying to escape the violent attacks of her children's father for the last five years. During that time she has been in four different women's refuges. She has also been rehoused twice, the first time in a flat abandoned by a black family before her who had been subjected to racial attacks by their neighbours. The same racist neighbours forced her to abandon her long-awaited home. She was subsequently rehoused in her ex-partner's old haunts, so that he located her and tried to burn down the flat by pouring petrol through the letter box. Again she went into a refuge. A year after we spoke, I returned to the same refuge and found she was still there, still awaiting rehousing.

CHARLOTTE is a 33 year old London-born woman who has lived with the father of her two young children for four and a half years. When they established their relationship she put all her own resources into a business with him, which failed — due to his gambling habits. He became increasingly abusive towards her over the last two years, subjecting her to constant criticism and derision day and night, and then becoming sexually and physically abusive.

> 'there was mental abuse as well. There were a lot of bad vibes generally. Bad communication, lots of complaints about everything — he would keep me awake all night going on and on criticising everything about me, my family, what I did, how I spoke, how I reacted to everything. That created a sexual problem which would bring out the violence as well . . . he would — you know — rip off my clothes and . . . (in a lowered voice she explained that she was raped).'

During her pregnancy with the youngest child she was subjected to extreme emotional and financial neglect. Another woman became pregnant by him at this point. His cruelty and neglect had deep effects on her during her pregnancy;

> 'It was very depressing. It leaves you inert and with no energy left to do anything. It took me a long time to realise the actual seriousness of the situation. That I was actually in that situation. Might sound funny but it took a long time for me to admit that it actually was a real nightmare.'

52

In retrospect Charlotte describes her partner as suffering from insecurity, and burdened with debts he had incurred. Their flat was in her name, and she also owned the car (which he prevented her from using).

> 'I think basically his problem is chronic insecurity, which is something I hadn't realised before . . . he comes over as quite arrogant and pushy actually. But he finds any type of rejection totally unacceptable.'

She left on two occasions, but returned, having nowhere else to go. Eventually she had to call the police for the second time to escort her to a women's refuge when he became frighteningly irrational one night. One of the reasons she gave for leaving were his threats to kill their children.

ZOEY was 23 years old and struggling to start a different life for herself after spending six abusive years with a man much older than her, who operated as a pimp. She spoke clearly and insightfully about her life. Zoey had been raised by an English family in the country and came to London 'in search of the bright lights' at the age of 16. She started working as a hostess in Soho clubs, where she met her partner — an influential man, quite different from anyone she had ever met, and who gradually took over control of her life.

> 'I thought I was in control of the relationship. He never worked — has never worked, so it was a completely different way of life. And I thought it was exciting, free — he showed me all different things, all the runnings* and everything . . . He was willing to show me how I'm supposed to be, and where I come from, my roots. I was to stop putting on make-up. I had been very into myself — into makeup and clothes. He was nothing like that. I never thought I would go for a guy like him. I was looking for something different I must admit. But I thought he was sort of soft when I first met him, cuz that style I had never come across — the black man's style. I think I came unstuck because he was so smart. He really worked his brain on me. He was very patient, so he got what he wanted. Everywhere he went everybody just hails him up- he's very popular. That's what attracted me to him. When I first looked at him I thought no, I was just looking into his wrinkled old face. I don't know what it was — it was his style, and after a while . . .'

---

* 'Runnings' is a Jamaican term for 'what's going on', and 'how things work' within a particular subculture.

Zoey had never experienced abuse prior to this relationship:

'The first time he hit me I left him. That's the kind of person I was. I was so shocked and appalled. But in the end I thought, well this is it. I'm in the bottom of hell, I can't get out of it. Now I'm the kind of person who gets beaten consistently and doesn't go, so I've gone mad between then and now. I'd gone mental, lost all contacts, and I had his child. And he knew all those things. He knew what he was doing'.

She concealed the reality of her situation from her parents and sister:

'To my parents I was playing happy families. They never knew the truth at all. Oh no. It would have been too appalling, it would be like a horror movie to them. That's unreal.'

Her partner was also violent to other women, and invoked the old testament in his general misogyny:

'He had no respect for women at all. He'd say that over and over again. Woman is Delilah, Satan. Woman is man's downfall and all this all the time. Woman is down there. He used to go on about Margaret Thatcher running the country — all these women running the country. When I took him to court I won an injunction. So he had 28 days to get out, and all these things just confirmed that it was a woman's country . . . He's got to have somebody to belittle all the time.'

The frequency of physical abuse varied:

'Sometimes it would be morning and night, morning and night every night for a week. If we was really at each other's throats, really arguing, and then he might not beat me for six months'.

She suffered extensive bruising and cuts from punches, kicks and being hit with furniture and other objects that came to hand. On one occasion he broke his toe kicking her. On another she was hospitalised with her head split open, and had to go to casualty on yet another. The police were called approximately 30 times in five years.

Most of their fights centred around money:

'He wanted money from me, from my work. He said he wasn't interested in the house because he was a Rasta and he was going to Africa. But he'd be willing to sit down and let me do everything financially — the food, housekeeping, bills and everything. He used to get me to give him money in the beginning, he said he would pay me back because I loaned him some. But then it got out of hand. For years and years — I can't begin to weigh up how much — thousands and thousands'

She had a friend who was in a similar relationship:

'Me and my friend used to laugh, for about three years we'd come down and laugh at ourselves. In the end that was our only pleasure. To run ourselves down. When we faced them we'd know that we'd been cursing them stupid — it was like that.'

Her friend left the scene and started a new life for herself some time before Zoey did.

'His word was God's to me and he knew best. He knew, you see? He was never supposed to be wrong. Whatever he'd encouraged me in, I would have done. That's why I'm here now. Because of sheer disgust in myself. Disgust. That's all I can say, in the end. Absolute disgust.'

ELSIE is a 25-year old woman of Caribbean and European mixed parentage who grew up in a northern English town. She has a particularly extroverted and dynamic character. The violence she was subjected to in her relationship was so bad that it drove her to attempt suicide. She had been in a relationship with Mike, the father of her child for 18 months at the time of interview. They had been living with his mother and his sister at his mother's small (two bed) council flat for the period of their cohabitation. They attempted to get council accommodation of their own on numerous occasions, to no avail.

Elsie has held a wide range of domestic catering and sales jobs, while her partner is a musician who goes for long periods without work, but felt that Elsie should stay at home and be a full time housewife.

'He wanted me to be a housey woman and I ain't housey at all. I'd rather be out working — not barefoot and pregnant over the stove . . . He used to go out for days on end, yet if I go out for an hour, he used to say — "where have you been?" I'd be wanting to ask him questions anyway, but alright. And when he comes in its "Where's my dinner, why aren't my slippers being warmed by the fire?" and all that bit. While I would tend to go about my business. Its a double standard that's been in force since Adam and Eve. I joke about it, but at the time its not funny at all.'

Most of their fights began with verbal disagreements which escalated into him being violent towards her: kicking her in the legs and chest and punching her to the face and head. He fractured her nose twice and she has a number of scars rendered with an iron bar on her arms and legs. At other times he would strike out suddenly over minor issues. Despite the severity of her injuries, Elsie partly blamed herself:

'I'm a very stubborn person, even now. I was partly to blame. But I don't think it was worth getting slapped in the mouth for it. I mean if it was that I'd done something wrong he could have said — "Elsie you shouldn't have done that," and that would have been it, I would have just said, "Yeah, alright then, I'll do it different next time", you know? It could be that I'd put too much salt in the dinner. That to him was a major mistake and I got a punch in the mouth for it. Such little things — okay, I was wrong about it, you know, but I'm not a cook, and I don't think that not being able to cook should get you a slap in the mouth . . . I'm stubborn and he's stubborn, so I wouldn't give in, because I'd been a single woman a long time before I met him, and like I moulded myself the way I like myself and I knew that. I told him before I moved in together that he was not going to like living with me.'

The situation got worse after the birth of their daughter, ostensibly because he was jealous of her. When asked what used to spark off these fights, Elsie responded:

'Money and sex. I mean I think he expected it to be like it was when we first met. Even though we were going through a bad patch. He still — he would like hit me at half past nine and at half past eleven when we were in bed he be all lovey and "Come on let's do it now?", and I'd say "No", and he'd wonder — but why? What have I done? . . . He wasn't sorry for what he'd done, because he didn't believe he'd done anything.'

Elsie explained her suicide attempt as being due to her partner's violence:

'It was hurting me that much. I didn't want to give him the satisfaction of killing me, so I thought — well, I'd top myself. But it didn't work — I was unconscious and they tried to put this tube down my throat and I thought — "Oh God, I'm going to die here".'

On one occasion when he was trying force her over the balcony, the neighbours heard Elsie's screams of 'Help — he's killing me' and called the police (see chapter 6). While she did not have any family support, she had met a number of Mike's friends; indeed he had introduced her to a particular woman friend of his who he had hoped would teach her the runnings, as he put it. As his violence became more and more extreme, his friends attempted to intervene, expressing strong disapproval of his behaviour towards Elsie, so that he refused to have anything more to do with them. Eventually, despite repeated visits and appeals to the council, unable to find anywhere else to live and trapped in a clearly life-threatening situation Elsie grew desperate and contacted the Samaritans for help. She was eventually referred to Women's Aid.

SARAH is 27 and has an 8 year old son. She had been in the refuge for 19 months at the time of interview and there was still no sign of her being rehoused. She had been going out with Maurice for about three years when he arrived one day with his bags:

> 'He virtually just moved in. I mean we were going out, and one day a neighbour came and said — "He wants you outside." And when I looked out of the window, he had taken all his things out of the car. He just moved in. We had been going out for about 3 years, but that didn't entitle him to move in automatically the way he did. But I didn't really say much. I just sort of asked him, you know, what was happening. He said he thought that was what I wanted . . . Apparently he shared a flat with another woman who had a child for him. They had apparently broken up, so I thought — you know — "what the heck?". She threw all his clothes out and then he came and said he thought it was what I wanted.'

Maurice was a self-employed decorator, while Sarah did full time office work. Their relationship deteriorated after he had moved into her council flat.

> 'He started abusing me and being aggressive, you know. I mean he'd never done it before — he always said "Oh I'll never hit a woman, I'll never hit a woman" and I always believed him. In all the three years I'd known him he'd never hit me before.'

They fought over 'silly things' — if she used the car (which was hers) when he wanted to, or being five minutes late to collect him, for example. This resulted in unexpected consequences:

> 'I went up the stairs to close the door and I just felt one punch on the back of my head. In my flat you go down as you enter the door, so I

went flying down the stairs and crashed into the wall. He just started beating me and kicking and swearing — fucking this and fucking that. I couldn't understand it — that I was too out of order, that he don't know who I think I am and all this. Until I was knocked out unconscious. When I woke up I was so mad, I wanted to kill him, but because he was so big and tall I knew that if I hit him I was going to get twice the hit I gave him back. I thought I was due to die that day because Wayne (her son) was at his aunty's. It was just me and him in the flat. Wayne was gone for the weekend. I was just so mad — I started trembling, I couldn't stop myself, I couldn't control myself. I just started to shake and then he said "Yeah, you fucking pretend you're sick, you go on and fucking pretend you're sick". And I said — "I want some water — can I have some water?" My lips just dried up and I was just trembling. He thought I was joking or something. Then he realised that I was genuinely shaking. I couldn't keep myself still. He ran to get the water and everything. And then they took me to the hospital — he took me to the hospital and everything — he lied to them and told them that I fell over and banged my head. I just told them that I didn't want him in here. He wouldn't leave because he knew that if he left me I would tell them.'

Assaults of this sort had longer term effects on their relationship; not only was making up and saying sorry followed by other attacks, but the nature of their relationship changed:

'After he started being aggressive I suppose I became afraid of him. But I always pretended — I never showed him that I was afraid of him. If he said anything, I always said it back, and that — "I'm not frightened of you". "Not frightened of me? I'll give you fright" he'd say, and I'd be sitting there thinking, "oh God, please don't let him hit me". He was always threatening before that incident . . . On the other occasion he didn't actually get to abuse me much because I jumped out of the window. I mean he would have killed me. He threatened and then slapped me in the face. I ran through the kitchen and locked the door and took the key. He ran round to come in through the front window, and I said to him you just put one foot through — he lifted his foot and I was over the balcony. I had on something skimpy, it was raining, I had nothing on my feet. Looked like a tramp. I didn't care — I just wanted to get away from him.'

Sarah explains his violence thus:

"I think he was insecure. He was jealous of the fact that — because I've always been independent, like now I'm a student and everything. I've been saving up money because I do people's hair at home and I charge them £50. I'd been saving up my money and I brought a car. He didn't like the fact that I always went out and got my things — whatever I wanted. He detested that you know — he always wanted me to have a baby for him. And I've always said no because I want my career first. "Fucking career" — he didn't like it. He did not like the fact, he just wanted me to be a slave to him. I don't know. He just seems really insecure.'

'Things got worse as time went along. He just got over possessive — he wanted me to be under his spell — at his beck and call sort of thing. I don't know why. I suppose because his parents — his mother always cooked for him and washed for him even though he was living with this other girl, he always went to his mother's for dinner. At Christmas everyone goes to his Mum's and she spoils them. And that's what he expected of me. Cook dinner every day and make sure its no rubbish.'

Violence also had a negative effect on her son:

"He was hyperactive. I had to take him to a child psychiatrist because of all the ups and downs; it disturbed him a little bit. Maurice would shout and Wayne was frightened of him. He used to say things like — "I don't like Maurice because he hits my Mum", you know — things like that. Sometimes when he got violent Wayne would wet his bed. It was obvious that that is what it was. He was frightened for me. When we took him to the child psychiatrist, I didn't go in with him, and the things he told her — I couldn't believe it. At the time he was about five — I thought what does he know about this. He knows everything and it affects him. I cried when she told me that.'

Meanwhile, the mother of Maurice's first child had another baby for him, much to Sarah's distress, since he had denied that he was continuing to have relations with her. She explains why she put up with him for as long as she did under those circumstances thus:

'I don't know. I must have loved him.'

MARY was interviewed at her council house in north London where she now lives with her three year old son. She has never stayed at a women's refuge. She is a 32-year old women of Jamaican origin who had a strictly religious upbringing in her Pentecostal family. She entered the church and engaged in missionary work in the Caribbean, and describes herself as having had very little experience of life when she met the man she married. She did not live with him before they were married, and they settled in Hackney. Since they could not find anywhere to live, they were grateful to be offered the use of Paul's sisters council flat. At that stage the relationship was far from violent. It was:

'Great — wonderful! It really was. If he swore he used to apologise — It was always — "oh I'm sorry!". I think it was because prior to that I had spent seven years in the church, so I was a total fool. He could see that, but I think that's the reason why he was so courteous and gentle — I think that had a lot to do with it. I jumped out of the church and into his arms! (laughter).'

After four years of highly sheltered married life, Mary found her life had ceased to have meaning for her. She left her husband and went to live in France for 2 years while they got a divorce. When she returned from abroad, she was again homeless, all her family having returned to Jamaica some time previously. She stayed with her now ex-husband for the time being. While she had been away he had met someone else, who he continued to see — an older woman who kept him supplied with the drugs that he had developed a dependency on.

'He wanted both of us — he didn't want to choose. So he'd be spending some of the time with her and some of the time with me.'

He went through violent mood changes and their relationship deteriorated again. On one occasion Paul took Mary's tape recorder to the other woman's house, and she angrily phoned him there. He returned and subjected her to her first serious assault:

'He came home, opened the door — I was in the kitchen and he just laid into me, left, right and centre. That was the very first time it had ever happened. I was in hospital for two days. I was traumatised and shocked. I had a lot of bruises — my eyes were out here, and I was just really lost. I was really dazed. My family had gone back to the West Indies. My mother had gone, my sister had gone — everybody had gone — I was completely alone. Well almost — I have a brother and sister here, but I couldn't really go to them — it was my younger sister and I don't think my older brother would have understood somehow. So I was alone — I did feel alone and more than that I felt ashamed, so I couldn't go to them. That was really bad. It was the shame more than anything. I couldn't understand it. I mean I had never experienced violence of that kind before. It had never happened — I've got five brothers and sisters — a large family, and I'd never known it to happen to them. I'd heard of violence, obviously, but as far as my father and mother — I'd never seen it. I'd never even met anybody who had experienced it. I think it was partly because I was in the church, and led a very sheltered life. I'd never expected it.'

After this painful experience, Mary reacted in a way not uncommon for isolated victims of domestic violence:

'When he realised where I was, where I'd gone, he turned up at 12.00 that night, but the nurse had told him to come and see me in the morning, and he came back the next day. After about 3 days, he was really contrite, he hadn't meant to do it and what have you. It sounds a really funny thing to say but, even though I knew what he had done, he was the only person I wanted comfort from. Do you understand what I mean? Although he'd put me in this position and what he'd done and what have you, he was the only person that I really wanted. I didn't feel to reject him. And I went back to him. And then I fell pregnant (laugh).'

It was after this that she discovered her partner to be a user of hard drugs, and their relationship continued to deteriorate.

'There were instances when we'd be in the car, and he'd just get into a rage — "why don't they get out of the way!", as if he wanted to kill everybody. Depending on his mood, I couldn't speak to him, without fear of being snapped at. He was on cocaine, and I think that had a lot to do with his violence towards me.'

In the end, and after further violence, even in her pregnant state, he agreed to move out. Since it had been his sister's flat however, he continued to visit and disturb her. All Mary's desperate attempts to be transferred by Hackney council failed (See chapter 4).

YVONNE is 25 years old and has three children. Her ex-partner, Roland, is a British Rail engineer. They cohabited for a couple of years, somewhat intermittently, after he moved into her council flat with her.

'He'd say I'm stepping out of line. I'm getting too big for my boots, I must remember I'm only little and things like that . . . I never had any broken bones, but I've been swollen up and bruised, which is enough. He was just sick. I remember one time I ran away, down to his Dad's house, and he even beat up his Dad so he could come in and beat me. He phoned the police. But by the time the police came he (his father) said — "It's alright — he's calmed down now — it was a domestic affair, its alright".'

The violent attacks to which Roland subjected Yvonne, particularly when he came out of prison after being remanded for other violent offences, were clearly life threatening. She was rehoused twice by the local council, and spent long period in reception centres. He found out the address of her second home before she had even moved into it, from the housing department. Yvonne has essentially been trying to escape from his violence for the last four years; this has included being attacked on the streets when he has spotted her. Their youngest son was born two days before Roland was taken into prison on remand for a different violent offence. Roland appears to have had some mental disturbance:

'About two days after Mikey was born he went into prison. When he came out he goes to me — "When did this take place? Where did this baby come from? Its not my baby". So I said to him — "During that space of time that you was in prison you have forgotten that I had a baby?". I said — "Obviously, as far as I know my two children got the same father, so if this one ain't yours, that one ain't yours". He told me that its either his Dad's child because he's got his Dad's name, or his brother's child. And then he started to name untold amount of his friends — it could be any one of them, so I was supposed to have laid down with all of them.'

His hostile feeling towards their youngest child erupted in one of his violent attacks:

'He claims he never saw the water boiling. We were having an argument, I was in the kitchen making a bottle for Mikey. I'd just turned off the fire, and the water was still there bubbling and he come in and brought the argument from one room through into the kitchen, and picked up the water and flung it like that. I had Mikey in my arms, I had him in my hand. He didn't hold it over me — he held it over Mikey — like that (demonstrates) and the water splashed upon me, but I didn't get burned. Mikey got burned from his head right down to his chest. All they did was give Roland a six months hospital order, and he kept running away, so he only served about three. After a while they said they didn't want him there no more . . . I phoned the ambulance — and I mean this is how stupid he was — he said to me I must tell them I was giving the baby a bath. Now stupid as some women are, they don't put a baby in the bath head first. When the ambulance men came they asked what had happened and that's what he told them. I never said anything in case he thump the ambulance man down and then thump me down afterwards. He wouldn't let go of the eldest one. He said I must go to the hospital with Mikey and get myself treated and Mikey treated and then come back. The ambulance man said — "Its alright love, I know what's happened", and he phoned the police on his radio thing.'

Perhaps the most alarming thing about Yvonne's case is the nature of intervention by the statutory agencies that were repeatedly involved in the case, but that is discussed in chapters 4 and 9. Her experience highlights the complete lack of protection available to black women, even when their assailants have both criminal convictions for violence and have been subject to psychiatric orders.

Domestic violence against women of Asian descent
SANGITA is a 22-year old Ugandan born woman who has a three year old son. Her family moved to Britain in 1971. She was staying at an Asian women's refuge when she shared her experiences with Ayesha. She was married to her husband, a Kenyan-born 28-year old at the age of 19, after he had visited her family for about 9 months. They lived with his mother for about a year until they were given a one-bedroom council flat. She describes her husband during the courtship:

'Before we got married he used to come around. We didn't go out, but we did sort of sit and chat. He was very shy. Very quiet. But he seemed a nice person. He never showed any signs that he'd be a violent person. Very quiet and shy.'

Three months after they had been married another side of his character emerged:

'Usually when he was drinking at pubs and all that, someone would say something to him and he'd hit — he'd blow his top. Or he didn't beat them up, he'd just get angry. With his brothers and sisters he didn't get violent — just get very angry . . . He hit my sister-in-law once because she was trying to protect me. And he hit his own Mum once, but that was because she was trying to protect me as well. He used to kick me, throw things at me. Kick me, punch me — he used to throw me about the room. He used to pull my hair to pieces . . . No broken bones, but I've had black eyes and I've got scars, loads of scars to prove, because he used to have quite long nails — he'd just grab hold of me and the skin would sort of come away . . . I always used to say if you want to hit me don't do it in front of the child because it would affect him. It has affected my son, but now he has calmed down a bit.'

Various, often trivial 'misdemeanours' sparked off violence:

'If he didn't like anything I was doing. If he didn't like the cooking — because he used to be a meat eater, if I made vegetables he'd just throw the pans everywhere — throw the food everywhere. If I didn't talk to his parents properly, his Mum properly. If I was talking to his sister — he didn't like that. If I went shopping without telling him. If I left the house. So I was just a prisoner in my own home. I wasn't allowed to go out anywhere.'

'When I did refuse to have sex with him, he'd say to me — Are you sleeping with another person? You must be. He was so suspicious. He'd often say to me — You must be sleeping with other men. And he'd sort of force himself on me . . . Yes, it was very painful.'

Interventions by Sangita's female relatives on her behalf only exacerbated the situation.

'My sister-in-law used to tell me, you know — Go to the doctor. But I was too scared to go out of my own house, in case he caught me going anywhere. I just sort of locked myself in. But I did tell my health visitor once. At that point I was really breaking — cracking up you know.'

Sangita was then referred to a community centre that did not assist her in any way. Eventually it was her mother and sister who helped her to escape to an Asian refuge in another part of town.

SMITA now 28 years old, has one daughter and is a community worker. She comes from a Pakistani Muslim family that settled in Britain in 1960. She was about to sit her O-levels when she was married:

'I was about 16 and he was about 30 years of age at the time, so I let my parents make the decision at the time. I think what they were looking for more than anything was that he had a good job — he was well settled and they thought I'd be looked after. That was all they were looking at — the material aspect of the marriage. I was very worried, but I didn't think I had a say. I think the way I was brought up was — I didn't have a choice. They were making the decision that they thought was right for me.'

She was subjected to her first assault the day after the marriage:

'Immediately after the marriage, because I'd offered my sister a drink. After the wedding she'd come to stay with me for a week. I'd offered her some orange juice and he said I didn't have the right to do that . . . It was bad from the start really. He was very oppressive, very authoritarian mannerisms. Thought he knew everything that was right for me, totally controlling. I was totally controlled and it was almost like living with one's father. I played a very menial role of cooking and cleaning and that's all. I wasn't asked anything and didn't have any friends. I wasn't allowed friends actually. I had no contact with the outside world. Virtually a prisoner in my own home. It was a very sort of numb feeling — that one wasn't really living — a horrible existence. I was kept indoors and not allowed any opinion even — suddenly my life had changed from being a free, easy-going schoolgirl to one that was almost a prisoner. I didn't think it was my fault, all this — I hadn't done anything to deserve this.'

The violence was severe, including:

'Kicking, pushing, threats of using a knife. He pushed me against the radiator once — he would push me against hard objects. Punching and kicking. I actually ran out of the house and my nose was bleeding. Yes I did have injuries — head injuries. I stayed in hospital for about 2 weeks. After that I suffered depression, and I had amnesia for a long time. Bouts of amnesia when I would forget things. I've been very depressed since it all. I used to get blackouts and just keep forgetting things. Frightening actually.'

'When I was six months pregnant he pushed me down the stairs. And then he just wasn't around when I'd had the baby. There was no caring in him at all; there was no love, there was no care.'

'When the baby was born, when she started crying too much he just put the pillow over her face. It was so awful to think that . . . In a way

65

I was getting in his way. I mean the fact that he'd married me, now I was getting in the way of him having other relationships — just me being around wasn't nice for him. I don't think I can remember a time when he wasn't being abusive. We couldn't have a conversation because he didn't think I was worth having a conversation with — I was too stupid to have intelligence. He was always putting me down.'

'There was another spell after that where I was beaten up on the street and he had beaten me up so violently that I again had a blackout and I was in hospital for about five or six weeks after that . . . He punched me and I fell against the concrete. I was very, very badly beaten up. No-one helped me, everybody walked away. They didn't get involved. That was the first day of my breakdowns. After I had recovered from the physical injuries I just lost control and I had a nervous breakdown in hospital. I was transferred to a psychiatric ward.'

Smita was put into group therapy, which she found intimidating. Her family do not appear to have been much help. In fact her father had been violent to her own mother for years, so that domestic violence was probably a normal and accepted occurrence in their family relationships:

'I think they were angry because I'd ended up in the psychiatric hospital, because they had all the old myths. Suddenly I'd lost control of my life and I wasn't an able citizen any more. I wouldn't say they were supportive really.'

'Although the marriage lasted for seven years we didn't really live together because he — his lifestyle meant that he stayed away mostly because he was having lots of affairs with other women and he had his own flat.'

When she went back to college after the birth of her daughter, his violence got worse. Prior to that she had courageously kept her books and tried to study for her O-levels in secret, a difficult thing to do in her mother-in-law's house. Smita then took a job to sustain herself and her daughter as well, since her wealthy husband had ceased to provide any income whatsoever.

After she escaped to a women's refuge, the court awarded custody of their daughter to Smita's husband, ostensibly because he could provide a better home. She is still involved in the court battles around custody and divorce, five years later.

MADINA is 20 years old, of Bangladeshi origin, with an enthusiastic character that immediately endears her to people. She went to school and grew up in Tower Hamlets and was married five years ago when she was 15, to a Bangladeshi man who came to Britain from Kuwait to marry and settle here.

'I'm brought up here obviously, so I didn't want an arranged marriage but I had no choice. I was forced into the arranged marriage bit and well — that was that. But I thought I could cope with going along with my husband and with the idea of a housewife and whatever. I thought I could cope with it, but at the beginning . . . He sort of . . . I don't know how to explain it . . .'

'He thought I was too Westernised. The violence started from the beginning. Every time I tried . . . I couldn't get myself to fall in love with him. Even though I pretended. I then tried to forget about that part of life and just be a complete housewife, but he . . . it just sort of . . . he used to see me in a peculiar way. He never acted to me as a husband — the way a husband should act. That's what I think anyway. Then after about two months of my marriage I just couldn't handle it any more. I wasn't happy! With the marriage, with my husband, with the way I was living. He didn't understand me, and I didn't understand him. I did understand him, but he didn't understand me. I left him and went to my Mum's after two or three months. I just left him because I couldn't cope with being depressed all the time. Four years of marriage was being depressed every day of it. I was married for four years and that was four years of being depressed all the time.'

Madina's family persuaded her to return to her husband several times in those four years, although her mother was fairly supportive. She continued to try:

'I had Sima, my daughter, but day after day it was as if he never noticed I was there. He used to work. I was there for the cooking, the cleaning, the um — for his bedtime, to look after Sima — that was all I was there for. I didn't exist as a person. I felt so depressed sometimes . . . He used to pick on anything he saw I was doing, whether it was right, wrong, even if it was right he'd find something wrong with it. He used to just pick on it to find a way of starting an argument with me. So we were always arguing and through the arguments he used to sometimes hit me.'

'I don't blame myself in any way, because — I mean I know I'm saying this — I'm defending myself, but he couldn't have asked for someone better. I did my role I was a mother, I looked after the kid, I stayed at his house all the time. I was a complete housewife. A complete Indian housewife! Even though I've been brought up in this country, but he just couldn't accept that. I don't know why.'

'He was so big-headed that he thought whatever he said and whatever he did was right, because he was my husband he had the right to hit me and abuse me and things like that . . . I was just an object for him.'

After Madina left him, her husband went to Bangladesh, making no attempt at reconciliation.

SHIREEN is the British born daughter of a Pakistani Muslim family. She is 19 and has a nine month old baby boy. She was married to a 25 year old man of similar background, just before her 16th birthday. She had planned to leave home at the earliest possible opportunity, having been subjected to violence and abuse at the hands of her father. Her mother had been coerced into being his second wife after an unwanted pregnancy, and had been forced out of the marital home by constant violence and abuse. Shireen's mother had to go to the police herself to try and stop her husband harassing her. So Shireen had borne the stigma of her mother's fate, and been raised by her father and his other wife. She had been promised to an older man, and when that fell through her father arranged her marriage and she was told of it a week before. Yet she looked forward to a way out of her miserable home life:

'I realised that I was going to be married and I thought, Wow! Brilliant! I'm going to break out of this vicious circle. When I got talking to my husband and had a nice relationship I thought it was fantastic. So I was really happy about it when I got married. But bit by bit his true colours started to come out.'

Shireen found her in-laws strict and begrudging towards her. There was a great deal of violence in the family, and it emerged that her husband had spent seven months in prison, out of a 14 month sentence for GBH. She discovered her husband to be having affairs, taking drugs, drinking and gambling. His violence started while his parents were in Pakistan:

'First it was once or twice a month. He was a part-time boxer and he's six foot six. I am not exaggerating he's really fit to look at — he's really handsome, proper — what a girl would want in a man. He beat me up and he used to do weight training at home. He used to lift the whole weight up in one hand and put the punch bag in the middle of the room and box that. Then when he used to hit me, it wasn't as if he was hitting a fragile woman. Women are fragile — its not as if it were man to man. He used to really lay into me, punch me about. He would hit like a man to a man. Punch me — really get the punch out as if he was in the boxing ring. I got beaten up so badly that he broke my nose. Blood clots and long strings of blood — the whole works.'

Shireen got no support from her own family. Rather she was further humiliated:

'My father used to stick up for my husband. He used to stand up for him and I always used to be in the wrong. The last time I saw my Dad he made me cry. He insulted me in front of the whole family, in laws too. Then they thought, well, if she's nothing in her father's eyes, then she's got no respect, no status. Then they started, you see. If my Dad had shown a bit of respect in front of them, it wouldn't have been that bad. Fair enough a father should tell his daughter off, but it could be done between us and I wouldn't have bothered. He could have said anything — he could have beaten me up or anything, but as long as it was done in private.'

Shireen was subjected to quite extreme violence, and lost her first pregnancy. It was therefore her second pregnancy that resulted in the birth of her son:

'When my son was born, my husband turned round to me and said to me, listen — I've got out of you what I wanted out of you and that was a son. After that that was it. There was nothing to our sex life and he had other women.'

On one occasion her husband dragged her down the stairs to throw her out of the house while she still had stitches in from surgery following a subsequent miscarriage brought on by the violence. Her father-in-law had accused her of aborting herself after she lost that baby. The neighbours called the police on several occasions. Shireen was driven to desperate actions:

69

'My husband beat me up so bad on one occasion that I was in the kitchen, and as he went out there was a glass bottle and I smashed it on the sink and started jabbing it in my arm. He got the bottle off me and took me to hospital and I had bandages. I couldn't look after my son so I left him at my mother's. She asked me what had happened to me and I said I fell over on the floor.'

One day, after a fight with her mother-in-law, followed by her husband punching her in her bed that night, Shireen took her son and escaped. She has since changed her name and plans to raise her son lovingly, and to study to become a lawyer.

SUNITA is a British born Indian woman who grew up in a suburban home. She was married to a man of similar background, in what turned out to be an attempt by his family to extricate him from a relationship with an older married Indian woman.

'He was in love with her before we were married, and then he was okay with me for a month. And then he became so distant. He just completely changed. At first he was loving and caring and would always consider me in everything. Then he just became distant and he would never be at home. If I wanted to talk to him he'd never be there. I was always just left with the in-laws, and he'd be away with this other woman. They have another house, which is my husband's . . . My husband told me himself that he had this woman and he loved her and he could never give her up. He was saying that he can't leave her and he wasn't going to leave me either. I'd have to stay at home — you know — stay there as I was doing.'

After two and a half years, Sunita left, with the help of a social worker. She has not had any family support throughout her sad marriage:

'My parents are very upset about it. They keep sending letters through my social workers and telling me to come home because its their reputation at stake. All they keep saying is "don't change". But I gave them all that time before for them to do something. I told them what I was going through. They said that they can't do anything. And now I've made a step, all of a sudden they're caring and want me back. I know my Mum cares a lot about what people say. She's just worried — what can she say to people, and back home in India what is she going to say. Its their reputation — that's all they're worried about.'

Her husband for his part has received the divorce petition:

'He just keeps saying that I'll end up being a slag, being used by men. That I'll end up being a very lonely person. He tells me to come home now, while both families want you. Later on in life nobody will want you and you'll be very lonely . . . I've told him he's a free man now — he can bring her home and she can look after his parents and be a daughter in law and bring their children up. He said I was just acting like an English person now. He thinks that men should do that. He goes "You think what I'm doing is bad. Loads of men do worse than that. People hit their wives. I've never hit you". He thinks what he was doing to me wasn't bad.'

HAMZA is a Kenyan born woman of Punjabi Sikh origin who fell in love with and married a Kenyan born man of Punjabi Hindu origin. Her family were unhappy about the marriage because her husband's previous marriage had broken down. He became extremely overpossessive and violent immediately after they had married.

'Right from the first day of marriage, he became so possessive suddenly. Very, very possessive. He just wanted to control me completely; he didn't want me to have any friends, he was jealous of everyone I knew or associated with. He didn't want me to wear this, that and the other. He completely changed. He kept saying "Now you're married, so you have to do this, now you're married you must not do that". I was shattered by all this experience, and I couldn't just go back to my parents because I was unhappy, they would just have said "We told you so!". I was completely in a daze. I just didn't know what to do . . . The first time he hit me was a week after the marriage.'

He wanted her to abandon her teaching job and stay in the house, although financially this was not a realistic option, and beat her for insisting that it was necessary that she continue working. In any case she was soon grateful that she had some life outside her unhappy marital situation. She left him several times because of the violence, but did not wish to be a burden to her own family.

'Every time there was a fight because he wanted me to leave my job. I said "No", because I knew we couldn't really survive without my income. I used to have bruises, but nothing that would really bleed — no cuts. But I would have lots of marks. Gradually as time passed he realised that if I was beaten on the face it left marks and then I had to

71

pretend I was sick. So I couldn't go to school and that created a lot of complications because my mother would come to visit me also. When he realised this, he started hitting me on my head and back, where it wouldn't be really seen.'

In 1982 they sold up and moved to Britain, where they brought a house jointly. Hamza hoped that they would have a fresh start. Unhappily, things only got worse, and she was now completely isolated.

'When he used to hit me it wasn't because we didn't have a good sexual relationship, but he used to complain many times that I was not — that I was frigid, he would say. I guess I couldn't respond ever because of the way he used to treat me . . . He would hit me at any time. It didn't bother him that I was pregnant. In fact he hit me with a stick once, when I was eight months pregnant with my first baby. I lost that baby anyway . . . I don't know whether it had anything to do with the beating but . . . it was born a bit early — four weeks — and didn't have a lung, so it died.'

In England, both of them were at home all day, since she never got a job in Britain, and her husband was self-employed. Hamza eventually found the strength within herself to take her children and leave her husband. She went into a refuge. She had been there for well over a year at the time of interview, with no prospect of being rehoused by her local authority, since they are awaiting the outcome of her divorce settlement (see Part II).

GEORGINA is of Malaysian-Chinese mixed origin. She has a five year old daughter and works for a local authority, having escaped from a violent husband and gradually rebuilt her life in the 10 years since their marriage. She had known her Nigerian student partner for one year, then they cohabited in a council bedsit for a year and then married and they moved into a one-bedroom Camden Council flat. 10 months after they were married, he became verbally abusive and threatening, and then subjected her to serious assaults on three occasions.

'The final attack came when I was four or five months pregnant. I remember I was asleep — he was out as usual — out all day and all night. The next thing I knew someone just dragged me onto the floor and kicked and punched me, and then all this verbal abuse while he was doing it. I was so shocked. Because I was asleep at the time it was like a nightmare. I wasn't sure it was really happening. But it was — I felt the pain and everything. I remember saying, "Don't come near me, right?". I remember grabbing a badminton racket and saying that, "If you come near me I will hit you". The next thing I knew was that he had overpowered me and took it from me. Then I was hit right down on my head. I had a cut on my forehead and I've a scar on my chin here. The next day I didn't go to work or anything. I was sort of at home. And then I started to bleed heavily. The doorbell rang, and when I went to the door it was his best friend. When I opened the door and he saw me, he just freaked out, and I remember him going to call an ambulance. He said, "I'm going after him, but before that I have to go with you to hospital". I went to hospital and had a miscarriage.'

Violence had other, longer term effects on her as well as the immediate and traumatising damage she suffered;

'My whole personality had changed from that violence. For two years I withdrew myself completely . . . I became isolated and kept away from everybody and everything. I was like a robot. I suffered from a lot of headaches.'

On being discharged from the hospital after her miscarriage, Georgina went to all the various statutory agencies for help, but was turned away unhelpfully, and often even more upset as a result of their treatment (see Part II). Her husband continued to be violent towards her until she found a particularly original way of handling the situation, with the help of her workmates and friends.[4]

SUI WONG is a 37 year old woman of Cantonese birth who has three teenage children. She was married for 18 years to her husband who is now 61 years old and worked in a take away restaurant while they were married. He became violent soon after the birth of their first child. Sui's husband turned out to be an alcoholic, and when drunk became verbally and sexually abusive and, like many alcoholics, incontinent.

Being a traditional Chinese woman, she lived with this for years, and was very reluctant to confide the extent of the horror she was living to family members. Indeed, her attempts to find a way out of her situation were largely in vain. She speaks very little English and could not afford the fees that a Chinese solicitor demanded from her when she enquired how to file for a divorce. She started doing piece-work at home to try and establish some economic security for herself and her children.

In sober moments, her husband denied all his terrible behaviour completely, even when she left the evidence for him to see, he merely accused someone else of making the mess. She received little family support:

'They all know that he has a drinking problem, but they think the men are like that. That I ought to accept it. They find it acceptable.'

Eventually, after 18 years of misery, during which she grew to thoroughly despise her husband. Sui heard of the Chinese Information and Advice Centre. She contacted them and was advised. She is now divorced and lives in a bed and breakfast with her children, as another homeless single parent family. She still has no family support:

'They used to think I was wonderful to cope with it, but they look down on me now that I'm divorced.'

Her husband won access rights to the children in court and visits every week. Sui says she hates him and wishes she could never see him again. (Interview conducted through translator in Cantonese)

SHUWEI is a 30 year old medical doctor who specialised in acupuncture. She originated from Shanghai. She married a man of Malaysian Chinese origin who was also an acupuncturist and they brought a house in his name and set up in private practice together. One month after their marriage, he became violent. All the money from their work went into her husband's account, and she was kept without money most of the time. Worse still her husband often did not bother to work: Shuwei worked at acupuncture during the day, and in a restaurant at night to try and keep things going. She also did all the household chores, while her husband watched TV and periodically assaulted her. When she became pregnant and stopped the restaurant work, her husband insisted that she have an abortion, as he did not want any children.

She describes feeling sick every day from being hit in the head and throat. After six months of this treatment, Shuwei was hospitalised with broken ribs. All her resources, and all that she had worked for were in his control. When she got home from the hospital, her husband asked her why she had come back and not died. Shuwei left, so beginning an alienating ordeal of staying in hostels and refuges, disadvantaged by her limited use of English. It was only after months of homelessness (see chapter 4) spent in racist and unsuitable temporary accomodation that she was able to find herself another job, which fortunately in the circumstances, had tied accomodation.

SU CHANG comes from a middle-class Chinese family and was going out with a fellow student of the same age from Hong Kong for about six months before she agreed to marry him, in secret, and against both of their families wishes. As a result for the first seven months of their marriage they did not actually live together, until Su told her parents she was going to live with four other Chinese girls, and moved in with her husband.

'Before we got married he was extremely nice, extremely understanding, extremely mild tempered. The things that he didn't like about me, came out after the marriage. Yet I was the same person before and after the marriage. Our problems were things that he had said he didn't mind. For example I smoke and he knew that I smoked before the marriage — he said, "Of course girls can smoke, why can't girls smoke — its fine." But after the marriage it was a case of — "My wife can't smoke, but girls can smoke." He had seemed very open-minded and liberated about everything. He never expressed anything in particular that was different from my own opinion. He was easy-going, very generous and very humorous as well. I'd been very honest with him about the things I had done in the past. I went out with a number of guys, and he went out with a number of people as well. We actually joked about the people we went out with. I didn't know at the time that he would remember everything I said about my previous boyfriends. He became an extremely possessive and very jealous person. I wasn't aware of that before because he had said that he didn't mind that I'd been out with people before. He didn't mind anything in particular. I didn't think I'd done anything wrong. Nothing out of the ordinary for girls over here as far as I know. Then after we got married, things started. If we were arguing about anything he would start quoting examples — "Why did you do this in the past, why didn't you do that." And then he would insinuate that I was cheap to have slept with people, although I stress that I only slept with people that I felt for. I don't sleep around, you know — for the sake of it.'

Her husband's jealousy grew worse as time went by;

'He started minding me going out with my friends. Especially ex-boyfriends. Some of them I still know as friends. He disliked them so much that it got to the point where I couldn't see them. If I made arrangements to see them he would make it very difficult when I got back. He would question this and question that. He was quite rude when he saw me with any of my friends. It got to the point where I avoid going out with my friends, and I hated bumping into people in front of him, because he can be very abusive as well.'

He used the fact that she had confided in, indeed married him, as well as physical beatings to try and exercise this type of control:

'I thought of leaving him actually, quite early on in the marriage. I threatened a lot to go for divorce. At the same time he would threaten me with going to my parents, and telling that I smoke — my parents didn't know that I smoke. And that I was married to him, and the fact that I had had an abortion as well. But that was because of him — it wasn't with someone else — it was with him. All these things that Chinese parents just couldn't take. My Dad has always been a very tough person to get around, and I've always been frightened of him because of his temper. I just couldn't face the consequences of my husband telling them everything that I did in the past. It was blackmail. As a result of that I gave up my friends, I gave up going out with the people that I used to know — they were all people that he knew. They all come from overseas and — especially the blokes — they've got very male chauvinistic attitudes.'

'I was smoking behind his back when he was away, thinking he wouldn't know. When he came back from Hong Kong he said — "Have you been smoking in the summer?" I said "No." He asked — "Are you sure you haven't?" And that's when I started to think — "Oh my God — he's found out." And then he said — "You've lied to me! You have smoked." And then he slapped me. He slapped me so hard he sent me flying across to the other end of the room. He pushed me around and swore at me, said that I'm cheap, I'm a prostitute, I'm all sorts of things under the sun, you know? — How could I be with someone who doesn't even earn my trust? And for two days he made my life hell. For some reason I was extremely submissive to him. I was just so scared of him going to my parents.'

'He just couldn't get it out of his system, that I'd been out with guys, that I'd slept with guys — he couldn't forgive me. Especially this guy who I had been out with who was still a friend. I don't know why, but for some reason he kept on thinking that I would be unfaithful to him. If I made a comment about someone on the TV — even how ugly they were — He would get so mad that he would start throwing the furniture around the house, breaking my china ornaments and things like that, just causing a complete mess.'

'At one time, before we moved, we lived in this grotty place near Bethnal Green. It was a really awful place, really dark, very scary. I'm just scared — so scared of being on my own and he knew that, so whenever we had a fight he would take the car and go off to stay with any of his friends, in the middle of the night and not come back for two days. Until I eventually phoned him, to beg him to come back. Going through the night on my own was the most frightening thing for me. I would have all the lights on in the house. Cry myself silly, until I was eventually so tired I was too exhausted to do anything but fall asleep. Then the next night it would be the same thing again. Until I couldn't tolerate it. Then I'd phone him and literally beg him to come back — I'd say it was all my fault, everything was my fault, I shouldn't have done this or that. It was a vicious circle.'

Su explains why she stayed in such a destructive relationship for as long as she did, beyond the blackmail already mentioned:

'I think I did actually believe time and time again that he would change when he cried and apologised. I thought about him every time, because he seemed so lost and helpless. I just didn't have the heart to tell him "No, I'm not going to give you another chance", when he was in such a state. He even tried to commit suicide, when I really threatened to leave him once. He's driven me to several suicide attempts.'

One day, in a fit of pique, because Su was visiting her family, he marched into the house:

'He just walked through the door and said to my Mum — "Did you know your daughter's married to me? Did you know she smoked and did you know she's sleeping around like a prostitute as well?" — you know — just one after the other, he just completely bombarded my Mum with it all. She was so shocked she burst out crying. She looked at me and said, "Will you tell me this person is lying to me?" I looked at her and I couldn't. I didn't know what to say. I wanted to die that minute.'

So ended the marriage. In the end Su was reconciled with her family and got a divorce, living with the terror of threatened underworld reprisals against her and her family on the one hand, and hardening her heart to her husband's pleas on the other. She suffered acute damage to her self-esteem as a result of her experiences:

'For a long time after my marriage I thought I would never go out with anyone again. I didn't think anyone else would want me.'

LINDA is a 31 year old Filipino woman with a two year old son. She met her English husband while she was working for a cosmetics company in the Middle-East. They went out together for about eight months, and then he returned to England but they kept in touch by post:

'We went out together — to dinner parties. He's a very nice man. I think that's why I fell for him. He is very gentle, very kind, very romantic.'

This 'gentleman' sent for her to join him in England and they were married. Within two months of marriage things changed drastically:

'When he's drunk he gets violent, even over just a small thing. Like he says he doesn't want me to wear jeans. Or use any word of American — like "kids". I mustn't say kids I must say children. And he is very jealous, for no reason. He's older than me — he's fifty-something.'

'The first time he beat me we were in America. He took a job for two years and we were staying in a hotel. We were just having a drink after working with some of his colleagues, and I was talking to one of the blokes and he didn't like that. When we got to our room he started calling me names and beating me and all. I tried to run away, but he found me in the station.'

'Whenever he comes home I feel edgy, like maybe he'll start again. Every time I say something, he'll say no, that's not right. He thinks I'm stupid or dumb, I don't know anything. He's always trying to teach me. You won't believe that he even tried to teach me to operate the cooker. How to put the bed sheets on the bed and all that. I couldn't believe it.'

'I don't think he trusts me. He's very insecure. Every time I go out he is with me. I can't even go out on my own — even to the butcher, or to go for my check up. After we came to London we confirmed that I was pregnant and we were both happy. I thought things will change. I

78

should give it a try. When I went for my check up he came with me, right inside the surgery. After that he had a bit of drink and then start an argument, calls me names and I just ignored him. I was so depressed. I thought — "My God, is this what marriage is all about?" I wanted to run away but I don't know how. I don't know anybody here and I got no money.'

It was the beating she received in her third month of pregnancy that drove Linda to run away:

'I had the beating and then he threw me out of the house. He said he doesn't want me any more. He called me all the names that you can think of . . . I had a few punches all over the place and he kept hitting my head against the wall, so I packed my things and left. I stood outside the door. I didn't know what to do. Hoping he would call me. He did call me back. Took my suitcase into the bedroom and apologised. He swore to me that he would never touch drink any more. He won't beat me again. So I believed him. But that was only for one day. The next day he was good. And then the next day again he started beating me. He came home drunk while I was cooking. I nearly burned my cooking. He kept calling me in the sitting room. I was very scared. I didn't answer because if I answered, whether I was right or wrong, I was still wrong. So I thought not to cause any argument I would keep quiet. But then he gets angry if I don't answer. I just kept moving away from him, that's all. And I was shaking. He punched me in my tummy. I was already three months pregnant at the time I thought I would lose the baby. He threw me out of the house. I didn't want to move. He said, "Get out, I don't want you any more, you whore." So he grabbed me by the shoulder and threw me out of the house. So I stood outside the door, and he came out and pushed me. He pushed me four times, until I reached the main road. The fourth time he pushed me I fell over and I had some bruises on my knee, and my wrists were bleeding. I was praying that one of the neighbours would come, and at least he would stop. But none of them came. I was just running on the road, shouting for help. None of the people helped — they just stared at me. He was running after me as well, but I was running faster than him because he was drunk and he was unsteady. I got to the crossing and I saw this police car coming. I stood in the middle of the road and shouted — "Help! Help!" And heard the screech of the car.'

Linda got little sympathy at the police station, but so began the long process of seeking a home for herself and her future child (see Part II).

Domestic violence against African women

MABEL is a 33 year old Ghanaian with two children; a five year old son and a four-year old daughter. She ran her own small business and lived in a council flat and has lived in London since 1974. Nine years ago she met Kofi, a Ghanaian tailor, who shared her strong Christian faith, and after two years they were married. She attributes some of their problems to his family:

'They didn't seem to get on with me. They interfered a lot, and I won't take that. I don't want anybody to tell me what I have to do in my own home and things like that. Kofi was pressurised by the family: they said I was having a good time, taking the money from him or whatever. I don't know what they were thinking of, because I always worked hard. Yes, most of the time I provided everything. And I didn't really demand of him. But because of the way they see me — I love to look good, that's me. So when they see me dressing up well, they think that it's from him.'

Her husband's violence was irregular:

'One week he's alright, and then the next he's like a monster. It was on and off for about 10 months.'

At other times he was:

'. . . a very nice man. A very nice father. He is wonderful. He really cares for his children. But when the monster comes, you know . . . Then he'd cry. Whatever he did, he'd start crying and asking — "Why did I do it?" — talking to the little boy as if he was a big man and all that . . . He is a believer, a Christian, and he didn't believe in psychiatrists or whatever they call them. He always believed in — well — we do have demon spirits anyway, so that could come in. Like those were behind everything. As far as I'm concerned, because he can be as nice as anybody and can be as nasty as a monster.'

'He would break down, he would kiss my feet like Jesus did and he would quote from the Bible — "The Bible says this, the Bible says that." But yet he'd do it again. I mean what can you do? "How long would that go on", I always asked him, "How long?".'

They turned to the church and to prayer, but to no avail. Instead Kofi went on to inflict quite serious injuries to her, and she saw the effect this was having on her children:

'I had to go to hospital for head X-ray. And I was taking tablets for migraines. He left me with bruises almost everywhere, bite marks and all that.'

'I didn't want my children to see us fighting all the time. It got to a time that whenever the two of us sat down to talk, my little girl, Suzie — at that stage she was only a year old — she would come and stand in front of us and sort of look at Mummy, look at Daddy . . . and the little boy, especially, when he was about 4 years old would start and shout — "Don't shout at Mummy, Daddy, stop talking to Mummy, go away! Don't fight Mummy, you want to kill my Mummy!" I really felt sorry for my son because I didn't want him to grow up and have that kind of thing in his mind at all — that one time my Daddy wanted to kill my Mum, or that he was beating Mum all the time. Otherwise he would probably — God forbid — grow up and behave like that. I just couldn't allow that to happen at all.'

Mabel persuaded her husband to move out, but could get no peace from him. Eventually she abandoned her flat and her business and went into a women's refuge, where she was staying when we interviewed her.

IYAMIDE was brought over to England by her husband in 1977. He was much older than her, but she had known of him in her community for years. Since living in London she continued her career as a nurse, while he worked in a large department store. They lived in a house they rented form their local authority, once they had the children. Their relationship deteriorated from the time he brought her to England;

'You know African men — when they've brought you here, they think that you are a slave. Especially when they are older than you. They want to make their power over you.'

Her husband, a teetotaller himself, took exception to her drinking an occasional glass of wine. She found herself alone, without friends or relatives in this country. Her husband worked and they had no social life at all:

"We go to work during the day. Then he goes to bed. I had nobody to talk to. We had no social life. It was a miserable life actually. Even if he came to sit down, he'd be over there sleeping. Since I joined him, we could never go out. He'd go to work, come and lie down and sleep.'

On the other hand:

'If I introduced any friends to him, he would be after them. After I went back home to visit, one of my friends who used to come — we used to be very close — she just cut off. When I asked her what was wrong, what have I done? She said to me — "Iyamide, you are very good to me, but all the time your husband is harassing me to make love to him".'

'I had three children for him, and the way he insults me! I can never stand it. Each time I thought about it I didn't want to make love to him.'

She was beaten and kicked repeatedly, on one occasion until

'My eyes were bleeding. When he saw my eyes were bleeding, saw the blood, he called the ambulance. By the time the ambulance had come, he had washed everything, cleaned the whole corridor. He didn't want the people to see that. When the doctor attended me he asked if my husband did this — because of the way they saw my eye full of blood. I went back because of the children. Since 1980 I was staying because of the children. They love him so much.'

Iyamide had to go to hospital three or four times, where she had X-rays. Her vision has been permanently damaged by repeated blows to her eyes and head.

'When the youngest baby was born he beat me. He tried to strangle me. My voice all went. I couldn't even talk. He was on top of me, holding my neck like this (demonstrates). After that I just tried to hold on to something and I banged him on the head. Otherwise he would have finished me that day. From that time until today we never made love.'

Iyamide left her husband shortly after this. I heard her disturbing account of what happened to her after that in what the council call 'temporary accommodation'. (See Chapter 4).

PATIENCE is a Nigerian store manageress who has been in a relationship with Ransome for nine years. They have a young son and got married a year and a half ago. She has left him many times because of his cruelty to her and their child.

'Last Easter he took me and stripped me in front of his friends. He was beating me, punching me and pushing me about. I had come in from the kitchen because I heard him saying some nasty things in front of his friends trying to be funny by making fun of me. So I came out from the kitchen and I told him he would regret the things he was doing. As I was going out he started rough-handling me — shouting and pushing me. As he was doing all that my zip had come down, and my breast was coming out — I didn't even notice — I was busy trying to restrain things so as not to display anything to those people. He started slapping my breast and shouting "Cover yourself!" All in front of his friend and the wife, while they were looking on'.

Ransome has been consistently unfaithful to Patience. Probably partly because she grew up in a polygamous home herself, what disturbs her most is his degrading behaviour towards her and his taste for pornography. When she leaves, he begs and cajoles her to come back.

'He hasn't spent long in Nigeria. His Dad is here and he's spent most of his years in this country, yet he says to me "Our tradition is that women should live with their men". He is not serious!'

She has been subjected to pressure from elders in her family (all men) who are concerned that she should have all her children with the one husband. For her own part she does not feel it would be in her interests to get a divorce from her student husband because as she put it, 'I have worked hard for him'. Custody or maintenance rulings in British courts would be of no use to her when they return to Nigeria, where (in her community) taking legal action against one's husband is not an acceptable way of solving marital problems. Her own friends have tired of advising her to permanently leave Ransome. Patience has been multiply abused; not only has her husband injured her on numerous occasions, but on one occasion when neighbours called the police to intervene, they took the opportunity to arrest her and subject her to racially and sexually humiliating ridicule and then assaulted her at the police station (see chapter 6).

Discussion

A number of themes emerge from this material, some of which were introduced in chapter one. The degree to which violence against women in their homes is tolerated in Britain has long been condemned by the women's movement here, but this has largely been from a Eurocentric feminist perspective. The class, race and cultural dynamics of agency responses to domestic violence have been grossly neglected by feminists, except for the more vociferous Asian women's organisations (such as Southall Black Sisters). Regarding women of African and Caribbean origin, community groups have focused on police brutality, rather than the more sensitive issue of woman abuse. Police brutality is less of a contentious topic within the black communities because it is an oppression delivered by the 'Other' — in this case the state. Woman abuse remains a shameful and buried phenomenon, like other forms of fratricidal behaviour, only made worse by its private nature. This privatisation protects the abuser and facilitates further violence. The collusive silence around the issue has the effect of limiting the options that abused women have. Seeking help from the authorities is often regarded as an act of betrayal and several women in the sample who had been forced to seek police assistance as a result of serious violence, now live under threat of death for doing so (as in Roweena's case). Black women are expected to bear their beatings (as if these too were not a betrayal of humanity), and actually to understand that they are a result of the black man's oppression. Yet, as many survivors have pointed out, being beaten by the man one has taken as a sexual and emotional partner is itself a crude and degrading form of oppression.

In October 1988 a black community meeting, entitled 'Violence Within the System' (and billed as the first ever), was held on domestic violence. During this meeting participants exhibited something of a consensual understanding that black men beat black women because they themselves are brutalised by state repression. While it is commendable that such a meeting was held and that discussions took place with seriousness, this kind of analysis can feed into the collective abdication of individual responsibility for brutal and anti-social behaviours. However, many people in the black communities recognise that it is now time to seriously address the problem of violence against black women in Britain, so that more organised collective responses can be developed.

Our findings demonstrate that high levels of violence and cruelty to women by the men they are or have been in relationships with, are being tolerated, by the communities themselves, as well as by statutory organisations.

The occurrence of domestic violence in all the cultural and religious groups we investigated was clearly demonstrated, and this evidence supports the observation made in chapter one; that violence occurs in all creeds, cultures and classes. The fact that this practice may have culturally specific content is also evident in women's accounts. In the examples above we saw Muslim and Rastafarian men using religion to assert their patriarchal authority and misogyny.

Women also often referred to tradition, but in their case it was usually to describe how they had tried to conform — to become the ideal wife — only to find that nothing they said or did satisfied their spouse, or stopped the violence. While women of Caribbean origin referred less explicitly to established orthodoxies, it was clear that the men they were involved with often held quite unrealistic expectations about how 'their' women should behave and conduct themselves, and often felt they had a right to use violence to enforce these. Women (who may well have been born and brought up in Britain) were often criticised and beaten for the 'crime' of being 'too Western', sometimes by men who had also been brought up in Britain. Some of these husbands, like Smita's, continued to have sexual relationships with English women throughout their marriage (presumably to meet their own 'Western' desires).

Others did not refer to religion or tradition, but simply held and tried to enforce expectations that the women found to be oppressive and unrealistic, for example not being allowed to have friends or go out, being expected to stay at home and cook (even when this was not economically feasible as in Hamza's case) and anger over the woman's cooking (as Elsie described) are just a few examples.

There were Asian women who had both arranged and 'love' marriages.[5] Contrary to what racist discourse would suggest, there was nothing to suggest that either form of marriage was less violent. What did emerge was that when a woman had married a partner of her own choosing, she had less access to family support if her choice contradicted her own family's wishes. Having made an individual choice, she also had to cope with the consequences of that choice on her own, so that such women sometimes found themselves in a more isolated and vulnerable position than they might otherwise have been. In other words it is not whether the marriage is arranged or not, but the woman's family's attitude to that marriage which affects how much support she will get.

For others, conforming had not meant exemption or protection from abuse, and often (as in Smita's case), respectability, and their daughter being suitably married meant more to her family than her safety or well-being. Many different cultural and relational factors can therefore prevent a woman's family from giving her any support after marriage. In Smita's case, her family's conformity and the fact that her mother had also been abused by her father meant that she got no support. In Shireen's case, the fact that she was the daughter of an abused first wife meant that she was held in contempt and beaten in her family home, so that her own family's behaviour towards her only worsened her situation after her arranged marriage to a sadistic man. In other words culture or 'tradition' comes into play through interpersonal (familial) relational dynamics, as well as through male assertions of power and urges to dominate.

Within the communities, extended families sometimes intervened positively, although on some occasions, they did not feel able to intervene (for example where the woman's father was dead or absent). In other cases the woman's own relatives made the situation worse (as in Shireen's case).

In some cases (women of Asian and African origin in this study), migration had meant being isolated from family and community support, so that violence reached dangerous levels. For example in Iyamide's case, violence began when her husband brought her over to England.

In-laws were often involved in exacerbating conflict (as in Mabel's case where they were jealous of her and wanted greater access to her husband's income), and sometimes as perpetrators of violence themselves, so that some young wives were multiply abused. In Elsie's case, her cohabitee's doting mother used to watch indifferently, so perhaps giving tacit approval, while her son assaulted 'his' woman. Several of the Asian women living with their in-laws had been married to men who had no interest in them, and continued to pursue their relationships with other women. As traditional wives, these women were expected to live in the family home to serve their in-laws and husband (when he appeared). Smita's wealthy husband actually kept a flat of his own where he continued to live as a bachelor, returning to terrorise and impregnate the young wife with whom he had no real relationship. Sunita's husband continued his relationship with a woman his family did not approve of, expecting her to be satisfied with having been married at all even if there was no relationship between them. He continued to threaten her with ostracism and condemned her as having 'Western' ideas when she finally left and told him to find the courage to bring the woman he was relating to into his family.

In short, double-standards which indulge abuse and neglect of women and wives are quite explicitly upheld by families and conformist elements within the black communities. This indulgence of sons of the community has detrimental effects on the women and children, who are expected to live with them while being denied many basic human rights in the name of 'respectability'.

Professionals within the black communities also often appear to condone violence. Recalcitrant responses to domestic violence have been observed in the white community, so it is perhaps not surprising to find that black professionals too, often adhere to patriarchal values and fail to assist abused women. There were incidents in which women were told by doctors from their own communities that 'women should not leave their husbands' (as in the case of 40-year old Mumtaz Begum, who sought help from her male Asian GP). Sometimes women who did not speak English sought legal assistance from lawyers in their own communities and were not given proper legal advice, as in the case of Sui Wong who could not afford the fees of the Chinese solicitor she went to, but who was also not advised to seek legal aid.

The lack of protection for women in the privacy of their homes and families emerges starkly. This applies even where the police have been, sometimes repeatedly, involved. In Yvonne's case, for example, it is clear that her assailant was mentally disturbed and a danger to both her and her children. Even when he badly scalded the baby, he was still able to return to continue terrorising her. (Police responses are examined more thoroughly in chapter nine). Other women were being battered by men who had drug addictions or criminal records for other crimes, yet few were encouraged to prosecute, and one woman who had attempted to prosecute (Yvonne, on a different occasion from the one cited here) had had her case thrown out.

This study also found that women are often unprotected from men they have ceased having a relationship with. Ex-husbands and ex-boyfriends were not deterred from assaulting women. This upholds the theme introduced in chapter one 'that once a woman has engaged in any form of sexual relationship with a man, his social dominance over her is assumed . . . and this includes the right to physically assault her'. In some cases indeed, the man only became more violent at the point when the woman tried to end the relationship or alter the terms on which it would continue. Yvonne and Roweena are only two of the examples where women had been coerced and intimidated for a long period (several years) after they had ended their relationships with assailants who kept seeking them out and returning to further terrorise them and their children.

The evidence from many of the women in this study (particularly those of Caribbean origin, but also from women of African and Asian origin) contradicts the Western feminist analysis of domestic violence which relates it to women's economic marginalisation, and concomitant dependence on their spouse's income. Many had been assaulted by men who depended on them. This indicates that men continue to emotionally and physically dominate women even when they depend on those women. Indeed, the evidence is that this can be an exacerbating factor. Many women cited the fact that they were working and had some economic independence, as a source of antagonism.

At one extreme were a number of women whose men contributed nothing to the homekeeping or upkeep of children, and assumed they had rights to the woman's earnings. Recall that Sukie's partner actually resented her using the money she earned, to buy clothes and food for their children. Zoey's cohabitee never worked, but pimped and beat her, accusing her of cheating him while he sold her sex to obtain a car and other material needs for himself.

Not all these men were without incomes of their own, and some exploited the sexism of the cohabitation rule to collect and control social security payments to the family. Sarah's partner earned several hundred pounds a week, and started assaulting her after he had moved into her flat. Only then did he feel confident enough to violently express the resentment he felt towards her for having a career instead of having a baby for him, even while the mother of his two other children had a third for him. Charlotte put all her resources into a business with her man, only to be kept in a state of near starvation during her last pregnancy, while he impregnated another woman.

This material also shatters the stereotype of the 'strong' or 'castrating' black woman. Rather, many black women are both providers and slaves whose labour supports men who then degrade and abuse them. It seems that when women have even a limited material advantage over the men they have relationships with, this in itself may in fact provoke those men to assert their male authority literally with a vengeance, through violence. This dynamic suggests that the frustration felt by men who are unable to conform to patriarchal standards, manifests itself in sadistic behaviour towards the women they live off. Thus we can see that socio-economic jealousy may operate in a way that parallels sexual jealousy and often links up with it.

Notes

1. While research is often conducted without any payment to people interviewed, it was felt that the women we consulted had a right to be compensated for their time, especially since many of them were already economically oppressed. Since the amount paid was so small, this was a symbolic gesture, in no way considered to be adequate payment for the time, trust giving and emotional turmoil that being interviewed meant for all those who took us into their confidence and made this study possible.
2. Only one woman declined to have her interview tape recorded, so her responses were filled in on the schedule and more detailed notes also made.
3. Parents are not eligible if their children have been taken into local authority care (perhaps — in a cruel irony — because of homelessness or bad living conditions that threaten their health and safety), or are living primarily with the other parent, or abroad with relatives, for example.
4. Georgina's workmates rallied around her by coming to stay and collectively ousting her husband.
5. 'Love marriage' was a term that women used to describe marriages to partners of their own choosing.

4. Shunned and shunted around: black women's experience of statutory agencies

Corporatisation and coercion

Introduction

In this section we shall examine the experience that black women have had when they have approached local authority housing departments with the urgent housing needs that often result from domestic violence and relationship breakdown. However, although this project focuses on housing, it is necessary to bear in mind the impact of other agencies as part of the context in which housing needs are met or not met. Certainly in terms of the women's experiences, one builds up a picture of individuals caught in a complex and often alienating web of state bureaucracies. It would therefore be reductionist and unrealistic to consider their relationship with one agency (local authority housing departments in this case) completely in isolation from the effects of various other agencies. This is particularly true as we see the growing interrelatedness — or corporatisation of state agencies in their practice. The interviews with both housing officers and women indicate that there is often a great deal of buffering and cross-referring between agencies. In recent years, welfare agencies have become increasingly involved in 'policing' the public, for example, hospitals and housing departments often ask black people for their passports in order to prove their entitlement to health care or housing, so linking up with and performing a function on behalf of the immigration service (Mama 1984 develops this argument).

Consumer groups[1] — in this case the black women in this study — often experience themselves as being passed around from agency to agency, or from one department to another, while being deprived of the one thing they actually need. Most of the women in the study were quite clear about what their needs were, but were involved in months and even years of struggle to attain these. In most of the cases this report draws upon, a secure home away from their violent partner is the most salient and immediate need. This 'need' is and must be recognised as being a basic human right: the right to live in a place where they will be free from violence or the threat of violence.

It may seem to be stating the obvious to point out that the police and legal agencies do have a responsibility to enforce the law in women's interests (see chapters 5 and 6). However, it has also become clear that even if these agencies performed substantially better than they do at present, other basic social and material support (including safe housing) would still be a necessary accompaniment to legal action. In a significant proportion of cases, black women do not wish for quite valid reasons (Chapter 6), to involve the police and/or the law courts and in any case, social and welfare agencies should be able to respond independently as well as in concert with law enforcement agencies. Addressing the social and emotional needs of black women should not be contingent on police and legal actions and processes.

The main argument of this chapter is that while it is important that multi-agency responses be developed, it is imperative that these do not merely multiply the pain and suffering that all battered women and their children go through. The evidence presented below indicates that for black women, the latter is what often happens. This must be understood as a result of the historically oppressive relations of the British State to black women, and the reproduction and reinforcement of these relations by the current political regime. These relations continue to operate in ways that are, for the most part, destructive towards black women.

This is not the place to do a detailed report of social services responses to black women who are experiencing domestic violence, though a few examples are included. Rather our purpose is to take proper note of the inter-relatedness of state services, so that we may better explore the possibilities of developing more effective responses to domestic violence. This research has indicated that while the police are often involved on an emergency basis, access to housing is often the most immediate and long term material need of women who have been subjected to violence. Other agencies (hospitals, GP's, social services and community and voluntary organisations) also have a valuable role to play. This positive role includes detecting domestic violence and making information, advice and support services available to black women leaving, or wishing to leave, violent men. Being referred to the specialised women's organisations, which are currently developing to address black women's needs will often be the first step towards them living without violence. There are not nearly enough such organisations, and their future success depends on increased and continued support from the state. However, they must not be pushed into a situation of righting all the wrongs of bad, ineffective policies, racism and insufficient resources. Rather it is imperative that the supporting and mediating role that these organisations seek to play must be supported, resourced and developed (see chapter 11).

The role of social services
The role of social services are discussed here only in terms of the contact that abused black women had with the departments and social workers in the course of their trying to leave violent situations and establish new lives for themselves.

One third of the sample (33%) had contact with social services, though this contact was not evenly distributed across the different groups of women. Half of the Asian women had contact, as compared to two of the six African women and only 20% of the Caribbean women (see Table 4.1). This index of service uptake reflected differences in the women's descriptions of their experience of social services; none of the Caribbean sample described this as positive or supportive, while some of the Asian sample did.

When asked if they had contacted social services, some responded by saying that they had found it necessary to seek financial assistance from the DHSS, an answer which suggested that some are not informed about the range of social services provision. Others had more contact with social services, but only if their children were deemed to be at risk. Several had been threatened with the removal of their children from the violent home, while some women had temporarily placed their children in local authority care while the mothers recovered from incapacitating injuries inflicted on them by their partners.

An earlier study of responses to domestic violence (Borkowski et al 1983) suggested that social work intervention was not viewed as likely to be of any assistance by other practitioners (eg doctors, health visitors). Black social workers we spoke to were very much aware of domestic violence as a problem, but did not have any clear idea what sort of assistance they might provide to a woman in this situation. Social workers have no mandate or statutory power to intervene unless children are thought to be at risk, and their professional role seems to centre around supporting the dominant, middle-class nuclear family form, often at a cost to the woman. On one occasion a sympathetic policewoman contacted a cultural and educational community project (the Africa Centre) for help over an African woman whose child locked the key in their tower block flat one Friday night. This woman was denied any sort of assistance by social services and told that the only thing that social services would do was to place her children in care, since as the tenancy was not in her name she had no tenancy rights in any case (case referred to this researcher). Certainly from this study it would appear that social workers will only get involved if there are children at risk, although in a few cases of young Asian women, social workers did facilitate escape from unhappy or violent marital homes.

Table 4.1 *Contact with Social Services*

Ethnic group	% with contact	(Number)
Asian	50	(n = 20)
African	33	(n = 2)
Caribbean	20	(n = 11)

It is undoubtedly the case that children are negatively affected by male violence in the home, even if not actually beaten themselves. It could be argued that all children in homes with violent men are at risk of being damaged. All the mothers in our sample were aware of the damaging effect that their partners violence was having on their children, although only a few of them said their children were also subjected to physical assault. For example Sarah described how her five year old son had needed psychiatric treatment, and how she had wept when the source of his disturbance was identified as the violence she was experiencing. Christine's seven year old son developed a speech impediment and bed-wetting, both of which improved while she was in the refuge.

Outside perceptions of social services (by housing professionals, for example) indicate that they are expected to deal with domestic violence. One housing officer helpfully remarked that perhaps I should be talking to the social services department rather than housing. The social workers whom the researcher consulted were aware of domestic violence as a problem in many of the black families they come across in the course of their work, but did express their involvement in child-centred terms. In the example below we have a case of a housing officer referring a homeless woman to the social services department for social work intervention.

Joanna fled from her violent partner in 1984. She was temporarily put up in a women's refuge with her two children and appealed to her housing officer for housing on medical grounds (one child was asthmatic) as well

94

as those of domestic violence. After nine months she had moved out of the refuge into temporary accommodation, knowing that this could mean a longer wait for a permanent home, but unable to bear inflicting refuge conditions on her children any longer. Part of the problem was bureaucratic:

'Once they've made enquiries, they're supposed to send you a paper called Section 64 which says they consider you homeless and will rehouse you. It took them six months to send me that paper. This paper is like a passport to lots of other things. You need it to feel secure, and they know you need it. Without it you can't convince any other borough or anywhere else that you have registered. It took six months, and in the meantime I had to keep phoning, going down there. When I rang up they used to tell me to stop bothering them, that they would send the paper. Nothing arrived, so I went down there in person, and I was told not to make any enquiries until I hear from them. I rang again and he put the receiver down on me.'

Finally she received the paper:

'They register you for a year, during which time they make you three offers of accommodation It took them another nine months [15 months homeless] before they made me the first offer and I was surprised and disgusted with it. It was a tower block, with three very small bedrooms and a very small kitchen as well. It was all cramped and the surroundings — being in a tower block — were not very clean. I felt that when they offered places they should consider the environment. In time I was made three offers. My God, they were all disgraceful. The next two were also in blocks of flats, and I thought drug pushers lived there. They were not really habitable, even to look at. One, I couldn't bring myself to go inside, it was so filthy.'

Joanna grew increasingly desperate, but continued to persevere with Lambeth housing department. Her persistence did not have quite the desired effect:

'After two offers I was so fed up that I went in and told them I was fed up with them all and that I didn't know what I was going to do. I contacted my housing welfare officer again, and he urged me to accept these places. At that stage I realised that my chance of being rehoused didn't exist any more. I said I just couldn't care what happened to me and the kids any more because none of them cared. That they had reduced me to this state. So my officer rang Social Services and told them. He stressed that he wanted to make an appointment for me to see a social worker. He came to my (temporary) flat and left a note saying that he had made an appointment for me the following Monday. I felt I didn't need a social worker because I didn't have a social problem, I had a housing problem. I didn't feel that a social workers intervention was necessary. So I didn't keep the appointment. The social worker got the police and together they broke down the door of the place I was staying at. When I came back the door was ajar and I couldn't lock it. They had left a note on the table saying that they had done this because I didn't keep my appointment with the social worker.'

Eventually Joanna had her standards of decency beaten down far enough for her to accept a damp and substandard flat on an old run down estate, where she still lives.

Unhappily, Joanna's experience is not unusual: many black women are subjected to social services interventions that are experienced as more coercive than supportive when their housing situation is desperate. While there is no doubt that homelessness or bad accommodation can drive women to desperation, there is doubt about what a social worker can do regarding a housing problem. In a number of cases social workers' concern for children has led them to remove or threaten to remove children from mothers who have been abused. Quite apart from the traumas of forcible separation, this further weakens the case with the housing departments who are far less likely to house women without children. Many women thus find themselves on the horns of a nasty dilemma, since their children can be removed from their custody where it is thought they are not providing proper homes.

We can see from the above examples that a woman may not want or need any social work intervention. Some housing departments may however ask for a social worker's report as evidence of serious housing need, particularly if no police or other reports are available. This has the effect of coercing women into relationships with social services, against their wishes, and may add to the oppressions of violence, homelessness and racism by further disempowering rather than supporting the woman. Furthermore the practice of using social work reports as a passport to housing, will operate to selectively deprive women, who neither need nor want social work intervention, of access to housing in the same way as demands for police reports do. Black women will often fall into this camp for one reason or another. More fundamentally, if a woman has decided for herself that what she needs is housing, and that no amount of social work will give her a home, surely she is within her rights to turn down social work intervention. Contradictorily, it is also apparent that many black women who may benefit from social work intervention are denied it. A great many others simply do not know what is available in any case, and if they do, how to go about getting it.

The social workers we consulted pointed out that housing departments did often 'pass the buck' by insisting that women saw social workers. Other agencies who may have been mediating between housing and the family sometimes found it necessary, for bureaucratic purposes, to send women to social services to obtain letters 'proving' there was a serious need, in support of their applications for housing.

Women have been cautioned that their children may be taken into care if they do not leave the violent home. This may be experienced as punitive and threatening rather than supportive. Furthermore, in the case of married women leaving the violent home may result in losing the custody of children to the violent father. Smita had this experience:

> After several years of brutal assaults and gross neglect by her husband she took her young daughter and fled from the house one night. The court felt that her affluent husband and his relatives could provide a better home than she could as a single parent in a women's refuge, and so awarded custody to the violent father. Smita was subsequently assaulted by her husband when she went on an access visit. Meena was returned to her mother some months later by the court. Five years later the court battles over the custody of her daughter (now 11 years old) are still going on. Smita was married at 16 and is now 28.

In some cases, the social services warn that they will remove a child who they feel to be at risk because the father is violent. This was Lily Ching's experience. Her young son was temporarily fostered when Lily had returned home from hospital too severely injured to look after him. In her exhausted and powerless state, she felt some anxiety when she was asked to sign papers that she had not found the energy to read. Subsequently she was cautioned by social service that if she remained in the violent situation, so jeopardising her son's safety, they may be forced to remove him from her custody. Once she left, she had to face the even more coercive threat of deportation. Lily did not have a negative opinion of social services, however, but attributed that anxiety to her own overall situation, and identified a need for black women to be better informed (empowered one might say) in order to have some control over the contact they have with the social services.

'At one point, when I was still in (the refuge) and Oliver was on the at risk register I felt that (threatened). But I can't really blame them. There was one time when I couldn't walk, and they arranged some sort of fostering for me, for one day. At that time they asked me to sign a paper and I was quite worried about it, because I was thinking that that might be some more points for them to take him away from me. They didn't really explain it very clearly to me, and I was very exhausted, and I didn't get round to reading all the documents and they just asked me to sign. That was quite worrying. You hear from the news how babies can be taken away.'

'The people I trusted were the people at Women's Aid. I kind of told them everything really. I told them that Oliver had been hurt, and I suppose they let a paediatrician know about it. They made an appointment for Oliver and I to go along and see them. The Women's Aid told me that, and said that the social services were about to hold a conference for Oliver's case, and asked me to go along. But I didn't go — I was transferred to another Women's Aid in Wales, and then to Birmingham. They also assigned a social worker to come and see me. I found that I was receiving special treatment in the sense that she would come and see me every day, which I find to be unusual. I feel that they were kind of keeping a close eye on me to make sure I didn't go back to my husband. Which I found to be fair enough — I needed the attention at the time. And she helped me get people in to help with doing up the house.'

'You find that you have to draw a line, and keep a distance from these people, and make sure about the kind of information you want to give them. I've learned a lesson from that. I think you have to know where you stand first, and before you do that you just can't tell anybody everything. Not even the Women's Aid.'

Yet in other cases where a child has actually been seriously injured by the man but no social work intervention was made, the response of other (legal) agencies means that the children and their mother remain very much at risk, as Yvonne's story indicates.

98

Yvonne has spent five years fleeing from the violent father of her children (see chapter 3). The police were regularly involved, and her partner Roland had been remanded in custody for other violent offences a number of times. According to Yvonne, when she called the police for help, a group of them would arrive and assault him.[2] On one occasion Roland returned to Yvonne's home after being remanded in custody for some other offence. He accused her of being unfaithful to him when he saw the baby that had been born two days before he had been arrested, apparently having forgotten seeing him. In the ensuing argument he took a pan of boiling water from the stove and flung it over the infant and her mother. He was sentenced to six months in a psychiatric facility. After three months he escaped and returned to continue harassing Yvonne, forcing her to become homeless again.

Selena described her social worker, as not wanting to know her after she had called in her violent ex-boyfriend to help her with the uninhabitable flat she was given, and was then subjected to further violence. There is a thin line between a social worker encouraging relatively powerless people to take a stand, and subjecting them to their own disappointment, perhaps after investing the time and emotion involved in trying to assist an abused woman.

The issue of what kind of intervention social workers could actually make in these cases cannot be addressed here, but evidence of this sort indicates that it is an issue that urgently needs to be tackled. As has been argued elsewhere, black families may well have good reason for not wanting social work intervention (Lawrence 1980), and there is growing awareness of the negative consequences of removing black children from their families, and placing them in the inappropriate or substandard environments that state care often consists of (Ahmed, Cheetam and Small 1987). The picture is not a black and white one; rather complex interpersonal relationships are often involved, and people's experience of these is often inherently contradictory. Social work support, in the few cases where it was accessible and forthcoming, was welcomed by the woman. This was true for some of the younger Asian women who participated in the study.

SUNITA, a young woman of Pakistani Muslim origin was born, grew up and went to school in Sussex. She was taken out of school and into an unhappy arranged marriage to a man who was in love with a woman he could not marry, and who had no interest in Sunita. His family had arranged the marriage in the hope that this would bring him back into the family. She was expected to stay in the house with her in-laws, performing domestic duties. Her own family and her in-laws initially tried to talk to her husband, to no avail. Sunita grew increasingly depressed. Her father in-law was being visited by a social worker who noticed the young wife and investigated her situation. Having established that Sunita wanted to leave, she came to the house with the police one day and escorted Sunita to an Asian women's organisation. This was two years after her marriage. She was subsequently rehoused by an Asian community project, and has continued to be supported by her social workers who have enabled her to keep in touch with her family by carrying letters between them, yet protecting Sunita's whereabouts from them.

When asked if she thought it had been necessary for the police escort (a policewoman) to accompany the social worker she replied:

> 'They wouldn't allow me to go anyway if it wasn't for the social workers, and she said she would rather be safe than sorry so it was best to have the police there as well.'

While we did not have the resources to do a systematic evaluation of ethnic differences in social service responses to abused women, it was notable that women of Caribbean origin in the sample did not have the positive experience that some (young) Asian women did, and where there was intervention, did not find it supportive. This observation suggests that there may be "play offs" between race and culture in statutory responses, (Mama 1989) and is an area that deserves further investigation.

To sum up then, it is clear that the different arms of the state do come together to act in ways that can have compounding effects on battered women. The treatment of black women by social services needs to be substantially improved on the one hand, while on the other, ways must be found to empower black women so that they are in a position to negotiate with them over how they can best be assisted to resolve their situations. The evidence suggests that this would best be done outside state structures, through black and ethnic minority organisations, or through women's organisations which are conscious enough of racial dynamics to be able to be supportive to black women.

Black women's experience of housing departments

In the light of all the evidence on racism and sexual inequality in housing (see chapter 5) one can predict that black women will generally be given a tough time at housing departments. The erosive impact of the situation has been summed up thus:

> 'Perhaps the single most important influence on our health and sanity, particularly for those of us who are unemployed, is the kind of housing we have access to. The cumulated effects of twenty-five years of racist housing policies have ensured that growing numbers of Black women are imprisoned on the upper floors of dilapidated tower blocks in every inner-city, with little hope of escape. If our white neighbours harass us, or if our men abuse us, we often have no choice but to leave, exposing ourselves and our children to the traumas of homelessness' (Bryan, Dadzie and Scafe 1985)

Black women's access to public housing is severely circumscribed through a range of mechanisms. The single black woman, the single black mother, the black woman with or without children and seeking to escape violence are all likely to be offered inferior housing, or none at all. Women who were still in violent situations often gave housing — 'I've got nowhere to go' — as the reason for staying. This was not always due to lack of knowledge about existing resources. Some, like Iyamide, had contacted women's aid but found no space available. Others could not speak English, did not know how to go about getting such provision, or could not bring themselves to go into a hostel. These facts underlie the observation that unknown numbers of black women remain in violent, even life threatening situations in which their childrens' lives are also threatened. The spectre of destitution on the cold London streets has more reality in the current decade with its growing numbers of homeless families than it may have had in the 1970s. For example:

> Lai Ha, a middle-aged Chinese woman who does not speak English, lives like a slave in her abusive husband's house. She is his third wife, and sees that the second wife is still homeless after a year and a half on a local authority waiting list.

Referrals to London Women's Aid alone, rose from 2,019 to 6,627 between 1984 and 1987, an increase of 22% over those three years. However, there are only 3-400 bed-spaces for women in refuges in London. There is no doubt that significant numbers of these are black women, even judging conservatively from the numbers of black women in refuges at the present time (Russell forthcoming). The shortfall of refuge space and the overall housing situation therefore function alongside

101

cultural pressures from within the black communities and societal racism to keep black women in violent situations.

Many women fall into groups that we did not reach at all because they have never heard of women's refuges, and so do not even call Women's Aid for help. This applies particularly to women who lead more secluded lives, as housewives, or in more closed communities, or who do not have a good command of English and the means to contact agencies that may be able to advise or help. The tragic death of Krishna Sharma indicated what can happen to isolated women (see Appendix).

When it comes to black women who are seeking to escape violent relationships, one would perhaps expect a slightly more sympathetic response than usual from the local state. After all, in recent years there has been a proliferation of policies on rehousing of women who have been subjected to domestic violence and many boroughs now have written policies stating that victims of domestic violence should be treated as a priority category. But where there are such progressive policies, how far are they guaranteeing that black women get rehoused, and when they do, that the accommodation they get is adequate? Are black and white victims of domestic violence being treated equally sympathetically and given priority to the same extent as one another? (One might expect so since there has also been a proliferation of anti-racist policies.) Or are the domestic violence policies being selectively applied to women who fit stereotypical notions of what a 'battered woman' is expected to be, and so excluding black women who often do not come across as 'victims' in quite the same way? In real terms, given the overall context of declining public housing, how effective can such policies be if — as most London Boroughs are now complaining — there are no homes to allocate to anybody anyway? However, local authorities should not be able to make this an excuse for doing nothing and attention should be paid to offering these women reasonable homes in the remaining housing stock, as well as considering more innovative ways of providing accommodation (eg through the housing associations they may turn stock over to).

The evidence below is the first of its kind. It indicates what the responses of housing departments to black women who have been subjected to violence actually are. Later (chapters 7-9) the development of local authority policies is examined in more detail, to examine the other side of the coin, so to speak.

It will be recalled from chapter 3 that most of the women in the study were staying in refuges at the time of interview, and so in a sense were in the relatively 'privileged' position of having an agency supporting their demands for housing. Many refuges have built up working relationships with the local housing departments, so that rehousing is facilitated to a degree (see (iii) below). Others have not been so successful in acquiring the cooperation of the local Housing Department, and in one borough (The Royal Borough of Kensington and Chelsea) the relationship was one of open hostility and non-cooperation.

For women not in refuges, approaching the housing department on their own and individually, treatment can be far worse. More often than not, their requests are simply shelved, leaving them to be subjected to violence until they abandon their homes and join the ranks of the homeless.

There are (theoretically, at least) three main routes to rehousing:

i) Transfers
Housing departments can respond to requests from women who are their tenants, and these are usually requests for transfers to another part of the borough. Applications generally go to the estate or neighbourhood office, and then, if deemed by housing officers to be a priority case meriting a management transfer, up to the district manager or equivalent office for approval. The details of the processes involved vary from borough to borough, and two boroughs are more fully discussed as case examples in chapters 8 and 9. Most of the sample were actually not able to live in their homes at all, as a result of violence, and so were effectively homeless. Seventy-seven per cent were already in one or other form of temporary accommodation at the time of interview.[3] Many of these had tried to get transfers for many months before actually being forced to flee onto the streets.

ii) Homeless Persons Units
The second means of obtaining housing after violence is available to women who are already homeless, having fled their homes, and being too afraid to return because of the danger of further violence.[4] This group includes women who have reported to the homeless persons unit (HPU), with nowhere else to go. They may be temporarily lodged in hostels, reception centres, bed and breakfast hotels, or women's refuges, all of which are designed to be short stay temporary accommodation, to keep people off the streets pending rehousing. The figures do not indicate the fact that many of these women had already left to stay with friends or relatives several times before finding themselves in temporary

accommodation.[5] This suggests that there are significant numbers of abused women in the hidden homeless population.

iii) From refuges

Women in refuges may be processed through either the HPU or the management transfer system, depending on their circumstances. In addition, some Labour boroughs have specific arrangements for rehousing women from refuges (eg Islington, Camden, Lambeth, Southwark). This may be done through either of the above routes, depending which borough the woman originated from, or she may be rehoused in the borough under a quota system. Usually quotas only apply to women not eligible under existing policies — for example homeless women with no children. Whatever 'category' the women fall into, approaching housing through a refuge is likely to be less traumatic — at least the burden of proof is somewhat lifted, and women may be accompanied to the housing department by a refuge worker.

Austerberry and Watson's 1983 study of women in hostels found relationship breakdown and/or domestic violence to be the single largest cause of single women's homelessness. For the single women they studied, not having children in their care meant they did not have access to the affordable rented accommodation that local authorities provide for families. The definition of 'family' is a highly ideological one, determined by dominant notions of what a family should be. This may well account for the concentration of single parent families on the worst estates, when in fact they actually have greater need of safe and decent housing. Women's generally low income levels mean that the majority cannot afford to buy or rent decent private accommodation, so that as a group, low income families (a significant proportion of whom are black and/or female headed) are at the mercy of the public housing establishment. This is particularly true of abused women who often have to abandon their jobs, in order to move away from violence, as well as having to become single parents.

The case material indicates in detail how the housing bureaucracy often operates in ways that punish women who do find the strength and courage to leave violent men. Whatever the causes and processes, for many black women, leaving a violent home may well mean embarking on a long ordeal of racism, homelessness and near destitution.

As will be explored below, while some women had held and were still holding local authority tenancies, a sizeable proportion had abandoned their tenancies and were seeking rehousing. A third group had not held

104

local authority tenancies in the first place, but lived in local authority accommodation and so had rights to be rehoused in some boroughs but would be treated less than sympathetically in others.

Whatever their situation during their experience of violence, once made homeless as a result of it, all those who had children were entitled to rehousing under Central Government legislation. This was recognised in those boroughs who had developed clear policies to deal with the problem and who at least attempted to implement them in Homeless Persons Units (HPUs). In other boroughs, more energies and resources appeared to be directed at getting around the legislation than in meeting the obligations it imposes on LA housing departments. Certainly the experiences that the women in our sample had with various LAs, indicate the human side of all the talk about scarce resources and 'really deserving' cases. The material presented below also indicates the consequences that the wide-ranging policy changes dictated from the central state are having on women and children. Since our research focused on an extremely desperate group of women and their children, who were already homeless as a result of domestic violence, implications about housing needs in general can only be drawn with caution. One can quite safely say, however that women deemed to be less desperate — who perhaps had not yet fled their homes — appear to be treated even more casually. Many of the women in our study had erroneously been categorised as 'less desperate' by housing officers and not rehoused because they had not yet fled violent situations and become homeless. Only after they had become homeless (and therefore been subjected to the additional stresses of that) did they move up to the top of the housing needs tariff but then only in boroughs that do proclaim to prioritise victims of domestic violence. In other boroughs (like Conservative Kensington and Chelsea) even being homeless was not sufficient to 'prove' a housing need serious enough to be considered for housing.

The first stage of applying for alternative housing sometimes involved applying for a transfer while still in the violent situation. Very few women in the sample had any success in obtaining transfers before becoming homeless as a result of domestic violence. In other words there appears to be no supportive response at all until things have deteriorated to such a stage that the women (and children) are homeless. Only at this stage can they expect to be heard at all, and then it may take months before they are even acknowledged and taken onto the waiting list.

Refuge workers and other workers in the field almost unanimously felt that black women were discriminated against by housing departments.

Their informed impressions by and large support the existing evidence on racism in housing.

An analysis of how officers respond to black and ethnic minority women will give us an indication of the mechanics of this racism, as well as the destructive impact it has.

Many of the women we interviewed did not initially articulate their experience as 'racist', though they certainly reported insensitivity if not downright hostility from officers. A significant proportion did not describe their interviewing officers as 'racist' or even unpleasant, but nonetheless got nowhere with their applications. Such women (perhaps after several months and many exchanges and 'lost files') later came to interpret their experience as having been connected with the fact that they were not white women. Although some women had a sophisticated understanding of the meanings and assumptions at play in their interactions with officers many did not. For example, Shaba, an Iranian woman exhibited this under-reporting of racism when she did not describe being told she should 'go back to Iran' by a housing officer as racist. This is a problem that typifies research on racism. However, in addition to the qualitative evidence presented below there were other statistical indicators which suggested that severe racism was texturing the experience of the women in the study.

Illustrations — gaining access
Visiting LA housing departments can be a harrowing experience at the best of times, not to mention when a woman is already suffering traumatisation, severe stress and/or depression as a result of being violently assaulted in her home.

MARY (see chapter 3) is a 32 year old single parent with a three year old son, and told of her experience in detail, calmly and patiently. She was being physically assaulted by her son's father, Paul. Paul had become addicted to hard drugs and insisted on continuing his relationship with another woman, who was also an addict. His behaviour became erratic and dishonest, as well as violent, until Mary could take no more and Paul moved out. However, since they had been living at his sister's council flat, he continued to visit and disrupt Mary's life and she went to the council to seek housing, during her pregnancy. So began a long struggle that was to last three and a half years.

106

'Up until that time I had not realised what the housing situation was. It was a shock. A real shock. I found that the staff, particularly at reception were unhelpful. I would even go as far as to say that some of them were overtly racist . . . Their attitude to black people was such that there was no other conclusion I could come to. Most of the people in Hackney housing office were black. It was dirty. There was violence going on. There was swearing. I used to go there practically every day and there was one particular man who talked to me as though I was nothing. The attitude towards black people — he was nothing less than a racist — "Do you think we are here to provide housing for you" — that type of attitude. There were lots of people there — the majority of them were women with children. I used to sit down and listen to what was going on. Some of them refused to speak to this particular man.'

After months of regular visits to Hackney Housing department:

'I was beginning to get really desperate. The situation was chronic, because by this time I had the baby. I couldn't claim supplementary benefit or housing benefit because the tenancy was not in my name. Then I went to social services and the DHSS and they'd ask — "Well who does the property belong to?" I was really living hand to mouth . . . I had applied for housing when I was pregnant, and then went again when I had the baby, because they don't put you down as a mother and child until you actually produce the baby.'

Mary had worked continuously up until the seventh month of her pregnancy, and henceforth survived on her meagre savings, and some handouts from her son's father. This extract is a further illustration of the manner in which different statutory organisations can act together to worsen the already desperate situation of a single parent living under threat of violence and harassment from her ex-husband. Mary spent a whole year trying to get housing from Hackney council. She went to the department 'practically every week'. During this period she was made one offer:

'I was told that they could only offer me bed and breakfast accommodation in Paddington. I just couldn't believe that this is what the situation really was. I was eventually offered one place in Hackney, in about September. I just could not take it. I'll describe it to you. It was off the beaten track, down all these little windy cobblestone roads, right off to the back of nowhere near the river Lee. When you walk

107

into the estate, all you can see is empty flats, lots of them burnt out, with graffiti and the dirt! Really filthy. They are these pre-war flats, with the oval entrance that is so dark — even in daylight when you are looking in its really dark. It was on the 4th floor, and there was no actual door on the flat itself. There had obviously been a fire there, and they'd cleaned it up to a certain extent. I think that these people (previous occupants) had literally burnt them up to get out of there, because I couldn't understand how there were so many burnt out flats in one building. I sat in the car. I didn't get out. That was my first reaction. There was no way I could have lived — just me and my baby — in a place like that. It wasn't near to any shops. There was no way. I wouldn't even get out of the car.'

So much for Hackney. Demoralised by her year-long experience, and seeing no prospect of ever being housed, but determined to find a decent home in which to bring up her baby son, Mary moved to Haringey. There she stayed temporarily with her nephew, who had moved in with his girlfriend, and applied for housing in that borough. She was interviewed by an officer she describes as sympathetic, and explained about the domestic violence and her experience in Hackney, as well as all her plans to study and raise her son properly. She was advised that she would have to move into a hostel and join the waiting list. She was thoroughly investigated by housing officers, and told to expect a wait of six to nine months. She phoned regularly for another whole year:

'After a year, I think he got thoroughly fed up with me and told me that he was nothing to do with my case any more — "If you want to know what's happened to your papers ring the area housing office". I had already approached them the same week that another girl who had come in two weeks before me received a letter saying she had been offered a place. She said — "Oh well — we came at roughly the same time, so it will be your turn soon". She was also a single parent — a white girl. After another month I went down to the housing office and asked them what had happened to my papers. I was told that they had not been sent to them yet. So I said "After nine months you still haven't received my papers?!" They said — No — that they were dealing with cases that came in nine months before mine. So I said that if that was the case, they should explain to me why my friend had been given a property. She looked up the name and said — "oh well, she had been in the hostel a year before me. So I said, well actually no -I don't think so — she came in two weeks before me, and not only that she was living

108

in better (hostel) accommodation". She tried to tell me that the girl had registered before she actually came to live in the hostel. So I said — Look, there is nothing you can tell me about this girl — she is a personal friend of mine. To make sure I hadn't got things wrong I went back to see Susan-Jane and checked.'

Susan-Jane confirmed that she had not registered before, verifying that the housing officers where lying to deflect Mary's case. On other occasions officers used junior staff to block her attempts to see them. On another she was 'unofficially' offered a place in a building full of squatting hells angels, which she refused (also verbally) only to receive the official letter offering her the place after the deadline for accepting it had lapsed. At the same time, the hostel warden was trying to force her into a smaller room, under threat of eviction. To cut a very long and angering story short, Mary was cajoled into living in Tottenham, and denied housing through a variety of dirty tricks. She persisted with her demands, eventually seeking the support of a local councillor. She then had to take the case up with a committee, pleading 'unfair treatment' (advisedly *not* 'racism'). She won her case, despite the attempts of the local housing manager to subvert it, and was promptly offered a decent place, in her words, in a respectable part of Haringey. The Haringey phase of her struggle took two and a half years. One year of this was spent staying with her nephew, and a further year and a half was spent in a grubby hostel, where she also had a bad time.[6] Her son was three years old by the time they had the home where I visited them.

Mary's case was not atypical, but the courage and tenacity with which she pursued it all the way up through the bureaucracy was. Many women are successfully deflected and stalled through an entire range of blocking strategies. Other women survive their ordeal in different ways. Often this involves being coerced into accepting the worst type of housing, and so having to cope with the long term problems of struggling to raise children on their own in a disruptive and dangerous environment. As we saw in Joanna's case, the children often develop medical problems as a result of damp and sub-human accommodation. Others are placed in danger of developing any of the whole range of social problems that typify the environments in which they are forced to live. The 'bad' estates in inner cities have very high crime rates, and are heavily policed, both of which present nightmarish problems for single mothers.

IYAMIDE is an African woman who had lived in council accommodation in a Labour borough and had worked as a nurse since joining her husband in this country, 14 years ago. Forced to leave with her two sons after years of physical abuse (she suffered permanent damage to her eyesight, migraines and was hospitalised more than once), Iyamide went to request housing and was told to stop being troublesome and go back to her husband, who the housing officer described as a 'gentleman', despite all the medical evidence of brutality that was put before him.

SHABA is an Iranian woman who lived in a privately rented room in Barnet with her husband and baby. They had lived in the borough for 12 years and been on the waiting list for four years. Her husband became extremely violent towards her about two years ago. She suffered a miscarriage and a broken nose, and she was hospitalised because of the injuries he inflicted on her. When she went to hospital to give birth to a child after that, her legs were so covered in bruises that the delivery room staff enquired. After the birth, he was also violent towards their baby daughter when she cried. In desperation Shaba continued to plead with the housing department. She attributes a lot of her young husband's violence to their extreme overcrowding in that one room, and the pressure the landlady put on them to leave (issuing an eviction notice). Eventually she was forced to run for her life after her husband tried to strangle her. She found herself out on the streets, with nothing except her baby daughter, and homeless. Someone she met advised her to contact Women's Aid. When she went again to the housing department she was callously interviewed by a white male housing officer who told her she should go back to Iran, causing her to burst into tears in his office.

This kind of abuse of power can be reduced by refuge workers. In both Iyamide and Shaba's cases, and those of many others, refuge workers subsequently accompanied them to the housing department to state their cases, which suggests that the direct victimisation of individual women like the examples given above can be prevented or challenged. However, both women (like most) were still homeless many months later when we interviewed them.

Time spent waiting
Strong evidence of discrimination also comes from the long periods of time it takes for different groups of women to be rehoused. Both black and white workers in mixed refuges observed that it was often the black women in the refuge who took the longest time to be rehoused. Lewisham refuge actually monitored the rehousing of black and white women, and

110

found racial differences which they submitted to the local authority. Statistical indicators do not reveal the emotional stresses that black women face in their struggle for homes. The observation that black women were rehoused more slowly, and in worse property was made not only in Conservative boroughs with no policies on domestic violence or race equality, but also in more progressive Labour boroughs. This raises serious questions about the successful implementation of such policies at all levels of the housing hierarchy. In at least one Conservative borough, the attitude was so bad that there was no rehousing from the refuge at all during the research period, indicating a point blank refusal to accept legal responsibilities to homeless women, regardless of race.[7] In other boroughs there was no refuge at all, which meant that there was nowhere for women to go and the borough's responsibilities to women fleeing from domestic violence could remain invisible, or simply left to others.

As has already been pointed out the vast majority of our sample (77%) were homeless (staying in the various forms of temporary accommodation) during the research period, and others were still in highly destructive situations. A few, like Mary had finally been housed, but most, like Joanna (after two years) had eventually been forced to accept very poor housing simply to stabilise their existence. Many other cases indicated that black women are presented with a choice between accepting disgusting accommodation, or remaining homeless indefinitely. Mary, like many others, was threatened that she would not receive any further offers if she did not accept a place she found to be quite uninhabitable. Mothers are reminded (although their situation is through no fault of their own) that the welfare of their children is at stake. In addition not only may they lose custody through being homeless, but the long term disruption of long periods of half-life in temporary accommodation is an additional pressure placed on them.

Others, like Carol and Delma, were still blighted by 'lost files' at the time of interview and still had no immediate prospect of being housed.

One case was the exception which proves the rule. Sunita, a young Asian wife was rehoused in two weeks, once she finally made the break. This was not thanks to any statutory body, but through an Asian housing association. This suggests that it is possible for community organisation and action to alleviate the situation of all the hundreds of others still trapped in the local state bureaucracies.[8]

To sum up this section, it is clear that black women are subjected to all sorts of bureaucratic obstructions after being driven from their homes by domestic violence. They are very often not only denied access to decent housing away from extremely violent men and kept in the half-life of homelessness for very long periods, but also subjected to the emotional traumas of racism, made all the more damaging because of the insidious ways in which these can operate over the months and even years of homelessness and powerlessness. These facts remain, and whatever the explanations of the highly political conditions producing this situation are, ways must be found to overcome it.

Power in relationships

In this section we shall look at the operation of culture and the state as factors 'inside' the relational situation which ensures that it is often the women and children who face the housing consequences of domestic violence. In chapter 3 we highlighted the appropriation of 'tradition' 'religion' and 'culture' by men dominating their womenfolk. Further examples are presented here, and then we go on to address the interaction between state power and individual male power. It is argued that black and white men can and do 'appropriate' state intervention for their own ends; in this case to further oppress the women they physically abuse. The fact that this appropriation occurs at all indicates that men who assault black women often use other forces, alongside physical strength to control, coerce and oppress them. Women also become further involved with the state in various ways when they attempt to protect themselves or escape violence, as we have explored to some extent above, but the evidence presented here indicates that this involvement is generally very different from the vindictive and oppressive ways in which some violent men involve the police and the immigration department. After looking at the collusion between male power in the home and the state, we shall go on to examine the role that the local state — as landlord — plays in domestic violence through an analysis of tenancy status.

Cultural appropriation

Husbands often exploited culture-specific (or more general) notions of morality to coerce their wives. Nineteen year old Sunita's unfaithful husband tried to force her back into his family home by warning her that she will be reduced to the status of a prostitute in the outside world. Some exploited the ignorance and isolation in which they kept their wives, to terrorise them from leaving or running away. For many women, conformity to 'tradition' and 'respectability' was a major factor in their toleration of extreme brutality. This fear is something that more liberated women, and many white women will find difficult to comprehend, never having been subjected to strong and overtly patriarchal traditional cultures.

Patience, a Nigerian store supervisor married to a Nigerian student, gave a clear account of the way in which male elders in her polygamous extended family kept persuading her to go back to her husband when they visited England, long after those closer to her had tired of supporting her attempts to leave her chronically insecure and sadistic husband. This compounded her problems at a number of levels. First it subjected Patience to cultural oppression in the name of 'our tradition' which undermined her resolve on the occasions when she did leave. She also suffered as a result of trying to negotiate two social and political contexts at once:

'At home the family frowns on a woman for calling police on her husband. That's why I haven't. Whilst we have been in this country for a long time, I still think of home. I got a court injunction, but at home its not like that. When you separate from your husband, the husband still maintains the children — you know the sort of separation I mean. That's how I want it to be. Over here you are the losers — the mother and the child. Its not acceptable to be depriving the child of the father, of knowing the father. And I will lose out. I worked hard for him and my son has to reap what I sowed in there.'

This is all the more ironic since Patience's husband had no qualms about getting the police to remove her from their home twice, or about listening to them deride her. The police assaulted her themselves on one of these occasions (See Chapter 6). Patience's reluctance to get a divorce is also based on her observation that whatever settlement is reached in a British court will be rendered redundant when they go back to Nigeria. Her repeated returns to her husband eventually isolated her from her good friends and relatives who lost patience with her:

'They keep laughing at me. They say — "You will go back, and then you will come back and start crying." Some of my relatives don't want to talk to me again. My relatives? Those who have helped me to pack out, and then I've been back, so many times. I'm not talking about petty issues, I'm talking about when they've seen me with my face puffed up with blood! When I'm crawling on the floor and I've lost my clothes — You can imagine the reaction of my relatives or friends who love me! Somebody helps you, and then another uncle will come and say — "Go back". An uncle who you respect will say — "Have I ever told you anything before? Go Back." And I will go.'

It weakened her position in the refuge where workers did not take her seriously and therefore would not give her a proper room. They also threatened to transfer her to another area, although this would have meant her losing her employment.

It also weakened her position with the local housing department who had previously allocated her a flat which she turned down after the birth of her baby during a period of reconciliation.

Thus we can see cultural oppression having spin-off effects all the way through the network of organisational and social structures that should be offering support. When these organisations are staffed by people who are often in any case racist, difficulties of this sort are used to justify non-delivery of supporting services and resources.[9]

Exploiting isolation and the racist state

'Imported wives' are also isolated, not so much by 'tradition' as by migration away from their families and communities. However 'tradition' may also make it quite impossible for them to return to their country of origin, should they be deported when their British husbands brutalise or otherwise reject them.

Even worse is the fact that those who do make contact with agencies outside the private hell of their violent homes may face not only a barrage of hostility and racism, but be threatened with deportation by officials in any of the service agencies, because of the 'no recourse to public funds' clause in their immigration status. It can be argued that it is misogynistic or totalitarian men who seek to import wives from the Third World in the first place, exactly because they have difficulty in finding the 'traditional' 'subservient' woman of their fantasies amongst today's European women. When they discover that their imported wives do not fulfil their fantasies, and beat them for this reason, they have the added confidence of knowing that foreign women are isolated from any community or family support.

Leove Bongay, a Philipino woman, was sent for by a white Englishman who had impregnated her during a holiday romance in the Philippines. He insisted that he wanted to marry her, and persuaded her to leave her job and home in the Philippines. A few weeks after she had joined him, he woke up and told her he was 'tired of her' and threw her out. He then reported her to the Home Office, saying he was no longer

114

responsible for her. She was taken in off the streets by a philanthropic woman and gave birth to her daughter in a hospital outside London. Having 'taken recourse to public funds', Leove faced the threat of deportation. A campaign is being waged for her to stay in Britain with her child. The voluntary organisation assisting her has since been sent a hospital bill for the maternity care she received after being left destitute.[10] Her ex's inhuman discarding of her is thus being effectively supported by more than one branch of the state.

Nahawa Keita, a Malian woman who did not speak English was brought over to Britain from Mali by a British man who married her. He turned out to be an abusive alcoholic and she was forced to run away more than once, but not surprisingly found herself unable to cope on her own in a strange country. Her husband constantly threatened her with the immigration department, in full knowledge of the fact that her community had completely rejected her and she was terrified of being sent back to face their wrath (*African Woman* No. 3).

It is not only white men who exploit the racist and sexist immigration legislation in this way. In Lisa Huen's widely reported case, a campaign was mounted to challenge the Home Office threat to deport her after she eventually left her violent husband (who was a British born man of Chinese origin). Before she finally decided not to return to her husband, social services had warned that if she remained in that situation, they might be forced to take her young son into their care, since he too was on the at risk register.

In Iyamide's case, her husband expected her to be grateful to him for bringing her to Britain and felt justified in treating her the way he did after she joined him and bore two sons. He was able to feel justified in keeping her completely isolated socially, beating her to obtain the money she earned and making passes at her friends until they too stayed away. It will be recalled from chapter 3 that he inflicted serious injuries on her and permanently damaged her vision.

In Patience's case, her husband was able to get the police to remove her from her home, after the neighbours who had heard her screams for help as he brutally assaulted her, had called them to intervene. As if she had not suffered enough violence, the police too sexually and racially ridiculed Patience in an extremely degrading manner and kicked her down the steps of the police station, where they locked her in a cell for the night (see chapter 6). Here we have a more explicit collusion of contempt towards an African woman.

These examples, because they are clearly vindictive, represent a further assertion of power by the man, and stand in stark contrast to the ways in which women got involved with the state. Women showed a marked reluctance to call in the state even for their own protection. Where they have involved the authorities it has been out of desperate need for physical protection — to stop themselves being beaten or even killed or in the process of seeking housing. Many refused to press charges, even when advised to do so. Others were fully aware that their husbands had married them to get into Britain, but did not think of having them deported to save themselves from violence. This evidence therefore challenges the prevalent (and historical) perception that black men have of women as 'traitors' who collude with the state to further oppress them. Rather it would seem that the opposite often occurs.

There is, however, some evidence that gender differentials — even within black peoples highly limited access to housing — lead black men to further resent black women, and thus to have no qualms about driving them out of tenancies. There is some irony in this, as it is clear that single black women have no more access to public housing than single black men and that it is only through their roles as mothers that black women gain any access at all. Often it is clearly a case of black men brutally resenting black women for catching a crumb that has slipped off the welfare table, and ironically housing is a crumb that women are only entitled to through being impregnated by men. Gender difference, and in particular women's reproductive work, is thus materially constructed into social difference through the public housing bureaucracy. This has policy implications concerning the effects that evicting violent black men has on black women, which are addressed in part II. At the emotional level, such punitive action, while apparently just in terms of individual male's behaviour towards black women, multiplies existing hostilities between those black men who 'blame' black women for all the injustices that they experience, in this context, because of racial oppression (Lucy Bonnerjee makes a similar point in her work on homelessness in Brent 1987). Many of the women in this study were left unprotected after the eviction of their violent partners, and felt that they were in even greater danger since the men would feel even more vindictive towards them. It has long been observed that broader social and political oppressions are often 'acted out' in various ways in personal relationships, and through violence (Fanon 1967, Staples 1982). In relationships where the woman

116

is not victimised, she will still bear the emotional burden of the black man's oppression in her capacity as 'his' woman, if not also as a material provider.

The impact of tenancy status

All these examples indicate the way in which women become trapped in a Kafka-like corporate network of state apparatuses. Beyond this, there is the terrain of the relationships themselves. The psychodynamics of violent relationships cannot be taken on in detail in this study, but we can look at the relation between the 'internal' power relations of the relationships and the 'external' or objective power of that relationship by examining the role that tenancy status plays in the housing circumstances of women who find themselves being battered by their menfolk.

Entering a relationship can affect women's already circumscribed access to housing. Marrying or cohabiting can be seen to have affected women's tenancy status in negative ways that are often compounded by LA housing department policies and practices. The processes through which this is so are addressed in the borough studies (chapters 8 and 9). For example, the issuing of a joint tenancy in cases where the woman was a sole tenant involves weakening her position in the event of relationship breakdown or violence, since the couple will then have equal tenancy rights in the eyes of housing officers (unless there are children in which case the parent with custody may be prioritised — in principle if not in practice). Under the Housing (Homeless Persons) Act of 1977, while LA obligations to house the homeless were made clear, it also became more difficult for LAs to evict tenants, even where they exhibit anti-social behaviour towards other tenants. Local authorities have developed a variety of policies to deal with anti-social behaviour (most commonly against noise nuisance). Some Labour boroughs have attempted to deal with the more serious anti-social (if not seriously injurious and criminal) behaviour of racial harassment and domestic violence. The housing legislation, generally speaking, can be seen to have been selectively taken up, in ways which have clear racial implications. In particular it would seem that 'noise nuisance' or damage to property are tolerated far less than racial harassment and domestic violence against black women by both law enforcement and housing officers. Georgina, a Chinese woman who (it will be recalled) did manage (with the help of friends and workmates) to get her spouse out of their council flat after he had beaten her so badly that she miscarried, found the police unwilling to intervene when the man

117

returned and tried to break into their flat, until she pointed out that he was in fact damaging council property.

The limited access that women have to housing, whether they have children or not sets up a situation in which women face a choice between two evils: that of remaining in a violent domestic situation, or of leaving it to face the trauma of homelessness. Women in the study had varying degrees of knowledge about what this actually meant when they actually left their homes to flee violence. Some knew that they would face a long wait in appalling conditions. Forty year old Lai Ha was one such case. She was still in her domestic situation (her husband's house) when we interviewed her in Cantonese. She spoke at length of the cruelty and harshness of her existence in her husband's house where he and his relatives (mother and sister) treat her like a domestic slave. It appeared that their treatment of her became even more punitive after she gave birth to a baby girl two years ago, since her husband had wanted a son. He had sons by his two previous wives, but they had both left and won custody because of the way he treated them. Lai Ha, who works as a part time cleaner and has no money of her own, knows full well the continuing ordeal of her predecessor who is still homeless two years after leaving the man who then married Lai Ha and brought her to Britain. She is currently being advised by a community organisation. Despite her distress at her present situation, she cannot currently bring herself to go onto a hostel or refuge where no-one would speak Cantonese and she would suffer abject poverty and isolation, not to mention the problems of negotiating her way through the mire of legal, immigration and social agencies she would have to deal with. She has never held any kind of tenancy (see d) below).

In terms of their tenancy situation, one striking finding of the research was that women who fled violence were often not women who depended on their violent partners for accommodation. This contradicts the Euro-feminist analysis of domestic violence as being inflicted on dependent wives by husbands or partners who have material advantages over the women they live with, particularly in terms of housing and income. The women in the study can be separated into three groups in terms of their tenancy status for the purposes of analysing the implications of this where their relationship breaks down or their partner becomes abusive.

Another way in which the limited access that black people and women have to affordable housing generates domestic violence is by producing 'cohabitations of convenience', in which couples may opt to live together before their relationship is sufficiently established at emotional level.

There were an alarming number of cases in this study in which a homeless man simply moved in to the woman's flat, without her consent. At the same time few women are heartless enough to refuse shelter to the man they have been going out with. In this way, black women's compassion[11] for the homeless plight of black men can result in them being driven out of their homes when the relationship, forced to levels of intimacy that it cannot sustain, breaks down or becomes violent. In other cases men, who no longer have access to public housing in their own right, appear to have used a woman (and her children) to secure accommodation (as happened in Zoey's case). In a situation in which many black men are forced down into the underclass of the unemployed and unemployable and have no other means of getting a permanent home, this is not really surprising, and suggests that black male homelessness has to be taken into account in considering the conditions which produce and perpetuate domestic violence. There were several women in the Caribbean sample who had been brutalised by an unemployed black man who moved between two or more women's homes for shelter (amongst other things). The instabilities and insecurities of such a situation, not to mention the deceits, betrayals, recriminations and guilts that are involved in this peculiarly modern and urban form of polygamy, can only be described as facilitating the destructive relational patterns that often deteriorate into violent assault.

In short there are a variety of scenarios behind the violence which, at the material level, involve the housing situation of black communities. Our consideration of the tenancy status of women who have fled or consider fleeing their homes because of violence should be viewed in this light.

Most (over 90%) of the women we interviewed had actually moved out of the violent situation at the time of interview (68% were staying in refuges at the time, and a further 9% were in other temporary accommodation). The tenancy status (defined as Hers, His or Joint) of the woman changed as a result of violence in 73% of the sample interviewed. The 73% figure does not include the further 23% who had their own tenancy during the violent relationship but still had to move (tenancy status unchanged because temporary accommodation tenancy also in woman's name). Change in tenancy status therefore indicates the number of women who moved from joint or his tenancy situations into holding their own tenancy, though in most cases this meant a tenancy in the overcrowded and substandard conditions of temporary accommodation. Most of the women in our sample had left violent homes,

Table 4.2 *Tenancy Status**

	During DV	At time of interview
Hers	23%	88%
Joint	29%	3%
His	33%	3%
Unclear	15%	6%
Total	100	100

* Out of the 88% holding their own tenancy at the time of interview, 68% were in women's refuges. Only 18% of the total sample had been rehoused in a permanent home. These 18% comprised of the African women, 32% of the Asian and only 19% of the Caribbean samples.

regardless of their tenancy status. While this often meant leaving a place where the tenancy was held jointly or by the man, in nearly a quarter of the sample it was actually a case of the woman having to leave her own tenancy.

a) Where tenancy was in the woman's name
All 23% of the cases where the woman held the tenancy turned out on further analysis to have been women of Caribbean descent. None of the African or Asian women interviewed were sole tenancy holders during their experience of violence, although in a few cases the women had held tenancies of their own before the relationship.

For the 23% who held the tenancy during the violent relationship, this appears to have offered them little protection. In some cases the relationship appears to have broken down prior to the violence, but the man had not been willing to move out. The effect of his violence in most of these cases was to force the woman out:

JOSEPHINE, a young single Rastafarian woman with 2 children became involved with a man who moved into her council flat after they had been going out together for a month. He then became violent and over-possessive, forbidding her to see her woman friends or go out. She became pregnant, but this did not lessen his violence towards her. In the end, 11 months after he moved in, she left because she feared he would damage or kill her unborn child. She had her baby daughter while at the refuge where she is having to stay in one room with all three children. She said that they constantly contract colds and stomach infections in the overcrowded conditions of the refuge that took her in, but she cannot risk returning to her flat, even if the council were to change the locks to exclude her ex-partner as a non-tenant. She is therefore waiting for a transfer.

120

SARAH (see chapter 3) lived in a council flat in Brent with her 8 year old son. She was having a relationship with a man who lived elsewhere (she later discovered, with the mother of his two children). One day he arrived with his luggage, announcing that he had finished with the mother of his children. She objected, but did not refuse to accommodate him at that point. He had never been violent towards her at that point: indeed his generosity made her the envy of her friends.

'We were going out for about three years, but that didn't entitle him to just move in automatically as he did. But I didn't really say too much. I just sort of asked him and he said he thought that was what I had wanted. She threw all his clothes out and he then came and said he thought it was what I wanted.'

This man subsequently had another baby with his first child's mother, although he had denied continuing that relationship. While living with Sarah, he became increasingly violent and over-possessive towards her, ostensibly because she would not stop her career and have children for him.[12] Sarah had been in refuge for almost two years when we interviewed her, and still had no promise of rehousing from the Labour borough where she had lived for most of her life.

SUKIE (see chapter 3), a tenant of Haringey, has been homeless for nearly two years as a result of violence from a partner who moved in to her flat after helping her to decorate it. During that time she has stayed in a number of refuges and bed and breakfast hotels with her children. She was forced to leave the area and so her job, fearing reprisals after her partner was given a six months suspended sentence for grievous bodily harm after he had tried to strangle her to death.

In cases like this, where the man is not officially a tenant, even eviction is not a policy option.

In a number of cases, the woman was the sole tenant and the man did not live with her. In other words she was subjected to violence from a visiting man she had never lived with. For others, it was violent attacks from an ex-partner that forced women (and children) to abandon their homes.

Women who are assaulted by men who do not live with them are worse off legally, since they do not come under even the limited facilities of the Domestic Violence and Matrimonial Proceedings Act, under which injunctions are commonly obtained. Although the law should protect women from physical assault simply as citizens like any other member of the public, it is evident in the case material that when a man attacks a woman in or outside her home, law enforcement agents still dismiss the matter as 'domestic' once they suspect or assume that there is or has been a relationship between the woman and her assailant (see chapter 5).

In other cases, as a result of sexual discrimination in social security law, the acknowledgement of having a male cohabitee (even part-time) jeopardises women's right to benefits that may be their only means of sustaining themselves and their children. For black women, however the men who stay are often not 'breadwinners' in the way that nuclear European family structures presume and in the case of unemployed men, increasing numbers of whom are homeless as well, they may simply not be able to offer any financial or material support to the woman they stay with.[13] Other men may choose not to deliver the 'family benefit' to the rest of the family even if he is cohabiting with the mother on a full-time basis. When the children in question are not his, but the result of a previous relationship, he may not feel any responsibility towards feeding them at all. Nevertheless the presence of any such man being detected by social security officials would result in the woman and her children losing their right to benefit.

The extremely oppressive scenarios that dispossessed black families live under ensure that even black women who do have a tenancy and take a man in, either through compassion or more positively because they like his company, are unable to take recourse to the law for their protection because they cannot risk losing their autonomous access to social security benefit. This entrapment is further evidence of the multiply oppressive effects of the corporatisation of the state.

Local authorities may refuse to consider such women as homeless as a result of domestic violence, since their assailant did not officially live with them. When it comes to rehousing 'Violence from outside the home' may not be accepted as domestic violence. Indeed the practice of some LAs is to treat women in this situation as 'intentionally homeless' and therefore not eligible for housing (whether or not they have children). The Homeless Persons legislation is sufficiently ambiguous on this matter for Conservative boroughs to be fighting individual cases right up to the Law Courts. In a racist context, black women, viewed with suspicion at the best of times, are more likely to be seen as 'trying it on', particularly if they already live in nasty accommodation that any normal person would be desperate to get out of.

122

b) Joint Tenancies

Twenty-nine per cent of the sample had joint tenancies during their experience of domestic violence. Many of these were women who held tenancies of their own prior to their relationships, but who had changed these once they started cohabiting. This change from sole to joint tenancy was often at the instigation of the LA housing officer, in the course of the couple transferring to larger accommodation. For example:

> MABEL, an African woman, lived in her own council flat until she got married, whereupon her husband joined her and she agreed to have the tenancy changed from hers to joint. Although he moved out after becoming violent, his continued harassment forced her to abandon the flat and go into refuge with their children.

> GEORGINA, a woman of Chinese descent, had a bedsit she rented from Camden council. Some time after her Nigerian student partner moved in with her to live, they obtained a transfer to a one-bedroom flat, but the Housing Department insisted that the tenancy be changed to a joint one at this point. They got married, and Georgina continued to be the breadwinner. She describes her husband as having been lazy. Her horrendous experience at his hands included severe beatings with the use of various weapons, rape, and on one occasion his violence put her in hospital where she had a miscarriage. After being discharged, she went to housing and was told there was nothing they could do for her. She had the locks changed and with the support of friends ousted her assailant and his property. She lived in fear for some time after that, with her partner returning to try and break in, and the lack of police protection.

In this case, as in others, the man was forced to acknowledge her claim to the home and moved out but continued to threaten violence after doing so. In joint tenancy situations where the man is persuaded to leave, there is always the possibility that the situation becomes one of 'violence from outside the home' with the attendant problems that we have already discussed in a) above. In some cases, this will be a successful manoeuvre, since many men will stop battering the woman once they no longer live together, and most manage to find themselves somewhere else to live, or someone else to live with. Indeed some LAs (those with policies in this area) encourage women to enter this category as much as possible, either by agreeing to evict the man for assaulting another tenant (a 'hardline' policy which may not be upheld in court), or through cancelling the joint tenancy and reissuing one in the woman's name only. However, if (as in many of our cases) the man continues to lie in wait for and otherwise harass or assault the woman, there is then less that the Housing Department can do to protect her, since the assailant is now no longer a tenant.[14] Worse still, sometimes the man becomes even more threatening if not dangerous, towards the woman who he feels has put him on the street, from a home to which he did have a tenancy claim.

c) Tenancy in the man's name only
Women who had no tenancy in the first place often 'did the normal thing' and moved into their partner's accommodation on marriage. While these were sometimes adjusted to joint tenancies, as in some of the cases where a man moved in with a woman, often the tenancy was simply left as it was. Policies regarding recognition of the housing rights of a 'non-tenant' vary between boroughs. In any case, for a cohabitee to have tenants' rights, she must be acknowledged by the LA. This may mean having lived there for a certain minimum amount of time. Wives are more easily accepted as being tenants, because of the dominant notion of a wife as a man's dependant. However, there is no evidence that wives are treated any better than cohabiting women in terms of rehousing away from violence. In some cases they may well be worse off, since some LAs will not rehouse wives until they see legal evidence of a divorce, or even details of any settlement.

Many of the black women in this study wished to live separately after being cruelly battered, but could not countenance divorce for religious and social reasons, fearing the effect this would have on their children as well as themselves in their community. The respect that women show for their traditions does not, however mean that they should pay the very high price of being forced to remain in violent situations. To make divorce a condition of rehousing is not only completely unreasonable to all women given the time and complexities of court procedures, but worse still, has definite racial and cultural implications for black women from traditional backgrounds. This means that the housing bureaucracy is imposing very limited and parochial notions of marriage and the family on people from complex and varied familial and marital systems. It amounts to using people's cultures against them to exclude them from housing.

In the context of the housing crisis and the limited amount of affordable accommodation for single women, just as with men, cohabitations of convenience occur. In these situations it is a case of the woman moving in to a place where her man has obtained a tenancy or otherwise gained

124

access to a home. These are often cohabitations born of dire need, particularly where the woman has become pregnant or has a child for the man. This sometimes means she can no longer stay in her existing accommodation, which may have been with her family, friends or private rented accommodation. With inferior earning power, decent accommodation can rarely be afforded by women on their own.

PATIENCE simply moved in to a council flat that her husband obtained through his relationship with a previous girlfriend. As a result his name was on the tenancy, but hers was not. His tenancy status was part of the situation, and presumably enabled him to use the police to remove her from the premises after she had been badly beaten on more than one occasion. This put her at the mercy of the police who then subjected her to sexual and racial insults, and assaulted her again themselves at the station (see chapter 6).

Apart from moving into a man's accommodation (an option only open to women whose partners do have accommodation), the broader housing situation of black women affects their options when relationships break down, often forcing people who would not otherwise remain to stay together. Given the appalling living conditions that many black couples have to tolerate, bad housing and homelessness has to be seen as a cause of relationship breakdown and domestic violence, as well as a consequence of it.

ELSIE became involved with an unemployed musician, and joined him when her family reacted negatively to her becoming pregnant by him. Paul lived in a two-bedroom council flat with his Jehovah's witness mother and younger sister, so that Elsie's arrival, while welcomed, did cause serious overcrowding (ratio of 5:2). They applied to the council for a place of their own to keep the family together, but to no avail. Under these circumstances, various relational problems developed, and Paul became extremely violent (see case description). Elsie suffered a broken nose and was hospitalised several times after being beaten with metal poles and other objects. When we spoke to Elsie in a refuge, she was still pleading with the council for housing, albeit under different circumstances from the previous waiting list application, since she now requires housing as a single parent. At the emotional level, she has not been able to decide for herself whether her partner would continue to be violent to her under better living conditions or not, and she may well take the risk of finding out the hard way once she does get rehoused.

In this way, we can see that for many black women, atrocious living conditions keep them multiply oppressed. These conditions make it extremely difficult, if not impossible, for them to make decisions about relationships which they may understandably feel have never really had a chance. Under these circumstances, objective material oppression is at such a level that relational dynamics have limited explanatory power, since normal (undestructive, mutually supportive) relationships have never had space to even develop.

Women who live under a man's roof, or under a tenancy in his name (33% of the sample) are perhaps the worst off in terms of even the few limited options available to the other two tenancy groups. Their situation is one of material dependency, whatever the relationship is like. The relational dynamics generating violence are also different, since it cannot be analysed as a male reaction to perceived material power as is the case when women hold the tenancy. It is more clearly a case of men battering women, who are not only physically weaker and socially subordinated to them, but also materially dependent on them. To escape their partner's violence women in this situation must become homeless. This applied to many of the wives in the sample, and some of the cohabitees. In some cases the woman had some resources of her own and had invested these in co-buying a house in the man's name. Then the woman's problems will be exacerbated because the LA will not rehouse her until they establish the woman's financial situation after the divorce settlement, although since the husband is contesting this will take years (see discussion of private sector women).

In other cases (Zoey), the man appears to have obtained a tenancy on the basis of a woman and children, but in his name. Even the subsequent cancellation of this because the woman was forced to flee from violence merely fuelled his rage at her. She was subjected to violence primarily over withholding her earnings from him, and then accused of taking his home away from him after he beat her repeatedly for the first 'crime'. She was not able to return there after winning the injunctions and his eviction, because one effect of the legal battle was to put her life in more danger than it ever was.

d) No tenancy
In a number of cases where the couple lived in LA accommodation, neither

party had an officially recognised tenancy. In some cases accommodation was obtained unofficially, through relatives.

MARY moved into a flat in which her husband had been staying but which was under his sister's tenancy, so that neither of them were officially recognised as tenants. When Mary appealed for rehousing, she was advised to stay in her ex-husband's sister's flat with her baby. In that instance she was still being subjected to harassment, and as she put it, her husband would always feel he had a claim and certain rights to her as long as she remained there.

In other cases, both partners were homeless, and moving around various bed and breakfast hotels, and private sector rentals when there was enough money between them. Generally they had no prospect of obtaining a permanent home from the local authority, or being able to afford one in the private sector, a situation which faces growing numbers of young couples in London today. Often the housing stress of eternal temporary accommodation exacerbates relational problems and must be considered a factor in the genesis of violence:

SELENA moved between various temporary accommodations with her violently jealous musician boyfriend, while working in clubs and as a singer herself. When she and her daughter finally did get housed, she was given a flat on a sink estate in Greenwich. The lack of amenities, isolation and sexual harassment, combined with the disgusting state of the flat she was given, all weakened her resolve and led her to call her ex-partner to assist with making the place habitable. She was later forced to flee his violence again, with even slimmer prospects of rehousing. By this time even her social worker (who had previously sent her to a psychiatrist) did not want anything to do with her.

In this case desperation bred out of the appalling housing she was eventually given, led her to call on her ex, and so opened her up to further violence. Social services are quick to tire of women for what they see as personal weakness. Where Selena did find the emotional resolve to leave her violent partner, this was broken down by the threats she received from neighbours, and the appalling condition of the flat she and her daughter were given. Yet even this apparent weakness may well be the result of Selena having lived the multiply oppressive half-life of homelessness and economic insecurity for many years.

127

Black women in temporary accommodation

Seventy-seven per cent of the women who participated in this study were in temporary accommodation during the research period. Although not all could be consistently followed up, by the end of the year it was clear that only a small minority of them had been then housed. The suffering that this caused to these single parent families would have to be multiplied hundreds of times to understand what black women and children go through to escape from violent and abusive men, in London alone. Worse still, what they go through before that — living in relationships with such men — should also be considered (this was indicated in chapter 3). There are various statistical indicators of what temporary accommodation is like. These are presented alongside examples drawn from case histories — some of which you already know something about — to illustrate what being homeless means for black women.

Statistical indicators

Only 18% of the whole sample (n = 100) had been rehoused at the time of interview. Most of the rest (77%) were in refuges, and a few were in bed and breakfast hotels or other forms of temporary accommodation. Refuges are the only form of hostel accommodation represented, although some women had also been in mixed hostels and reception centres at some stage. Those rehoused represented 32% (13/40) of the Asian women in the study, as compared to only 9% (5/54) of the women of Caribbean origin. None of the 6 African women had been rehoused when we interviewed them. This represented a significant number of children in temporary accommodation; a total of 125 children still lived with their mothers when we interviewed them. Twenty-nine did not because mothers had lost custody, or left them with their fathers, or because the children were adults. Others had been placed in care.

These women were of all ages, ranging from late teens to women in their 50s, some of whom had tolerated violence for years. For example Bernadette, a 49-year old woman of Caribbean origin who had been married to a soldier had been brutalised most of the 14 years of her married life, but had not known of refuges. Tragically, after her divorce (won on grounds of unreasonable behaviour) her ex husband continued to harass her until she was driven out of the LA flat she had been given in 1974 and in which she raised all five of her children. She then lived the half-life of moving from one hostel to another experiencing various forms of harassment, until she was informed about refuges only a couple of weeks before we interviewed her.

There were several types of temporary accommodation, none of which were ideal. Women in our sample found refuges less harrowing than other forms, and many expressed deep appreciation of the emotional support they received and what it had meant to them. It was the mixed reception centres and hostels that women had the worst things to say about. This is important in light of current housing policies which are likely to see growing numbers of people pushed out of public and private housing to live permanently in such hostels.

Mary (whose story has been mentioned several times already) spent a year and a half in one hostel and described the pressures she was subjected to by hostel wardens. She observed that white homeless families in her area were not only rehoused quicker and in better homes, but also sent to a different class of hostel while they were homeless:

'There were two hostels where they particularly sent single parents at the time. One was in Highgate and one in Crouch End. What I noticed was that in Crouch End, where I was staying it was absolutely filthy. There was no floor covering — you basically had four walls. The room I was given you could go like that (stretched out her arms) and you were touching the walls. My first impression was that if I was ever to go to prison — this was exactly how I imagined it. But by then I knew I wasn't going to be housed any other way. I later went to see a friend who had been moved to the Highgate hostel after a quarrel with the warden. She had been the only white girl at Crouch End. When she was there I had occasion to visit her and it was like walking into Laura Ashley — a designer place. And all the residents, with the exception of two, were white.'

Lily Chang was also very unhappy with the hostel the police took her to:

'The first time I left home they took me to this hostel — run by the government I think. They didn't want me to stay there too long — so the warden told the police. I still don't know why, but the people in the hostel were not very nice. I found them a bit racist. They kind of gave better treatment to the English people. You had to share the kitchen and common room. One of the women was picking on me, so I tried to complain to the warden, but it was me who got told off.'

Yvonne's main complaint about the reception centre where she was placed was that there was no security, so that her ex was able to find her and continue to terrorise and assault her there.

Iyamide, still in temporary accommodation, was particularly distraught because of the effect staying in one cramped room at a bed and breakfast hotel, was having on her children.

'Seven whole months. It's a terrible thing. The children — you know children. When they want to play, they (other residents and staff) shout at them — Go inside and shut the door! So we were there like a prison. I don't even want to think about it . . . I had to get up at half past six to get them to school.'

The reception used to allow her husband in, a situation which he used to further upset their two sons:

'The children used to run away. They didn't like to stay in that bed and breakfast, so they kept running away so you can see the advantage he was taking. Sometimes he would take them without telling me. And he would tell them he was coming to see his wife and I would find him upstairs. I would tell him that I was not here for him — You are not the one keeping me here, so don't come again. I kept telling him not to come, but he just kept on coming. He always comes — even here [in LA-rented temporary accommodation] — says he's coming to pick up the children.' (Custody is shared, so Iyamide has not got the option of not seeing him at all).

Sukie too had a nasty time in a Bayswater hotel with her two young children. It may be recalled that her boyfriend moved into her council flat and drove her out with violence that got him a conviction for GBH. He was given a suspended sentence which meant that fearing reprisals, she had to flee from her flat after the court case:

'I went to the emergency department and they put me in a bed and breakfast down in Bayswater, Inverness Terrace. I had three beds in a little basement and it was infested with cockroaches. I kept complaining to the manager and he kept saying they were going to fumigate the place. Every night they were all over the floor, moving all over the bed. I was so terrified that I had to go to Social Services and tell them I was not going to take that.' (She was then referred to Women's Aid).

The accommodation that the LA placed her in was so far from her place of work and her children's schools that she had to leave her job to look after the children. She was therefore forced to depend on social security benefit.

Several other women in the sample had found hostels quite unbearable and experienced racial harassment from other homeless families and/or sexual harassment from male residents. Many (including Sukie) pointed out that they were already relying on small social security payments, and the absence of cooking facilities in bed and breakfast hotels made it impossible for them to give their families a balanced diet, since they had to live on expensive take-away food.

The material we have indicates that the temporary accommodation in which black women find themselves, ranges from bad to appalling. Almost by definition, it is a transient and insecure situation, which compounds the economic, social and emotional stresses that homeless families are in any case under. In addition to the problems identified by Austerberry and Watson's (1983) study of single women's housing problems, black women in mixed accommodation are frequently subjected to the racism of people they have not chosen to live with, and this can be compounded or even surpassed by racism from wardens. Black women are likely to be in this unenviable situation for longer periods of time as a result of the widespread discrimination in housing departments.

All of this experience is compounded by the length of time it takes to get rehoused at all, and the hopelessness of moving from hotels to refuges to hostels in some cases. This gives us some idea of the general hardship that homelessness inflicts on families headed by black women. This combines with the trauma of having been subjected to domestic violence, perhaps over a long period of time, and increases their vulnerability to the multiply oppressive forces dictating their fate as they quietly struggle to survive and build lives for themselves away from violent men.

The numbers of homeless people (particularly single homeless people) have continued to rise very dramatically, and are going to continue to do so for the foreseeable future. There were actually women in the sample who, like Selena, had never had permanent homes, largely as a result of never earning enough, and not having access to council accommodation since they did not have children (although Selena did have a daughter). This reflects in the long term a broader lack of vision. In Britain, housing has not developed to accommodate the changing lifestyles of the modern era, in particular that large numbers of people live as female-headed households, or as single people, and a great many (a third) of marriages break down. This changing situation means that greater flexibility is necessary. More immediately, however it is also a direct result of the

131

present regime's policy of deliberately returning housing to the control of 'market forces' and the undermining of social planning that this entails. This forms part of a more general pattern of the erosion of local government power by Central Government.

Black women in the private sector

This group of women are particularly important in the context of the widespread privatisation of housing under the present government. As a result of the 'Right to Buy' and other forms of privatisation, we can already see not only a rapid depletion of the public housing stock, but also that what is left is of the worst quality. With the abandoning of any government commitment to providing decent and affordable housing through the public sector, we can predict that the numbers of women being forced to remain in violent situations will continue to grow. The housing stress that in itself is a causal factor in generating domestic violence is rapidly worsening, and at the same time, the routes that have been available in progressive boroughs for the rehousing of women who have survived violence are being overwhelmed and undermined. Here, the broader housing crisis has undermined any possibility of these policies being implemented, so that implementing them at all, let alone implementing them for black women is a possibility that grows increasingly remote.

The rehousing prospects of black women who experience domestic violence in the private sector can be summed up as being generally worse than that of women in public sector accommodation.

Black women in the study, who were subjected to violence in homes in the private sector, all faced the struggle of entering the public sector by obtaining council tenancies as homeless persons, which we have seen to be an increasingly long and stressful process. Despite the legislation on homelessness, some (notably Conservative boroughs who are more often in favor of Central Governments housing policies) still refuse to take on women escaping violence as new tenants. This puts additional pressure on those boroughs that have developed policies to facilitate the rehousing such families. None of the boroughs take on single women with no children, so that this group have to find ways of paying private rent, or need to have enough earning power to be able to afford to obtain a mortgage on their own.

In our sample, most of the women in privately owned homes were in fact staying in homes owned by their husbands or their husband's family. Most were Asian, economically dependent wives, who were not allowed

132

to go out to work. Sometimes the house they lived in was not in the husband's name, but in the name of his family, which would have implications for any divorce settlement.

A small number were buying or had brought homes with their assailants and had been forced to abandon their investment in order to escape violence. Some were too traumatised to have even considered recouping any of their material losses at the time of interview. Others (like Hamza) were being refused LA housing pending the outcome of a divorce settlement. In cases where the woman did not wish for a divorce, but simply a home for herself and her children away from a violent husband, this was effectively a way of denying her access to housing.

In all cases where the woman had been in the private rented sector, she effectively had no tenancy rights and the only route out of the violent home was to become homeless and appeal to LA Homeless Persons Units. At best, if her request is lodged in a borough that does recognise its responsibilities under the Homeless Persons Act 1977, she will be given temporary accommodation, pending acceptance for housing. Thus she will be embarking on another long and soul-destroying ordeal (see below) as one of the growing number of long-term homeless on waiting lists. If she is not accepted by the borough she is applying to, legal battles may be necessary to force them to accept her, and sometimes even to allow her to remain in temporary accommodation. As if this were not bad enough, even the worst temporary accommodation constitutes 'recourse to public funds' so that it may result in deportation for women who do not have full residence rights under current legislation.

Getting accepted on to a borough's waiting lists alone can involve months of struggle, not to mention the subsequent wait of up to two or more years to actually obtain a permanent home.

SHABA, an Iranian woman was married and resident in Barnet with her husband for 12 years, in one rented room. They had a child and were on the waiting list for council accommodation for over four years. During this time they were served with an eviction notice and told by the housing department to go to court to remain in the one overcrowded room they had in their landlady's house. Things got so bad that she was eventually forced to run away from her young husband when he became increasingly violent. She described him as being shocked by the blood he spilt at first, and then getting so used to it that neither that nor her screams and pleading had any effect. He also used to cover her baby daughter's face with the pillow when she cried, or rocked the cradle so hard that little Roya's nose bled from hitting the sides. She returned to the housing department, now homeless, and was told to consider going back to Iran, whereupon she broke down in tears and left (Shaba wept during the interview, recounting her sad experience).

HAMZA, a Kenyan-born Asian woman who accompanied her husband to Britain in the 1970s had been in the refuge with her teenage children for over a year at time of interview. She had been forced to leave the home she and her violent husband had brought together when they arrived here from Kenya. She has no prospect of being rehoused, since the local authority are refusing to accept her as homeless until the divorce settlement is made and her financial situation made clear to them. Hamza has never worked in this country and has no prospect of working since she is now a single parent and it is a long time since she left her teaching job in Kenya, so that she is hardly likely to be able to afford a mortgage on her own in any case.

Other women in our sample had no claim to properties held in their in-law's names in any case. For all of them, local authority housing is the only option. The exhausting process of obtaining LA housing is probably most difficult of all for women who have never held LA tenancies in their names, and therefore involves creating a new tenancy rather then transferring an existing tenancy.

Summary and conclusions

A number of theoretical points and practical implications emerged in this chapter which will be briefly summarised here.

When a housing department requires a police report, this has particular consequences for black women who are as a group, more reluctant than the wider population to involve the police in their lives. It effectively blocks those not willing to involve the police in their problems from access to rehousing or housing. For black groups who often have negative experiences of statutory organisations, cross-referring can have multiply oppressive effects, as the case material presented above illustrates.

The increased policing of welfare services must continue to be a source of concern, particularly in relation to groups as desperately in need as the women in this study. For example, the increased stringency of immigration legislation has been accompanied by the growing obsession with controlling the 'aliens' inside the country already, and restricting our access to public resources. Public service employees are encouraged to question the eligibility and integrity of clients; so being granted a license to carry out racist passport checks on those they most suspect of being alien: black people.

This increased coming together of different parts of the state — corporatisation — appears to be something that will continue, particularly with the technology that has become available, and raises serious civil rights issues.

In this chapter we have seen that the increased corporatisation of the British state can have dire consequences for oppressed groups, in this case multiplying the oppressive and discriminatory practices to which black women are subjected. The negative consequences appeared to overrule the other possibility, which is that of developing efficient and humane multi-agency responses in the interests of the clients. The case material indicates that public 'services' can quite easily become coercive rather than supportive, particularly with the linking up between the police state (police forces, immigration service) and the welfare state (housing, social services, healthcare). Service delivery appears to be dominated by 'police' concerns over eligibility and exclusion when the client groups are black women, instead of being concerned with delivering an egalitarian service. This raises more general theoretical questions about the nature of advanced capitalist states, where welfare services are functioning to reproduce and compound social divisions so efficiently.

There is clearly an enormous need for safe and decent housing for black women. The evidence is that there is a grave shortage of provision for many social groups, but that black women in particular continue to be excluded from existing services, or are made to pay very dearly before getting even the most undesirable kind of service. The anti-racist project within state apparatuses must be continued and supported to try and change this situation. However, since it is taking so long, specialist provision for black women must be immediately developed to meet the very pressing needs that statutory organisations are failing to recognise let alone to meet. A number of different strategies must be pursued simultaneously, and these are elaborated further in later chapters.

The analysis of tenancy status indicated that black men's lack of access to housing is one factor producing violent situations. The conditions we found black families to be living in were so bad that we were forced to the conclusion that the general discrimination in housing is obviously forcing black people to live together in overcrowded and bad quality housing, conditions which are likely to produce and increase violence. It also indicated that holding a tenancy does not in itself protect women from violence. However, women with no tenancy at all were even worse off. Establishing independent access to affordable housing for black women is a necessary condition for reducing levels of domestic violence in black communities.

The experience of black women in the private sector indicates that the broader restructuring of the housing market, in particular the privatisation of public housing will make things much worse. Private renting would not be a solution to the housing crisis, even if black women were to be able to afford the necessary rents in London. Many abused women will also be becoming single parents, and the lack of childcare support in Britain will in any case make earning a wage, let alone the high wages necessary to buy a home, quite impossible for the vast majority of black women.

Notes

1. Any group of citizens demanding resources from the welfare arms of the state constitutes a consumer group in contemporary terminology which wishes to emphasize consumer choice, negotiation and bargaining in accordance with the 'free market' ethos of Thatcherism. It is therefore something of a misnomer during a period in which the welfare state is being eroded, and is used rather ironically here since this study involves a consumer group who the state has been preoccupied with excluding from services and resources. Other terms used include 'client', borrowed from legal agencies, or 'users'. Many groups experience the welfare state as a large alienating bureaucracy, and I have argued elsewhere that the Thatcher Government has exploited such sentiments to erode services (*Feminist Review* no.32 Summer 1989), so making this experience increasingly negative and heightening the historical paranoia of this 'small and overcrowded island'.

2. According to one ex-police officer, this is common practice — 'What do you expect us to do when you arrive and find the walls covered in blood', was his response to further questions.

3. This was because of the way in which we contacted interviewees: women in this group were under-represented in our sample because it was heavily weighted in favour of women who had already left to stay in refuges.

4. The Housing (Homeless Persons) Act of 1977 obliges local authorities to accommodate women made homeless because of violence or the threat of violence in their home.

5. Black women who are homeless but temporarily staying with friends and/or relatives were under-represented in our sample because of the methods used to contact them.

6. Her experience of temporary accommodation is discussed later on in this chapter.

7. Given the resistance of statutory bodies to accepting anything other than crude numerical evidence, a long-term follow up study which would compare the different experiences of black and white women is in order. The present study was not designed for this purpose. Instead, and in the face of our limited resources, we prioritised the need for a fuller understanding of what black women go through in their struggle for housing.

8. Lai Ha says that if there was a Chinese refuge, she would go there.

9. There have been a number of tragic deaths of women in black communities in recent years, which illustrate one outcome of social tolerance of domestic violence (see appendix). Many of these were murders of women who had unsuccessfully sought help in a number of ways. These are not included in the main text so as not to locate them too closely to the living women who participated in this study. Krishna's bruised body was found hanging in torn clothing on 8 March 1984. Later enquiries revealed that Krishna, mother of two, had been in a violent marriage for eight years, and had called the police only the night before her death, pleading for help. The coroner returned a verdict of suicide. Chandra Mohan Sharma's house was subsequently picketed by angry women from that community, who clearly had a different opinion about Krishna's death (*New Statesman* 1 June 1984).

10. Information from the Commission for Philipino Migrant Workers.

11. In psychological terms, what I have called compassion here could be further explored: what we are talking about is the psychological make-up of women — which may include a 'need' (or willingness) to nurture and provide for a man.

12. The worst injuries Sarah sustained however where the result of an unexpected blow to the back of the head with a bottle, delivered by her cohabitee's 'ex-partner'. She still bears the long scar where her scalp was stitched. She was therefore subjected to multiple abuse. Many women are in fact multiply abused; at the hands of their partners and the police, or their partner and his relatives, or their partners and their employers. The fear of being multiply abused adds to the conditions coercing them into remaining in a violent situation, increasing the feeling that there is no escape from violence.

13. Staying with several different women may be a male coping strategy, enabling them to retain something of their 'manhood' while at the same time not giving any single woman the power of being sole supporter. In any case many women may not wish to accommodate a dependent man full-time. The structure of this manhood is conformist, and like the structure of the femininity that needs a male to nurture at any cost, needs to be further explored. In the present oppressive social situation, the material conditions and emotional expectations of the two sexes are often in direct confrontation, so much so that relational problems are bound to develop. In many cases, violent assaults on black

women is just one — completely unacceptable — enaction of these contradictions.

14. Local Authority housing has a very bad record in the general area of tenant protection. Council housing estates (particularly the worse ones in the inner cities) are very unsafe places at the best of times, and it is a long term fact that in the slow process of running them down, safety has been neglected, making fear of violent attack a major source of dissatisfaction.

PART II: Statutory Responses

140

5. Woman abuse and the law

Introduction: law and domestic violence in international context

The international nature of woman abuse was indicated in chapter one. Many of the ex-colonies discussed there have legal systems that are derived from British law, so that their inadequacy in combating domestic violence stems from the coming together of a number of traditions. In Kenya for example it has been observed that:

> 'in reference to wife-beating, customary law and African traditions and statutory law and English traditions interact with new concepts of the family and social organisation to completely transform the phenomenon' (*The Nairobi Law Monthly*, Feb 1988 p8).

The same could be said of many African and Asian countries. In Islamic states, for example, religious legal systems derived from the ancient text of the Koran prevail. In many Commonwealth countries there are customary and religious legal systems existing alongside the governmental (historically colonial) law as is the case in Nigeria and India, for example. When it comes to violence against wives, customary and religious laws in most places accept physical abuse as grounds for a woman to divorce the perpetrator, even when the law is extremely discriminatory in many other ways (see Ibrahim 1978, Akande 1979, Bello 1985). This contradicts the Western assumption that the British law has generally been and is 'more advanced' than other (for example African or Islamic) legal traditions. As the evidence in the next section indicates, it is only very recently that laws specifically aimed at protecting women from the men they live with have been introduced in Britain. In fact many women, especially black women, are still not adequately protected (see also chapter 6), since these laws are not enforced or applied by law enforcement agencies.

As we noted in chapter one, the legal systems of many of the countries which the subject group of this project have connections with, are based on English Law. What is notable, when we come to consider the protection of women from violence by the men with whom they are involved, is the wide variation in the development of the written law, in both its application and enforcement, across different countries. Even within Britain, the law has often been very lenient with, or altogether reluctant to convict husbands who have physically abused their wives or cohabiters (Dobash and Dobash 1980, Edwards 1986). Historically English law has condoned some degree of physical chastisement in much the same way as, long after the flag independence, the law in many ex-colonies still does.

In many cases the assailant and the woman may not have had their marriages registered under the national law, but rather in accord with Sharia or customary law. If this is the case, it may be necessary for the wife to seek protection, divorce or redress under whatever legal system she was married under, since she may not be eligible for protection under national law. In Nigeria for example, women married under Sharia law cannot seek redress or child custody under the national law when they get divorced, but only in the Alkali courts (under the same Sharia law).

In many countries, women who are cohabiting with men, as 'common law' wives, can only appeal to the criminal law when they are assaulted, since they are not protected under civil law. In some countries women cannot give evidence against their husbands, and in others they will not because it would not be culturally acceptable for them to do so, and may not be in their own interests.

There is also substantial evidence that many women are assaulted by men that they do not, or no longer, live with. Family and marital legal codes generally do not cover cases in which there has already been a divorce, or a legal separation, or where the man never lived with the woman whom he assaults in her home. This means that ex-wives and ex-partners, like women who are not legally married to their assailant, can only seek redress under the criminal law.

In some contexts, as we saw in chapter one, attempts to reform the colonial law in the direction of improving provisions for dealing with domestic violence have been blocked on the basis that woman abuse is in fact some sort of indigenous 'tradition'. Others would argue that the problem calls for a return to 'traditional ways' as if only the degree of violence is the problem. Traditional curbs on woman abuse have indeed been undermined by urbanisation and other major social upheavals, so that wife-maiming, wife-murder, and other forms of woman-abuse are actually on the increase in many countries, in rural as well as urban areas. This does not mean however, that the pre-colonial set up was necessarily satisfactory, simply because women were not beaten 'too hard' and were not therefore maimed and killed by their partners as often as they are now. Rather it can be argued that 'traditional' (for example African) cultures (in common with other patriarchal cultures) contained the potential for the violence that we are now seeing unleashed by the underdevelopment process. This would seem to be more likely, particularly since non-action and toleration of violence are now being called for precisely in the name of 'tradition'.

The evidence that woman-abuse is a serious problem with very high social costs, has resulted in some response from international agencies, particularly since the United Nations Decade for Women. During the decade, with its themes of Equality, Development and Peace, the need to create an environment that fosters respect for the dignity of the individual was stressed.

The 1986 United Nations Report of the Expert Group Meeting for example, includes the UN guidelines on what the legal provision for dealing with domestic violence should be, in the written law, in police practice and the rest of the Criminal Justice system.

International research under the auspices of the Commonwealth, has been conducted into the legal aspects of domestic violence (Connors 1986). This is relevant to this project in a quite specific way, because of the historical fact that the legal systems of most Commonwealth countries have their origins in British law, and also because a significant proportion of Britain's black population originate from, or have connections with, Commonwealth countries in Africa, Asia and the Caribbean. In a paper presented to a meeting of Commonwealth Law Ministers in Zimbabwe 1986, Connors identified a common pattern in the legal response to wife abuse:

i) Most countries allow for divorce and judicial separation remedies which may well be the principal response to domestic violence. These remedies however, are of course, applicable to married spouses only.
ii) All countries in the Commonwealth render physical assault between spouses as being as criminal as if such activity had occurred between strangers. In all countries, criminal prosecutions may be brought by the state or the victim may bring a private prosecution.
iii) Quasi-criminal remedies derived from breach of the peace provisions exist in most Commonwealth jurisdictions. Their potential

as a remedy for domestic violence has only recently been recognised.
iv) Injunctions are available in all Commonwealth countries as ancillary proceedings to a matrimonial cause or a civil action. A number of countries have, however, gone further and enacted special legislation to provide protection for women who are the subject of domestic abuse, while others are contemplating such a step.

Generally there are a range of relevant legal provisions which fall under the Criminal Law or the Civil Law.

Criminal law
In cases involving injury, or death, to the woman, criminal law often has provisions for dealing with violent abuse. However, all the evidence points to the reluctance of legal agencies to implement the provisions of criminal law when it comes to dealing with men who assault the women they have or have had sexual and/or familial relationships with. Violence against the person is apparently taken less seriously when it can be dismissed as 'domestic'. The particular reluctance of the police to uphold the law in relation to domestic violence has received some attention (Edwards 1986, 1988), not least because they are the agency with the most obvious potential for intervening to reduce physical assaults on women in their homes. In general the research suggests that their reluctance to act is the result of a number of factors. The organisational culture of male-dominated police forces, with for example, the stereotyping of women as 'hysterical' or 'nagging wives', has been identified as particularly patriarchal and therefore tending to give priority to male rights rather than women's safety. The prosecution-oriented nature of 'police work', combined with the casual treatment of domestic violence by the courts, and the reluctance of women to go to court and see a prosecution through, have also been identified as sources of police non-response. So too has the identification of domestic violence, by the police, as a 'social' and therefore non-criminal problem. While the whole picture is quite a complex one, the police do have a responsibility to enforce the right of women to protection from violent assault in the home and to take action themselves when the law is broken. Furthermore, the police also have a responsibility to properly advise women on the relevant existing legal provisions. In practice however, research in Britain indicates that the police forces consistently neglect this responsibility, and therefore discriminate against women who have been subjected to domestic violence and in favour of the perpetrators of this particular crime. Worse still, and as was noted in

144

chapter one, the police and other law enforcement agents themselves often commit violent crimes against women. This is particularly so in countries where there are high levels of violence generally, and where the state is authoritarian and has little regard for the human rights of women in particular (eg in South Africa with regard to African women, and in Nigeria, India and other neo-colonies).

In the few (and therefore exceptional) Commonwealth jurisdictions that have concluded that domestic violence is a crime, specific legal provisions have been enacted. In Canada, for example, stiffer penalties have been imposed for all crimes of violence. More specifically, the police have been empowered to place a criminal charge even if the woman would prefer not to, so removing the burden of choice and proof from the already traumatised and often intimidated woman. This contrasts to the situation in England where the burden of proof not only lies on the woman, but where it has actually become possible for judges to sentence women to imprisonment for being too frightened (after being threatened and intimidated) to give evidence against an assailant (*Observer*, 12 March 1989).

Generally speaking, the reluctance of the police to act in relation to domestic violence in itself produces a reluctance by women to call on them to intervene and in consequence produces a breakdown in law enforcement.

Another consideration to be born in mind is the overall levels of violence in people's lives. In contexts like South Africa and many of the independent but extremely oppressive peripheral capitalist countries, extreme disparities characterise the lives of the people, so that structural violence is an integral part of daily life. As was noted with reference to Kenya:

'Kenya like any third world society has extremes in all spheres of human existence which profoundly test the social human fabric. There are vast gaps between the rich and the poor, urban and rural, and powerful and powerless. This situation of disparities means that violence is inherent. The individual both male and female . . . exists in a state of violence, with the weakest either economically, culturally, socially or otherwise bearing the brunt of the violence.' (*The Nairobi Law Monthly*, Feb 1988).

This description could be one of almost any peripheral capitalist country. More disturbing is the fact that the most affluent Western nations (upon which the peripheral capitalist countries are modelling themselves) are also characterised by structural inequalities and have very high levels of violent crime. For example it has been pointed out that North American culture is intrinsically violent, and in many ways has been predicated on violence throughout its history (Staples 1982).

Civil law

There are various possibilities within civil law that can, if properly used and enforced, be used to protect women from domestic violence. As I noted above, injunctions are available throughout the Commonwealth. However, in many places, an injunction will only be granted when other legal courses (divorce or judicial separation) are already being pursued. This means that injunctions are not remedial either by design, or in practice. Furthermore, in several jurisdictions, some groups of women cannot obtain protection orders eg Muslim wives in Malaysia and Nigeria). In others provisions for injunctions only apply to married couples and not to cohabitees, or where violence is inflicted by other relatives.

The use of injunctions in relation to domestic violence has been facilitated by supporting legislation in a number of countries (see Connors 1986 for a comprehensive review). In most Commonwealth countries however, even after a woman has gone through the ordeal of the courtroom and obtained an injunction, there is inadequate enforcement of injunctions by the police. It is also extremely difficult for women to get exclusion orders, which order the perpetrator to keep off the premises, presumably because of reluctance by the courts. Few judges (most of whom are male) feel that violence is sufficient justification for ordering a man out of 'his' home, even in order to protect a woman.

In summary, it is clear that injunctions are at best only a temporary measure, offering some protection to women whose assailants are in the first place likely to be deterred by the law. However, without adequate enforcement by the police, it is apparent that taking out an injunction may exacerbate the situation without providing any real protection for the women experiencing domestic violence. More fundamentally, the law in this area is extremely complex, so that in Britain for example, even lawyers have to be specialists in the area to be effective. Internationally, it remains the case that injunctions are not a viable option for the vast majority of women. According to Connors (1986), the provisions of civil law are not being successfully employed by victims of domestic violence in Commonwealth countries. In some countries legal amendments are still required for this to happen.

146

In all countries, provisions in civil law require a more supportive social context than that currently prevailing. This can be achieved initially by:
i) improving police responses to domestic violence;
ii) the provision of sheltered accommodation (perhaps like the women's refuges in the West); and
iii) providing legal counselling for victims of domestic violence.

Because what actually prevails in many ex-colonies can be traced to colonial law, as can the application of British law in relation to black women in Britain, it is useful to look at this legacy in more detail.

British traditions of women abuse and the law

'When Katie gets saucy, she gets nothing but a box on the ear' (Martin Luther[1] 16th century).

'A woman, a spaniel and a walnut tree, the more they are beaten, the better they be' (Old English saying, circa 1600).

'Our women are like dogs, the more you beat them the more they love you' (19th century)

Current work in the area of woman abuse and the law indicates that there is a general recognition that the law is inadequate in protecting women from physical abuse by the men they live with, or otherwise relate to. This can be attributed to the character of the written law, or to the interpretation and enforcement of the written law by law enforcement agencies: the police, courts, lawyers, and the wider society in general. Available evidence suggests that there is substantial room for improvement in all these areas.

Historically both the law and its enforcement can be seen to have been imbued with patriarchal values which have asserted the necessity and desirability of women's subordination to men. This is particularly so in the case of wives, and the record shows that this subjugation has not only been demanded, but that men have been legally empowered to enforce it by a number of means, including physical 'chastisement'.

This has not always been universally the case, and in Europe the subordination of women within the family has clearly gained ascendancy with the development of the nuclear family and the modern state. Even before this however, it has been observed that:

'. . . by the thirteenth century, feudal law was firmly established, with its hierarchy of land holding and personal loyalties based on military service. With the break up of the family as the basic social, economic and political unit of society, women's position changed dramatically. Because men's power stemmed from land-holding and inheritance, women were important only for the provision of legitimate heirs.' (Atkins and Hoggett 1984 p10).

In feudal and mediaeval times, the larger extended family form prevailed, often with its own fortifications, and the national state structure was not the centre of administrative, military and political power in the way that it is today. Similarly, although class hierarchies clearly existed, the division between private and public; between domestic unwaged labour and public waged labour were much less in evidence. With the growth of the centralised state came the development of a range of other social institutions which mirrored the patriarchal and class relations of the state on a smaller scale. Engels' thesis relates the origin of the nuclear Western family to the development of private property and the state (Engels 1972). The nuclear family has long been identified as the principal site of both biological and social reproduction in capitalist societies (eg Zaretsky 1976, Barrett and McIntosh 1982). This perspective has been developed extensively in recent years, particularly in the evaluation of economic and social development in capitalist societies (eg Mies 1986). Mies writes of the 'housewifization' process, and its relation to colonialism, focusing on the exclusion of women from the waged labour force and all aspects of public life, and her confinement within the private sphere — the home and family. It is clear that with the growth of wage economies, domestic labour became 'women's work' which, as unwaged work, is also devalued.

Women's legal status in capitalist and peripheral capitalist countries reflect the sexual inequalities that have characterised their status in all patriarchal social formations. In England, once a woman became a wife she abdicated any independent claim to whatever property she had, right up until the Married Women's Property Act of 1895. She also gave up a number of other rights she had as a single woman, and gave her husband the right to inflict corporal punishment upon her. The expression 'rule of thumb' for example, has its root in the ancient law allowing a husband to chastise his wife with a stick no wider than his own thumb. At no time in history has the wife had any right to chastise her husband.

With the growth of Protestantism came a growing emphasis on individuality, the sanctity of marriage and male authority. Christian

148

marriage highlighted the conjugal pair united by love, but at the same time, a woman's obedience to her husband became more than simply what was expected: it became a moral duty. In the 16th and 17th centuries the status of women reached a new low.

The Lutheran inspired Reformation began in 1517. While Luther was more progressive than many of his predecessors, preferring to think of women as 'friendly rivals' rather than profane inferiors, he also retained many of the old ideas:

'Men have broad shoulders and narrow hips, and accordingly they possess intelligence. Women have narrow shoulders and broad hips. Women ought to stay at home; the way they were created indicates this, for they have broad hips and a fundament to sit upon, keep house and bear and raise children'.

'. . . Scripture and life reveal that only one women in thousands has been endowed with the God-given aptitude to live in chastity and virginity. A woman is not fully the master of herself.'

It is not therefore surprising that moderate physical chastisement was condoned and practised by Martin Luther.

Calvinism contained the same contradictory mixture of companionability and domination of husband over wife. John Knox went through the scriptures quoting them at length to 'prove' that God had ordained women's inferior status. While 16th century marriage manuals did not uphold the use of violence to keep women in their subordinate place, popular sentiment did. Mary Wollestonecraft's famous book *The Vindication of the Rights of Women* was published in 1792.

During the 17th-19th centuries, it continued to be acceptable for men to beat their wives, with the community exerting only a limiting effect; that is to say, only the extent of beating was at issue. The evidence suggests that abuse had to be extremely severe before any intervention was likely, and that this prevailed across all classes. Truisms of this period included the notion that women enjoyed being beaten; that a man was not a man unless his wife was entirely subjugated, and that the more a man beat a woman the fonder she became of him. Many of these beliefs are still echoed today, and not just in Europe.

As Foucault's work shows (*Discipline and Punish*, 1977), the 18th and 19th centuries were very much an age of flogging. Discipline and obedience to authority and the moral order of the day were enforced by beating and whipping in the schools and prisons as well as the home. In some places excessive physical cruelty to wives was publicly ridiculed, but not to the same extent as were disobedient women who 'did not know their place'. Dobash and Dobash (1979 ch. 4) report that the ducking stool, public whipping or the branks were used to punish nagging or scolding women (the brank was an iron bridle with a padlock and a spike to enter the mouth which was forced onto the offender).[2]

Only in the 19th century do we see the emergence of widespread resistance to the husband's absolute right to chastise his wife. The act giving the husband such a right was erased from the statute book in 1829, although this did not in any way prevent or punish wife assault. The fact that a few years after, women were specifically excluded from voting under the First Reform Act of 1832, indicates that removing the husbands right to beat his wife had little to do with enhancing women's status, since they were still not regarded as citizens. It still remained virtually impossible for a woman to sue for assault. Only in 1895, when the Married Women's Property Act was passed, did it become possible for a woman to get a divorce on the basis of her husband's conviction for assault. It was around this time that the sale of wives was also finally prohibited. Early women's rights campaigns were underway, emerging particularly out of the abolition movements of the period. In 1840, somewhat ironically, male abolitionists refused to allow women abolitionists to participate in the first anti-slavery convention held in London, relegating them to the gallery.

The widespread abuse of women continued unabated, and probably inspired the struggle for women's emancipation that middle class women began to wage. The extreme oppression of working class women may well explain the middle class character that the early women's movement was to have. Witness the testimony of Betty Harris, a Victorian wife who worked pulling her husbands wagon through the coal mine wherever there was not space for a horse:

'I have a belt round my waist and a chain passing between my legs, and I go on my hands and feet. The road is very steep. The pit is very wet where I work . . . my clothes are wet through almost all day long . . . I have drawn till I have had the skin off me; the belt and chain is worse when we are in the family way. My feller has beaten me many a time for not being ready. I were not used to it at first, and he had little patience. I have known many a man beat his drawer'. (Dobash and Dobash p68)

In 1853 the situation was such that Fitzroy could put it to the House of

Commons that the nation should treat married women no worse than domestic animals (Dobash and Dobash p68).

1869 saw the publication of *The Subjection of Women*, and John Stewart Mill's plea in the House of Commons for women's right to be equal under the law, and five years later a discussion in the Commons led to the appointment of a Parliamentary committee to investigate serious assaults on wives and children. The figures collected indicated a high level of brutal assaults by men on women and children (6,108 in 52 counties between 1870 and 1874). These did not include what were referred to as the 'ordinary' domestic assaults presumably also occurring on a daily basis. Three years later Power's shocking account of *Wife Torture in England* was also published. According to this, in the 3 years since the Parliamentary report, 6,000 women had been 'brutally assaulted that is, maimed, blinded, trampled, burned or murdered outright'. Below are some extracts from this report:

'Frederick Knight jumped on the face of his wife (who had only been confined a month) with a pair of boots studded with hobnails.'

'Charles Bradley . . . set a large bulldog at her, and the dog, after flying at the upper part of her body, seized hold of the woman's right arm which she lifted to protect herself, and tore pieces out. The prisoner in the meantime kept striking her in the face, and inciting the brute to worry her. The dog dragged her up and down, biting pieces out of her arms, and the prisoner then got on the sofa and hit and kicked her on the breast.'

'George Ralph Smith, oilman, cut his wife, as the doctor expressed it, "to pieces", with a hatchet, in their back parlour. She died afterwards, but he was found Not Guilty, as it was not certain that her death resulted from the wounds.'

'Michael Copeland, who threw his wife on a blazing fire' (all cited in Dobash and Dobash).

The historical situation regarding the abuse of women in Britain is aptly summarized thus:

'Legislation on women's rights and the response to these laws were a reflection of a long history in which the husband had complete authority over his wife and was given the legal and moral obligation to manage and control her behaviour. The use of physical coercion was simply one of the "legitimate" means traditionally used to achieve such control.' (Dobash and Dobash, p74)

To sum up this section, we can see that the violent physical abuse was directly related to women's subordination in all spheres of social life, regardless of whether she worked or not. This or similar situations prevail in a large number of countries today, including large parts of Africa, Asia and the Caribbean, as has been discussed here, and in chapter one. In Britain there have been many legislative changes in the 20th century. Yet woman and child abuse both continue, and in recent years appear to be on the increase. The vast majority of such instances go unreported and unchallenged, often out of respect for the privacy of the family and in keeping with the old adage 'Every Englishman's home is his castle'.

Even when law enforcement agencies are contacted, there are often no legal or social reprisals of any kind. This suggests that regardless of what legal reforms there have been (and these are discussed in more detail below), the law is still not able to protect women from abuse. It also indicates that the old attitudes to wife abuse will continue to survive and influence legal, judicial and social behaviour until they, along with the patriarchal value system of which such practises are a fundamental part, are more fundamentally challenged. However, it is also clear that even modern law is far from adequate in terms of protecting women from violent assaults in their homes. For example, there are still circumstances in which a man is entitled to use 'self-help' to force his wife to have sexual intercourse with him (Atkins and Hoggett 1984 p127). The history of English law has substantial bearing on the present legal situation, and the implementation or reluctance to apply the law in relation to domestic violence.

Present day British law

The present day legal situation is one in which there have been quite major improvements in the legal status of women. Nonetheless the patriarchal character of the Law has not been fundamentally altered. Furthermore, the uptake and implementation of the letter of the law inevitably depends largely on the values of the wider social sphere, and this too has remained patriarchal enough for wife-abuse to have remained a phenomenon that is largely tolerated and ignored in British society, as elsewhere. Despite the equal pay legislation, women workers are still restricted in terms of their access to certain forms of employment, and as a group, still earn substantially less than men. Without a concomitant domestic revolution, women workers will continue to be responsible for childcare. Without the provision of day care nurseries, this means that mothers still cannot work, unless they are affluent enough to purchase childcare. Britain provides less creches and day nurseries than most other Western European countries, and is moving towards providing even less, so that sexual equality legislation is quite simply ineffective.

In relation to domestic violence, the written law needs to be developed substantially to be effective in reducing and preventing woman abuse. Furthermore, the interpretation and selective enforcement of the law continue to make it very difficult for women to use the written law to protect themselves from violence in the home. As recently as 1976, a leading textbook on family law expressed the view that 'no spouse ought to be allowed to rely on the other's past conduct as a justification for living apart, when there is no probability of recurrence.' In other words, violence could only be grounds for divorce or separation if the court felt it was likely to recur (see Atkins and Hoggett, p128).

The same authors identify the question of "toleration" as a second problem. In the past, a wife could not complain of behaviour that she had previously tolerated. There is evidence that some justices still give considerable latitude to husbands, particularly if they are from the working classes who are widely believed to indulge in a little "horseplay" with their wives. While courts are now instructed to ignore the fact that the couple may have continued to live together for six months since the last act complained of, recent cases indicate that a woman may be refused relief on the grounds that she had 'accepted the situation as part of their married life' (Atkins and Hoggett, p129).

The concept of provocation is the most insidious of all those characterising legal practice relating to violence against wives. So-called nagging by the wife, or neglect of household duties, or denial of 'conjugal rights' are examples of behaviour that may be deemed provocative. In situations where the man is the breadwinner, with the woman economically dependent on him, as well as being physically weaker, the strategies that are left to her to resist any of her husband's orders or decisions are limited. For refusal to perform housewifely duties to be deemed to be "provocative" in the eyes of the law is to deny women even the subordinate negotiating strategies that are available to her.

There is not the space to give a detailed account of the relevant areas of the present day written law — this is already available elsewhere (see eg Smart and Smart 1978, Edwards 1985, LSPU 1986). Rather this will be summarised for the purposes of looking at the uptake by black women, of the legal provisions that do exist and at how effective their attempts to gain protection from violence through the law have been.

Black women and the law

The relevant legislation falls into several areas of law. Under civil law these are; marital law, assault and trespass law, and most recently the domestic violence acts. Under criminal law the normal provisions regarding assault and grievous bodily harm, manslaughter and murder theoretically apply. Housing law is relevant to the housing consequences of domestic violence, and for some groups of black women, immigration law is also relevant. Race relations legislation may also be relevant regarding the response of statutory and voluntary agencies to black women who are entitled to any of their various services. Many of these different areas of law have overlapping consequences and some or all have wider implications than might meet the eye. This means that offering sound legal advice to black women who have experienced domestic violence may require legal expertise in a number of different areas.

Immigration law, for example, has consequences in all aspects of welfare and housing provision, not only through the 'no recourse to public funds' clauses that apply to some black women who live in Britain, but more insidiously through the policing of immigration law by schools, hospitals, social security offices, housing departments etc. Many of these apparently unrelated organisations and services may conduct passport checks on citizens, and are more likely to do so when black people request services. This can cause particular inconveniences to black women who may have been forced to leave their homes without their documents, or whose husbands retain them. It also has the consequences outlined in chapter 4 for women who have not been granted any independent immigration status in Britain.

Black women in this study had various experiences when they sought legal help in dealing with their problems. Some of these experiences are detailed below.

Criminal law

In theory, assaults between men and women who live together could be treated the same as assaults between strangers. The Offences Against the Person Act of 1861 defines four principal kinds of assault;

154

i) Common assault (section 42)
ii) Assault occasioning actual bodily harm (section 47)
iii) Malicious wounding (section 20)
iv) Grievous bodily harm (wounding with intent to cause serious harm) (section 18).

Only common assault is not an arrestable offence, which means that the police who arrive at a home and find a woman visibly injured, are empowered to arrest her assailant on the spot. This very rarely happens, as Edwards' work has demonstrated. Rather the police habitually play down serious injuries by not arresting the man or by advising the woman to take out a private prosecution and so deterring her, even where the Crown Prosecution service could itself prosecute. For example, Krishna Sharma, whose case is documented in the Appendix, sought help from the police but was advised to take out a private prosecution, shortly before her death. As the LSPU Police Monitoring and Research Group noted:

'While in theory the criminal law does not distinguish between domestic and other assaults, the police in practice prevent the criminal law from being effective in this area' (1986 p15).

Even if police reluctance does not succeed in discouraging women from taking legal action, there are other hurdles for her to deal with.

There is substantial evidence of sexual discrimination in verdicts passed and the sentencing of violent crimes between men and women (Edwards 1984, Smart and Smart 1976, 1978, Carlen 1976, 1985). The facts are that there is a high incidence of murder between spouses, and that the majority of these are murders of women by their husbands. Edwards (1985) cites that between 21% and 29% of all homicide victims in the ten years between 1972 and 1982 had been in relationships with their killers (spouses, lovers, cohabitees or ex-partners in any of these relationships). Out of a total of 576 victims of homicide, a shocking 104 were women murdered by their spouses in the domestic setting. Women are also grossly over-represented as victims of male violence in the other categories of violent crime (attempted murder, manslaughter, wounding and assault). In some cases the woman's death may have resulted from violence, but the husband had not been convicted for murder (see Appendix). It is therefore little wonder that the Parliamentary Select Committee on Violence in Marriage (1975) recommended that the police should keep some statistics on domestic violence, so that at least there would be some record of the phenomenon and its prevalence.

Statistics or not, women like Krishna Sharma (whose bruised body was found in 1984) and Balwant Kaur Panesar (stabbed to death in a Brent refuge in 1985) had sought police protection from their violent husbands before their deaths.

Many of the women in this study had suffered injuries that were serious enough to have resulted in convictions for GBH or assault, but this very rarely happened. Only 15% (8 out of 53) of the women who had contact with the police because of their partner's assaults on them, took legal action under criminal law. Of these, four were of Asian descent, four were Caribbean. One quarter of those who did press criminal charges subsequently dropped them. Out of the six who did press charges, five resulted in guilty verdicts, and one was found not guilty. The five guilty verdicts resulted in the following sentences. The most serious sentence was one of three years imprisonment for GBH, another got six months for assault, a third was given one month for assault, while the remaining two were not given custodial sentences — one was given a suspended sentence and the last was bound over to keep the peace. The not guilty verdict was surprising since it was one in which a policeman testified in support of the woman's evidence (Yvonne's case, chapters 3 and 6), and after a long history of serious violence in which injunctions had been issued. One of the suspended sentences was for an incident which the woman (Sukie, chapter 3) felt was actually attempted murder (she bore the injuries and scars from a strangulation and knife cuts to the court). Since the court offered no protection to the woman, she then had to flee from home (with the children), feeling more endangered as a result of having tried to take legal action against her assailant, as happened in a number of other cases where injunctions were taken out but not enforced by the authorities.

Since the *Police and Criminal Evidence Act 1984*, the police have been empowered to compel women to prosecute, a change that was fiercely opposed by women's organisations at the time. This is in keeping with other moves which have increased police powers, but not necessarily in ways that are in the interests of women who have been subjected to violence. While it is right to be critical of the lack of seriousness which prevails in the treatment of domestic violence by the law courts, this cannot be improved by judges acting punitively towards women. In a controversial recent case, Judge Pickles sentenced a white woman to a week in prison for refusing to testify against her assailant, a black Rastafarian man. In this instance, the judges unusual zeal for a conviction led him to punish the woman for not upholding the law, while her assailant walked free. Michelle Renshaw had retracted her evidence on the basis that she was scared and had been threatened by her partner (*Observer*, March 12 1989), after which the case against him (wounding and assault causing actual bodily harm) was dropped.

Rape and marriage

Until recently it was deemed that rape could not occur when the perpetrator and his victim were married. The 'right to rape' was codified in 1736 were it was asserted:

> 'But the husband cannot be guilty of rape committed by himself upon his lawful wife, for by their mutual consent and contract the wife hath given herself in this kind unto her husband which she cannot retract' (quoted in Edwards 1985 p 193).

This was subsequently tested in the courts in the 19th and 20th centuries. For example, in R v Jackson (1891) where the husband enforced his conjugal rights, it was held that a husband could be convicted of assault, but not of enforcing his conjugal rights. This century certain exceptions have been made. In 1949 Mr. Justice Byrne decided that a husband could be found guilty of raping his wife if a separation order — a revocation of conjugal rights — had been granted. A few years later Mr. Justice Lynskey ruled that a husband could be found guilty of rape if there was a separation agreement between husband and wife which included a non-molestation clause (Edwards, p 193-4).

In 1980 the Criminal Law Revision Committee Working Paper recommended that rape in marriage be recognised as an offence, but that only the Department of Public Prosecutions be empowered to bring prosecutions. More recently the Criminal Law Revision Committee has recommended that the offence of rape be extended to include cases of forced intercourse when the couple are no longer cohabiting.

In short, the law on rape in marriage has been developing in a generally favourable direction, although women who live in the same premises as their attacker are still highly unlikely to be protected by existing law. Furthermore, put in the context of rape prosecutions generally, it is extremely difficult for the woman to win such cases. In view of the fact that domestic violence frequently involves rape and other forms of sexual abuse, Edwards is correct to advocate further reform.

Certainly our own research yielded evidence that domestic violence often includes sexual degradation and humiliation, with rape sometimes being the culmination of a violent episode (see for example Charlotte, chapter 3). Most women (like Maleka, chapter 3 and many others) found it extremely difficult to talk about their experience of rape at the time of interview, and were not pressed to do so. Most could well have benefited from specialist counselling support (seldom available in refuges under the present circumstances) to help them cope with this particularly painful and humiliating degradation.

Black women and civil law

Domestic Violence and Matrimonial Proceedings Act 1976; Domestic Violence and Magistrates Courts Act 1978

The Domestic Violence and Matrimonial Proceedings Act of 1976 was something of a breakthrough, since it was the first time that legal remedies specifically for dealing with domestic violence were made available to women in England. Prior to 1976, married women could only get injunctions as part of divorce or custody proceedings. Unmarried women had to rely on getting injunctions for assault or trespass. The uptake of this legislation is indicated in the statistics; in 1984, 15,619 injunctions were granted in England and Wales. In London alone the figure was 3,259, out of which 1,230 (38%) had powers of arrest attached (Judicial Statistics 1984).

Both these Acts afford women some limited protection within civil law from violent husbands or cohabitees, enabling women to seek injunctions against their assailants. This was a lengthy procedure under the 1976 Act, and the 1978 Act presumably aimed to address this by enabling applications to be put through magistrate's courts. The latter Act also empowered the court to evict the assailant from the matrimonial home under an exclusion order. Women who are not married to their assailant can only use the 1976 Act, but not the 1978 Act. Women who do not actually live with their assailants cannot use this provision either. If there are children involved, a woman may be able to get an injunction under the *Guardianship of Minors Act 1971*.

Injunctions can last for varying periods. Non-molestation orders last until cancelled by the court, but ouster injunctions last three months, or are terminated if the couple start having a relationship again. Powers of arrest are usually set to last for three months, but can be made to last for as long as six months.

In theory, once an injunction has been granted, if the man against whom it has been made breaks this injunction, then he is in contempt of court and can be ordered to court and possibly committed to prison for doing

158

so. Injunctions may simply order a man to stop molesting or harassing a woman, or they may exclude him from the home (ouster injunction). They may or may not attach a power of arrest. In any case, the police can use their discretion to arrest any person violating an injunction. There is a wide variation in the readiness to issue injunctions, and most solicitors choose to go to the county court (and therefore utilise the 1976 Act), possibly because they feel that injunctions are more likely to be granted here. There is also a wide variation in the courts' treatment of men who do contravene injunctions — some may send a man to prison for doing so, while others may simply caution him (see LSPU 1986 for a fuller discussion).

Jan Pahl's (1982) Bristol study found that:

'The majority of women said either that the injunction had proved an effective measure, or that its existence had been enough to prevent further violence. Injunctions seemed to serve three main functions: they indicated unequivocally to husbands that violent behaviour towards wives is not acceptable; they served to label the women as people whose complaints to the police ought to be taken seriously; and they gave an effective remedy to the police if violence recurred'.

This differs from the experience of the black women in this study who had taken out injunctions, suggesting that for them, injunctions may not be effective deterrents. At least 18 women in this study had tried to gain protection through injunctions, sometimes on more than one occasion. Some had theirs renewed by the courts over a period of time. Most were very critical of the procedures, condemning them as ineffective, since the police did not enforce them.

Many of the women in this study were not married to their assailants and therefore could not use the 1978 Act, which meant the lengthier process of going to County Court. Many did not live with their assailants and so could only seek injunctions under the Assault and Trespass laws.

The major weaknesses in the law regarding injunctions (protection orders) seem to centre around the reluctance of law enforcing agents to make use of the provisions, and to inform the women concerned about them. A common pattern was for their assailant to attempt to gain entry, but to flee before the police arrived. The police would then say there was nothing they could do since he was not there for them to apprehend, and the man would then return once they had left. On no occasion did the police subsequently seek and arrest the man for contempt of court. In some cases they did assist the women to move to a safe place with the children.

For some of the women in this study (including Roweena and Sukie, chapter 3), going to the police or the courts simply made their immediate situation even more life-threatening and dangerous. Others, like Zoey (chapter 3) and Yvonne (chapter 3 and 6), went to court on many occasions before finally leaving their homes to try and build new lives for themselves elsewhere.

Most black women in this study did not take any legal action. This may have much to do with the police responses, and the poor relations prevailing between black people and law enforcement agencies, which may well make black women more reluctant to involve them. In some cases, women were forced to take recourse to the law (some housing departments demand legal action before considering rehousing), and this has merely worsened their immediate situation, sometimes making it even more life-threatening:

ROWEENA (it may be recalled) has spent five years on the run from a man already wanted by the police but not apprehended. His whereabouts are unknown since he has never had a fixed abode. This man was the father of her first two children, and a heavy drinker who inflicted serious injuries on her. They did not live together, but he frequently forced entry into her flat, beat her with his fists and any object that came to hand and threatened to cut up her face while holding a knife to her throat. His five-year campaign of hatred included numerous assaults and threats on her life. The police had been called on many occasions. After she had left for the first time, Roweena had been placed in a bed and breakfast. A friend told her ex-partner of her whereabouts, so that she was forced to flee again. The refuge she stayed at, and the local authority housing department insisted that she take out an injunction, although Roweena, being aware of his attitudes was very reluctant to do so. She gave in to this pressure and applied for an injunction, but insisted that she could under no circumstances return to her flat, since he now knew where she lived. The refuge (an all-white refuge not affiliated to Women's Aid, which had a three-month length of stay rule) evicted her once she had the injunction. Luckily Roweena found a space in a Women's Aid (WAFE) refuge, and was eventually rehoused. Unfortunately for her, she and her children were then subjected to racial attacks by her neighbours. She once again became homeless and went through the long process of being rehoused. This time the council rehoused her, against her will, in her ex-partner's old haunts. It did not take long for him to locate her, and attempt to set fire to her flat by pouring petrol through the letter box. When I interviewed her she was back in the WAFE refuge. By this time Roweena had stayed in refuges four times and had been rehoused three times in the same borough during a five-year ordeal. She was trying to get accepted for housing in a Conservative borough on the other side of London at the time of interview. She was still waiting to be rehoused a year after the interview.

Other women point out the ludicrousness of a situation in which they have to get the papers for an injunction and then go home to hand them to the very man who has assaulted them.

Ouster injunctions are particularly hard to obtain, presumably because magistrates are reluctant to make men homeless, even if they have been assaulting the women with whom they live.

As with the criminal law, the main weakness of civil remedies appears to be due to the police reluctance to enforce them. It is still an open question whether or not the police are more or less reluctant to enforce injunctions for black women. They may be motivated to do so, for example if there is a prospect of getting a conviction against a black man, or less likely to do so if the man is white (for example, as Shaheeda asserts in the next chapter).

The large areas of divorce and custody law are also relevant to women who have been through domestic violence, but cannot be addressed here. The length of judicial processes are often complained about, particularly when housing and other immediate needs are hinged on the outcomes of divorce hearings, as was the case for women like Hamza (chapter 4). Other women did not wish to get divorces because of the negative effects it would have on both themselves and their children in their community, but did need to be rehoused since they could no longer live with their violent spouses. Custody is often a long battle that may continue for many years, as was the case with Smita (chapter 4) who is still battling over her daughter five years after leaving her violent husband. In her case the father was initially awarded custody of their young daughter, a cruel blow for any woman who has been forced to flee from violence at the hands of their children's father. In court, the living circumstances of both parties are taken into account in considering which parent will provide a better home. Since it is usually the woman who has become homeless, her living conditions are seldom likely to strengthen her case, until after she has been rehoused. Similar problems arise where children are taken into state care. Widespread prejudices against women not seen to be displaying 'appropriate female behaviour', including single mothers and homeless women, affect judgements at all levels of the judicial process. Ensuring that good legal advice and support is available to black women seeking to escape violence would be a major contribution to their struggle to survive and lead full lives (with their children) away from abusive partners.

Immigration Law in the service of violent men

This was discussed in chapter 4 and will not be elaborated here, other than to reiterate that the current immigration laws of Britain clearly compound the situation of some black women who are assaulted by the men they live with. In their case they leave the violent situation only to find they can then be deported. Worse still, the situation is actively exploited by men, who either use it as another form of coercion inside the relationship, or to 'get rid of' women they have lost interest in, or to further intimidate and threaten women who have left them.

Housing Law

The *Housing (Homeless Persons) Act 1977* recognises women who experience violence or the threat of violence as homeless. The relevant part of the Act (section 1 (2) (b) reads:

'A person is homeless for the purpose of this Act if he has accommodation but —

b) It is probable that occupation of it will lead to violence from some other person residing in it or to threats of violence from some other person residing in it and likely to carry out the threats.'

The interpretation and response of local authorities to this aspect of the Act has varied considerably, as the two borough case studies will illustrate (chapters 7-9).

Conclusions and recommendations

The evidence presented in this chapter supports the argument presented in chapter 4; that the different branches of the state can, and often do, act together against the interests of black women. Here we have seen quite clearly the collusion between the criminal justice system and those wider societal attitudes which justify and excuse the violent abuse of women by their sexual and emotional partners. Where the law has been developed, through the Domestic Violence and Matrimonial Proceedings Act 1976 and Domestic Violence and Magistrates Courts Act 1978, the provisions have been largely contingent on legal separation, or preferably a divorce. In the case of the 1976 Matrimonial Proceedings Act — the provisions are contingent on the woman also claiming financial redress. Those women who are not married cannot seek protection under the 1978 Act. We have seen the ineffectiveness of injunctions in many cases, and the consequences of police failure to enforce even the existing laws.

For black women, there is the same reluctance to involve the law that white women show, but for black women, as for all black people, this is compounded by the historical relations that have prevailed between the imperial and colonial armies and police forces and black people, not to mention the present day police repression of the indigenous black communities. This theme is explored further in the next chapter. There is ample evidence to show that the police, the judiciary, lawyers and the courts are often racist in their daily practice, so that black people's mistrust of the legal system is based on objective circumstances. Full and proper law enforcement should therefore be coupled with making specialist legal support and advice available to black women, through the various black community networks, projects and law centres, as well as in mainstream advice centres like citizens advice bureaus.

Black women need to be able to find legal representatives they can trust to look after their interests, if they are to be assisted in not staying in life-threatening situations. If they wish to use the law in their quest to find ways of stopping their partners violence, they should not have to pay the price of homelessness and all the other consequences documented in this report. The provision of specialist legal advice is already being undertaken in the few black women's centres that currently exist (see chapter 10). To be effective this work needs to be properly resourced, and extended to a much wider range of community organisations and projects. It should also be supported by a general initiative to inform and raise people's consciousness in legal circles as well as in black communities.

This chapter, like chapter 4 indicates the desperate need for multi-agency responses to domestic violence, and the care that must be taken to ensure that when agencies do link up they operate together in ways that support women, rather than oppressive in ways that merely compound the many other problems they experience as a result of domestic violence. In chapter 4 it was noted that in the case of black women certainly, there is a great deal of linking up that is multiply oppressive and coercive, rather than supportive, and that this functions to force women to remain in violent and sometimes life-threatening situations (with their children).

Notes

1. Martin Luther started the Protestant Reformation in 1517. Lutherans propounded the view of wives as helpmates and companions, which was revolutionary for the period which had previously been characterised by extreme misogyny. Lutherans did however reinforce ideas of women's 'natural' inferiority and 'God's intention' that she should play a particular (subservient) role.

2. The researcher observed this practice being re-enacted as a tourist entertainment in parts of the colonies today (Bermuda), with visitors being encouraged to throw rotten tomatoes at the black woman (or 'wench' as she is described) being ducked.

6. Black women and the police: a place where the law is not upheld

Introduction: policing and black women

'Although violence against women in the home is a "crime" the police are highly unlikely to arrest the man, preferring instead to advise the woman to take out an injunction against him. If the man is Black, however, they are more likely to arrest him, but Black women are confident that this is motivated by racism rather than out of any concern for the woman's safety. If either the woman or the man is Black, the entire case may become one not of protecting the woman, but of an immigration investigation' (McGuire 1988).

In recent years, a substantial amount of criticism has been directed at the responses of the police forces nationally to domestic violence. Edwards has conducted the most substantive research into police responses in London (Edwards 1986, 1988). Her findings reveal the widespread recalcitrance of the Metropolitan Police when it comes to upholding the law, where the crime is deemed to be 'just domestic' by police officers called to the scene. 'No-criming' of this particular form of assault (often serious enough to amount to attempted murder), appears to be widespread. Records of calls not being kept (and where incidents have been recorded, information has often been incorrect), reports not being submitted, and violent incidents not being categorised as crimes, have all emerged as common practice in the areas of London included in her study. Edwards' research indicates that the police receive approximately 58,748 calls concerning domestic violence every year in the GLC area. Her work also indicates the wide variation in police responses, and in their implementation of the 1987 Force Order. Research like this has also precipitated the recent establishment of two 'Domestic Violence Response Units' in Tottenham and Lambeth. These too need to be critically assessed, particularly because of their location in areas that have been subjected to particularly coercive policing, and where black women have been the victims of such policing in at least two deeply disturbing recent incidents; Cherry Groce (paralysed from the waist down after being shot in the back in a police raid) lived in Brixton and Cynthia Jarret (who died of a heart attack during a police raid on her home) lived in Tottenham.

Prior to Edwards' work, a number of feminist criminologists had already raised the serious questions around gender and the law (Smart 1976, Smart and Smart 1978, Edwards 1984, 1985, Carlen 1985). This work has tended to concentrate on analysis in terms of the patriarchal character of capitalist society, and has shown, for example, that women convicted of crimes are likely to be treated as 'mad' or 'sick' rather than 'bad'. It has also been demonstrated that women are sentenced particularly harshly when their behaviour contradicts gender expectations (for example in the case of women convicted of violent crimes). In this work much of the sexual inequality prevailing in law and law enforcement are attributed to the fact that males dominate the police forces and the criminal justice system, and that the dominant social values within these institutions, as in the wider society, are still anti-feminist and even misogynist in their ideological content. It is these values that inform police perceptions of domestic violence as being 'not real police work' and that lead to it being accorded only low priority, since it is not viewed as being the kind of work that will lead to promotion. The evidence also suggests that policemen often abuse their own wives.

Little of this work has attempted to address the differential treatment meted out to different groups of women, (ie class and racial inequalities being reproduced by the same institutions). One of the few studies to incorporate racial as well as sexual considerations into criminological study in Britain was an investigation into the imprisonment of women, commissioned by the GLC women's committee in 1986. *Breaking the Silence* did not however, look at the 'service delivery' aspects of policing or the criminal justice system, since it was a study of the processes by which women generally and black women in particular end up in prison, and their treatment once they are inside.[1]

This researcher is not aware of any existing research that focuses on the issue of police responsiveness to crimes committed against black women. This chapter then, will be the first time the subject has been addressed.

In considering black women and the police, this study suggests three major areas of concern which need to be taken into account:
i) The reluctance of black women to call in the police even when serious,

166

if not life threatening, violent crimes are being committed against them;
ii) the reluctance of the same police to enforce the law in the interests of
black women when they are called in to do so, and most disturbingly,
iii) the evidence that the police themselves perpetrate crimes against black
women.

Statutory and voluntary organisations that have been set up to monitor
the police in the public interest (eg Local Authority Police Units and
organisations like Newham Monitoring Project and Southall Monitoring
Group) have uncovered widespread abuses of women by the police. Many
of the cases they deal with stand in contrast to the sociological literature
which frequently chooses to highlight 'man-to-man' confrontations
between 'black youth' (who are invariably male) or black men and
members of the police force (eg Pryce 1979, Cashmore and Troyna 1982).
This is unfortunate in that it does not facilitate the development of the
broader political understanding of the relations between coercive state
apparatuses and the civilian population, that a race, class and gender
analysis highlights. As a result, police ineffectiveness and lack of
accountability is a problem.

More alarmingly, even police assaults are individualised and
marginalised from considerations of how to develop police services in the
interests of the citizenry. In the current political climate, policing is
becoming increasingly coercive and intrusive, and police powers have
been massively increased to the detriment of civil liberties by the Thatcher
regime (Christian 1983). In other words developing a better police 'service'
in the interests of the population has not been of as much concern as
increasing police power. The wider socio-political context, in which police
powers have been massively increased without much effective opposition,
has been explored elsewhere (eg Hall 1988). It is necessary to note
however, that the mobilisation of popular opinion in support of rather
than against increased police powers, has for some years relied on racial
constructions of rising crime (see Hall et al 1978). As Paul Gilroy puts it:

'The discourse of black criminality has been articulated not just by the
police, who have sought to mobilize popular support for the increase
of their resources and the expansion of their powers, but by the extreme
right who have organised marches and protests against the levels of
black crime and sought to link these fears to the argument for
repatriation' (Gilroy 1987 p 111).

There are a number of studies into police-black community relations,
many of which have been generated or inspired by police attacks on black

people (Lambert 1970, Humphrey 1972, Roach Family Support Committee 1989). In recent years there have also been a number of campaigns over police brutality and deaths of black people in custody, and against increasing police powers, though the success of these campaigns is hard to evaluate (eg the Roach Family Support Committee, the Brixton Defence Campaign, the Campaign Against the Police and Criminal Evidence Bill). The inner city disturbances up and down the country during the 1980s, and some more recent abuses of power, have also generated enquiries into policing practices, particularly with respect to the black communities (eg Lord Scarman's enquiry into the Brixton disorders of 1981; Lord Gifford's enquiry into the Broadwater Farm disturbances of 1985).

However, the male character of much of the existing material is self-evident and needs to be criticised.[2] Nonetheless, despite the gender-blind nature of this work, there is sufficient evidence to show that it is not only black men who are subjected to the peculiarly coercive and aggressive forms of policing most evident in inner-city areas.

The Institute of Race Relations recently published the alarming catalogue of evidence that they presented to the Metropolitan Commissioner Peter Imbert in October 1987. This documents the prevalence of police misconduct towards black people in their own homes, on the streets and in police stations. Thus, for example, when black people attempt to report crimes, they are frequently subjected to harassment, and/or their cases not taken seriously (see also Gordon 1983, 1986). Amongst the hundreds of cases included in the IRR evidence, are a number involving police brutality towards women. A few of the better known examples are quoted below:

'On 5 October 1985, Floyd Jarrett was stopped by police as he was driving through Tottenham, North London, and arrested for suspected theft of a motor vehicle. The police, who had no grounds for suspecting Mr Jarrett of stealing the vehicle then proceeded to search his family's home for stolen goods.

The search of the house was carried out by four officers, with a District Support Unit held in reserve. The officers let themselves into the house with keys taken from Floyd Jarret while he was at the station — but when asked how they got in they told the family that the door was open. The home was occupied by Mrs Cynthia Jarret, Patricia Jarrett and two young children.

During the search an officer brushed past Mrs Jarrett, pushing her out of the way. She fell, breaking a small table. The police continued the search while Patricia Jarrett called for an ambulance. The officers then left the house. When they realised Mrs Jarrett was seriously ill, an officer returned to the house to give her mouth to mouth resuscitation. Mrs Jarrett was dead on arrival at hospital.

Although the police deny Patricia Jarrett's statement that at no time was a search warrant shown, the Broadwater Farm Inquiry was not convinced that the police had a search warrant, and believed it was possible that one might have been filled in only after Mrs Jarrett had died.'(IRR 1987, p25)

Other accounts suggest that Patricia Jarret asked for assistance and was ignored, which would imply that they either did not take any notice, or worse still, that they knew of Mrs Jarrett's condition and did nothing.

'On September 1985 a team of armed officers went to the home of Mrs Cherry Groce in Brixton, South London to arrest her son Michael, who was wanted for armed robbery. In fact Michael Groce no longer lived there. The officers smashed down the door with a sledgehammer and then an inspector rushed in shouting "armed police". He put his finger to the trigger. Mrs Groce says the officer suddenly rushed at her, pointing a gun at her. She tried to run back but he shot her. She is now paralysed and confined to a wheelchair.' (*The Times*, 16 Jan 1987) (IRR 1987, p 26).

'In February 1984 Linda Williams lodged an official complaint after the police arrived at her Peckham home and demanded to see her son, Errol. Mrs Williams says that when she asked to see their search warrant she was dragged downstairs by the hair and, while down, was repeatedly kicked in the back, while another policeman stood on her legs. Mrs Williams was pregnant at the time (*West Indian World* no 649, 8 Feb 1984)' (IRR 1987, p 24).

In April 1983 an Instant Response Unit arrested a black youth, Emile Foulkes, who was sitting on a wall near his home in Waltham Forest, East London and accused him of taunting a group of white youths. According to Emile, the police grabbed him and called him a 'black nigger'. When his mother Mrs Esme Baker, attempted to intervene, she was forced into the van, her dress was torn open and her breasts exposed. An officer prodded her in the breasts with his truncheon and said: 'I didn't know a nigger woman had breasts.' Both Emile and his mother were later acquitted of charges of threatening behaviour and assaulting the police. (*Searchlight* no 89, Nov 1982) (IRR 1987, p 18).

Other cases of police and immigration officers misconduct (including denying women much needed medical care while in custody, planting heroin in homes, coercing African immigration defaulters into having anal intercourse with them) were identified by the women's imprisonment project (Mama, Mars and Stevens 1986), and need not be repeated here.

Lack of protection in the community

Black women being subjected to violent assault in their homes may well have no alternative but to become involved with the police. Often, the police arrive at the scene as a result of neighbours calling them. A significant proportion of the women in this study were single women, many of whom lived in quite isolated conditions. For many others, their assailant was the person who lived with, was staying with, or who was visiting them. Often children tried to intervene, but clearly are unable to protect their mothers. It will be recalled that children were sometimes also injured by their mother's assailant (accidentally or deliberately). Black women are particularly isolated if they live in white areas. While some of their white neighbours might adhere to the stereotypical view that such things constitute 'normal behaviour' for black people, others may simply lack concern when it is black women who may be being beaten to death.

In black communities too, however, black women are no more assured of protection against violence. There is evidence to suggest that many black people have internalised white stereotypes, or have come independently to believe that woman-abuse is 'black' behaviour, so that black neighbours may also choose not to intervene. It may also be the case that people living in 'ghettoes' or on sink estates in inner city London, are forced to become accustomed to high levels of violence. In such circumstances they may also decide that domestic violence is something they will have to grow accustomed to, and therefore will not intervene or call the police. Here, however, we also need to consider the history of black people's relations with the police. It has been observed, for example, that black people who have been subjected to race attacks are sometimes subjected to further abuse and victimisation by the police. More commonly, the police refuse to enforce the law, and so do not protect black people from white racial violence and abuse (IRR 1987, chapter 2). As the studies referred to earlier have shown, this forms part of a broader pattern within which black people have been abused, victimised and harassed by the police both on the streets and in their homes. It may well be then that black neighbours who have themselves had bad experience at the hands of the police, are reluctant to have any further contact with them.

The reluctance of neighbours and friends to intervene when they hear cries and screams, while perhaps being understandable at some levels, does need to be questioned and investigated further. Many of the women in this study found themselves in life threatening situations with absolutely no other form of support available to them on a 24-hour basis. Some, like Linda and Sulochana ran out onto the streets to escape (Sulochana clutching the youngest child) or, where they could, ran into neighbours homes (like Shaba and Patience, chapters 4 and 3 respectively). Men often assaulted the women in this study during the night. Sometimes neighbours or other concerned parties called the police, either to complain about the noise, or because they feared for the woman's safety.

Nonetheless there are many cases of violent assault in the home that the police are not called to (nearly half of the women in this study), or where their intervention is too late. The tragic death of 24-year old Denise Moncrieffe in October 1988 is a case in point. Her fully clothed body was found one Monday afternoon, in the ground floor flat she shared with her cohabitee. She had suffered internal injuries after being kicked and punched repeatedly in her stomach. Police interviewed 50 neighbours, many of whom remembered hearing her screams, but did not interfere. Her common-law husband, a 28-year old mechanic was charged with her murder and remanded in custody (*Hackney Gazette* Oct 7 1988).

Many black women in this study also described being attacked on the streets in broad daylight, without anyone responding to their cries for help.

YVONNE for example was kicked down the stairs of a bus in Brixton after the man she had abandoned her home to get away from, spotted her and the children as he drove past. He leapt onto the bus and proceeded to attack her while onlookers observed.

SELENA was followed on her way back to the refuge in which she had sought shelter, and attacked in Shepherd's Bush market in broad daylight, but nobody intervened.

This does not only happen when women are attacked by partners or ex-partners, but far more generally, since when a woman is attacked, members of the public may assume that her assailant is someone she knows, especially if they are both black. Or, again if the attacker is black, they may be particularly afraid to intervene because of the general racist paranoia about 'violent black men'.

> HINDI, a 23 year old student of mixed Nigerian and European origin was harassed and assaulted, by a Caribbean man she had never seen before, on a bus on her way home from college while her (white) fellow students looked on and did nothing.[3]

Women in the study also reported instances of respected members of the community, who were asked for help, refusing to assist. Mumtaz, one of the women in this study, had an Asian GP who told her that 'women should not try to leave their husbands'. Meena, a 42 year old mother of two also sought help from her Pakistani GP who sided with her husband and kept her addicted to tranquillisers instead of helping her. Others like Shireen knew better than to confide in their family doctors. The fact that other women in this study were advised and assisted by their GPs indicates that GPs, like other members of the community, can play a more positive role. Medical practitioners who, after all have sworn oaths to protect life, have a responsibility to be supportive to women they know to be being abused.

In those cases where the neighbours are concerned or disturbed enough to do something, they may well opt for calling the police, rather than attempting to directly intervene and perhaps put themselves at risk. In addition, given the fact that quite often nobody intervenes at all, many women find themselves in a situation where the police are the only agency that can be called upon to deal with the immediate problem of them being violently attacked, either in the home or on the street.

Police involvement

The experience that Britain's black population have of the police forces perhaps goes some way towards explaining why nearly half (47%) of the women we interviewed had not had any contact with the police throughout their ordeal. This is a high percentage when one bears in mind that most of the women in this study had already been forced to leave their homes. A significant proportion of the remaining 53% who did have some contact with the police did so only because neighbours or friends had called them. The fact that the majority of this group also subsequently became homeless, suggests that even where the police were involved, their response did not assist the woman sufficiently enough to prevent her from

172

having to flee her home for her own (and/or her children's) safety. Despite the extreme violence that most of the sample had been subjected to, and despite the fact that there may have been nowhere else to turn, it is notable that very few had called the police on their own account. This suggests that many black women will be severely injured, and face the other dire consequences of violence (see chapters 3 and 4) rather than involving the police or making use of the law.

Quite apart from the poor opinion that women, and particularly black women, have of the police, there is also some evidence to suggest that fear of reprisals combines with a sense of loyalty to deter black women further. A few of the women also had violent partners who were engaged in other criminal activities and women feared they would take it very badly if they were 'betrayed' by the woman they already disrespected enough to physically and emotionally abuse. For example:

At the age of 15, Marlene became involved with a much older man of Caribbean origin who dealt in drugs. On one occasion she had served a prison sentence for possession of drugs found in this man's flat while she was staying there. They fought a lot and his extreme violence culminated in an incident during which he threw her from the seventh floor of the tower block they lived in. She spent seven months in hospital, several of which were spent in traction, and was left permanently disabled by an incident that went down as 'attempted suicide'. In her case the fear of her partner combined with her own experience of law enforcement agencies, prevented her from exposing her partner. After her release from hospital, Marlene was rehoused in the same area. However, the same man later broke into her flat and smashed the place up so badly that she left and went into a refuge.

Women who expect little from the police or the law, for example, because they have been brutalised by police and prisons themselves (and/or because they have been involved with men engaged in non-legal activities, and perhaps participated in these themselves) are likely to try and find other (legal, illegal or extra-legal) ways of dealing with their assailants.[4] However, a number of women in this study have also developed such an attitude because legal avenues had failed them dismally (see previous chapter) or made their situation much worse in the past.

A number of women were in relationships with men who they knew had already been harassed and brutalised at the hands of the police.

GEORGINA MING (see chapter 3) for example was one of the women in the sample who gave the fact that she and her Nigerian partner had been stopped and harassed by the police as a reason for not calling them sooner than she did. When she did call on them to assist when her ex-husband returned to the flat and tried to break in, they refused to come until she told them that he was 'damaging council property'.

It is sometimes suggested that black men beat black women because they are themselves brutalised by the police, unemployment, and other manifestations of racism.[5] The question of where this leaves oppressed black women is more of a sticking point. So too is the question about the community loyalties of black men who assault their sisters (or tolerate and condone the domestic violence of other men in their communities), in the confident knowledge that being a 'right on' black woman, she will not seek police protection, and so risk incriminating a violent black man.

When the police were called, their presence sometimes did have positive effects. For example:

Charlotte (see chapter 3) called the police on an occasion when she felt her partner was going mad and had threatened to kill their children. When they arrived she was able to collect a few possessions and be escorted out of their home to a women's refuge in another part of London.

Kiran's neighbours called the police when they heard her drunken husband beating her. The police came and took her to a local black women's centre. The workers found her a place in a women's refuge.

Responses of this type are immediately helpful to the woman and constitute good emergency procedure. It would also be desirable, however, for the police to advise the woman that there are various possible courses of legal action, in case she is interested in pursuing the matter and, for example, retaining her rights to the home. This happened in some cases, but there were many where it did not. There were also instances in which the police had dumped the woman in a hostel where she was not wanted or accepted. This may sometimes happen out of necessity, when local refuges are full, but it also happens when the police do not even know that refuges exist, or are reluctant to use refuges for reasons of their own. Lily Chang and Shuwei (chapter 3 and 4) both had unpleasant experiences at hostels to which they were taken by the police, who insisted that they be taken in. They did not get sympathetic or supportive treatment. Lily felt that the wardens were racist because of the way she was treated, and Shuwei did not speak English. For Shuwei it was a particularly unpleasant experience because her arm had been broken and the hostel she stayed at made all the residents stay out during the day time, so that she was forced to walk the streets endlessly.

In another very disturbing case (see chapter 3), the police were called to Yvonne's home on numerous occasions as a result of the repeated and severe violence she was subjected to by her partner, Roland. Roland had a long record of offences and was intermittently remanded in custody for other offences, including assaulting police officers and GBH, but either he did not get custodial sentences, or had already served enough time on remand when he went to court. Yvonne described a typical police response:

> 'They say "come on lads, its (nickname) again" and all ten of them would come out and put on their steel caps ready to come and get him.'

The police themselves would assault Roland, but on one occasion they did get as far as the court. To quote Yvonne again:

> 'When the policeman was in court last time he said to the judge "Really and truly she's been in front of you before. What are you going to do? Wait until he takes her guts out and they're lying on the street, before you lock him up?" The policeman told him it was a mockery, and the judge said he'd have him for contempt of court, so he said he could have him for what he liked.'

This is clearly an instance in which the police were quite zealous in their response, but found themselves frustrated at the courts. To recap, later, Roland was imprisoned on remand for another offence. When he returned, he appeared to have become quite paranoid, and to be hallucinating — seeing and hearing things. In a fit of jealous rage he accused Yvonne of being unfaithful to him and dashed a pan of boiling water over the baby. On that occasion the ambulance men consoled Yvonne that they did not believe him when he said she had burned the baby while bathing him. Roland was later sentenced to six months in a psychiatric facility, where, according to Yvonne he went on hunger strike to avoid the drugs they were prescribing, and was forcibly injected. He escaped and returned to her home after only three months, still in a disturbed state. Yvonne abandoned her home once again. She had been rehoused twice, after staying in reception centres and refuges when we interviewed her, but Roland had found her addresses (once from the housing department) and

175

she had to move on each time. She has since moved to a different part of the country with her three children.

Her case illustrates the fact that women and children can be left unprotected even from mentally disturbed men. It also illustrates the hopeless inefficacy of the responses of the police, the law courts and the mental health facility in which he was placed. It seems that he will be left until he kills someone, and then locked away in a top security hospital indefinitely.

To give one final example of police responses in cases which appear, on several occasions, to have warranted arrest of the man or at least some law enforcement action, let us consider Elsie's experience. Her assailant had broken her nose twice and split her head open so badly that she had to be hospitalised. On another occasion bystanders called the police when they saw her partner trying to force her over the balcony:

'One of the police officers took me outside the flat and sat me in the van. One asked him his side of the story and one asked me my side of the story. Then they conferred notes, and agreed that it was just a domestic argument and lets go home — "Why don't you kiss and make up?"'

He found her after she had moved into a refuge, and the refuge workers called the police:

'They came with a big van, so [the police took him into the van]. I was saying good — take him away, and then these two young coppers got out of the van, and they said "Why don't you sit down and talk? Come on you sit here and you sit there". They took us into this van, and we sat opposite each other and the two coppers stood at the doorway of the van and they kept us there talking for about an hour. "What was the problem?" The copper would say . . . At the end of this hour of conversation they agreed with me, and then this young copper said "Why don't you just kiss him goodbye?" . . . They were more like marriage guidance counsellors than coppers — saying "well actually I had a little row with my wife, but I didn't hit her".'

Elsie described their reaction to the situation as 'pathetic'. When asked if she thought they realised the extent of the problem she replied:

'Yes, I've been in there with black eyes and blood trickling down my face all over my white T-shirt. I mean Mike followed me one day into the police station and told the policeman that he'd done it. He said,

176

"Yeah, I did it. She wouldn't cook my dinner so yeah — I licked her round the head with it." And the blood was trickling down my back.'

The police did not inform her about Women's Aid or take any legal action, yet they found time to take up amateur marriage guidance. Their apparent amiability should not be allowed to mask their failure to enforce the law.

Use of the Police as a weapon by men

'If there is one thing the police enjoy more than assaulting and locking up black people, it is finding ways to deport us instead.' (Black community worker)

Historically the British authorities have often employed the policy of incarceration and the subsequent deportation of 'undesirables' eg poor people, unemployed and casual workers, convicts, mad people). Certainly, the penal colonies which later became Australia and America were a happy synthesis of the European law and order traditions of incarceration and deportation, which were also about class control. Today many persons who would simply have been deported on conviction are incarcerated first, and then deported at the end of their sentence. Since foreign prisoners do not get parole, they often serve longer sentences, as well as having the extra punishment of deportation (Mama, Mars and Stevens 1986, D'Orey 1984). In other words, even these days some prisoners get both — incarceration and deportation. Perhaps it is this historical legacy which generates the curious play offs that sometimes occur when police are called to a scene in which a black woman is being assaulted, and have to decide a course of action. They may choose to enforce the laws outlawing assault, or they may turn the whole affair into an immigration investigation (see also Gordon 1981). A solicitor specialising in domestic violence who we interviewed, pointed out that in some of her cases the police have been known to arrest the woman, pending enquiring into her immigration status.

In this study it emerged that not all woman-beating men shun the police. In a number of cases, men actually threatened their wives with the police and the immigration department in the course of their disputes.

Jameela is a 21-year old Pakistani woman who was married by arrangement in Pakistan to a biochemist with British nationality. Jameela was brought into Britain as a fiancée in 1985, although they were already traditionally married. Her problems began soon after they started married life in the family home, when her brother-in-law tried to rape her. Her husband was himself sexually violent and abusive to her, and did nothing about his brother. On the one hand, he regularly threatened to have her deported back to her family in Pakistan in disgrace, while on the other told her that if she tried to leave the room, in which he kept her locked for days (with no toilet), the police would catch her. Even during her pregnancy, her husband refused to allow her to see a doctor, and kept her so malnourished that on one occasion she fainted from hunger. Her only relative in this country is a sister in a very similar predicament, who is married to a relative of Jameela's husband. They live several hours away and cannot see each other. Jameela was deeply depressed when we found and interviewed her at a women's refuge.

In a number of cases the husband was able to mislead the woman about her immigration status and terrorise her with the threat of deportation, when she did in fact have independent status, or did not know what her status was.

Arifa is a 50 year old Afghani woman whose Indian husband used her sheltered upbringing against her. Since she knew very little about the law or her rights in Britain, he was able to stop her from getting a British passport and so keep total control over her. They were married for over 20 years and he was violent to both Arifa and their children. He often used her economic dependency on him punitively, making them go hungry for days on end.

In view of the number of recent cases, where the Home Office has actually issued women escaping violent husbands or partners with deportation orders, there is in effect a collusion going on between the patriarchal power that men wield over their families and the state power of the British authorities, against the interests, if not human rights, of many black women (see chapter 4).

In some of these cases the man has dominated the interaction with the police, because he is male (or perhaps because he has a better command of English) and they have therefore elected to listen him rather than to the woman he has assaulted, so that once again they turn and leave perhaps after a few words about disturbing the neighbours.

Shaheeda is a 27 year old Asian woman who was abused by her father. At 15 she ran away to London and ended up in a homeless persons hostel. There she met a white English man from a middle class family, who was himself a 'problem child'. Eventually they set up home together. Their relationship was 'rocky' from the start and once they lived together he became physically violent. Shaheeda had three children, one of whom was taken into care and later adopted. She tried to leave a number of times and the police were involved, but according to Shaheeda 'they always took his side because he is white'. Eventually, during her third pregnancy he assaulted her so badly, that she did leave and go to a refuge.

Mei Ling is a 32 year old Chinese woman whose husband became violent to her after she gave birth to a daughter when her husband wanted a son. He beat her repeatedly seizing upon whatever trivial excuse he could find, and subjected her to violent rapes. On two occasions he threatened to kill her, and she called the police. They did not offer any assistance. Eventually he began torturing their baby by blowing a whistle loudly in her ears, so that Mei Ling ran away with her baby. She still lives in a bed and breakfast, and is very isolated and unsupported, but visits a local advice centre. She has not been able to get housing, and her husband still refuses to give her a divorce.

In other instances, the man has instructed the police to remove the woman. One man actually pointed at his wife and suggested that the authorities should deport her for him. The police duly arrested the woman pending enquiries about her immigration status (Radford and Co solicitors case eg).

The general point is that men are able to use the police and immigration to terrorise women. In many cases they are merely exploiting a situation in which racist and sexist immigration legislation and policing practices do mean that these agencies are often threatening and coercive towards black women.

Consequences of Police non-response: When a non-response is a response

In a number of cases the police have arrived at the door having been called by neighbours who heard the screams and thuds that accompany domestic violence. Even this sometimes made the men seek vengeance on their victim. More often than not there was a lack of response on the part of the police, so that when they left the scene, the man felt even more confident.

If the police are called in and do not respond in a way that cautions the man to the effect that assaulting the woman will not be tolerated by the law, this can have punitive effects on the woman. Indeed, her assailant may punish her further if the police have humiliated or unnerved him without also taking steps to prevent further violence. For example, Iyamide (chapter 3) described how her husband's violence towards her was actually reinforced by the police coming, but refusing to take any such action.

One Asian woman in this study described how the police responded when she called for help. They sent an Asian community policeman, who told her off severely in her own language and then told her to stop misbehaving and to try to be a 'good obedient wife'.

Non-collaboration by the woman

When other parties have called the police, the woman sometimes did not admit that she was being assaulted prior to their arrival, in which case the police often take her word for it (sometimes even when there is obvious injury), and leave.

> Shireen is only 19 years old, but she has tried to kill herself twice. Her husband beat her severely throughout their married life, on two occasions so badly that she had miscarriages. Her in-laws turned round and accused her of having abortions. Her husband tried to drive her out of the house, but she did not know where to go for help. On one occasion the neighbours called the police, but Shireen refused to press charges against her husband. Her husband was later sentenced to seven months imprisonment for assaulting someone else. Shireen subsequently left him and stayed in a number of refuges.

For an economically dependent wife, pressing charges may not appear to be in her own interests. She may be afraid of being left destitute and disgraced in her own community. Others fear reprisals, or have had negative experiences of the police's response in the past, as discussed above. Or it may be that the manner in which the police respond is off-putting to an already frightened and traumatised woman. Uniformed male officers may be the strongest deterrent to a violent man, but they may also frighten the woman. The police guidelines on domestic violence issued on June 24 1987 recommended, amongst other things, that more women officers should be used. However, since only 10% of the force are women, this will be difficult to implement. Police responses should bear in mind the fact that many women, particularly black women will be too terrified or suspicious to trust them.

Changes in the law, and in the practice of the courts (see chapter 5), in the direction of coercing women to give evidence are not necessarily the best way of tackling the problem. Worse still they may well serve to further deter women from reporting violence and seeking legal support. Black women are right to be concerned about the potentially negative impact the sweeping increase in police powers introduced in the 1984 Police and Criminal Evidence Act, will have on black people.

We have already discussed the evidence that police often refuse to take violent crimes defined as 'domestic' seriously. Under these circumstances, if the police are repeatedly called to a woman who then denies that there is a problem, they may well use this as an excuse for not taking any action in the future. If women do deny that there is a problem when the police come, it may also worsen her situation by giving her assailant more confidence. Even worse, racist police may take the opportunity to harass her themselves (see below).

Punitive Police responses to the woman

In some cases, the police respond in ways that are more actively punitive and abusive to the woman.

Patience is a Nigerian woman married to a Nigerian man who had been raised in Britain and who subjected her to violent abuse and other forms of degradation. She often slept in the factory where she worked rather than risking further assaults at home. Her husband's violence did not stop. On one occasion, the neighbours called in the police when they were disturbed by screams and bangs. When the police arrived her husband (who had a better command of 'the Queen's English') told the police that she had been damaging property in his flat and instructed them to arrest her. The police ridiculed the pair of them. Patience quoted the police as saying 'Eenie meenie minie mo, catch a nigger by the toe' while they decided who to arrest. They opted for Patience, and dragged her off in a half-clothed state, refusing to allow her to collect her bag or proper clothing. When they arrived at the police station she was roughed-up and then kicked down the stairs into the cells, where she was locked up all night, shivering with cold. She was ridiculed and racially humiliated (remarks about her husband not wanting to 'fuck' her any more, about a dirty smell in the station etc). A woman police officer witnessing all this laughed with amusement, telling her colleagues to 'take it easy lads', while Patience wept and pleaded for mercy. In the morning she was driven to the edge of the borough and dropped on the street. No charges were brought against her.

Horrific experiences like this can only be understood in the context of police assaults on black people, most of which continue to go unchallenged.

Conclusion

It is clear that police responses to the women in this study were very mixed. They ranged from being helpful and supportive (for example assisting women to collect their children and belongings and leave the scene), to the worst type of intervention which was damaging and abusive. In most cases better legal advice and support could have been given. Only a minority of the women in this study who had contact with the police said they were in any way encouraged to press charges or prosecute, suggesting that the police often assume that they will not pursue the matter.

For many black women (as for white women) the police often become involved whether the woman calls them or not. It is therefore imperative that work is done to improve the ways in which the police respond. This work has already begun through, for example, the exposure of the inadequacy of police responses by Susan Edwards (cited above). None of this work, however, has examined the race and class dynamics of police responses.

The findings of this research do suggest that police may be particularly insensitive, and on occasion brutal, towards black women. The experience of Patience is particularly disturbing, as are the experiences of women threatened with deportation, under existing law.

The most helpful police responses relied on the existence of black women's centres and refuges. Specialist facilities are far from adequate, and those that have been established are struggling to stay open in the face of cutbacks in funding. The importance of the work these do in supporting black woman must be recognised, more must be established, and the police must be encouraged to refer black women to these agencies. The experiences of women like Shuwei and Lily, who were dumped in quite unsuitable and unsympathetic hostels which did not provide any of the necessary support, demonstrate that it is important that the police refer black women to the right places.

Encouraging black women to make use of the law for their own protection and in their interests is another role that the police should play. The police should also refer black women to other legal agencies, who they might find less intimidating, regardless of the women's willingness to press charges. The police should be equipped with lists of lawyers who specialise in this area of law, as well as law centres and women's centres that they can advise women to approach, perhaps after recovering from the immediate trauma and when they feel strong enough to do so.

Generally, it is clear that the police role should centre around appropriate, effective and efficient enforcement of the law as it relates to domestic violence. The issue of the police not following up cases or taking appropriate legal action to enforce injunctions and other aspects of the law, remains an important one. The Police and Criminal Evidence Act of 1984 empowered the police to compel women to prosecute. Similarly, the Police Force Order of 1987 aimed to encourage police to act, and to prosecute violent men, even if the woman does not wish to pursue the matter. However, since the police were already empowered to arrest assailants prior to this legislation, (the main problem has always been police non-response or under-response), it is somewhat paradoxical that it was decided to extend their powers further. In the light of the evidence on police racism, there is good reason to fear that this extended power will be used against black people. Certainly, it may well serve to further deter women, particularly if they or their partners are black, from calling the police. From the perspective of the women whose experiences have been documented here, these recent changes are also of concern because of the evidence that the police are often racist and punitive towards black women. There must be some doubt that increased and ill-defined police powers, bearing in mind the lack of accountability particularly of the Metropolitan police force, will operate in the interests of black women. Indeed these developments may well present black people generally and specifically black women, with particular problems.

Notes

1. *Breaking the Silence: Women's Imprisonment*, (researched and written by Mama, Mars and Stevens in 1986) was subsequently republished by the Women's Equality Group of the London Strategic Policy Unit and is available from the Campaign for Women in Prison.
2. Having witnessed first-hand the violence meted out to black women, as well

as men, during the Brixton uprisings of 1981, this researcher has no illusions that being female counts for much in relations between black women and the police in Britain.

3. This woman was not one of the sample for this project, and had not experienced domestic violence, but recounted her experience to the researcher, in the course of explaining why she was afraid to go out alone in London.

4. Generally, black women (including those who have committed very minor crimes) are left with a deep mistrust and suspicion of both the police and the courts, often because they feel they were unfairly treated and took extra punishment in one way or another. This is not surprising, given the treatment of black women at all levels of the criminal justice system and the racism within women's prisons (Mama, Mars and Stevens, op cit., 1986).

5. This attitude was, for example, evident amongst some of the participants at a black community meeting entitled 'Domestic Violence Within the System' held in Lewisham on October 8 1988, organised by the International Women's Day Planning Committee.

7. Local authority responses to domestic violence and relationship breakdown

Race, gender and public housing

Women's limited access to housing has been the subject of a small but growing number of publications in recent years (Brion and Tinker 1980, Austerberry and Watson 1982, 1983, 1986, Levison and Atkins 1987, Brailey 1986, Institute of Housing 1987, SHAC 1985, 1986, Shelter 1987). This attention is long overdue, particularly when one considers that women are the primary consumers of public housing (as of other social services). This statement is based on the fact that women's roles as homemakers, childrearers and carers have meant that women spend significantly more time in the home, in order to perform all the daily tasks that guarantee the reproduction of the workforce from day to day and across the generations.

As a result of the socially circumscribed roles of women, they are collectively those most directly affected by housing policies, by housing design, by housing shortages and currently by the housing crisis.

In addition to the disproportionate direct impact of everything about housing on women, the class, gender and race divisions of society also circumscribe the access that different groups of people have to homes. The dominant notions about what forms 'the family' should take have had particular consequences in terms of access to housing, for all groups not 'fitting' in with the white, middle class notion of the nuclear family. This includes single people, unmarried women, black people, migrant workers, travellers, and many others. Black women are denied access to housing on several counts: as women, as black people, as members of the working classes, often also as single people and single parents.

Inefficient and ineffective housing policies, and substandard accommodation disproportionately affect women. The direct negative impact that bad housing practices generally have are particularly acute when class, race and gender dynamics are also brought into play, as they are in the case of black women.

Access to housing does not function on its own, but in accordance with economic power. The determining power of the financial factor is such that all the groups one can identify as having restricted access to housing are also economically underprivileged. The patterning of access to better quality homes mirrors the earning power of various social groups. The group we are most concerned with here falls into three underpaid sectors of the labour force. They are black, women and mostly working class, and as a group have been consistently identified as being the lowest paid members of the workforce (Phizacklea 1983, Mama 1984).

Not so for our access to housing. A literature search revealed virtually no publications in the area of black women and housing and British black women do not appear to have been included significantly, even in 'international' women and housing events where women have been invited from abroad.[1]

The access that black women have, or more accurately have not had, to public housing can best be understood as the logical outcome of a number of different dynamics operating at both material and ideological levels. These can best be articulated through some understanding of the historical context out of which public housing policy and practice has emerged. This is a history of contradictory discourses in the general areas of welfare, race, empire and the family, which goes back a very long way. The Victorian period will be briefly discussed below, on the basis that it is most directly relevant to the present situation, in view of the resurgence of the ethos of that period in the Thatcherite Britain of today.

This is not the place to do justice to the subject, but it is possible to highlight the conditions under which the most relevant discourses and practices which exclude black people emerged. There is also however a broader context in which these dynamics take place.

At the present time, public housing of all forms is coming under government attack. This in itself is the result of underlying contradictions in British debates around the provision of public housing, and the rise to ascendance of a particularly conservative approach to social welfare, including housing (Jacobs 1985). This does not however negate the importance of the race and gender dynamics of housing policy and practice that I will be focusing on in my analysis. Indeed, race and gender dynamics underlie many of the discourses around welfare, empire and the family, whether this has been explicitly articulated or not. Every time the 'ideal family' is mentioned, the 'other family' or alternative family is also invoked, often in a threatening manner. Each time 'the deserving' are given anything, there is a simultaneous concern with excluding 'the undeserving' from that provision. Dominant ideas exist as such only in relation to alternatives; subversive and repressed ideas that often threaten the hegemony of the ruling ideology.

Here it is argued that throughout the history of 'public' housing there has been a preoccupation with excluding certain sections of the public from it. This preoccupation is constructed out of dominant ideas including moralistic stereotypes and specific racial and sexual evaluations which are part of the culture in which housing officers operate, and which inform and guide their housing practice leading them to deliver their service in prejudiced and discriminatory ways. To exclude the preoccupation with excluding certain groups from analysis of housing policy implementation, as so many housing experts have done, is to give an ethnocentric and incomplete picture of the subject.

Here we shall look at the race and gender dynamics in the history of public housing, for it is through these that black women's access to public housing has been particularly restricted.

After that we shall go on to see that the research we conducted for this project, demonstrates not only that black women's access to housing continues to be circumscribed, and with increasing effect as a result of broader political changes, but also that for black women who have been subjected to violence, this has appalling and long term impacts on their lives.

Race and gender dynamics in the history of public housing

The history of public housing owned and managed by local government dates back to the turn of the century. The Housing and Working Classes Act of 1885 and the Housing of the Working Classes Act of 1890 heralded this development. The Tudor-Walters Report of 1918 contained the first detailed proposals for local authority house-building programmes while the 1919 Housing Act, obliging local governments to provide some rented accommodation, signalled the beginning of modern council housing. This history has been documented in a number of places already and will not be detailed here (see Schifferes 1976, Merret 1979, Holmans 1987). The contradictory class relations out of which public housing has emerged have also been described in some detail (Stedman-Jones 1971).

The broader socio-political backdrop to the emergence of public housing includes the major social transformations that London underwent in the 19th century as a result of the industrial revolution and imperial expansionism. As the capital city of a large and rapidly expanding empire, London developed an insatiable demand for labour, drawing working people from all over Europe, and later from the empire. At the same time London became a cultural centre for both the aristocracy and the newly developing middle classes. The luxurious affluence of opera houses and ballrooms stood in stark contrast to the squalid slums and rookeries of the less privileged classes. The latter was the London that inspired Dickens' socially critical work and it was from the situation of the lower classes that Dickens drew his images of cruelty and exploitation, and brutality towards women.

In terms of housing, overcrowding was a serious problem: by 1848, the Statistical Society found that on Church Lane, St Giles, there were *on average* 40 persons per house and 12 persons per room, and this was not exceptional by any means. The population continued to soar, more than doubling in central London between 1821 and 1851. At the same time there was massive dis-housing, as slums and houses were cleared away to make room for railways, docks and warehouses. Inevitably it was the undesirable areas inhabited by casual workers and poor people that most offended the sensibilities of the middle-classes and their delicate lady-folk. Massive street clearances targeted the very areas in which the workers, needed by the factories, lived. Combined with the then growing demand for labour, overcrowding increased, and Malthusian population theories haunted the sleep of the well-to-do, with spectres of swarming hordes of degenerates overrunning 'civilised' society. The Metropolitan Board (the London Regional Governing body that later evolved into the Greater London Council) stuck to its conviction that brutal mass eviction was justifiable as a way of forcing the poor to move to the suburbs and house themselves. Industrial capitalism, from its inception was clearly interested in the labour of the worker, but not in the welfare of the rest of his or her body.

The punitive attitude of Victorian legislators towards the human needs of exploited workers is clearly visible in the Common Lodging Houses Acts of 1851 and 1853. Rather than taking steps to provide accommodation for workers, these Acts required local authorities to register and regularly inspect common lodging houses, to enforce minimum standards of hygiene and remove sick persons to hospitals. Despite their intrusive powers however, both Acts failed to contribute to an improvement in standards, if that is indeed what they were intended to do. Lodging houses remained hazardous places — filthy and overcrowded — throughout the 19th century.

188

Between 1872 and 1885 over 75,000 persons were officially cleared from the centre of London, setting the scene for a major housing crisis in the 1880's. Statements written reflect the ethos of the times, and the morally righteous concerns of the middle-classes. Overcrowding was seen as a threat to the Christian mission, encouraging fornication, prostitution, and the mixing of the 'honest poor' with 'thieves and wantons'. Welfare was seen as encouraging parasitism by middle class reformers like Lord Shaftesbury and Octavia Hill.

The housing situation of women during the industrial revolution and since has not been as well documented (but see Watson and Austerberry 1986). It is notable that women did not have the right to own property in their own right until the Married Women's Property Act of 1882. Women from the lower social classes would not in any case have had the financial wherewithall to purchase dwellings, although a minority may have inherited houses. Some of these women had to turn their homes into boarding houses. In London certainly, women's accommodation depended largely on their marital situation and the ability of their spouse to gain access to housing. Women migrated to the cities to find work, just as the men did, and faced the traumas of the housing problems. Many relied on cheap lodging houses, but in the context of Victorian middle class morality, women were excluded from the vast majority of these. Furthermore women's wages were very much lower than men's, increasing their need for cheap accommodation of a decent standard. Despite the fact that a high proportion of lodging houses were in fact owned by women seeking a means of sustenance through renting out rooms, letting rooms to anyone, but particularly to women, was frowned upon and thought to be unrespectable and shameful. This may well have been because taking in lodgers entailed a lack of the privacy that was so integral to the nuclear family, and encouraged other types of relationships. Witness Mrs Booth:

'any arrangement which, by supplying cheap accommodation encourages young women to leave the shelter, however poor, of their own home and offers them an opportunity of living without any restrictions or oversight . . . exercises a decidedly harmful influence' (Quoted in Davidoff 1979).

As Watson and Austerberry (1986) argue, the underlying preoccupation seems to have been the loss of control over women's sexuality. Certainly the hegemonic discourses restricting women's rights on the basis of particular notions of female sexuality and morality, are reflected in the legislation of the period. Prostitution was seen as a symptom of poor living conditions and lack of housing but, having identified it as a problem, legislation victimised women, rather than attacking the sources by, for example ensuring that decent accommodation was available to women. The Contagious Diseases Acts of 1864, 1866 and 1869 forced prostitutes and women suspected of being prostitutes to undergo compulsory medical examination and to register with the police, a move which resulted in public outcry and demonstrations (Watson and Austerberry 1986 p34).

Tied accommodation was another source of housing for women workers. The scullery maids who lived in the basements or attics of the homes of the well-to-do, draperies and dressmaking workshops, were attached to the workplaces.

Casual wards, or workhouses were the worst and final option, acting as a form of detention, with a system of rules that made it impossible for the resident to find work. In 1886, 21 per cent of the occupants of casual wards were women. Towards the turn of the century, the Salvation Army took to providing rescue homes for 'fallen women'. By 1890 there were 13 such homes accommodating 307 women.

The evidence suggests that there were significant numbers of black women in London at this time (Fryer 1984) Africans where brought to Britain during the transatlantic slave trade, and the importation of black women did not cease when slavery was made illegal in 1807. A significant proportion worked as domestic servants and therefore had some form of tied accommodation. After the abolition of the transatlantic slave trade, other nationalities were also imported from various parts of the empire to serve similar purposes. Visram comments that

'. . . Indian domestics provided a cheap source of labour and, like African servants, Asian valets and footmen came to be quite in vogue for fashionable British families in the 18th century. With "full-blooded" Asians available, there was no longer any need to dress African servants in Oriental costumes.' (1986)

The same author notes that throughout the 18th and 19th centuries, large numbers of Asian servants, particularly children's nannies or 'ayahs', were discharged in London after being brought over to serve and child-mind for their employers on voyages back from the colonies. Many were simply discharged and left to fend for themselves on the alien and often hostile London streets. So disgraceful was their plight that what became effectively an Ayahs home was set up in Aldgate at 6, Jewry Street by a Mr and Mrs Rogers (Visram 1986 p 29). This offered accommodation for a small fee while these women sought a way of working their passage home.

During this period, it can be seen that there was a lack of adequate housing for workers generally, but particularly for women and black people. There is little mention of black women in the historical literature, but it can be deduced that the few places that were available for women were restricted to 'gentleladies' and as such would not have been available to black or working class women. Mary Seacole's status as a doctress would not have been typical of most black women in Britain at the time. If black men were restricted to the poorest quality slums, abandoned shacks, and often the streets of London, then black women would also have found it extremely difficult to obtain accommodation. In the struggle to survive, some would probably have been forced into prostitution as one form of tied accommodation that was available to outcast women, or into poorhouses, or even deported to penal colonies along with other 'disreputable' members of 19th century British society. What evidence there is suggests that the modern day preoccupation with deporting black women, and otherwise excluding them from the fruits of advanced capitalism is but a continuation of this early penchant for deporting and/or containing (through incarceration in institutions) the underprivileged sectors of British society — most of whom are in fundamental ways not only rejected but also victimised by the punitive practices of the governmental and administrative apparatuses of the society to which they belong.

At the beginning of this century, there continued to be a massive shortage of cheap and decent accommodation and what there was, was generally out of the reach of working girls and women. Those who were shop assistants or worked in the drapery and allied trades are reported to have slept in overcrowded dormitories above the premises and to have put up with very poor facilities. In 1909 300 women are reported to have signed a petition to demand that the London County Council erect a hostel for them and other homeless women, an action that was repeated around the country, leading to the formation of the Association of Women's Lodging Houses in the same year. Women activists like Mary Higgs also wrote and campaigned about women's housing problems at that time. Her commendable aim was that:

'there shall be no town throughout the length and breadth of our land where the poor stranger woman cannot find safe shelter, a place which if her need is great, she may call "home"' (Quoted in Watson and Austerberry 1986 chapter 3, p 42).

One is left to wonder if 'stranger women' was ever intended to refer to black women — unmentioned in the early campaigns and subsequent studies. Watson and Austerberry's own study of women's homelessness is the strongest existing source on women's housing in Britain, and makes the same omission, concentrating on a narrow feminist perspective that does not take cognizance of differentials within 'women' other than in terms of their status with respect to the dominant nuclear family form. When they do quote one black woman whom they interviewed, it is not to indicate that racism makes the housing problems of black women even worse, but rather to suggest that expectations of decent homes are culture specific.[2]

Homelessness has long been associated with black people, even in the imagery of a title which conjures up particular notions of Africa to indicate what a dreadful experience it is. Mrs Chesterton's *In Darkest London* describes how she left her middle class home to experience the horrors of life on the streets of London (1928, cited in Watson and Austerberry).

A land fit for heroes: race, gender and municipal housing between the wars

It was only after the First World War that the notion that the government had a responsibility for housing gained sufficient ascendance to actually produce political resolve. This was closely tied to the fact that large numbers of men who had been in the casual and 'undeserving' classes before the War now returned home as war heroes. The previously mentioned 1918 Tudor Walters Report contained the first detailed proposals for local authority housing and building programmes, and the 1919 Housing Act ushered in the beginning of modern council housing, with the local authorities becoming responsible for providing some rented accommodation.

It should be noted that council housing was not initially housing for the poor; it had never been intended to be provided on the basis of need. Rather, it was for the waged worker who could pay the rents, which were at that time significantly higher than rents in the private sector. Bitter and protracted political battles were fought over the issue of government responsibility for housing anyone at all, and it was not until the 1930s that a consensual acceptance of council housing as a permanent institution emerged (Schifferes 1976). The consensus over public housing that did emerge in the 1930s was, however, a qualified one, masking fundamental contradictions between the Labour and Conservative views. These contradictions have resurfaced in the 1980s. The Conservatives, then as now, remained largely in favour of subsidising private enterprise with public money. Labour on the other hand, particularly under Wheatley's government aimed at eventually replacing the private rented sector with publicly owned renting for the entire working class if not beyond (Schifferes 1976).

Another significant factor in this history was the growth of a tenants movement, initially organising rent strikes in the private sector, but then during the 1920s within the public sector as well. Ironically, it was often the presence of black people that inspired white tenants to organise themselves at all, just as it was often the presence of black workers that inspired early labour organisation.

As we can see from this brief discussion, the debates around housing were not at all concerned with need, indeed public housing emerged very much around male interests, as the discourses around men returning to home and hearth, encapsulated in the expression 'Every Englishman's home is his castle', indicate. If women were to benefit at all, this was only through their marriage to returning heroes, or through their position at his hearth.

In fact the end of war period was a bad time for large numbers of women, many of whom had been widowed or remained single, and who now found themselves being pushed back out of the jobs they had performed during the war. They were expected to quietly retire to the domestic servitude they had so willingly left behind at the call of Queen and country.[3] In a situation where women did not have independent access to housing, many — even if in full-time employment — would have been forced to contract 'marriages of convenience' simply to keep a roof over their heads.

The inter-war years, during which public housing came into its own, were also years which saw a growth in British racism, exacerbated by the economic slump and nurtured by the growth of fascism across Europe. Older Black people who lived in Stepney at this time can recall Mosleyites organising marches on the multi-racial community, but being barricaded out and doused with pans of hot water, as in the famous Cable Street battle. Black people did not in any case have access to public housing until much later. Rather they lived in small concentrations in areas that white working class people moved from as soon as their own situation allowed. These were mostly private lodging houses and evacuated slums providing the kind of appalling living circumstances that had earlier prompted a Parliamentary enquiry in 1910 to examine the plight of 'Distressed Colonial and Indian Subjects'. Even so, black people were resented and hated. This hatred erupted as soon as the war had ended, with the white working class attacking black people in the 1919 race riots in Liverpool, Cardiff, Newport and Glasgow. The government responded to these race attacks, not by disciplining the perpetrators, but by deporting some 95 West Africans.

The post-war years

Black people's struggle for housing continued in the post war period. At the same time, immigration was being encouraged because of the need for cheap labour during the economic boom of the 1950s and 1960s. Black men and women were brought over from the Caribbean and Africa in particular to staff the expanding welfare state and industries, a process which has been documented by Peach (1972). Although labour was needed and imported from the colonies, black people continued to be excluded from public housing by residence qualifications. When the Empire Windrush arrived at Tilbury on June 22, 1948, with the first full shipload of workers, there was no accommodation provided. After the Mayor of Lambeth had welcomed the arrivals, they had to be accommodated in the Clapham air-raid shelter. They and all the other immigrants had to join their predecessors in the private housing sector. The colour bar ensured that even here, black people only had very limited access to the poorest quality accommodation. Landlords openly advertised that they would accept 'No Coloureds' (Glass 1960). The result of such widespread exclusion meant that most black people had to find homes for themselves on the private market, and often had to rent out rooms amongst themselves. So developed a situation in which black people lived for the most part in run-down multiple occupancy dwellings which they either owned or rented. There they were subject to all forms of victimisation and hardly, if at all, protected by legislation designed to curb Rachmanism and other abuses. These dwellings later became the target of compulsory purchase orders and slum clearances in the later 1960s.

Black people remained too weak both numerically and politically to have much positive influence on policy, and both local and central government remained accountable to the white electorate and shared the racism that periodically erupted. In 1954 black people in Camden had to defend themselves against white people whose weapons included petrol bombs. In 1958 black people in Nottingham were similarly attacked by

194

white mobs, in a climax to a series of individual attacks in the preceding months. In the same year, the black community in Notting Hill was attacked by gangs of white residents, demonstrating continuing race hatred. Although black people have continued to be politically marginalised, their presence in Britain continued to have deep effects on the wider political agendas as well as on social policy and administration.[4]

The 1961 Commonwealth Immigrants Act ushered in a new era of racial immigration controls that have continued to the present day, long after primary immigration has been stopped completely. By the time the Race Relations Act of 1969 was drawn up, immigration was already so tightly controlled that governmental concern was able to shift away from incoming black people to the administration of race relations on the home front.

Eventually black people could not be excluded from public housing by residential qualifications, since they had lived here too long. Slum clearance programmes also meant that some of those whom local authorities were obliged to rehouse ('decants' in housing terminology) were black people, who lived in the worst places which inevitably became the targets of slum clearance programmes. Even compulsory rehousing provoked rent strikes by white tenants incensed by the black presence on council estates.[5]

Within the public housing sector too, black people were allocated the worst forms of accommodation by the local state, which was constantly placatory towards white residents who constantly accused housing departments of 'favouring coloureds' even though nothing could have been further from the truth. For example, Burney (1967) described Lambeth's Labour Council as having a 'defeatist attitude' towards the housing of black people right from the start and documents the situation in that borough.[6]

The 1969 Cullingworth Committee marked the development of policies intended to disperse black people and to break up the communities that had developed partly because of racist housing practice. Their recommendations may well have been inspired by fears that the race riots erupting across the Atlantic in the ghettoes of the United States would start up in the deprived inner-cities of Britain where black people were being forced to live in similarly squalid conditions.

Thus we can see that racism has had long term and deep effects on the type of housing that black people live in, across all sectors of the housing market. The continuing dynamics of racism within housing have been the subject of a number of recent publications and will not be repeated here.[7]

It is however important to note that modern housing departments have been born out of this history of racist exclusion and paranoia. This is partly masked by the bureaucratic character of local state bureaucracies in general, which is briefly described in the next section. Then we shall go on to look more specifically at the impact of housing policies on women, and evaluate the impact of these on black women. After that we shall look more specifically at the impact of housing policies on women, and evaluate the impact of these on black women.

Organisational character of housing departments

Housing departments have many characteristics common to large hierarchical bureaucracies. Communication across the different departments and up and down the hierarchy is generally problematic in structures of this sort. Regarding the interface with the public, there are various bureaucratic layers that any particular demand has to penetrate before decisions are taken, usually at managerial level by an officer with whom the public will have no face-to-face contact. One gets the impression that large amounts of paper are passed up and down and across the various segments for processing, with their human implications being buried in the interests of appearing to be efficient and professional. Decision-makers seldom have face-to-face contact with those whose lives are subject to their decisions and a main role performed by those heroically termed 'frontline officers' is that of protecting their managers from direct interpersonal contact with the public. Such direct contact has become increasingly confrontational in recent years. This has led to the construction of thick security screens designed to protect interviewing officers from the wrath of the consumers (their clients). Visiting the Housing reception to see one's housing officer is therefore rather like visiting a top security prison, complete with microphones for communicating through. Lambeth, for example was like this at the time of the research, and shortly afterwards Brent housing staff went on strike to demand similar protection from their own irate clients. The lack of privacy for women who may be there to ask for housing on the basis of an issue as sensitive as domestic violence, must make seeing housing staff even more of an ordeal.

This is not the place to do a comprehensive review of the racial make-up of 'frontline' staff, but it was pointed out to the researcher that there are more black women being employed in this capacity, so that as workers within the bureaucracy, black women appear to be placed between those needing housing (often other black people) and the state. Since

196

interviewing officers are at the bottom of the housing hierarchy, they are not in a position to affect policy or practice substantially. However, black officers' position at the interface between the public and the local state will make it more difficult for the consumer to accuse the housing department of racism.

Officers on the whole display a high level of ego-involvement with the institution and various degrees of identification with its broader policies and interests. While some expressed a degree of criticism of their institution's policies, they were not prepared to go on record expressing their frustrations. Some seemed to feel that they were in a position to improve things 'through the system' to an extent sufficient for them to want to remain in their jobs, while others are said to have left or been encouraged to leave, but were not interviewed in the present research. Most did not appear to identify closely with their client groups. Some of those interviewed gave the impression that this would be seen as 'unprofessional' and not conducive to smooth and efficient performance. The definition of professionalism here is constructed out of the concerns with efficiency, financial considerations and limited resources which have prevailed under the Thatcher regime. The local bureaucratic culture is thus reinforced at top level; by the central state, even as LA powers are being withdrawn.

Policies for women in the public sector

Our discussion of the history of race and gender dynamics in the history of housing, and the development of public housing in particular, indicates the deeply rooted nature of both gender and racial discrimination in housing. With the development of municipal housing, women have been able to obtain affordable rented accommodation to a degree unprecedented in previous epochs. Gains have been won in the development of local authority housing policies that have tried to militate against the disadvantaged position of women in all sectors of housing. Yet despite the sometimes bold initiatives in, for example, the struggle for victims of domestic violence to be given priority for rehousing, women's access to public housing has continued to be significantly circumscribed by their roles as mothers and wives, as studies of the housing situation of single women without children and single mothers illustrate (Austerberry and Watson 1983). Women-headed households still constitute approximately 70% of the homeless households.

Women, as the major beneficiaries of 20th century public housing, are also going to be the most affected by the assault on public housing that is currently being waged by central government. The London Housing Unit (LHU) has pointed out some of the gender implications of the Housing Bill (1988). Since women still earn significantly less than men, they are economically disadvantaged in the private sector, so that for most women there is no real alternative to council rented accommodation Moreover, the private sector has a very poor track record in relation to those women who have had to depend on it, as has been the lot of the very many single and childless women who never gained access to council accommodation. The rent increases that are expected to result from the restructuring of the housing market will in any case further reduce the access that such women have had to private rented accommodation, putting greater stress on the already overcrowded and uncongenial hostels.

Owner-occupation has continued to be beyond the means of the vast and growing numbers of women-headed households.

In London (1987 figures), 64% of black women and 54% of white women earn less than £125 per week, yet the average market rent for a 2-3 bed property is £159 per week and average weekly mortgage repayments in London for a similar property are estimated to be about £162 (LHU Jan. 1988 p16).

The assault on the public housing that women rely so heavily upon, is occurring at a time when family forms have been consistently evolving in ways that make ensuring women's access to decent homes at affordable prices a rapidly growing concern. The divorce rate multiplied six times over between 1961 and 1983 and has continued to rise. As many as a third of all marriages are now likely to end in divorce. Premarital or long-term cohabitation are increasingly favoured options. Changes of this type produce an increased and growing need for flexibility in tenancy arrangements, so that changes in relational situations can be absorbed without greatly increased suffering and homelessness, and so that women can have access to housing in their own right. Despite advances in matrimonial law, women and children are still often the ones to bear the housing costs of relationship breakdown. The present study indicates this to be the case beyond a doubt so far as black families are concerned.

Similarly, in their survey of women's hostels and refuges, Austerberry and Watson (1983) identified marital breakdown and domestic violence as the commonest reason for women's homelessness.

198

Some women more equal than others

While the development of a public sector has meant more women than ever before can live in affordable rented accommodation or even rent homes for themselves, it is notable that within this gain, some women have benefited more then others. Without a doubt, those in the best quality council accommodation are members of the favoured family type: wives and mothers in nuclear families of the northern European type.

Other groups of women's housing rights have not been so easily recognised. Single mothers, for example tend to be concentrated, not in the better estates where they may enjoy the support of a secure community, but on the least desirable estates in the inner cities. Homeless families are also likely to be offered worse accommodation than those already in council homes. The implications for homeless single parent families are grim.

It has been repeatedly demonstrated that black households are concentrated in the poorest quality accommodation and in the most deprived inner city areas. This pattern is evident in the location and quality of accommodation afforded to black single mothers (CRE 1984, Henderson and Karn 1987).

It has been argued that these inequalities in housing are reproduced in part because housing officers offer the least desirable accommodation to those they perceive to be the most desperate, on the basis of a 'beggars can't be choosers principle'. The concerns of housing management are held to be the source of these policies, which have led to the creation of sink estates; dumping grounds for rejected and underprivileged groups of people (See Lawrence and Mama 1988).

As we saw in the last chapter, women interviewed in the present study described how their standards where forced down by long periods of homelessness and coercion from hostel staff as well as housing officers. The 'beggars' principle therefore appears to work, and this has the consequence of reproducing existing concentrations of underprivileged groups in the worst quality housing and in the most deprived inner-city estates. It also has the consequence of guaranteeing that those in most need of decent accommodation are the least likely to get it. It is through these dynamics that inequality is reproduced. This reproduction of inequality has particularly disturbing consequences for black women who are already vulnerable as a result of having been battered and who are seeking to escape violent partners, or who are seeking alternative accommodation as a result of relationship breakdown.

Impact of the women's liberation movement

The general struggle for liberation waged by the women's movement over the last decade has included active campaigns on the issue of violence against women. The physical subjugation and coercion of women by men has been a frontline concern of all those seeking human rights for women, whether in the battles over the violent crime of rape and other forms of sexual abuse and degradation, or over the more private crime that used to be called wife battering. The international nature of this struggle was highlighted in chapter 1. Here we shall briefly address the impact of the struggles against the torture of women in the home on, the local and central state apparatuses in Britain.

Active campaigns against the abuse of women by their sexual and emotional partners have had some impact on the central state. This became apparent when in 1983 a Parliamentary Select committee was appointed to look into the problem of domestic violence nationally. The Select Committee came up with a range of recommendations which included the provision of refuges as temporary accommodation, and recommendations around the rehousing of women who have been subjected to violence in their homes. Yet in 1989, very few of the recommendations have been met in real terms. In fact the housing situation can be seen to have worsened substantially over the years since that committee published its findings and recommendations. A wide range of Central Government welfare policies have contributed to making things even more difficult for battered women through the broader changes in taxation, social security and housing. The fact is that even the conservative recommendations of the Government's own committee have been overridden by politically motivated, wider policy changes that will have devastating effects on women's access to housing and the self-help initiatives taken by the women's movement. This suggests that the very existence of the Select Committee was tokenistic and of very marginal concern to the government. The only area addressed by that report that can be said to have been taken up at all is the police role in responding. This narrow concentration on law and order considerations is far from adequate, as the present research indicates. We noted in chapter 6 that changes in police responses to domestic violence need to be evaluated in the context of broader increases in police powers and threats to civil liberties. The changes should also be evaluated in the context of the undermining of all the other (non-coercive) responding agencies; the housing, health and welfare services, because it is in these support services that the long term solutions lie. The need for positive and less oppressive multi-agency responses was stressed in Part I.

The most concrete and concerted action to have emerged out of the vibrant campaigns against violence against women waged in the early '70s has been the development of the women's refuge network catering to the most immediate need that being assaulted in the home produces; emergency accommodation for the women. Refuges also offer emotional support in a woman-centred environment, and assist women in dealing with the various large and often unsympathetic bureaucracies of the Department of Health and Social Security (DHSS), housing, social services and legal bodies. They function as safe houses and are run for the most part exclusively by women (see chapter 11).

One effect of the refuge movement has been the sensitizing of some local authorities to the housing needs of women who have been through domestic violence. Refuges in local authority areas have provided bases from which women have been supported by experienced refuge workers in their claims for permanent homes away from their violent partners. As such they have been invaluable in getting women's claims for housing recognised in the boroughs in which they are based, by forcing the issue onto the local government agenda where possible, as for example in Islington, Lambeth, Haringey, Camden and Southwark.

London-wide strategies

One effect of the Women's Movement has been increased participation of some women in local state bureaucracies, particularly through the establishment of women's units and the appointment of women officers. In most of the boroughs that have developed policies aiming or professing to improve the situation of women in society, this has been the result of concerted activity by women activists with footholds in the mainstream establishment, as will be discussed below. Evaluating these policies (and their impact on black women) is made particularly difficult because of the barrage of changes that the Thatcher regime has forced on all statutory organisations. Apart from the wide-ranging attack on the institutions of public housing, welfare and social security, the local state itself is being eroded. The abolition of London's government heralded further centralisation of power that was to be followed through with further curtailments of local state power through rate-capping, the Local Government Act and a number of other changes.

A range of policies have been developed by local authorities in response to the housing problems resulting from both relationship breakdown and domestic violence. However, rather than developing a London-wide initiative, what has happened has been a proliferation of diverse policies in the different boroughs, with varying degrees of political will and commitment to their effective implementation. This variation between boroughs has negative consequences since those with progressive policies become overwhelmed with demands while other boroughs are able to shirk their responsibilities to the homeless with virtual impunity.

In 1980 security of tenure was extended to the public sector, a development which had substantial impact on the options that LAs had available to them regarding the housing management and allocations problems that result from relationship breakdown. Under the 1980 Housing Act, 13 grounds for possession of the tenancy were specified, but relationship breakdown was not one of them. This omission affected cohabiters in particular, since there are no legal proceedings for establishing which partner should retain the tenancy. In the case of domestic violence, court action against the assailant is not always, as we have seen, in the best interests of the victim. Furthermore, the length of time that legal settlements and custody battles take (up to five years in some instances) means that legal action would in any case not preclude the need for housing policies to be developed to deal with both the immediate and the long-term consequences of both relationship breakdown and domestic violence.

The Greater London Council's 1983 survey examined the impact of the 1980 changes to the Homeless Persons Act on borough policies and practices in the area of relationship breakdown. The survey attempted to examine what the effects were and made many recommendations. The GLC's work in this area was taken up by the London Strategic Policy Unit's (LSPU) Women's Equality Group (see WEG's 1987 Review of Borough Practice and their 1988 Report on Race and Gender Monitoring).

Since the abolition of the GLC, and then the LSPU, work in this area has been continued in a much more limited fashion by the LHU, and the London Race and Housing Research Unit (LRHRU) (which was also closed down in March 1989). The LSPU's Women's Equality Group commissioned a review of London refuge provision before being closed down (Russell forthcoming), and the LHU commenced a survey of borough housing policies on relationship breakdown in 1986/7, but this work was regrettably never completed because the relevant officer's post was cut.

The Women in Housing Forum established at that time has however, continued to wage an uphill struggle for coherent guidelines to be accepted by the Association of London Authorities (ALA). In April 1988 the ALA's Housing Committee failed to accept the guidelines that LHU recommended on behalf of the Women and Housing Forum. These are reproduced here to indicate the areas of concern.

1. Each borough should produce a clear written policy statement and a detailed procedural note on relationship breakdown.

2. Information about policies and procedure should be provided for tenants, for example in a leaflet available at local housing offices.

3. Specific training on borough policy and procedure should be provided for appropriate staff.

4. Women applicants should be advised that they may be interviewed by a woman housing officer if they wish and sufficient women officers should be made available.

5. Cohabitees and married couples should be treated equally; cohabitees should not normally be required to demonstrate the previous stability of their relationship, nor should a time limit be applied to the relationship before assistance is given.

6. Gay and lesbian couples and heterosexual couples should be treated equally; borough information on their policies should make this explicit.

7. The word of both partners or the partner applying for a move should be sufficient confirmation of relationship breakdown; legal confirmation should only be insisted upon when the (same) relationship has broken down on several occasions.

8. Partners of sole tenants and joint tenants should not be treated differently.

9. Rent arrears should not deter authorities from applying the same

policies and practices applied to other applicants.

10. Any requirement to pay rent arrears should take into account the historic and current financial ability of each partner to fulfil their rent obligations. Clear guidance should be provided for staff on apportioning rent arrears or writing off debt.

11. Cases where violence has occurred or has been threatened should be treated as highest priority and alternative safe accommodation provided urgently.

12. Violence or the threat of violence should not be the sole determining factor in investigating and accepting relationship breakdown cases.

13. Applications from and rehousing of relationship breakdown cases should be monitored by ethnicity and gender; the information collected should include length of wait for rehousing and type of accommodation offered/accepted.

14. Sexual harassment clauses should be introduced to all tenancy agreements.

15. There should be an adequate appeals procedure for relationship breakdown rehousing cases. Women officers (at the appropriate senior grade) should be fully involved in decision-making on appeals cases.

The Department of the Environment (DOE) set up a working party and also commissioned a London-wide survey of policies on relationship breakdown, the findings of which were not available. Verbal communications with those involved in the working party indicated that the survey had not been successful, but that the DOE were considering conducting another one.

In the course of this project the researcher attempted to conduct a survey of the policy situation across the various boroughs, but received only five responses to initial enquiries made to all 33 local authorities in the GLC area. Time and resource constraints made it unrealistic to pursue the matter beyond establishing the reasons for the various attempts at the much-needed and overdue London-wide survey and policy review, not being more successful. For the present purposes it was decided to focus attention on two boroughs (one Labour and one Conservative) as case examples of the policy situation regarding the housing status of people with needs resulting from relationship breakdown and/or domestic violence. It was felt that only then would it be possible to build up an understanding of the situation thorough enough to facilitate the more detailed analysis necessary to evaluate the race implications of these policies. Even with this modification of the original research brief, the complexity of the local authority housing bureaucracies, and their ambivalence towards research of this nature, will have had effects on the information made or not made available to the researcher.

The following two chapters are presented as independent investigations of the two local authorities selected for special attention, and are designed to present the local state side of the coin. The choice of boroughs does not reflect their deserving any special attention as compared to other boroughs, but rather a decision to span the London-wide variation in both policy and practice. Thus we have a Conservative borough with almost no policy in this area, compared to a Labour borough which has been developing policy over a period of years. Since the Central Government is also Conservative, the Conservative borough's policies and practice are more in keeping with the broader political agenda of the current period. The Labour borough is in a crisis that other Labour LAs are in or entering unless they forestall this by voluntarily adjusting their agendas to suit the Central Government.

Notes

1. In addition to this study, the London Race and Housing Research Unit (LRHRU) also commissioned a study of black women's housing needs, also to be published shortly.
2. For example they quote a black women as saying
   'It would be different in India or somewhere, but here you're brought up to expect a place of your own'
   to make the peculiar argument that:
   'the last woman's comment expresses the social and cultural determination of the concept of homelessness: she would have felt differently had she been living in India, her country of birth' (p 98).
3. This is the theme of the film *Rosy the Rivetter*.
4. These deep effects cannot be elaborated here, but it is clear that 'the race card' was a factor in the election of the Conservative government in 1979. It is also apparent that spectres of 'black criminals' played a part in the public acceptance of increasing police powers, regardless of the fact that such powers compromise the civil rights of white as well as black people. The complex relations between

race, class and nation is explored further in *There Aint No Black in the Union Jack*, Gilroy, 1987.

5. In 1961 for example, white tenants organised a rent strike in Smethwick over the fact that an Asian family had been rehoused after the local authority took over their house.

6. Burney's study is a useful source on this period, since she did a case study of Lambeth. Also see Sidney Jacobs, 1985 article, 'Race, Empire and The Welfare State: Council Housing and Racism'.

7. Good sources on racism in housing in the contemporary period include Karn (1983b) 'Race and Housing in Britain: The Role of the Major Institutions' in N Glazer and K Young (eds) *Ethnic Pluralism and Public Policies* and Henderson and Karn (1987) *Race, Class and State Housing: Inequality and the Allocation of Public Housing in Britain*.

8. The Royal borough — blindness as policy

Introduction

In this chapter we present the first of the two borough studies which were conducted to enable us to look at the development of housing policy and practice on relationship breakdown and domestic violence, and the race implications of this. While our case material was limited to women who had been subjected to domestic violence, the policy study was conducted more widely — to include relationship breakdown — because in many boroughs, domestic violence policy is a development of relationship breakdown policy. There is also some mention of tenant harassment policy because this has influenced the development of domestic violence policy. Racial harassment policies are mentioned as an instance of tenant harassment policy and in recognition of the fact of racism and in particular, the frequency of race attacks by white tenants in many parts of London. The fact that race attacks have a long history in Britain (and London in particular) was one of the things that emerged in chapter 7 where we examined the struggle that black people have had to wage for housing. Elsewhere the long history of domestic violence is also highlighted, and both these areas of history form the backdrop to the present study and constitute the terrain on which public housing responses to black victims of domestic violence exist.

The Royal borough of Kensington and Chelsea was selected because it is politically Conservative, and has a significant black population. In addition, previous research attempts had been unable to extract any information about the borough's policies or practices in cases of relationship breakdown (with or without domestic violence), while reports from the voluntary sector concerning the housing department's practices in these areas were for the most part extremely negative (see chapter 10). North Kensington Women's Aid had completely broken off all relations with the Housing Needs Section at the time of the research, and workers at the Westway Housing Advice Centre were positively scathing. Local solicitors were accustomed to confronting the Housing Department's officers in the law courts over their refusal to accept people as homeless (this included victims of domestic violence).

With regard to race and gender dynamics in local authority policies and practices, the situation is one of complete suppression of information; no statistics are available, so that the numerical picture supplies very limited inferential information. There were also no written equal opportunities policy guidelines that would have facilitated the addressing of equalities considerations. This meant that to assess the race and gender implications of existing policy and practice, we had to develop a consultative research method that relied on interviews and discussions with a wide range of relevant people, rather than on a statistical profile. In addition the historical referents that feed into institutional practices were incorporated into the analysis presented below.

Historical profile: race relations in the Royal borough
Black people have resided here in significant numbers since the post-war primary immigration of the 1950s and 1960s.[1] The vast majority of the early black residents lived in cheap private rented accommodation and in multiple occupancy homes. The Royal borough of Kensington and Chelsea (RBKC) has always had a large private-rented sector and as such has been the home of immigrant and student communities over the recent historical period. It is also a borough well known for the property speculation and tenant harassment of property barons; from Rachman, whose practices as a landlord gained him notoriety in the 1950s,[2] to Baron Hoogsraten in the 1980s.

The history of race and housing in the borough merits a great deal more attention in the light of the current wider trends in housing policy, not least because it has the largest private rented sector and the highest proportion of housing association homes in London. These facts, combined with RBKC's loyalty and allegiance to the Thatcher regime in Central Government make it a good place to look for indicators of where current policies are leading.

Black access to public housing in RBKC was initially most effectively circumscribed by residency qualifications, but also through a variety of other mechanisms. The treatment of residents of properties marked out for slum clearances has long provoked outcry from black residents. Local activists assert that there has been a policy of 'removing' RBKC's black residents out of the area altogether, and a history of betrayed promises to the black tenants moved out during redevelopment and slum clearance programmes. The toleration of harassment by landlords may well have facilitated such a dispersal, but in such a way that the local state could not be held directly accountable. Administrations are seldom called to book for the excesses committed in the name of private enterprise. In this instance a 'removal policy' need not have existed, but not enforcing tenant protection legislation and indulging private speculators would ultimately have had the same effect, through illegal evictions and Rachmanism. Indeed the toleration of landlord harassment continues to the present day. At the time of writing, the Council's failure to tackle landlord harassment made headline news in the local press, with the *Kensington and Chelsea Times* publishing allegations that the Council's tenancy relations department was so short staffed it could not cope.[3] Housing Advice Centre workers point out that the council does not initiate any action against offending landlords, while tenants are often not in a position to do so. The Council confirmed that it had not had any successful prosecutions the year in which the research was conducted.

Through means that demand further investigation, the borough appears to have succeeded in concentrating many black residents in the less desirable council properties to the north of the borough, as is visibly obvious to any visitor to the borough. According to older black residents, there has also been an undocumented history of black struggle within the powerful white-dominated housing associations operating in the borough.

The Royal Borough has also been the site of more overt community conflict throughout the recent historical period. Much of this has been between the police and local black residents and their families, but there have also been attacks by elements of the white civilian population on the black residents. Notting Hill, situated to the North of the borough has the dubious distinction of having been the site of the 1958 riots, during which the black residents were subjected to mass attack by local whites and, in the initial absence of any police protection or intervention, were forced to defend themselves. The racial murder of Kelso Cochrane in May 1959, was one in a series of more isolated race attacks. His killer, like so many perpetrators of race attacks, was never found (Fryer 1984, Dadzie et al 1985).

Poor police-black community relations can be seen to have developed throughout the 1960s and early '70s, through repeated police attacks on black social and cultural events and repeated and often violent raids on private social events such as post-wedding house-parties, blues and shebeens. This police activity has often resulted in black retaliation and subsequent arrests. The regular harassment of the Mangrove Restaurant on All Saints Road led to a peaceful demonstration in August 1970 during which the arrests leading to the famous Mangrove Nine trial occurred. The Metro Youth Club was also a target for perpetual police harassment during the same period. Nor was black cultural and social life tolerated on the streets. Random stop and search and arrests of young black people by police patrols have not improved what are locally referred to as community relations.

The Black People's Information Centre was established in the early 1970s, in response to persistent police attacks on the local black community, and set about providing legal defence advice to the Caribbean community concentrated in the Northern part of Kensington and Chelsea.

The Notting Hill Carnival has increasingly become a main focus of controversy between the black community and sections of the white establishment. According to one of the earlier analysts, from 1966 onwards Carnival was actually supported by the establishment (including the police) as a welcome race relations exercise (Gutzmore 1978). In the early 1970s black and white individuals and organisations struggled over the control of the Carnival and Arts Committee. Black people as a group did not actually ever win control. Those black individuals that did penetrate the Carnival Arts Committee had the backing of more powerful local white organisations like the North Kensington Amenity Trust. Nonetheless, the cultural content of Carnival changed significantly over the years, diversifying to include militant reggae and sound systems alongside the steel bands, calypso, soul, lovers rock and salsa. There was also considerable growth, both in the size and in the international reputation of Carnival. Black and European people alike took to this more diverse contemporary display of music, masquerade and internationalism. Whereas in the Caribbean and the Americas, carnivals have always been an independent and central part of the culture, in Britain it is treated very differently by the State. Like other black social gatherings, Carnival is perceived as threatening by the establishment, and so subjected to increasingly heavy-handed policing. This struggle has continued down to the present day. It was in the mid-70s that the Council first called for its abolition, but such calls have continued, particularly from the police forces and the Conservative lobby. The production of Carnival-police violence during that period is discussed in more detail elsewhere (eg Gutzmore 1978).

210

Ten years on (1988), saw the most hysterical pre-Carnival media coverage ever, and within that we have been treated to an unabashed display of the more explicitly racial concerns around which establishment antagonism towards it have always centred. The intense hostility currently manifesting itself around this event emphasize a relationship between Carnival and 'black criminality' and the more general 'threat' that the white establishment appears to feel in relation to it.[4] In Kensington Town Hall, debates are held about the future of Carnival in an atmosphere dominated by the police and by alarmist constructions of both the event and its meaning. Racial ideas in the local area are unable to escape being tarred by the same brush.

RBKC comprises 21 Wards stretching from the Harrow Road in the North down to the river Thames in the South, and covers 1,195 hectares of valuable land. Royalty and members of the aristocracy inhabit the Central and Southern parts of the borough from Holland Park and Hyde Park down to Knightsbridge, while the armed forces can be found in Chelsea Barracks at the southern-most end of the Borough. The Conservatives hold a safe majority of seats — 39 compared to Labour's 15. In June 1986 the population was put at 137,400. There are no ethnic or racial statistics available in this Conservative stronghold, since the

Statistical Profile[5]

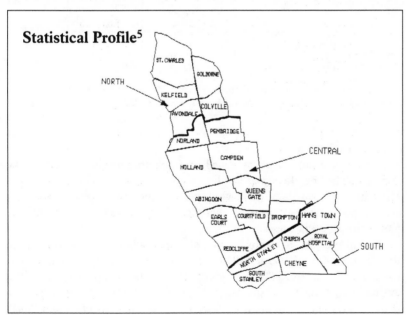

211

political leaders have held out against all forms of monitoring and operate on what officials call a 'colour blind' and 'gender blind' principle in all areas of policy. As will become clear throughout this chapter, 'blindness' is effectively a policy to mask and conceal inequalities and to stifle dissent and criticism, by simply not keeping any relevant information. As such RBKC exists beyond the racial numbers game, and yet remains preoccupied with numbers at all other levels of housing practice.[6]

There are marked class contrasts in the Royal Borough. In the affluent streets off Kensington High Street the Local Authority has luxurious properties that require a 20-year residency qualification, as part of the allocation criteria. This contrasts starkly with the extremely poor condition of the worst estates located primarily to the North of the Borough around Ladbroke Grove and towards the Harrow Road where the black population is concentrated.

RBKC has the largest private rented sector in London. Twenty nine per cent of all households fall into this category, compared to 10% in London overall. Local Authority tenants constitute only 31% of all renters in the borough (compared to 67% for London as a whole), while housing

Table 8.1 *Households by tenure type*

Tenure	Kensington & Chelsea %	London %
Owner occupier	45	54
Private renter	29	10
Local Authority	12	31
Housing Association	15	5

Source: *Housing in Kensington & Chelsea*, London Research Centre

associations (HAs) and charitable trusts account for 27% of all renters (11% for London as a whole).

The owner occupiers in the Royal Borough are for the most part in the higher income brackets and tend to have at least one person working. More than two-thirds of them were born in the UK. No other statistics are available, but it would seem that most of them are white and from the more affluent social classes.

Most of the private sector tenants are small adult households living in flats or bedsits built before 1919. Fifty per cent are headed by persons born outside the UK, 14% are students and just under a quarter have lived in the borough for less than a year. A significant but unknown proportion of private renters are migrant workers from the Mediterranean and North

Africa, and their situation is discussed elsewhere.[7] Over two-thirds of private renters have no rent book and a disturbing 12% say they have signed no written contract with their landlord. Eighteen per cent of owner occupiers and 14% of the boroughs private renters are said to have second homes.

The public sector contrasts markedly. On average LA tenants have been in the borough longer than any other tenure group. Nearly a third are pensioners, 20% are unemployed and LA tenants form the largest households in the borough with nearly a third having children. Sixty per cent of LA tenants receive total or partial assistance with their rent and rates, as compared to 15% of private renters.

Regarding the housing conditions in RBKC, the housing survey found lack or sharing of basic amenities to be almost exclusive to the private rented sector, and the worst heating problems to be amongst young private renters.

In the light of Central Government moves towards the privatisation of housing, it is noteworthy that private landlords were less often seen as ideal landlords than the council or a housing association. A startling 92% of council tenants who wanted to continue renting said that the council was their ideal landlord, while none said a private landlord. In terms of the 'Right to Buy' it is significant that nearly two-thirds of those wishing to buy could not even estimate the maximum price they could afford to pay, while a further 23% expressed a price well below that of a one-bedroom property in the Borough. Only 8% had sufficient savings for a deposit on the smallest property in the borough and 11% for a deposit elsewhere in London. Fourteen per cent had an income high enough to buy a property somewhere in London. Twelve per cent of owner occupiers had bought their property from their landlord, and only 4% had bought from the council. Eighteen per cent of council tenants had considered buying their homes. Some of these tenants had already given up the idea. In short, most of those residents who wish to buy will have found that their 'Right to Buy' may well be contingent on them removing themselves from their borough of residence, if not out of Central London altogether.

Nearly 13% of households in RBKC do not use English as their main language and a third of these felt things would be easier if the council staff could speak their language and forms were printed in their language. Spanish, Portuguese and Arabic are the commonest preferred languages.

It is striking that over 37% of the boroughs residents were born outside the UK (1981 Census).

Table 8.2 *Preferred language*

	%
Spanish	26
Portuguese	10
Arabic	10
Italian	7
Polish	4
French	5
Moroccan	2
Bengali	2
Other	34
Total	100
Sample size (prefer language other than English)	53

Source: *Housing in Kensington & Chelsea*, London Research Centre

Housing Survey included both 'Arabic' and 'Moroccan' as languages which must be an error since Moroccans speak Arabic, so that the figure for Arabic should be 12% and Moroccan not included as a separate category.

Table 8.3 *Birthplace of RBKC residents*

	Total	% Borough
UK	78,382	62
Eire	5,235	4.2
Old Commonwealth	3,409	2.7
New Commonwealth/Pakistan	9,464	7.5
Other Europe	13,764	10.9
Rest of world	15,638	12.4
Total	125,892	100

(From 1981 Census)

It should be pointed out that neither birthplace nor language figures give any real idea about the size of the black population, since they do not take account of either those who are English-speaking or those who are British born.

The invisibility of black groups is a matter of top-level policy in the borough and constitutes a major obstacle to research and understanding in the area of race and community relations in general. At the time of the research there was only one harassed and stressed officer employed in a 'community relations' capacity to handle all matters around race and

214

ethnicity for the entire borough. There is no race unit, nor any officers with a brief to work on developing race equality in policies or practices.

RBKC employs no officers to address problems of sexual inequality: there is no women's unit nor any posts with a brief to work on gender issues. The voluntary sector is similarly impoverished, with not a single women's centre operating in the entire borough, and only one women's refuge. The women's refuge is the only organisation focusing on women's interests, and as a small and highly specialised facility that is not open to the public, cannot be expected to meet the various needs of local women in any way whatsoever.

In terms of both race and gender implications of borough provisions and policies then, the picture looks bleak.

Organisational and policy aspects of RBKC housing practice

'If one person is perhaps more liberal, everybody's going to go there so there's going to be a remorseless pressure to let more get through . . . What you've got to make sure of is that the really deserving cases do get offers.' (District Manager, RBKC)

'We have a long history of only housing the really deserving.' (Head of Housing Needs, RBKC)

Both of these remarks contain assumptions that have a history, as well as reflecting certain contemporary housing concerns. In chapter 5 it was argued that throughout its history, public housing has been concerned with excluding certain sections of the public. Under the current political regime, these ancient concerns have gained new currency. For housing officers, trapped at the interface between an increasingly dishoused public and the unrelenting State, the old spectres of homeless hordes that haunted the dreams of the Victorian middle classes, have returned, and this is reflected in the attitudes and concerns of housing bureaucrats.

In RBKC court battles waged between the LA and individuals demanding housing are a source of excitement, and some officers seemed to regard them as challenges if not a kind of game or fight to be waged from the safe protection of the institution they serve. This indicated a marked insensitivity to the effects of homelessness and legal battles on clients, who were basically being regarded as 'trying it on' in pressing their demands for housing. Other (more ambivalent) individuals found them equally stimulating, but did appear to exact some sort of satisfaction from court verdicts in favour of 'the other side' (usually a homeless family). In the best known recent case, a Scottish woman, Mrs Hamner challenged the borough's refusal to house her when she fled from a violent ex-husband. At the time of the research the local authority had been ordered to house this woman, but was going to appeal to the high court for a reversal of the courts decision.

RBKC officers at management levels appear to have a significant amount of power regarding policy matters. They are confident that they will be supported in their decisions — all the way to court if necessary — by the LA and its legal department, and managers viewed themselves as having freedom to operate as long as they were acting within the law, and in ways that were politically acceptable. Both the domestic violence policy and the racial harassment policy were developed by the Head of Housing Needs and the Special Housing Needs Officer respectively — during the research period — as their initiatives and then formally approved at director and committee level. If, as in these cases, an officer chooses to respond to public pressure by drawing up a written policy, it appears s/he is free to do so and take it to the relevant committee and the director for ratification. Little opposition was anticipated from committee, since neither policy would affect the numbers of people getting housing. The researcher observed committee meetings to be conducted formally and ritualistically with little substantive debate.

The recently appointed Special Needs Officer (a black man) had an established work record within estate management before being moved to fill this post. However, if the casual treatment of his attempt to draw up a racial harassment policy by the committee is anything to go by, (members were visibly bored, most appeared not to have read the policy paper and some actually appeared to be asleep, while a single black councillor attacked it as being grossly inadequate), then it would appear that the post can at best be described as a tokenistic one lacking institutional back-up. This was perhaps not surprising, since devoting significant resources to 'special needs' (as they are termed in contemporary LA jargon) would in any case be somewhat at odds with the political will displayed in RBKC's declared gender and colour blind position on all issues and policy matters.

Policy for the most part however, is undeveloped compared to other boroughs. The law is used as a rule of thumb guiding practice to a surprising degree, in view of the ambiguity of many aspects of it. Awareness of other boroughs' policies in the area of concern seemed to be limited and underlined with contempt for 'liberalism'. Officers did

216

seem to follow case-law fairly closely; indeed they need to keep up with whatever precedents are being set by the courts, since the legal situation is what guides their practice. RBKC in general takes the most stringent possible interpretation of housing legislation, to minimise their obligations to the homeless as far as possible. Since court action is not in the overall interests of the vast majority of homeless families, this policy alone operates as a major deterrent on applications. In addition the LA fight cases tooth and nail (appealing all the way to the high court if necessary) to set precedents that will enable them not to be held to be responsible for housing particular categories of people.

Evading responsibilities to London's homeless in any way that falls short of breaking the law appears to have been a substantial concern guiding past borough practice. Solicitors practising in the area say that the borough breaks the law frequently because they know that few homeless people have the will or wherewithall to take the matter all the way to the courts, and the borough can therefore afford to be confident about shirking their responsibilities with impunity in the vast majority of cases. For their part, the acting head of the HPU complained that a particular solicitor kept taking up cases and then dropping them before the court hearing. This could be interpreted however as a case of the solicitor playing the same bluffing game by applying pressure tactics to try and force the local authority's hand in their client's interests, where the solicitor feels the LA should recognise a legal obligation to rehouse and where a client is not necessarily prepared to go through the time consuming ordeal of court procedures.

The law and how to interpret it in ways that can restrict access to public housing therefore emerges as a major consideration in RBKC housing practice. The rationale for this position predominating, rather than 'meeting people's needs' or 'delivering an equal service to all people' appears to lie in an all-pervasive concern over 'scarce resources', and the wish to ensure that only the 'really deserving' get into council properties. Who the 'really deserving' actually are remains a very grey area, and tends to be left to the discretion of officers. Competing needs arise from existing tenants (requesting transfers) and incoming tenants (homeless families). RBKC's policy states that homeless families are to be prioritised. It is however clear that lack of mobility within existing stock eventually contributes to homelessness. In particular, we found that relationship breakdown (initially a transfer problem) often develops into domestic violence and/or homelessness, so that a spiral is set up, simply by the fact that one is pitted against the other. Demands for transfers are not met on the basis that space is to be given to homeless families. The validity of pitting such different needs against one another in this way needs to be challenged, since it is around this that poor provision — which also results from bad policies and practices — are generally excused. Poor provision is also excused, and equality considerations ignored, on the basis of the Thatcher government's politics and policies which are reducing the affordable rented housing stock in both public and private sector. RBKC's rehousing strategy 1988/9 reflects this:

'The key feature of rehousing activity within the Borough is that of declining supply of low cost homes in the public and private sector. This has resulted in increased demand for diminishing public resources.'

Nobody would doubt that LAs are being encouraged, if not forced to decrease their housing stock through the introduction of more 'market forces' in all the recent housing legislation. The shuffling of who gets in to this shrinking space has become a prime concern.[8] Clearly the emphasis on priority needs and the proliferation of policies in LAs in recent years are largely about relocating and restricting access to public housing in the society. This relocation employs various criteria, but is most susceptible to discrimination in councils that do not develop equality policies and practices as a basis on which to allocate homes. In this situation, the highly dubious 'discretion' of officers is brought into play alongside their institutional concerns. Existing work has indicated 'discretion' to be the terrain on which racial discrimination is most effectively and unquestioningly reproduced (eg CRE 1984, Henderson and Kahn 1987). In other words an absence of effective policy will continue to yield and perpetuate racist practice, since all other things are not equal in 20th century Britain. Officers tend to defend discretion, not only because it empowers them in otherwise alienating jobs, but also against what they experience as excessive bureaucratisation ('paperwork'). This is a key area in which officers resist race and gender equality. For this reason the methods through which policies are implemented need to be evaluated in ways that identify and tackle sources of frontline resistance rather than simply dismissing such officers as 'anti-progressive'.

In the area of policies on relationship breakdown and domestic violence, most boroughs have developed policies that go well beyond their legal obligations and onto the terrain of identifying needs and trying to respond to them in ways that minimize the suffering of homelessness or impossible living conditions. RBKC however has not invested time or resources into

218

developing more humane policies. Nor has the borough taken up the policy initiatives already developed in other boroughs. Yet there is little hesitation in investing resources in fighting cases in court, which must be one of the more expensive ways of developing policy.

There is evidence in committee reports (supported by the Housing Advice Centre workers) to suggest that RBKC had in the past successfully evaded its obligations to rehouse homeless families through imposing a three-year residency requirement. This was reduced to 12 months as recently as 1986 on new applications and meant that until that time families accepted as statutorily homeless could be precluded from local housing. Instead they were forcibly relocated through the Greater London Mobility Scheme (GLMS). GLMS was designed to facilitate transfers between boroughs, and the abuse of its facilities by some boroughs, who used it as a 'dumping ground' for homeless families, was one of the factors that has resulted in quotas for some boroughs being more substantially reduced than others in recent years. RBKC's quota was reduced from a maximum of 462 in 1983/4 to 70 in 1987. In 1987 the London Area Mobility Scheme's (LAMS) Members' steering group approved measures aimed at 'restricting the forcible relocation of homeless households.' These recommendations curtail residency requirements of individual boroughs and so will have a limiting effect on the extent to which the borough can forcibly nominate on to LAMS the families it has had to accept as statutorily homeless.

Women's Aid found it necessary to refuse to accept any direct referrals from RBKC both to the local refuge, and to the London Office, to prevent a similar abuse of refuge provision by the Royal Borough. The Homeless Persons Unit (HPU) had developed a tactic of making women go into refuge as a matter of course before being considered for rehousing, and regardless of whether they required the particular facilities that Women's Aid provide. This tactic had the effect of filling up London's already inadequate refuge provision with women not requiring that facility, and so effectively depriving women needing their specialist support. This, combined with the housing department's extremely unsympathetic treatment of those who have experienced domestic violence led to a complete breakdown of communications between the refuge and the department. At the time of the research, the refuge workers and housing officers were still not on speaking terms. This meant that no women from the refuge were being rehoused locally, which had dire consequences for some of the women we interviewed.

219

From all this it is evident that 'gatekeeping' is a major preoccupation of many aspects of RBKC housing policy. Regulating the access of 'outsiders' from other boroughs to their limited and shrinking housing stock was described as a main concern of frontline officers, whom the Head of Housing Needs described as being resistant to some policy developments because of their being haunted by a fear that hordes of people from all over London will start swarming over their desks. This did not seem to be a rational fear, since RBKC's HPU was one of the quietest and emptiest the researcher visited. One can only conclude that this particular spectre was part of the institutional ethos taken up by officers, to such an extent that they have managed to reduce public demands on the Homeless Persons Unit.

RBKC is one of London's smallest boroughs, so that the managerial and bureaucratic inefficiencies dogging larger LAs are bound to exist to a lesser extent. The Council's expressed primary aim is:

'to fulfil its statutory duties towards the homeless and decants . . . to consider its role as the largest single landlord while maintaining its social objectives of meeting need within the wider community.'[9]

The same report proposes a target of meeting all demands from homeless households (recognised as such in accord with the stringent criteria employed). Yet RBKC's rehousing strategy for 1988/9 identifies the key feature of all rehousing activity as being the 'declining supply of low cost homes in the public and private sector'. In other words there is increased demand for diminishing resources that will further diminish under current Central Government housing policies. This means in turn that there is no prospect of 'meeting need' whatsoever. Nor is there any prospect of scarce resources being expended on equal opportunities considerations. More particularly there is no prospect of any improvement in their treatment of women and particularly black women, seeking housing away from violence.

Statistical indicators of RBKC housing practice

The figures on households in temporary accommodation in RBKC[10] indicate an increase of nearly 100% over the two-year period between October 1985 and September 1987. This is in keeping with the overall housing crisis that inner London is experiencing. The only type of temporary accommodation not showing this increase were RBKC's own hostels, presumably because there has not been any increase in provision over the period, so that a growing proportion of the boroughs increasing homeless households are in bed and breakfast hotels, voluntary hostels, short life and Women's Aid hostels located in various parts of London.

In the year 1987/8, 298 statutorily homeless households were rehoused within the council supply (RBKC stock, Housing Associations and nominations via mobility schemes). This figure represented 73% of the recorded homeless demand, and 92% of the recorded demand identified within the year. As noted above, applications are only accepted (and therefore on record) if the interviewing officer feels there may be a statutory obligation on the borough to rehouse them. The above figures then are not an acceptable estimate of homelessness in the borough.

Time spent in temporary accommodation in the year is reported as averaging 17.25 weeks (just over four months) in the year 1986/7, a period not at all representative of refuge residents at the time of the study. Refuge workers put the average time of stay in their facility at 12-18 months. The figures are not directly comparable however, since a sizeable proportion of refuge residents are not accepted onto the borough's waiting lists in the first place, and so are not on the borough's records and are never rehoused locally. Out of those households in temporary accommodation between April-Sept 1987, only 35% were deemed to be eligible for permanent rehousing, as compared to 65% who were not. The destinations of 52.6% of those in temporary accommodation during the same period were not known, since no records are kept of where people evicted from temporary accommodation by RBKC go to. Of those who were rehoused, only 27% were allocated RBKC dwellings and 5% into HA homes. Only 4% were housed through LAMS (presumably as a result of the quota reduction). The rest returned to a previous home or obtained private accommodation and one household returned to an institution.

Of the 396 people who applied for temporary accommodation during the same six month period (April-Sept 1987), 27 (almost 7%) are on record as having done so on the basis of having had a violent dispute with their spouse or cohabitee. Twenty four of these were admitted, only five (1%) on the basis of a non-violent dispute, and two of these were admitted into temporary accommodation by the borough. One cannot conclude from these low figures that domestic violence and marital breakdown are not occurring in the borough. Rather these figures indicate that not many women appealing to RBKC's housing department on this basis get on to the statistics. An inestimable number probably do not appeal to the housing department at all, some of these will remain in the violent situation, because they have nowhere to go and no hope of getting

221

alternative accommodation. We did indeed come across one such woman who remained in an extremely abusive situation, with an alcoholic Englishman, after having her appeals for separate housing rejected. In view of the preceding discussion of the department's policy and ethos to date, and the refuge workers experiences of women's housing prospects in the borough, it would appear that in RBKC most women who have been abused are unlikely to get beyond the front door. This situation would particularly apply to black women who are likely to be perceived as undeserving in any case.

One may conclude from the above figures that the borough can afford to be congratulated on its efficiency as compared to other inner London Boroughs, but such congratulations can only be in terms of the borough's internal logic. All the above figures are in the first instance products of existing borough policy. They cannot be used to evaluate the treatment of homeless families by the borough, and far less to evaluate the more specific treatment and processing of women seeking accommodation as a result of relationship breakdown and/or domestic violence. Nor can they indicate levels of need arising from these sources, in the Royal borough. While the statistics they do keep are accurately compiled and accessibly presented, and undoubtedly serve their bureaucratic functions quite well, they are of no use in assessing the policies themselves, since they are a reflection of those policies. They are also of no use in determining the impact of the borough's policies on women as compared to men, or on black people/ethnic minorities.

Policy and practice on relationship breakdown and domestic violence

Prior to 1988 there was no written policy either on relationship breakdown or on domestic violence. Instead a series of practices had developed out of the casework of the housing department.

As in other LAs, relationship breakdown and domestic violence cases come to the attention of officers through one of two routes, each of which have their own criteria and systems for dealing with such applicants. Either they approach estate officers, usually as tenants requesting transfers, and may then be referred up to estate manager level and then to the district manager. Or they approach the department through the Homeless Persons Unit. Once a request has been accepted and approved, it will be dealt with by the allocations department which is situated within the Housing Needs Section. The Head of Housing Needs and the District Managers report to the Assistant Director of Housing and Property Services.

The Homeless Persons Unit

The emptiness of the HPU mentioned above was explained by a Housing Advice Centre worker (and verified by a district manager) as follows. Many people are passed to the overcrowded Housing Advice Centre (HAC) by the housing department. The poor prospect of even getting hold of a form to fill in appears to have disheartened the public to such a degree that only those with the most hard and fast cases will even bother to attempt to get housing at all. Applications that will not be granted are not recorded. Applicants are told that there is no hope and they are not given the form to fill in at that stage. Even if they insist on filling in an application, it will be discarded and not recorded. It is in this context that the efficiency indicated by the borough's rehousing statistics should be qualified.

Applicants are interviewed by officers to determine their eligibility for housing. As will now be apparent, the most stringent criteria that are thought to be acceptable under the law are applied in determining whether an application form will even be given to the applicant to fill, and then again before their application is actually registered. RBKC will not house anyone who they are not obliged to house under the Homeless Persons Act. While the residential criteria used to forcibly remove homeless households from the borough in the past have been reduced, the attitudinal legacy of that policy appears to persist in their practice. In the context of this research, the same stringency was being applied to rehousing victims of domestic violence, a fact which places RBKC amongst the least sympathetic London Boroughs in their policy. Prospects for any real change in this or any other area look bleak, since meeting very narrowly interpreted statutory obligations has been prioritised. This means that only legal precedents will affect existing RBKC practice and thus many demands for housing will have to be backed up by specialist legal advice to be effective. At the same time, as late as 1988, there were properties earmarked for 'ex-higher income earners' with a 20 year residency qualification governing access. Many of these were empty because those eligible could not cope with the stairs as a result of their age.

The ethnic breakdown of HPU staff indicates a usual pattern. There are some black staff but this cannot seriously be taken as a significant index of racial implications of policy and practice, since within the

223

organisation black individuals are not empowered; they too have jobs to keep and hierarchies to conform to within the bureaucracy.

Once an application is filled and accepted by the borough, homeless families are placed in temporary accommodation pending rehousing (see table above).

Few people approached the HPU on the basis of non-violent relationship breakdown (we noted above that in the six month period April-Sept 1987 five applications were recorded and only two of these were admitted to temporary accommodation). Any such applications would have been assessed on the basis of RBKC's narrow interpretation of the legislation on homeless people generally, and would very likely not be regarded as homeless. They would face problems proving that they cannot return home if their partner has not had a long and legally documentable history of violently attacking them to the point where they fall into the domestic violence category (see below). Under the legislation (1980) granting security of tenure to LA tenants, relationship breakdown is not a ground for terminating a tenancy, so that RBKC are not under any legal obligation to do anything as the landlord. Relationship breakdown is not treated as grounds for issuing a new tenancy in RBKC.

In the cases where there has been violence, there was a similar lack of policy until 1988. While the researcher was conducting her enquiries in the latter half of 1988, NACRO held a public meeting to address the problem of domestic violence in RBKC. Representatives of various organisations that encounter the problems were present, and it was attended by representatives from the Housing Needs section, who were subjected to the righteous outrage of solicitors, refuge workers and residents, and others. The Head of Housing Needs, clearly in a hot seat, then announced that a policy had been drawn up and would be made available to interested parties.

The policy document however, does not go beyond a careful interpretation of the existing legislation, with a few public relations considerations added to ensure that the existing legislation is implemented as smoothly and humanely as possible.

The most significant development it does contain concerns recourse to the law. Previously borough practice had developed along what can only be described as the most punitive possible route, often with highly damaging effects on victims of domestic violence:

'women were requested to take recourse in legal remedies and obtain a non-molestation order or ouster and return to their home. Failure to

224

take such action frequently resulted in temporary accommodation being withdrawn and no long term housing duty being owed.'[11]

Women who refused to be coerced into taking legal action were likely to be defined as 'intentionally homeless' and therefore not eligible for rehousing. Women who left their homes to escape violence and gave up their existing tenancy before being accepted by RBKC as statutorily homeless were likely to be similarly defined. This account of what has prevailed is supported by voluntary sector workers and solicitors who also pointed out the inestimable damage that this practice has caused to women and their children. The brand new policy states that insistence on legal recourse should not be considered as the only remedy and no-one should be forced to take legal action and return to their home against their will. Rather women's perception of the problem is to be given more consideration — on paper at least. The questions about how this development is to be implemented cannot be answered at this stage.

At the public meeting, where this change was announced, scathing disbelief was the reaction of some of those present (particularly refuge workers and solicitors — those most in the know in their daily work), and lawyers stated that they were at that time handling cases where the victim of violence was still being forced to take legal action. Clearly the new policy had not been applied at that time.

The written policy does not address the definition of women who abandon existing tenancies, and if existing practice is not changed, such women will presumably continue to be defined as intentionally homeless.

What I have referred to as public relations aspects of the policy paper also include:

— Requests to be seen by a woman adviser are to be 'honoured wherever possible', and advisors are told not to request to see injuries.

— If she is too distressed to be interviewed, only basic information is to be taken down and there is provision for her to be placed in temporary accommodation for not more than two days and for an appointment arranged within that time. Failure to keep that appointment will result in cancellation of the temporary accommodation unless there are 'extenuating circumstances'. These are not specified.

— The need for speed of action is stressed, particularly if the woman needs to take out injunctions to return to her previous home.

The main limitations of the policy are spelt out in the discussion at the end of this chapter.

Estate management: no transfers away from violence

The district manager we interviewed was unaware of the HPU's written policy on domestic violence. The following excerpts from that interview indicate what the practice of estate managers is.

'If there's a relationship breakdown, we don't actually rehouse both parties or either party. What we essentially say is that that's a matter for them to sort out. They have to decide between the two of them what they're going to do about it.'

'We would obviously have regard for the children. Obviously we would expect whoever stays to accept responsibility for providing a home for the children. That's one of the reasons why they got accommodation in the first place.'

'If the man was refusing to move out, and perhaps she was coming to us saying he was being anti-social or something, we would advise her of the remedies available to her — obviously if there was a crime being committed then the police should be involved.'

'The policy is that they must sort it out themselves.'

Although there is no written policy on relationship breakdown, both the district manager and the special needs officer (an ex-district manager) were quite clear on how they treated cases, and confidently referred to their practice as the policy.

Since the domestic violence policy focuses on homelessness and the provision of temporary accommodation it does not in any case address the housing management problems that arise from domestic violence, prior to a woman actually becoming homeless.

District managers appeared not to be aware of the policy. This combined with the fact that it does not address the housing demands that are made through estate officers, suggests that the Estate Management and Housing Needs sections of the Housing Department function quite separately. However, recommendations for transfers that are approved at district manager level (of estate management), or by the Assistant Director of Housing and Property Services, go to the allocations section which is part of the Housing Needs section. Some consistency at the policy level, at least regarding definitions of homelessness, would be necessary to prevent people being passed between the two departments due to their differing interpretations of the policy, or of the legislation.

226

It is safe to conclude that for the time being the prevailing practice in the management of requests for transfers on grounds of relationship breakdown or domestic violence, has not been altered by the writing down of the domestic violence policy in Housing Needs Section. Still it appears instead to rely on managers' interpretation of the legislation. Since district managers both work out of the same Town Hall Office, they are likely to confer and have very similar positions. In the course of discussions, the police and legal provisions were referred to constantly by managers, and it emerged that referring women elsewhere — to the police, law centres and advice centres, was the dominant practice.

At the most general level, the percentage of tenant transfer requests being met has fallen significantly in recent years. Only those applications with a 'recognised priority' are currently likely to be successful. Competing demand from homeless families is most commonly given as an explanation for this decline, although it has also been attributed to decreasing opportunities through housing association and mobility schemes.[12]

Allocations reflect the broader housing strategy which prioritises demands from homeless households and decants. Rehousing through the waiting list has similarly declined as a result of its low priority within the allocations system. Projections for 1988/9 advocate increasing the emphasis on homeless families in the allocations strategy, with correspondingly poor prospects for transfers (steady at 0% of the net supply) and waiting list applicants (from 36%-24% of net supply).

The problems that are presented to and dealt with through the estate management channel are by and large those that exist prior to one or other party actually becoming homeless as a result of relationship breakdown and/or domestic violence, and do demand a different response from the housing department.

If a woman (with or without children) approaches her estate officer saying she cannot return home she will be referred to the HPU if she is thought to fall under RBKC's interpretation of their statutory obligations to the homeless. At the HPU she will be assessed and then processed according to the practises of that department. Alternatively she may be referred to the Housing Advice Centre on the basis that she is no longer a housing management problem since she is homeless.

If she does not appear to fall into RBKC's interpretation of who is statutorily homeless — for example if her word is doubted and she has no legal evidence to support her claim, or if she has no children, or if she is not recognised as a tenant, she will be referred to the law centre and perhaps advised to take recourse to the courts to resolve her situation. She will not be transferred, or referred to the HPU.

Women who have not yet been forced to abandon their homes, but are going through non-violent relationship breakdown and no longer wish to live with their partners will be told that housing is a matter for them to decide between themselves. The borough accepts no obligation to rehouse anyone as a result of relationship breakdown. The couple have to reach their own decision over who retains the tenancy, and the departing partner cannot expect to be housed in the borough from whom they have been renting accommodation If both parties refuse to abandon the tenancy (perhaps because they both find it economically impossible to obtain other accommodation), the housing assistants will suggest that the children be considered; in other words the partner providing a home for them should be given priority.

In terms of enforcing this advice, there are no measures taken, and no policy that any should be taken. If there is no violence, then there are no legal remedies available to the couple. Even if they get a divorce, the housing problem will be dealt with as part of the settlement and most likely the person winning custody will be awarded the tenancy. If the couple are not married, or not divorcing, there is no legal remedy for their housing problem, and single adults (men or women) are not counted as statutorily homeless, so that there is no LA obligation to house them.

In instances where the man becomes violent, the response is not much different. Women contacting their estate officer will be advised to contact the police or other legal agencies 'if there is a crime being committed' and take legal action, regardless of the documented fact that this may not only not assist, but may actually put battered women at greater risk (chapter 6). They will not be recommended to management for a transfer unless they provide substantial corroborating evidence. Battered women are not a recognised priority category.

The policy is to refer a woman to legal agencies to take court action to oust a violent man — an option rejected by most women in this study as likely to endanger their lives, or at least fail to resolve the problem. Ouster injunctions are in any case an extremely difficult thing to obtain. In many cases such a move often merely alters a woman's situation from being a victim of domestic violence to being a victim of 'violence from outside the home', which is in some ways an even worse position both legally (chapter 6) and in terms of rehousing possibilities.

The harassment clauses in the tenancy agreement are also referred to. Here again these can only be enforced by the law. There were no cases in

Royal Borough memory where a woman had succeeded in having a violent man evicted on the basis that violence constitutes harassment. In fact the District Manager had such difficulty in comprehending the question that he suggested that we discuss 'noise nuisance' instead, because that was something he had experience of. The possible racial implications of that diversion will not be gone into here.

The tenants handbook mostly devotes five times more space (one third of a page as compared to one and one third pages) to noise nuisance than to family break-up. The same small amount of space is devoted to 'Gardens and Flower Boxes'. On domestic violence (under 'Family Break-up') it has very little indeed:

'In any emergency (for example, if you are threatened with violence) call at the local Social Services Office. Outside normal office hours go to your local police station.'(p4)

If a request for a management transfer got as far as the District Manager's desk (which is described as a rare occurrence and no figures are kept), he told us that it would not be considered without substantial corroborating evidence. If this was available, then he would recommend it to the Assistant Director of Housing for approval. If sufficient evidence is not furnished with the request, it 'may or may not' be asked for. Presumably if it is not made available and not asked for, the request will not be considered.

When asked if there were any circumstances in which he would actually recommend a management transfer in the case of women being subjected to domestic violence the District Manager answered thus:

'I think it would be fair to say that where we get into the area of management transfers — where I would recommend to the assistant directorate for a management transfer, is where somebody has gone down those avenues. Perhaps they've been to the police — we've had cases where they have been to the police and somebody's been locked up for six months, there have been injunctions against them and still he comes back. They've really explored all avenues they can and they genuinely still have got a problem. That's the sort of area.'

The rationale for such apparently inhumane and suspicious criteria was also provided:

'If you haven't got the properties to offer, then the really genuine cases

229

are in the league with everybody else aren't they? I used to work for Greenwich so I know.'

This position does suggest an underlying assumption that there are significant numbers of cases that are not in fact 'genuine', and this is a preoccupation that has not been, and is not likely to be challenged in RBKC as it has been in other boroughs. It is not a belief supported by any real evidence that women are in the habit of faking physical abuse in an attempt to deceive the Council into providing them with accommodation. Our discussion of the history of public housing did indicate however that this attitude towards the public has deep roots in the class and racial antagonisms of British society.

Discussion

RBKC's housing policies and practice, regarding women who are subjected to domestic violence, are unsympathetic if not harsh. There is no uniform policy across the different sections responsible for housing allocations (HPU and Estate Management). Instead the HPU has a newly written policy, while estate managers continue to use the stringent criteria described, basically not granting transfers to women tenants who are being assaulted by the men they live with. Becoming homeless is therefore the only option RBKC offers to the vast majority of battered women, including those who do follow the advice and take initial legal action.

This is a pity, to say the least. Treating housing needs at the transfer stage would forestall a great deal of the suffering that homelessness inflicts on women and children who have become so desperate that they have fled their home to escape from intolerable if not life-threatening situations. Obtaining a transfer on the basis of relationship breakdown could also prevent the situation degenerating into physical violence. Being forced to live together (perhaps in overcrowded conditions) long after a relationship has broken down features significantly in the causes of domestic violence. In RBKC it would appear that men can actually force a woman out of her home with impunity. Worse still, situations arise in which this is the aim behind the abuse. In one of our cases the husband, after many years of marriage adopted this strategy following his decision to buy their home in order that he could sell what had become a valuable property on the private market. In pursuing this strategy, he went to the extent of bringing other men in to sexually harass his wife, now in her 50s.

230

The limited access that women have to housing has to be counted amongst the things that lead a man to feel he can violently assault the woman he lives with. The evidence suggests that he is right to be confident that neither the law nor the LA will not do anything to him, and that his victim will have nowhere to escape to. If she does run away, he can remain confident that she will eventually be forced to return, humbled by her experience of long term homelessness and her treatment by the housing department. This is particularly true if they live in RBKC or any of the other boroughs that stand on the narrowest interpretations of the law. The option of living separately would militate against violence in the first place and reduce the likelihood of it being tolerated thereafter.

Housing management has a major role to play at these preventative levels, long before the victims — women and children — are subjected to the suffering that we have documented. This argument presumes, or demands that housing management include some level of social responsibility.

RBKC's written domestic violence policy only applies to married or cohabiting couples, where women are being subjected to violence from the man with whom they live. This is minimal in comparison to other boroughs who also recognise that women may need to be rehoused as a result of violence from a man they do not (or no longer) live with. This situation is categorised by RBKC as 'violence from outside the home' and is not covered by the policy. When questioned on this matter, the HPU's acting Head described a hypothetical scenario in which a man could go down a street banging on all the doors and the borough would be obliged to rehouse all the women in those homes. This suggested an alarming lack of awareness, as well as a quite unsympathetic attitude.[13]

Violence from in-laws and other relatives does not qualify for consideration under the policy as it stands, which has definite ethnic implications. Lesbian and gay couples are not mentioned at all in the policy.

Women who do not have children will not be rehoused. The most they can hope for under the new policy is two days in temporary accommodation, and to be informed of their legal rights (which do not include any obligation on the LA to rehouse them).

Mental cruelty will not generally be considered as cause for permanent rehousing under the domestic violence policy because as the borough sees it, 'this is a very difficult area as it is difficult for the Housing Adviser and indeed the law courts to make judgement.' This most clearly excludes all cases of non-violent relationship breakdown where the woman no longer finds it possible to continue living with their partner. This covers the vast majority of cases, since thankfully not all relationship breakdowns include violent assaults on the woman. This does not mean that her life will not have been made intolerable: beating is only the crudest exercise of power; for many women the emotional anguish is far harder to bear (as the present research supported).

Several points are made in RBKC's new policy document concerning whether previous injunctions have been taken out. The document correctly notes the fact that some women may not feel protected by such measures, and that non-molestation orders may in some cases place them at greater risk. However, while the document draws attention to these facts, it does not specify how cases should be treated.

The 'new' domestic violence policy does not attempt to effect any fundamental changes. It emerges that it will continue to be the norm to keep women in temporary accommodation pending legal settlement, 'unless deemed reasonable to do otherwise in consultation with senior officers'. Nothing is said about what should be done in cases where legal action is not taken, as may frequently be the case where the couple were not married, or the woman simply does not wish to take legal action immediately. Failure to address this issue concretely, leaves open the possibility that her rehousing prospects will continue to be jeopardised in cases where she is not taking legal action against her assailant/partner.

From our own research, this has clear ethnic implications: many women do not file for divorce for religious and cultural reasons, even though they will remain permanently separated from their spouse. Furthermore cohabiters do not have all the same legal provisions available to them under civil law, regarding both injunctions and settlements. Others are not protected by civil law at all because they do not cohabit with their assailant. More generally, women made homeless by violence frequently do not recover sufficiently to engage in court battles for many months after they have left home. This means that under the 'new' policy, they will not be eligible for rehousing until proceedings have not only been initiated but completed; a process which may take several years. In addition, the stress and hardship of temporary accommodation are likely to militate against women recovering, since one ordeal is often simply replaced by a set of other social problems arising out of her poor accommodation situation.

The new policy also notes that in the case of owner-occupiers it may take considerable time to establish what equity will be forthcoming from the marital home and suggests therefore that it may be relevant to consider this and anticipate the settlement and whether this is likely to be sufficient to secure a home for the woman! This would appear to be very dubious terrain: housing officers are hardly in any position to anticipate the results of often highly complicated divorce court proceedings, let alone to make decisions on that basis that will have major effects on people's lives.

Regarding violence from outside the home, the policy document advises that in case of violent husbands trying to force entry or threatening to murder one of their woman tenants, it may be appropriate 'only in exceptional cases' to offer temporary accommodation for one or two nights, while legal action is taken. In other words it is clearly not regarded as a housing problem. Instead the buck is passed over to legal agencies and the borough accepts no responsibility for the safety of its tenants in such cases beyond a night or two in a hotel or hostel, and that for exceptional cases only. She will not be regarded as homeless and her likelihood of being granted a transfer as discussed below, is also negligible.

Regarding implementation of the domestic violence policy as it stands, eight of the interviewing officers (all women) had been to Chiswick Family Rescue for training on domestic violence. We are not in a position to comment on how effective and appropriate that may have been with respect to the particular policy in question.

When asked about the ethnic implications of the policy, however, the Housing Needs and HPU officers confessed frankly that they had not thought about that at all.

Conclusion

In the absence of independent documentation, the accusations of community activists, old residents and advice centre workers are hard to substantiate, but they do indicate community perceptions. In Kensington and Chelsea, these sources for the most part reflect widespread dissatisfaction with the housing department. This was something the community relations officer and some housing staff were aware of, but excused on the basis that it was beyond their power to do much about it. This may well be the case, but in the meantime such an attitude merely serves to excuse and justify the practice of the housing department staff. As we noted, other staff were less concerned about community attitudes, accepting it as something that came 'with the job' as it were.

The evidence from housing management implies an underlying attitude that relationship breakdown and domestic violence are not the business of housing management, but should be dealt with by individuals or, if they can't 'sort it out for themselves', by the police and legal system, or perhaps by social services. Our discussion of the legal responses to domestic violence and relationship breakdown, through both civil and criminal law , indicate s that law enforcement officers also feel that it is not their problem if the matter can in any way be designated as 'domestic'. Even if they do respond, the housing problems remain. Clearly what we have is a case of social institutions that have some of the power and the means to make provisions in the interests of citizens, passing the buck and refusing to accept such a role. This is a political position that has gained ascendance under the present regime, and which underlies the erosion of public housing. Happily not all LAs have taken such an extreme position on relationship breakdown and domestic violence, as we shall see in the next chapter.

Notes

1. See Peach 1968 and Glass and Pollins 1960.
2. Rachmanism, the term used to describe the ousting of longstay tenants through coercive means (moving in anti-social neighbours, allowing property to deteriorate below any level of human decency etc), owes its currency to that particular private investor.
3. *Kensington and Chelsea Times*, 28.10.88. no 288.
4. The exploitation of the spectre of 'black crime' by government was documented some time ago (Hall et al 1978). Yet the same card was played to usher in the Police and Criminal Evidence Act after the inner city disturbances of the early 1980s.
5. Main sources used here were RBKC's 1988 Housing Survey; 1981 Population Census; interviews and correspondence with housing department officers.
6. This is a reference to the preoccupation with numbers in the immigration legislation and subsequent internal controls discussed in earlier chapters (and see Peach 1968).
7. LRHRU commissioned a project on the housing situation of migrant workers in RBKC, the results of which were made available to the researcher (forthcoming LRHRU publication).
8. See LRHRU's Housing Allocations Project research report.
9. Report by the Director of Housing and Property Services to the Health and Housing Committee 16th May 1988).
10. Statistics supplied from RBKC's own reports.
11. RBKC Written Policy on Domestic Violence, 1988.
12. See 1987/8 Director of Housing's Report.
13. The court case between RBKC and Mrs Hammel in 1988 was over this matter: Mrs Hammel sought housing near her sister (local connection fulfilled) on the basis that her ex-husband continued to subject her to harassment that made

234

it necessary for her to leave. The borough regards her as intentionally homeless and when the court rendered a verdict in her favour, officers said they would be appealing to the High Court for this to be reversed. This suggests the 'floodgate theory' was motivating officers to take quite extreme positions and fight for them all the way to the top.

9. Lambeth — policies struggling towards equality

Introduction

Lambeth was selected for the comparative study in contrast to Kensington and Chelsea because it is politically Labour, and therefore has been involved with the equality initiatives that Labour boroughs have developed. Lambeth Council has promoted equality initiatives directed at various social groups; black people, women, lesbians, gays and people with disabilities and the effectiveness and appropriateness of equal opportunities policies is being constantly discussed. Such policies, and the availability of material places the London Borough of Lambeth in a far more advanced position, compared to RBKC. Like RBKC, Lambeth has a significant black population. In contrast to RBKC, social and demographic information on the black and ethnic minority population is not suppressed or left out of research reports, as will be evident below. Since policies on race and gender equality exist and are being developed and implemented in a number of policy areas, there is also substantially more information available for a discussion of the specific policies on relationship breakdown and domestic violence, and their race implications. Several of the women in this study were tenants of Lambeth, and their evidence suggests that, for them at least, the policies have not enabled them to obtain decent accommodation. Rather it seems that many black women still remained homeless for very long periods, and were then only being offered squalid and overcrowded accommodation. During the research period there was a team of local authority officers and voluntary sector workers — the Women At Risk Team, which was working on development and implementation of the written policy on rehousing women at risk of violence.

Historical profile: race relations in Lambeth

In contrast to RBKC there has been some research and writing on Lambeth's black communities. Early studies were very much from the white liberal race relations perspective of the 1950s and '60s (eg Burney 1967, Glass 1960). Nevertheless, the struggle that black communities had in getting access to housing has at least been documented in the Lambeth area (see Burney, cited above).

The *Empire Windrush* brought the first shipload of 492 Jamaican workers to Britain, arriving at Tilbury docks on 2 June 1948. They were accommodated in Lambeth, in the Clapham air-raid shelter, since although they had been recruited to work in Britain no accommodation was provided for them (as noted in chapter 7), and they were to remain virtually completely excluded from public housing until the Race Relations Act of 1968. Early immigrants looking for accommodation were therefore left to the private sector, where they encountered what was then called a 'colour bar' in which 'Whites only' signs were put up all over London (Glass 1960). Legislation later made such open displays of racism illegal, but racial discrimination in the private sector continues through landlords' prerogatives, and through the professional practices of mortgage companies and estate agents. Black people were charged extra for being offered anything at all, or were met with apologetic grimaces and slammed doors. The areas in which black people did find homes during the 1950s and '60s were by and large those already being abandoned by the white working class, many of whom were now able to move to more salubrious areas — the suburban parts of the borough around Streatham, Norwood, Herne Hill and Dulwich. Black people, on the other hand, were restricted to cheap lodgings and multiple occupancy dwellings in the old Victorian houses in the most run-down parts of Lambeth, mostly in and around the Brixton area.

Public housing remained closed to the majority of black people through various bureaucratic devices. There is evidence for example, to suggest that Housing and Public Health legislation was only selectively enforced, along racial lines. As Patterson (1965) noted, the overcrowding provisions of the Public Health Act were not enforced by Lambeth council because 'any coloured person evicted would have gained priority on the housing list'. Jacobs (1985) cites other examples of councils unashamedly giving racial reasons for adjusting policy specifically to ensure that they did not house 'too many' black people. Slum clearance programmes often avoided the areas where black people were concentrated. Such strategies ensured that black people continued to live in the most squalid conditions, and remained vulnerable to landlord harassment and victimisation, not to mention poor health.

Burney (1967) describes Lambeth Council as having adopted a defeatist attitude towards black people from the start. Patterson (1965) also notes that the local authority pandered to racist paranoia, constantly reassuring locals that they would not 'favour' those black people who did get onto the waiting lists. She quotes Councillor Nathan Marock in 1955 as saying:

'Even though some coloured families are living in miserable conditions, they will get no more housing priority than the people of Lambeth'

Clearly black people were not 'people of Lambeth' to his mind, a least when it came to housing. Yet at the same time the Council were using the black presence in Lambeth to lobby for money from Central Government.

In 1965 Lambeth, along with other boroughs with sizeable black populations, came high on the Milner Holland list of rapidly deteriorating boroughs (Milner Holland Report 1965). Soon after publication, the borough stated their case to visiting Labour party dignitaries (Mr Mellish, Head of the London Labour Party and Mr Foley, Minister responsible for Race Relations at the Home Office), so making explicit the argument that a black presence produced the housing problems that had actually long preceded their arrival. When this appeal failed, the borough continued not to do anything about the appalling conditions in which black people were forced to live. Instead they concentrated on using the housing shortage as a justification for racism. Council officers upheld widespread societal racism, and perpetuated it by dutifully translating it into their policies. A housing officer involved in the scandalous Geneva-Somerleyton Road slum clearance in the '60s expressed the attitude succinctly:

'We lean over backwards not to give them facilities that other people in clearance areas don't have. Once you give them better property, they won't have anything else' (Burney 1967 p144).

The Council also published a pamphlet blaming immigration for the intolerable housing situation in the borough.

If Labour administrators in Labour boroughs like Lambeth were racist and exploitative in their relationship with local black communities during this period, Conservative ones were very likely worse. However, as we saw in our discussion of Kensington and Chelsea in the last chapter, comparable material is not available because information has continuously been suppressed, and comparable research has not been conducted or published.

During the 1970s the problem of black homelessness continued. Squatting, originally a middle class response to housing shortage, was taken up by homeless young black people in the Lambeth area. *Race Today* reported over 100 black youth occupying empty council properties in 1975 (*Race Today* 1975). These were for the most part single people who the council was (and is) under no obligation to accommodate, and who continue to face the greatest housing problems. In recent years a number of hostels have been established in Lambeth, some of which specifically accommodate young black people.

More recently some work has been produced by black organisations engaged in publishing (Race Today Collective, Black Ink). The existence of black publishers, bookshops (such as that run by the Sabaar Collective on Railton Road) and writers' collectives in the Brixton area made Lambeth something of a focal point for black cultural organisation in the '70s and early '80s. Community centres like the Abeng Centre also hosted numerous black social, political and cultural events.

The Black Women's Group started in 1973, and eventually established the first black women's centre in London in Brixton in 1980. Lambeth was a place where black women first set up organisational roots. Early campaigns about the various abuses of black women were waged from this base during the early 1980s, through the Brixton Black Women's Group, the Black Single Parents Project, the Black Female Prisoners Scheme and the Black Young Families Project. There were a number of other black campaigning groups set up in the area, tackling problems of state repression (like Blacks Against State Harassment (BASH)). Later the Brixton Defence Campaign arose out of police brutality and abuses of civil liberties before, during and after the so-called Brixton riots of 1981.

Police-community relations in Lambeth have not been good in recent years. The Brixton area in particular has been the focus of the particularly coercive and intrusive policing practices that have been indicted for provoking the civil disturbances that later erupted in other inner-city areas around the country (see eg The Scarman Report 1981). Community policing was born out of the acknowledgement, brought about by mass resistance to the police, of the drawbacks of blatantly repressive policing practices.

The shooting of Mrs Cherry Groce in the back by the police during a raid on her home in Brixton left her paralysed and confined to a wheelchair. This event was just one in a series of police attacks on black people in the area, and provoked widespread criticism. This suggests that

240

coercive and intimidating policing practices continue, despite the talk about 'community policing' (see chapter 6).

Borough profile

Lambeth comprises 22 wards stretching from Clapham in the north to Brixton in the south, covering 6,835 statute acres of land. The population was put at 244,143 in 1984. It is therefore a much larger borough than RBKC. This has implications for all aspects of policy implementation and housing management since more personnel and more units are involved. It is also different politically, since Labour hold a safe majority of 40 seats to the Conservatives 21. An outsiders impression of the borough cannot escape being influenced by media representations. It is therefore generally perceived as being a borough of high black concentration, criminality, poverty and high unemployment. In fact only 29% of the population are black. This 29% are somewhat concentrated in the most deprived Angell ward. The wealthy owners of the salubrious properties in the more prestigious parts of Crystal Palace, Norwood and Dulwich appear to attract less attention in the popular press. Lambeth, like RBKC, is a borough of stark class contrasts but it is the high rate of poverty, the black population and the crime figures released by the Metropolitan police which have attracted the attention of researchers and the press. In 1986 it was estimated that some 15,000 (one in seven) households had gross household incomes of under £2,600 a year and four in ten households have incomes under £5,200 a year (1986 Housing Needs Survey). The correlation between poverty and blackness is evident for all to see, and empirically supported by all available statistics. Of the 29% of the population that are black, disproportionate numbers rely on supplementary benefit, live in poor and overcrowded conditions, and express dissatisfaction with their housing situation.

The low incomes of the majority of households in Lambeth severely restricts their housing options. The private rented sector has dwindled down to 15% (cf 29% in RBKC).

The private rented sector appears to be more secure than in RBKC since 89% of private tenants have rent-books as compared to only one third in RBKC. Four per cent of private tenants in Lambeth have no written agreement (as compared to 12% in the Royal Borough), and are therefore at the mercy of their landlords.

Table 9.2 indicates the change in the relationship between ethnicity and tenure type over the last 8 years.

Table 9.1 *Households by tenure type*

		Local Authority	Housing Assoc.	Owner Occupier	Private Rented	Total
Local Authority	No	176	9	31	9	225
	%	41	10	9	5	21
Housing Association	No	9	20	5	5	39
	%	2	22	1	3	4
Owner occupier	No	10	3	120	12	145
	%	2	3	33	6	13
Private rented	No	99	31	136	100	366
	%	23	34	37	50	34
Living with parents	No	51	12	33	31	127
	%	12	13	9	16	12
Other	No	30	6	17	27	80
	%	7	7	5	14	7
Don't know	No	57	11	22	15	105
	%	13	12	6	8	10
Total	No	432	92	364	199	1087
	%	100	100	100	100	100

Source: Housing Needs Survey 1986 in Lambeth

Table 9.2 *Tenure by ethnic origin*

			Local Authority	Housing Assoc.	Owner Occupier	Private Rented	Total
1986	Black :	No	277	35	131	46	489
		%	30	23	19	15	23
	White :	No	634	116	565	279	1,585
		%	69	76	80	85	76
	Total :	No	918	153	707	317	2,095
1981	Black :	No	8,364	1,165	4,980	2,232	16,741
		%	20	22	20	10	17
	White :	No	33,017	5,277	20,461	20,188	78,943
		%	80	78	80	90	83
	Total :	No	41,381	6,442	25,441	22,420	95,684

Note: 1981 data is from the Census. Here, 'black' refers to households whose head was born in the New Commonwealth or Pakistan. All data is in households.

Source: Housing Needs Survey 1986 in Lambeth

Of particular note is the fact that during this period the number of black tenants living in council accommodation has risen to 30%. In view of the early resistance to allowing black people access to council accommodation, at the gross level of getting into public housing, this indicates slow progress. It also may indicate that black people are not keeping up with the broader shift towards owner occupation, particularly since the proportion of black owner occupiers has not increased. More generally it is notable that far more white households (80%) compared to black households (only 20%) are owner occupiers and this has not changed since the introduction of the right to buy.

In the light of central government's moves towards privatisation, the continuing racial differentials between tenure types indicate that black people are benefiting least from the right to buy. Some of these differences may be due to the fact that in addition to their poorer economic situation, black people are still living in accommodation of such poor quality that they do not want to buy their homes.

Lambeth has higher rates of homelessness than RBKC. Regarding gender differentials, it is significant that 72% of homeless households in Lambeth are single parent households headed by women (Women in DHPS Conference Papers, Lambeth, January 1987). A significant proportion of these will be women who became homeless through violence or risk of violence. No comparable figures are available for RBKC because it is gender blind as well as race blind.

Ethnic data
An ethnic breakdown of Lambeth's black population is presented below:

No direct comparison can be drawn with RBKC because of the official invisibilisation of black people there. Birthplace and language data can be crudely compared, however. Just over two thirds of Lambeth's population were born in Britain, while nearly a third were born outside the UK, whereas in RBKC, a higher proportion (37%) were born outside Britain. Birthplace should not be taken as an indicator of race (although official figures often do this). The more detailed data on birthplace that is available is problematic and is not therefore reproduced here.

In Lambeth, 5% of households use a language other than English as their main language.

This compares to 13% in RBKC, so that proportionately two and a half times more people do not use English as their first language in RBKC.

Other ethnic data in Lambeth's 1986 Housing Needs Survey indicate the racial disparities in socio-economic terms. For both men and women,

Table 9.3 *Ethnic Origin of Lambeth Residents*

Ethnic Origin	M	F	T	%
African	135	112	246	4.6
Asian	159	158	317	5.8
Caribbean/West Indian	314	366	680	12.6
UK black	66	86	152	2.8
Other black	77	100	177	3.3
Total black	750	822	1572	29.1
UK white	1614	1638	3252	60.2
Irish	127	137	264	4.9
Other white	130	145	275	5.1
Total white	1871	1920	3791	70.2
Don't know	20	17	37	0.7
Total	2641	2759	5400	100.0

Notes: i) Asian = Indian, Pakistani, Bangladeshi, Other Asian
ii) Other black = Chinese, Middle East, Cypriot, Mauritian, Hong Kong, Japanese, Vietnamese, S. American, Mixed Origin
iii) Other white = American, East European, West European, Mediterranean

Source: Housing Needs Survey 1986 in Lambeth

black unemployment rates are approximately double the rates for white people. Within the black community, male unemployment is significantly higher than the rate for black women, although there are generally problems in identification of women's employment status because of their movement between unpaid domestic and waged labour.

Poverty varies between the different types of tenure. 60% of LA tenants have a household income of less than £5,200 per anum as compared to 38% of private renting households and only 11% of owner occupiers. Twice as many black households depend on supplementary benefit as white (27% and 13% respectively). Black households in council accommodation are particularly badly off with 40% in receipt of supplementary benefit.

The findings on household size indicate that black families are larger, live in more overcrowded conditions and more often have children. Nearly half (49%) of 'Afro-Caribbean' households are families with children (see Footnote 1). Since 70% of Lambeth's households have no children, the borough's children are concentrated in black households. Interestingly, only 18% of Lambeth's households are of the conventional nuclear type (two adults and one or more children).

Six per cent of Lambeth's households are single parent families, but this figure is based on a very narrow definition which for example,

Table 9.4 *Languages Spoken*

	Main language spoken		Other language spoken	
	No	%	No	%
Gujerati	17		7	
Bengali	3		—	
Hindi	2		4	
Punjabi	5		2	
Urdu	4		4	
Sub total (Asian)	31	30	17	10
Chinese/Cantonese	5	5	4	2
French	8		45	
Greek	7		3	
Italian	9		11	
Portuguese	2		6	
Spanish	7		10	
Turkish	4		4	
Polish	1		8	
Sub total (European)	38	37	87	51
Ibo	1		2	
Yorubo	5		16	
Arabic	4		7	
Other	19		39	
Sub total (other)	29	28	64	37
TOTAL	103	100	172	
English	1955		89	
No-reply/DK	37		58	
TOTAL	2095		319	

Source: Housing Needs Survey 1986 in Lambeth

excludes children living with a relative who is not their parent and single parent households with children over 15. In any case there does appear to have been a large increase (of 46%) in single parent families between 1981-85. More than half of the single parent families in Lambeth are 'Afro-Caribbean' households. Single parent households are by far the poorest, with 64% having incomes of less than £3,900 per year, which makes them collectively worse off than pensioners. As noted above, women headed single parent households are disproportionately represented amongst the homeless. Black single mothers therefore fare badly on a number of different indices.

Organisational and policy aspects of Lambeth's housing practice

'I think a lot of authorities try to shirk their duty. Under the Act you can approach any authority you like because you've had to flee, and they have a duty to accept you if they're satisfied that you're homeless and at risk, so the [borough of] residence doesn't count. We would have to interview and take them on like any other case.' (Senior Officer, HPU).

Like all LA housing departments, the structure is that of a large hierarchical bureaucracy, and likely to have the same basic characteristics as described for RBKC, probably to a greater degree on account of being larger (see chapter 7).

In Lambeth there are a number of units and personnel who are relevant to race and gender considerations. There is a Race Unit, a Women's Unit and a Police Unit, although all are quite small and constantly lobby for more resources. More specifically there is also a Crimes Against Women Officer, and a number of housing and other concerned officers and voluntary sector representatives have come together as the Women at Risk Group which has been working on developing the domestic violence policy, addressing its race implications and agitating for and working towards ensuring its proper implementation. This is in marked contrast to RBKC's complete lack of any such structures and the isolated Special Needs and community liaison officers.

The housing department in Lambeth, like that in RBKC was about to be restructured at the time of research. The process of decentralisation and its likely racial consequences were discussed in chapter 7. In Lambeth, some officers felt that decentralising allocations would undermine anti-racist strategies and compound existing inequalities. There was evidence of some staff shortage in the neighbourhoods, with posts not being filled when people left. Housing officers in Lambeth generally seemed to be under somewhat greater pressure than in RBKC. This may have been because of their expressed concern with meeting the needs of the local communities, which contrasted with the latter's intransigence towards the public. There was none of the scorn that RBKC estate management expressed for 'liberal' attitudes, which follows since Lambeth is clearly one of the boroughs that would be identified as 'liberal'. Officers were generally willing to be interviewed and helpful, but top management did not give official support to the research.[2] This may well be because the Central Government (and the political environment generally) is far more hostile to Labour local authorities like Lambeth which have come in for repeated attack, and this has fostered a high level of defensiveness.

The atmosphere is however, very different from that in RBKC, no doubt also partly because it has a Labour majority. Labour boroughs are in the situation of being overruled and having their powers eroded by radical Thatcherism, in ways with which for the most part they are in fundamental disagreement. As a consequence, an atmosphere of siege and alienation from Central Government pervades the corridors of the Town Hall and neighbourhood offices. Frontline staff are in the undesirable position of having being employed and trained to deliver a public housing service that is currently being completely undermined and overwhelmed. Housing departments in general are increasingly failing to meet their statutory obligations, and are obliged to cope with the human stress that results from being increasingly unable to deliver the service for which they were established. One would therefore expect the high stress levels and anxiety that are being felt amongst staff.

It was interesting that housing staff all the way up to director level in both Lambeth and Kensington and Chelsea were critical of Central Government policies regarding public housing. It was the specific grounds for their objections that were different. In RBKC criticisms were expressed as feelings of hurt, since the borough has shared and been loyal to the radically conservative policies of the Thatcher government. In Lambeth criticisms were more often articulated in terms of frustration about being prevented from delivering a fair and proper service as a result of wider constraints. For example non-replacement of staff creating shortages and stress for workers, or impending decentralisation creating a climate in which decisions were left in abeyance for too long.

As in RBKC, the key concern is over the contradiction between declining stock and rising demand, which suggests that this very narrowed perception of housing is a result of the wider central government-orchestrated crisis of public housing in general, and not just one of political orientation.

Both the history of the borough and the available information indicate that racism has long prevailed in the housing service. The recent period has seen a proliferation of Equal Opportunities policies which include anti-racism. However, during this research, officers' reports about the successful translation of policies into practice varied. Some felt that racism was still widespread, and attributed this to the lack of detailed guidelines for implementation of anti-racist policy. For example there was said to be 'clearly a difference in assessment of Nigerian families' who, at least until 1985, would be asked for their passports, and generally treated with more suspicion than other groups. Racial steering of applicants towards particular areas was also identified in the allocations practice. In this instance, it was suggested that assessment officers were found to be advising people where they were more likely to be rehoused, on the basis of rules of thumb (including racial differentiation) rather than real knowledge.

Other officers felt that racism was a thing of the past in Lambeth and emphasized that there had been anti-racist training, ethnic monitoring and the setting of targets to address inequalities. Committee and conference reports indicate an awareness that equal opportunities is still more of an aspiration than a reality in the borough. In the present climate, lack of adequate training and resources for equal opportunities are excused on the basis of the wider crisis and lack of resources more generally.

Whatever the case, there was more detailed understanding and discussion of race and gender equality concerns in Lambeth as compared to RBKC. In comparing the two boroughs, the researcher came to the conclusion that race equality policy development was like rolling back a carpet. The further it was being rolled, the more dirt was being exposed, and thus had to be dealt with. In Lambeth there was still a great deal of dirt, but at least a corner of the carpet had been lifted. By contrast, in Kensington and Chelsea the carpet was being nailed into place, covering at least as much dirt. Lambeth may choose to succumb to wider pressures and set back the changes that have at least been initiated over the last decade, or continue the struggle to implement race and gender equality. In order to achieve the latter, radical and innovative strategies may well be necessary to combat the negative impact of broader changes in the housing market.

Policy and practice on relationship breakdown and domestic violence

'Lambeth Council has gone some way in fulfilling its statutory obligations to women who have suffered threats or actual violence. However there are shortfalls and firm commitments are needed from all Councillors and Chief Officers to ensure the safety of women in the community' (Women in DHPS Conference Papers, Lambeth, January 1987).

In recent years Lambeth has hosted a number of conferences for women, including one on Black Women and Housing in 1987. The level of understanding and discussion of race and gender aspects of housing policy and practice is predictably much more developed than in boroughs which are gender and race blind as a matter of principle.

Policy on relationship breakdown and domestic violence is at a much more advanced stage than in RBKC, having been on the LA agenda for some time. What emerges most is the way in which policy development itself uncovers new areas for future development. Despite the more obviously disturbing effects of the housing crisis, the officers we interviewed and met with were valiantly continuing to struggle for improved practice, training and implementation of the guidelines on domestic violence. This work was being continued at the end of the research period, through the Women At Risk team and the Crimes Against Women Officer.

In Lambeth, the policy is being developed under the general title of 'At Risk Policy', and applies to persons suffering a range of threats or actual violence both from inside and outside their homes. This dates back to 21 October 1986 when the police committee agreed a report which recommended:

> '. . . the setting up of a team of officers and representatives of women's groups to formulate council policy or make recommendations for change in a number of areas with regard to violence against women.'

Women not living with their assailants and women suffering at the hands of other relatives (eg in-laws) therefore come under the same policy. This makes it very different from RBKC who do not recognise single women without dependants or women suffering violence from other relatives, and who were still fighting in court *not* to recognise women as homeless due to violence from outside the home.

The Women in the Directorate of Housing and Property Services Conference in January 1987 was attended by over 200 women employed in Lambeth (it goes without saying that women's conferences of any sort would not be countenanced in boroughs where it is policy not to recognise women's oppression). An 'At Risk' policy team was set up in Lambeth and operating by that time, and a workshop specifically addressing the issue of domestic violence and other women at risk took place. This was so full that it had to be split three ways, indicating the high level of concern amongst women in the council. This workshop:

> '. . . strongly felt that the Council should openly recognise violent episodes as being a violation of women's rights, simultaneously making

a policy commitment to provide *all* women, regardless of dependants, age, race, creed, sexuality, disabilities etc, with a place of safety.'

Concern was expressed over a number of anomalies in the policy as it stood at that time. These included the differential treatment of council tenants as compared to non-tenants; of single women with no dependants as compared to women with children; over women at risk from men who do not live with them. Concern was also expressed over police responses, and over the fact that long periods in temporary accommodation had particularly disturbing effects on families who were being rehoused under the At Risk policy. This led to the recommendation that

'A major policy review must be instigated to provide a coherent Council strategy to cover all women presenting for rehousing as "at risk" (to include public and private sectors, priority and non-priority applicants).'

There were also urgent calls for a written procedure to be provided, for appropriate training of women and compulsory training for men to counter their attitudes towards women workers and clients. Furthermore, the resource implications of such actions were specifically addressed.

At the time of the research some of these recommendations had been taken up. The Women At Risk group were still working on the policy guidelines, and on the development of a standard form for the various departments encountering women at risk. However, the apparent need for a comprehensive training package had not been addressed. Even more disappointingly, no guarantee of resources for it had been obtained at the time of writing. Differences between departments — the practice of the HPU and that of Estate Management — were still very much in evidence. Estate management operate much stricter criteria, and generally require a proof of violence (eg legal action such as an injunction) before considering women for transfers.

The male estate and rehousing managers interviewed were unaware of the Women At Risk Team's work, although the two (women) neighbourhood officers we interviewed were not only aware but involved with the team. This suggests that the problem of inconsistencies in the policy have yet to be dealt with at the management level.

Committee reports recognise black women as having particular vulnerability to violence from both sexual partners and racists, and the exacerbation of their circumstances by racism and sexual harassment:

'The statistics indicate that a higher than average proportion of women at risk of violence are black and this must be borne in mind throughout the report. Black women also experience a combination of racial and sexual harassment which can render their situation particularly acute.' (1986)

This awareness leaves no excuse for policy development in Lambeth not addressing the race implications, but of course does not guarantee that the policy will be equally applied to all groups of women unless appropriate measures are taken and the implementation monitored for race equality considerations.

Homeless Persons Unit

'Lambeth always gives the benefit of the doubt to the applicants'.

'If a woman comes in and she hasn't got any visible bruising, we don't say "You can't prove it — you haven't got a black eye so you've got to go back". We don't do that here. I know some authorities do. They may require a woman to go to court for an injunction.'

In response to the question of whether women used violence as a means of obtaining or moving to another area one of the HPU's senior officers replied as follows:

'If a woman is accepted as being at risk, whether she was a tenant or not — if she's going to spend six to nine months in a grotty Bed and Breakfast, then she must be desperate for a transfer. I would say that the vast majority of people that work here would say the same.'

This response indicated that staff are less suspicious of the public than their equivalents in RBKC and regard anyone desperate enough to go through the homeless channel and into Bed and Breakfast hotels as being in sufficient need of housing to warrant being rehoused. The attitude is more humane and very different from that exhibited by officers in RBKC. Despite the severe housing stress in the borough, the housing department staff did not share the worry about 'letting people in'.

The HPU is constantly crowded (cf RBKC's emptiness), and recently the growing stress between 'frontline' officers and the public has taken physical form. As a result of repeated assaults on officers by a desperate public, workers went on strike to demand better protection. Interviewing rooms were subsequently equipped with thick glass protective screens.

This gives them the unfortunate appearance of top security prison visiting rooms. The HPU's Senior Assessment Officer who showed the researcher round expressed concern about the lack of privacy for women being interviewed about their need for housing.

The law and police were not constantly referred to by housing staff and Lambeth has relatively developed policies of its own, rather than relying on such stringent interpretations of legislation that housing requests have to be fought out in court. Committee reports indicate that Lambeth Council's Police Unit has repeatedly expressed concern over policing practices in relation to violence against women in the home.

The HPU works closely with the local refuges and no doubt because their situation is readily apparent, are reported to treat women from the refuge as clear cut cases compared to women approaching the HPU individually.

Estate management: limited transfers away from violence
As was the case in RBKC, the estate management channel is more stringent than the HPU in accepting women as being at risk. However, whereas in RBKC, the estate manager indicated that it was virtually impossible for women to obtain transfers on the basis of violence, in Lambeth there is a policy to accept such women for management transfers, although legal or medical evidence is generally still required. Violence against women was described as 'endemic' and a product of a 'culture of violence'. Certainly it was something that the estate management were familiar with and had developed procedures for, again in contrast to RBKC. The Women At Risk policy applies, so that violence from outside the home, or from other relatives would be included under it, although the district manager we spoke to felt that violence from outside the home should be dealt with by the HPU, and not through the transfer process. He regarded 'Management Transfers' as a service that was supplementary to the HPU, functioning as 'a satellite' with respect to At Risk cases. This, and the evidence from HPU officers suggested that each felt the other should do more than they did, but this was more strongly voiced by the HPU who were very critical of Estate Management's much more stringent criteria.

The managers and neighbourhood officers we spoke to acknowledged that neighbourhood staff are not trained or equipped to conduct the highly intrusive interviewing made necessary by the stringent criteria for granting transfers. The two neighbourhood officers interviewed were both sensitive to the issue, but it is the district managers who have the decision-making power to decide who is accepted for rehousing and who is not. In Lambeth, such decisions do not have to be passed by the Assistant Director of housing, as was the case in RBKC.

In Lambeth, in severe cases, women will be placed in temporary accommodation, pending the supplying of evidence, but still be processed as management transfers rather than as homeless. It was pointed out however, that diminishing supply means that only serious 'life-threatening' cases can actually be successful these days, whatever the policy situation. It was also recognised that a lot depended on how the case was presented, which passes responsibility back down to the senior neighbourhood officers. The district manager we interviewed for example, said he looks for at least one corroborating source, but that he would rather be conned many times than make a wrong judgment and risk somebody's life. He was much less suspicious of people 'trying it on' than his equivalent in RBKC, and said that evidence was needed for consistency. In cases where an individual requested multiple transfers, questions would be asked on the third or fourth time because there was a need to stop the taking up of other people's priority need. In any case this was described as a very rare occurrence.

The policy on relationship breakdown is also significantly more humane than in RBKC where, it will be recalled, the borough's policy is 'that they sort it out for themselves' and the outgoing partner has no chance of obtaining any housing. In Lambeth, one offer is made to the outgoing partner, a policy which goes beyond the LA's statutory duty. If the outgoing partner is a single man he will be offered hard-to-let accommodation

Liaison between refuges and the housing department
It is important to note that there are two refuges open to all women, and an Asian refuge in the borough. The Asian refuge also has a house for young single women (mostly daughters escaping cruel or violent families). The majority of women in the refuges in Lambeth are already homeless and so will be processed through the HPU as was discussed above. Liaison between refuges and the HPU did exist, but could be improved. The Asian refuge in particular seemed to have developed a working relationship with the HPU. All refuges complained about the increasing lengths of time it was taking for women to be rehoused and the (black) women we interviewed complained about the poor condition of some of the offers they received (see below).

Liaison with estate management is not so developed, which suggests that transfers will be more difficult, quite apart from the fact that they operate more stringent criteria even though they are not having to create new tenancies.

In Lambeth then, unlike RBKC, there are (in theory at least) working relationships between all three refuges and the housing department. In 1984/5, refuges were granted a quota of 50 places available for rehousing of women from the refuges. The quota is supposed to be used by refuges to nominate households who would not otherwise be accepted by the council (for example single women). There was evidence to suggest that liaison between housing and the refuges needs to be improved, particularly on the refuge side where the workers did not seem to be fully cognisant of the housing process and particularly the quota system.

Discussion

Little appears to have happened in the last two years, although the procedural form had been finalised by the Women At Risk Team by the end of the research period. Training on the implementation of the procedure, and the proper use of the new standard forms are the next step forward.

A comprehensive review of the At Risk Policy and regular evaluations of its implementation are still very much needed. In Lambeth, at least the statistical material for such an exercise will be available as a result of specific monitoring procedures already introduced in the HPU. Estate Management have yet to take on the task of monitoring At Risk cases specifically, although the necessary information is on file. Since we were not granted access to files, it was not possible to conduct a full statistical analysis of the situation as a part of this research (see Footnote 2).

Evidence given by refuge workers and the women seeking rehousing in Lambeth however strongly suggests that the implementation of the commendable written At Risk Policy could be greatly improved. This applied particularly in the case of some of the black women we interviewed. Some had suffered as a result of their files being lost, or necessary letters taking many months to be written. Others had waited 18 months (and were still waiting at time of interview) for decent accommodation. Some had simply been forced to accept very poor housing. In one case, a very violent man found out the whereabouts of the woman he had abused through the housing department, albeit by masquerading as her brother.

In short the case material indicates that the practice is still lagging a long way behind the policy. In the light of the dedicated efforts of the Women At Risk Group, this is most probably due to a lack of political will and lack of any institutional backing for the proper implementation of the policy. It is therefore vital that the Directorate of Housing give the problems still evident in the housing of women at risk of violence — particularly black women — the priority they deserve, and make resources available for proper training and evaluation of the developing policy.

Notes

1. *Research Note*

   Categories used in Lambeth present serious difficulties for finer analysis. On the one hand there are the ethnic origin categories (eg Asian, West Indian and African), while on the other there is a 'UK black' category which may relate to ethnic origin, or place of birth. In other words, birthplace and ethnic origin have been conceptually conflated in the design of these categories. Then there is an 'other black category which is said to include Chinese, Middle Eastern, Cypriot, Mauritian, Hong Kong, Japanese, Vietnamese, South American, mixed origin'. Few of these are likely to identify themselves as black, and some may rightfully consider themselves to be Asian (eg Chinese). The classification of for example Mediterranean people as 'other black' is also rather strange. Others — the Mauritians — are African in geopolitical terms but may be of Asian, European or mixed ethnic or racial origin. It appears that in Lambeth there is still some basic conceptual confusion over race, nationality, geopolitics and ethnicity/culture. This undermines the usefulness of their ethnic monitoring.

   The Census figures which are cited in the Housing Needs Survey also conflate birthplace and ethnicity, but are misleading in a different way: the 1981 census only included 'East African New Commonwealth countries' which omits most of the continent, including the populous part, West Africa, which is where most Africans coming to Britain are from. The result is that the African population erroneously appears to have shrunk from 3.4% in 1977 to 1.1% in 1981 (this error is footnoted in the Housing Needs Survey). Furthermore 'country of birth' has not been properly defined in the data, for example, Africa is included as a country.

   Elsewhere other terms are used without being defined. For example the figures on single mothers refer to 'Afro-Caribbean', but it is not clear if this includes African and Caribbean people, or if Black British, Indo-Caribbean and mixed origin people are included in this group. In other words, it is not clear whether the term 'Afro-Caribbean' refers to birthplace, nationality, race, perceived ethnic origin or self-identification.

In sum, while Lambeth may be commended for conducting ethnic monitoring, the data does not hold up to finer analysis beyond the broader category of black people. Since ethnic monitoring is supposed to be just part of an anti-racist strategy and necessary to combat discrimination against black people in general, the general category 'black people' is the most important. However, it is this researcher's opinion that the numbers in this category are likely to be somewhat inflated by inclusion of some Europeans as 'other black'.

This will raise political problems that become evident in discussion of Lambeth's anti-racist initiatives. For example, when it comes to targeting, presumably the claim that the 35% of new homes allocated to black people is being reached is based on a definition of black that includes Southern Europeans and other groups that may well face discrimination, but are not generally defined as black people.

2. Official clearance was sought at Director and Assistant Director level, and then several months later, taken up with the Housing Committee through the Race Unit. It was eventually turned down by the Directorate at the very end of the research period. By this time the research had been completed, since we had elected to proceed pending bureaucratic clearance. An early draft of this chapter was sent to the Director of Housing for comment several months before publication, but no reply was received to this, or to our other enquiries concerning fuller use of interview material.

This section of the report has therefore been compiled on the basis of interviews that had been conducted with housing staff in the HPU, District and Allocations Managers and Neighbourhood Officers, and with the full cooperation of and liaison with the Women at Risk Group and the Crimes Against Women Officer. It has, however been written without directly quoting individuals who had agreed to be interviewed, pending clearance, in order to protect them from repercussions. Not getting official clearance meant that we were not given access to existing statistics on rehousing women at risk and ethnic breakdowns therein.

A survey of the voluntary sector and interviews with black women who had applied for rehousing after being subjected to violence were also sources of data and information (as in RBKC). This makes the sources of information slightly more extensive than RBKC, in terms of numbers of persons interviewed (both from the LA arena and from the voluntary sector and black women's arena).

Generally the existence of monitoring policies and the work of the Women at Risk Group meant that substantially more information was available, and Lambeth personnel were better informed on the housing and other consequences of relationship breakdown and domestic violence than were their counterparts at RBKC. Given more time to pursue the matter of clearance and conduct more detailed research, a more comprehensive study could easily have been made public, and would have been in the interests of the LA as well as the voluntary sector. This would have provided the LA with insight into the constraints on and possibilities for policy development, at no cost to themselves.

PART III: The voluntary sector

10. Community organisations

Method Note

This part of the project involved examining the kinds of support that is available from the voluntary sector to black women experiencing violence in the home and the resultant problems.

The first stage of research in this sector involved identifying and contacting a wide range of voluntary sector organisations, in order to establish which of them were actively engaged in work with women, and particularly black women, subjected to domestic violence. This chapter presents a summary of the research findings on the voluntary sector.

More than 40 black women's centres, organisations and projects in London were identified and written to, informing them about the project and inviting participation in it. These letters were then followed up by telephone. Discussions were held with the few that were successfully contacted and who identified themselves as being involved in work on domestic violence.

In the second stage, a range of black community projects were contacted by telephone. Most were not doing specific work on domestic violence, so this survey was not pursued. However, more general surveys of the voluntary sector were conducted in the two boroughs selected for further study, primarily to examine the possibilities for developing support work on domestic violence.

By far the most significant voluntary sector provision was found to be women's refuges set up specifically to meet the most immediate and urgent needs of abused women. Since they turned out to be the only agency working on domestic violence in most places, chapter 11 is devoted to discussing the responses of the refuge movement to black women.

Black women's organisations: committed but not resourced

The long history of black women's autonomous organising is documented in Dadzie, Bryant and Scafe (1985). The late 1960s and the 1970s saw the establishment of a number of black women's organisations in the various black communities in Britain. Some of these were anti-imperialist and internationalist in emphasis, like OWAAD (Organisation for Women of Africa and African Descent, which later became the Organisation for Women of African and Asian Descent). Others focused on the race and gender oppression of black women in Britain. Initially small voluntary groups, a number of these established black women's centres. Some of these retained the focus on African-Asian Unity (eg Brixton Black Women's Group), but others focused on the needs and concerns of Asian women only, or African and Caribbean Women (eg East London Black Women's Organisation, Camden Black Sisters). At least one started out as an African-Asian organisation, but later split.[1]

There is also one organisation which primarily addresses the situation of women from the African continent and supports women's initiatives on the continent (Akina Mama Wa Afrika), and two which work on healthcare (eg FOWAAD and the Black Women's Health Action Group).

The majority of black women's organisations on the mailing lists we compiled had either ceased to exist, moved or were no longer obtainable by telephone. Only those whose work did take up the issue were visited, to establish what type of work they were able to engage in around the issue of domestic violence. All black women's organisations were found to be well aware of domestic violence as a major issue of concern, and expressed support for the project. Several expressed regret that they did not have the resources or expertise to provide a more substantial service to meet the needs of women who approached them. It became apparent that the majority of black women's organisations are small, under-resourced and understaffed projects on low and decreasing budgets. Some had already suffered losses with the abolition of the Greater London Council; and a number were facing funding cuts or being threatened with cuts in their already skeletal workforces at the time of the study. Reliance on volunteers meant that they were for the most part unequipped to take on, on any significant scale, the detailed casework involved in meeting the needs of women subjected to violence. Under these circumstances, most established black women's organisations offered some emotional support and advice, and referred women to specialist women's refuges, or to the regional office for London refuges, or to hostels for emergency accommodation. This referral service is in itself valuable, particularly since as Part II of this report indicated, statutory organisations often did not inform the women approaching them for assistance about the existence of refuges, black women's resource centres.

Black organisations

Most of the black organisations contacted were not actively involved in work on the issue of domestic violence. Historically, failure to address sexism within black organisations and issues affecting black women specifically, has been one factor that since the end of the 1960s, has led black women to organise autonomously. Several concentrated on longer term campaigning and educational work, or on political-ideological work, rather than on servicing the immediate needs of their communities (eg Headstart, Black Liberation Front, Black Unity and Freedom Party). Others did not identify domestic violence as a problem. For example, one individual merely asserted that domestic violence was just another means that the state used to divide and break up black families, and indicated that he was concerned with reconciling rather than dividing black people. Some however, are beginning to address the issue of gender in the black community more seriously: for example the International Women's Day Planning Committee organised a public meeting on domestic violence in October 1988.

Other London-wide community organisations served particular ethnic groups (eg the Commission for Philipino Migrant Workers (CPMW), the Chinese Information and Advice Centre (CIAC) and the Moroccan Advice and Information Centre). All three of these unequivocally declared domestic violence to be a major problem that they frequently encountered in their communities and did work on, including facilitating the establishment of support groups.[2]

The voluntary sector in Kensington and Chelsea

The Royal Borough has the negative distinction of funding not a single independent women's organisation or women's centre. Within the LA apparatus there is no women's unit and not a single officer in the local authority has a brief to work specifically on women's issues, making the Royal Borough one of the most backward in the Greater London Area when it comes to resources for women. There are some black organisations (Grassroots Bookshop, Black People's Information Centre, Unity Community Association) but these do not work on domestic violence.

There is no black women's organisation, group or project in the borough that could be developed and resourced to work on domestic violence in the local black community.

According to social and advice workers reports, there is a substantial amount of domestic violence occurring in the local black community, but no agency appears to deal with all the various problems faced by women who are being subjected to violent assault, or to offer social and emotional support. Women in this situation are obliged to seek support in other boroughs or from London-wide provisions.[3]

Advice Services

Citizens Advice Bureau

The CAB receives all its funding from the local authority and is located in the Westway Information and Advice Centre under the M40 motorway, alongside the Housing Advice Centre, the Community Relations Advisor's Office, the Victim Support Scheme and a variety of other advice organisations. 31% of the staff are black or from ethnic minorities (mostly from migrant worker communities). Like most CABs, the North Kensington CAB operates primarily as a referral and advisory bureau, and does not have any specific training or resources to respond to domestic violence. The expertise they have in this area is based on the experience and the understanding of individual workers.

Housing Advice Centre

The Housing Advice Centre situated in North Kensington, is also completely funded by the local authority. 30% of its employees were black or ethnic minority at the time of visiting, and all the workers are at the same level. They were consulted generally about their handling of women who present to them with housing problems that result from domestic violence, and what services they provide. HACs generally function by giving housing and legal advice, and taking up cases with the local authority where they feel this to be necessary. They are also in touch with local interpreters for the benefit of clients not speaking English.

The HAC workers had a very low opinion of the RBKC's housing practice in general, but particularly in relation to women subjected to domestic violence, as noted in chapter 8.

This can clearly be seen to have deterred women from going to the Homeless Persons Unit, so that the HAC often functioned to inform women of their rights and to persuade and support women in approaching HPU.

The HAC had a number of cases of domestic violence on their case records, and felt very strongly about the borough's lack of policy in this area. According to one HAC worker, the lack of policy has meant that legal action often has to be taken against the borough to get anywhere in pressing even quite valid claims for housing. The long and arduous processes of the courts, against the high-powered legal experts employed by the local authority, meant that the HAC could seldom advise their clients to go through such an ordeal, even if they felt that there was a case to be won. This applied particularly to women who have already been traumatised by violence. In other words, advice workers feel that RBKC's housing department has perfected the art of refusing to house people. Nor were they impressed when the Housing Department proclaimed that it had a written policy on domestic violence.

North Kensington Law Centre

Situated on Golbourne Rd, this organisation aims to provide a free legal service, and to serve information and education functions. Forty four per cent of its employees were black/ethnic minority at the time of the research, but more than half of these are only part-time workers and two are in lower grade jobs. The Law Centre does not do any specific work on domestic violence, although it is something that they encounter regularly. They do refer women to a nearby solicitor who has specialised in the relevant areas of law.

Victim Support Scheme

The Victim Support Scheme has a somewhat different character to the organisations so far discussed. It relies almost completely on volunteers, having only one and a half full-time posts. Victim Support exists as a national network, with 42 offices in London (320 nationally). They are predominantly a white, middle class organisation. Each scheme has a certain amount of autonomy, doing its own fund-raising, although this is the 2nd year in which they have received generous Home Office funding to support their work.

The (voluntary) co-ordinator described their work as 'crime-based'. They appear to have a close, if not intimate relationship with the local police. This is not surprising in view of the fact that the vast majority of their referrals come from the police, and the local Constabulary in fact fund raise for the VSS by holding an annual sponsored swim. RBKC also supplies a grant, with an extra sum for 'coping with Carnival', to the VSS. Most of their 30,000 referrals per year come from the police, and are mostly victims of robbery, burglary, street crimes and rape. Victim Support is a short-term crisis intervention organisation, and in RBKC, by agreement with the police, they do not accept cases of domestic violence. Both the co-ordinator and the worker expressed concern at the lack of provision in the borough, pointing out that they simply do not have the resources to put their volunteers into such difficult terrain. They clearly acknowledge that they play a crime reporting role; that is, they encourage victims of crime to press charges and so support police work. It was stated that:

'We would love to have Moroccan volunteers to help in the reporting of crimes that are hidden at present'.

Other community organisations in the area include the Family Welfare Association and the Family Service Unit.

The voluntary sector in Lambeth

At first glance there appeared to be number of organisations to meet the needs of black women in the borough, but only the three women's refuges and Lambeth ASHA, an Asian Women's resource which refers clients to the Asian refuge, work on particularly on domestic violence.

The Black women's centre in Stockwell was established in 1979 by one of the earliest Black women's organisations in Britain (founded in the 1960s by women disaffected with sexism in male-dominated black radical organisations). It was the first Black women's centre in London. It closed down as a result of management problems earlier this year (1988).

There are a number of hostels for black women, for example, Ifeoma hostel which takes young black women deemed to be 'at risk of offending'.

Black organisations
In terms of community organisations, there were a number in the borough with different target communities, but few did any specific work with women, let alone women subjected to domestic violence.

Women's centres
South London Women's Centre: has five workers, three of whom were from ethnic minorities when we visited. It has recently been hit hard by cuts, like many women's centres. As is noted in their annual report,

although the borough has continued to fund them, monies due are often late. Both this and the insecurity of their premises (the landlord requires the property back by spring 1989) mean that the workers have to spend a greater proportion of their time on the dispiriting task of chasing up the LA and seeking new premises. There is unsurpisingly, under these conditions, a high turnover of workers. New workers, assisted by volunteer workers that they recruit, resolve to do their utmost to ensure the survival of the women's centre and overcome inherited problems that are part and parcel of working in the LA-funded voluntary sector in Thatcherite Britain.

Other women's projects include the Black Female Prisoners Scheme and the Single Parents Project. Many of the women they service have been subjected to violent attacks, which include racial and sexual harassment on estates.

It is clear that substantial resourcing and development of specialist provision would be necessary if black women who have been subjected to domestic violence are to be provided with adequate support. This is especially true for women of African and Caribbean origin for whom there is no specialist support.

Lambeth VSS

The Lambeth VSS differs somewhat from the RBKC VSS both in ethos and practice. They do offer support to abused women referred to them by the police, a significant proportion of whom are black (for example, in May 1988, out of 21 women referred by the police, 6 were black).

There is also a Housing Advice Centre and a Law Centre in Lambeth.

Conclusions

The voluntary sector in Lambeth is far more developed than that in Kensington and Chelsea. Provision for women subjected to violence, while comprising three refuges and accommodating a high proportion of black women (from all over London) is still far from adequate. The houses were in need of repair and improvement. In particular, more outreach support work and childcare support are needed. There is a need for a resource centre open to black women which could offer advice and emotional and social support to women not in the refuges.

Notes

1. Southall Black Sisters established the Southall Black Women's Centre which

continues to serve both communities, while some of the Asian women established a separate office which services Asian women, but retained the name of the original mixed group -Southall Black Sisters.

2. All three were visited by the researcher and women who worked there interviewed. Linda To at the CIAC and Margaret Healey at the CPMW both supported the project further by connecting us with women to interview.

3. The Moroccan Advice Centre which accommodates a Moroccan Women's Group is situated in North Kensington. Amina Hutchinson, the women's worker there pointed out that most women would be too afraid to come there because of the location which is on the main street, next door to a Moroccan cafe which the local men go to, so that no women from that community can go there without risk of being reported to her husband or family.

11. Response of the women's movement: refuges for women

Method

This section of the report has been compiled in consultation with the Bristol-based National Office of the Women's Aid Federation England (WAFE), the regional office for London refuges and with 18 local refuges in 12 London boroughs. All London refuges were written to (through the London regional office) at the beginning of the research, but thereafter attention was primarily concentrated on liaising closely with those refuges which had significant numbers of black women living and working in them. Consultations were held with workers and some members of management in these 18 refuges in the Greater London area. Four of these 18 were refuges for black women. Black women living in the general refuges and all women in the refuges for black women were approached for interviews about their experience of violence and their treatment by statutory and voluntary agencies. One section of the interview addressed their experience of women's refuges. This meant that data was gathered from both the refuge worker/management viewpoint, and from the perspective of black women who have lived in refuges.

Growth of a movement

The refuge movement started in Britain in the early 1970s. The earliest refuges, functioning as 'safe-houses' for survivors of domestic violence, were set up by women activists in various local communities across the country. They signified the translation of women's protests into political practice. Inspired by the wider women's liberation movement, and equipped with some of the tactics of popular protest, small groups of women, many of whom had been subjected to violent abuse themselves, came together in women's groups to occupy buildings, by squatting where necessary, and otherwise setting about the business of providing refuges. Initially, women simply took refuge in the women's centres that had been established by feminist groups, provoking publicity and building up concern that women should not be forced to remain in a home where they were being subjected to mental and physical cruelty.

So began the long struggle for resources to establish women's refuges and support groups, to provide the two most immediate and long neglected needs that abused women have: the need for somewhere to go (accommodation) and for a sympathetic and supportive environment in which to organise their lives and make decisions for themselves.

By 1974, it had become clear that a national network would facilitate the work that individual refuges were doing, and the National Women's Aid Federation (NWAF) held its first national meeting in London in the spring of that year. By the 1975 meeting there were 82 groups, 25 of which had refuges.

The movement continued to grow in strength and in numbers. By September 1978 there were over 150 refuge groups running approximately 200 houses, not all of which were affiliated to NWAF (Binney, Harkell and Nixon 1981). These accommodated about 900 women and 1,700 children at any one time.

In 1975, the Parliamentary Select Committee on Violence in Marriage had recommended that refuges be supported and increased to provide one family space for every 10,000 of the population, a modest target that has not nearly been achieved a whole 13 years after. Shortfall of refuge space remains a serious problem, and one that is likely to grow substantially worse in the years to come. Only 28% of the Select Committee's modest target has been met to date.

The growing involvement of black women with refuges has raised the issues of race and cultural difference within the movement. Although the women's movement may have started off as a predominantly white and middle-class feminist initiative, the development of refuges in the metropolitan areas heralded a greater participation of working class women. For working class women who had tired of consciousness-raising and short-term campaigning, the refuge movement provided both a practical political project, as well as a means to obtain skills and confidence in a supportive environment. Black women have increasingly become actively involved in refuges throughout the 1980s, both as residents and as workers. This reflects the fact that large numbers of black women too are subjected to violent assaults by their sexual and emotional partners and husbands and have nowhere else to turn. It also reflects the WAFE

270

practice of employing significant numbers of women who have themselves lived in refuges and may also reflect a growing awareness in the various black communities about the existence of refuges over the years.

The involvement of black women in refuges is a central concern here, as it has implications that are important not just for black women, but for the women's movement as a whole. Refuges, where large numbers of women find themselves living in very close proximity to one another and one another's children, while at the same time coping with the many other stresses that characterise the situation of women leaving violent homes, provide a powerful test of the movement's anti-racist commitments. The extent to which the organising principles of refuges have enabled them to meet the challenge of combating racism amongst not only workers, but also among the highly-stressed women who come to stay in refuges, will be critically examined below.

In addition to this challenge from within, as organisations which interact with a range of statutory bodies, refuges have a responsibility to combat the inherent racism of these organisations, which was documented in the earlier chapters of this report.

WAFE is also an example of a decentralised organisational structure that operates on the basis of general political principles of autonomy, collectivism and self-help. It therefore provides us with an example of one alternative to the large hierarchical welfare bureaucracies of advanced capitalist states. It is important to assess the extent to which these principles enable organisations of this type to meet the challenges of resisting falling into practices that reproduce the existing divisions within society in the way we have seen the Welfare State to have done (chapter 4).

WAFE estimate that they accommodated over 20,000 women and children, and dealt with 75,000 contacts in England during 1987. There are currently approximately 175 groups running 225 houses (1988 WAFE figures), not all of which are affiliated.[1] This indicates that the growth of the movement has not continued at its early pace, despite the ever-growing need for the overstretched and under-resourced provision that exists. National provision is still far short of the conservative recommendations made by the Parliamentary Select Committee back in 1975. In fact the DHSS actually terminated its funding of the National Office in 1985. WAFE has therefore only survived as a result of the unpaid efforts of those committed to keeping the organisation going. As has been noted elsewhere (CRAWC 1988), the fact that refuges have continued to be characterised by precarious funding is clear evidence of a lack of public will. They too urge the Government to take note of its own 1975 Report which recommended 'that funds are maintained and increased to ensure that refuges do not close'.

It would seem that the repeated calls for resources have fallen on deaf ears, and continue to do so long after the case for proper resourcing has been established at Parliamentary level. Every year refuges close through loss of funding, even while elsewhere others struggle to open and establish themselves. Every year hundreds of women are told there is no room for them, and some of these suffer repeated attacks while they wait for somewhere to go. Most alarming of all is the fact that in this situation, some of these women contemplate suicide, or may even be killed by their partners (see Appendix). In 1987, the DHSS finally re-awarded a grant to the WAFE National Office, but far greater resources continue to be needed if the service is to continue, let alone expand to adjust to impending and growing problems faced by abused women.

The urgent problems facing refuges, and all the women they serve, as a result of recent legislation and cutbacks in public resources present the most serious challenge to its survival that the refuge movement has yet had to face. These and other developments are discussed in the conclusion to this report, because black and white women alike stand to lose the hard-won gains that have been made if these challenges are not met.

Women's liberation and black women

It will be apparent that commitment to the liberation and development of women has guided the development of WAFE, and that this has remained implicit in policy development and implementation. WAFE refuges employ women and provide a woman-centred environment that creates an organisational culture quite different from the wider society. This is completely in keeping with the goals and aspirations expressed and developed by the women's movement in Britain and internationally. Feminist philosophy guides the policies and practices of WAFE refuges.

Feminist philosophy however, encompasses a rich and diverse set of philosophies, united at the most general level in their commitment to the liberation of women. In terms of the social relations between men and women, feminism can be depicted as ranging from the radical feminism which holds that patriarchy is the most fundamental social division and men the main enemy, through to socialist feminism, which incorporates class analysis. This is not a simple continuum of ideologies, but rather a complex and multi-layered set of ideas that manifest in various ideological combinations that cannot be fully discussed here. A great deal of debate surrounds this range of political ideas, and they all have implications for political practice. At risk of oversimplifying, those with more radical feminist leanings are likely to have identified men as the primary oppressors of women, and to implement this philosophy in separatist practice (see eg Firestone 1970). At the other end of this continuum, socialist feminists are likely to identify the ruling classes as the oppressors of the people, and men as oppressors of women, by virtue of their predominance in political, social and economic life (see eg Barrett and MacIntosh 1982). They are more likely to favour historical materialist accounts of social reality than essentialist or idealist ones, and less likely to regard separatism as the only means of effecting social and political change. Many socialist feminists are politically committed to fighting the oppression of women, on the broader basis that this will be in the interests of society in general, while many radical feminists are committed to fighting the oppression of women on women's terms, and are less interested in working in alliances with other oppressed groups to do so.

Recent years have seen the articulation of black feminism. Black feminists are as diverse as feminists along the radical-socialist axis, but generally give anti-imperialist and anti-racist struggles a lot more priority than the mainstream feminism that many black women have been active within (see eg *Feminist Review* 17, 1984 for a discussion of some black feminist perspectives, Thiam 1978, 1987 for a discussion of feminism and oppression in Black Africa). There are also substantial numbers of black women who demand certain rights for women, but continue to reject feminism as a 'white woman's thing', much in the way the many black men do. Such views are unsurprising, and find resonance with those white feminists who persist in writing as if they 'own' feminism. At one level this reflects the degree of alienation from the broader women's liberation movement that many black women experience. At another level they draw attention to the fact that black women often have very different sets of priorities as a result of the historical experience of black people in the West, as well as in Africa, Asia, the Caribbean and South America.

Working class women have also challenged what they see as the middle-class and elitist preoccupations of the women's movement. Nonetheless black and working class women's struggles have fed into and sometimes been appropriated by the broader but white dominated women's movement, both in Britain and internationally. As is now being acknowledged, much of the conceptual language of the women's movement was appropriated from national liberation movements in Africa and Asia and the Black Power movements in the African diasporas of

Europe and the Americas in the 1960s and 1970s. Terms like womanpower and women's liberation (as compared to the 'emancipation' the European suffragettes and suffragists fought for in the 19th century) are all examples. This makes it very difficult to argue that feminism, which has taken so much of its inspiration from political struggles waged by black people worldwide, is something over which white women have a monopoly.

However, the inspiration that the women's movement has taken from other liberation struggles can be described as appropriation when the women's movement fails to meet the challenge of confronting and combating racism and imperialism in its ranks. This ethnocentric tendency has been dubbed 'imperial feminism' by black feminist critics (eg Amos and Parmar 1984), and continues to be debated within the international women's movement.[2]

For the most part, many women who would consider themselves to be feminists have expressed some commitment to not being racist, but this has been accorded varying priority by different women's organisations. Where it has been forced onto the agenda, it seems fair to say this has been as a result of the efforts of those black women who have sufficient respect for the goals and achievements of the Women's Movement to invest their intellectual and political energies in such challenges. Within the black women's organisations that sprung up across Britain in the late 1970s, and early '80s autonomous organising was given priority over anti-racist work in white dominated forums. Similar principles underlie the struggle for autonomous black refuges, although in London these have not retained the commitment to African-Asian unity in the way that the first Black Women's Centres and the national Organisation for Women of African and Asian Descent (OWAAD) had. The black women's movement, through national and local conferences and the setting up of black women's groups and projects, gave black women valuable space to articulate their own concerns. These often turned out to be quite different from or even antagonistic to, those articulated by white women. For example, white middle class women articulated the Right to Abortion Campaigns, while black women found it necessary to campaign against the improper use of Depro-provera and forced sterilisation. These diverse concerns were then re-articulated as a struggle around 'reproductive rights' (Angela Davis 1981).

Today there is a more discursive relationship between some black and white women in and around the politics of women's liberation. There is still a great deal of sorting out of relations between black and white women to be done at all levels of philosophy and practice. White women still need to be made aware of the fact that it is by virtue of the international domination and exploitation of black people both in the West and in our countries of origin, that they continue to have greater access to jobs, energy, resources and time than do black women. Such an awareness would enable some to stop reacting defensively to challenges to the authority that only their relatively privileged position has enabled them to assume. This applies, not only in the West, but also in Africa, Asia and the Caribbean. Black women need to keep the pressure on to survive the current period of global reaction, as well as to continue to wage political struggles on a number on different fronts. The European anti-racist struggle is taking place in many organisations and in many different forms, and WAFE is not exceptional in this.

Organisational character of WAFE

Constitutional objectives

The Federation was set up for the benefit of its members and is co-ordinated through the national office in Bristol. The constitution sets out 5 objectives:

'1) Promoting the development of a network of autonomous locally based groups to provide temporary refuge on request for women and their children who have suffered mental, emotional or physical harassment in their relationships, or rape or sexual harassment or abuse.

2) Encouraging the development of facilities which offer advice, support and practical help to any woman who seeks it, whether or not she is a resident of a refuge, and which gives continuing support and after-care to women and children after they have left the refuge.

3) Researching into and campaigning for the provision of facilities which meet the emotional and educational needs of the children of women who seek refuge.

4) Providing information and assistance to local groups who are members of the Federation and to create a forum for the exchange of information and ideas on all aspects of the objects of the Federation.

5) Educating and informing the public, the media, the police, the courts, the social services and other authorities with respect to the violence women suffer, mindful of the fact that this is a result of the general position of women in society.'

Structure

Women's Aid groups are autonomous and by and large determine their own practice, although to affiliate to WAFE, women's aid groups have to be women-only independent voluntary organisations who support the constitutional objects and endorse the policies and guidelines for affiliation which have been voted on by the Annual General Meeting of WAFE.

There are a number of unaffiliated refuges in the country, often because they have not yet got around to it, or else because they are unaware of, or there are misunderstandings about WAFE policy. For example workers in one Asian refuge had been given to understand that endorsing the 'open-door' policy would mean that they had to service white women, while Southwark Women's Aid had a disagreement with the regional office for London refuges. Chiswick Family Rescue has never affiliated. Disaffiliating individual refuges is the only sanction that WAFE has in relation to individual refuges who choose not to adhere to the policies. Clearly this is not a sanction that can be used lightly in view of the fact that WAFE's foremost aim is to bring refuges together to operate as a national network. The regional office for London refuges does not exclude non-affiliated refuges from the telephone referral system. Nor does the national office exclude non-affiliated refuges from subscribing to the newsletter, or being on the annually updated contact lists, so that unaffiliated refuges are not excluded from WAFE's networking and lobbying work, although they do not pay their annual dues. Unaffiliated refuges do not however participate in the collective decision-making and skill-sharing that occurs through WAFE.

The Bristol-based national office operates as a co-ordinating body and does not exercise economic or managerial power over individual groups. Rather it plays a networking and administrative role that is designed to facilitate and promote all aspects of WAFE's work. For example, national office supports and assists new groups to establish refuges and obtain funding. WAFE's national office is also concerned with assisting policy development, active campaigning and fund-raising, research, and the organisation of AGM's and national conferences. The WAFE Conferences and Annual General Meetings are held to bring local and national concerns together. In addition to the above, the national office is also specifically funded to inform the public, organisations and individuals on the issue of domestic violence, and to enable training internally and externally.

The degree of contact between individual refuges and the national office varies, but formally exists through participation in the regional meetings at which all affiliated refuges have representation. For WAFE's purposes, the country is divided into 12 regions, each having an elected representative. Regional meetings are held on a quarterly basis to bring together representatives from all the refuges in a given region for consultation at the local level. Regional representatives are elected at these meetings and have the task of transmitting information between local refuges in their respective regions, and to both the National Coordinating Group (NCG) and the National Office.

The NCG comprises the 12 regional representatives and is the decision-making body of WAFE between AGMs. It bears responsibility for co-ordinating consultation in the regions and in representing the views of groups at national meetings. The NCG is both internally and externally accountable and requires the support of local and national workers to be effective. In addition to the NCG, there is an Employment Group and a Finance Group. All three are accountable to the National Conference and AGMs and are essentially concerned with the democratic management of WAFE as a whole and of the national office, and rely on the active participation of those elected into these groups.

In addition to the above there are also a number of other national working or special interest groups. These currently comprise the black women's group, the lesbian group, an anti-racist group and a research group.

Local refuges have a wide variety of structures. Not all of them have paid workers, and many that do still rely heavily on the active work of volunteers who may well shoulder substantial responsibilities. Refuge groups can be characterised as having four main elements: paid workers, unpaid volunteers (who do day to day work but may not want management responsibility), voluntary management committee members and women who live in the refuge. In many refuges some women play more than one of these roles and most management committees are likely to contain something of all four elements. The role of management often goes well beyond that of supporting and advising the paid workers, ensuring that policies are implemented properly, and where necessary, developing codes of practice to ensure this. In London there have historically (at least until recently) been more grants for paid workers and greater local government involvement in management committees, making them more like traditional voluntary organisations than some of the refuges in the rest of the country.

In short WAFE functions as a democratic and decentralised organisation and has a well developed structure along these lines, which is compatible with the policies and aims of the organisation outlined below.

Active involvement of refuge workers at all levels in this structure is the guarantee of WAFE's success locally and nationally.

National policies on race

WAFE's written policies express the organisations commitment to self-help, self-determination and democracy, which are articulated as 'all women having a say in the decision-making process'. They also stress the commitment to autonomy: that refuges are run by women and for women, and that men are not included in the decision-making process or as paid or unpaid workers, although there is provision for engagement of male casual workers eg plumbers, maintenance workers etc, should this be necessary. Single women (without children) are to be accepted and groups are committed to an 'open-door' policy; they will not turn a woman without assistance away. It is also policy that Women's Aid groups support the basic demands of the Women's Liberation Movement.

Prior to the establishment of written anti-racist policies, WAFE had other policies which had (and continue to have) race implications. For example, the open-door policy meant that initially black refuges did not affiliate because their understanding was that they were, by definition, unable to operate such a policy. This policy was not used to exclude black refuges and has since been developed to make that clear.

A second 'incidental' race implication of WAFE policies lies in the extent to which the policies on collectivism and local autonomy facilitate the anti-racist struggle by establishing more equal interpersonal relations between different groups of women. Since refuges are women's organisations, sexual inequality no longer absorbs the energies of women living and working in WAFE refuges. The whole environment is one in which women are helped to overcome physical and emotional abuse; one particular consequence of sexual inequality. In theory at least, this should mean greater space to develop positive and supportive relationships between women, and this should apply to women from different classes as well as women of different races and from different cultural backgrounds. The evidence indicates that women do indeed benefit from the supportive all-woman environment of refuges (Binney et al, CRAWC, both cited above), but these studies have not addressed the experience of black women specifically. The absence of any discussion on race suggests that in the early days it was perhaps assumed that racism, being based on inequality would not arise in the egalitarian context of refuges. But has this proved a valid assumption? As was noted above with respect to the broader WLM, the early naivete which enabled many western women to assume sisterhood would unite women irrespective of class, race, nationality and culture has been challenged by black women in recent years, both internationally and in Britain. This suggests that it was not a valid assumption for women in the refuge movement to make.

Recent years have seen the development of anti-racist policies. Four out of the total of nine written policies now concern race, and these are reproduced below.

'5) Women's Aid groups will not discriminate against any woman on the grounds of race, class, disability or sexuality. A full equal opportunities policy should be developed.

6) WAFE is committed to recognising and combating racism in refuges. It is therefore essential that workers and management receive training internally or externally. Anti-racism must be shown to be part of working practice.

7) WAFE recognises the need and supports the idea of establishing refuges for specific groups, where it will be particularly beneficial (ie *where there are language or religious barriers*) [emphasis added].

8) WAFE supports positive action in individual refuges in the recruitment of workers, and management, in respect of race, to ensure a fair representation.'

In addition to the above, WAFE has produced a separate Equal Opportunities Policy which addresses the employment practice of the organisation and does not differ significantly from those drawn up by Local Authorities, drawing heavily on the legislation. This includes a statement of intent:

'In all its activities, WAFE is striving to eliminate all forms of racism, sexism, class exploitation and discrimination on grounds of age, sexuality and disability and to actively promote equality of opportunity and good relations between women of different colour, ethnic group, class, age, sexuality, mental or physical disability. WAFE intends to ensure that no woman should be disadvantaged in seeking employment, or for any reason during their employment on the grounds of colour, ethnic origin, national origin, sexuality, disability, age class, creed or marital status. WAFE is committed to taking positive action to fight discrimination in all areas of its work.'

Copies of all WAFE policies are made available each year to all refuge groups attending the conference, and recently some funding has been made available for one-day regional anti-racist training workshops (personal communication from WAFE co-ordinator). In the course of the research, it appeared that some refuge workers had managed to find time to attend racism awareness training sessions in their locality, but often there was neither the time nor the resources for any substantive training.[3]

The Employment Group had responsibility for monitoring the implementation of the equal opportunities policy and for reporting back annually, until the 1988 AGM. During the 1988 conference, the Black Women's Group held a black women only workshop on anti-racism. Other (white) women convened a second anti-racist workshop. The black women's workshop (which I participated in) addressed various possible strategies for implementing anti-racism at all levels of WAFE operations. The participants (all black women) were clearly dissatisfied with the existing situation and articulated a range of personal and collective experiences of racism within Women's Aid. Subsequently national office endorsed the anti-racist workshop's request to become established as an Anti-Racist Group, which would take responsibility for monitoring and improving anti-racist policies in WAFE, and for producing training materials, guidelines etc. The Anti-Racist Group will be working with the national workers to develop ethnic monitoring mechanisms as part of monitoring employment and service delivery in refuges (personal communication from co-ordinator at national office). The Black Women's Group has also continued to meet and discuss the problems faced by black workers and women in refuges.

WAFE guidelines for recruitment practice, including ethnic monitoring, are clearly written out and training of all existing and newly employed staff is stipulated. However, it is this researcher's impression that while discrimination may be down in writing as a dismissible offence, it nevertheless has to be proven in practice. Like rape, racism can be hard to prove, especially when the burden of proof lies with the black women subjected to it.

London refuge provision

In London there are approximately 41 refuges operating. There is such a serious shortfall of space that the regional office for London refuges estimates that they turn away 50% of the calls they receive because there is no space to accommodate the women. This means that the women either remain in the violent situation, or rely on their local authority to place them in a reception centre, hostel or bed and breakfast, where they may well be further traumatised (chapter 4). As we have seen in our discussion of statutory responses, there are, and will increasingly be, many women for whom local authority housing departments will not accept responsibility, and who will have nowhere to go. Others may be accommodated for two days (as in RBKC) and then evicted, if they fail to furnish the LA with the right kind of evidence.

Of the seven refuges for black women in London, six specialise in servicing women from South East Asia. The Lambeth, Brent, Greenwich and Newham refuges for Asian Women were included in the research. Southwark ASHA ceased to operate at the beginning of the project as a result of losing its funding, while the refuge for Asian women in Haringey declined to participate in the research. Waltham Forest's Council-run Asian refuge opened after the research was conducted. The UJIMA refuge for black women opened in February 1988 and is open to all black women. In practice, women staying there are primarily of Caribbean and African descent. A Latin American refuge had just gone into operation at the time of writing, and other ethnic minority women's groups and community organisations currently have plans, in some cases with applications being processed, for establishing helplines or specialist refuges. Not all such initiatives are successful however, for example, an application to establish a Chinese Refuge was advised to compile statistics and apply for a telephone helpline to 'prove' the need for a Chinese refuge, even though it is evident that there is a large Chinese community in London, and that their needs are not being met by existing services or refuge provision.

A London-wide survey of refuge provision and its uptake by different groups of women was undertaken by the Women's Equality Group during the research period (Russell 1989). This study has found large discrepancies in the funding of the specialist black refuges as compared to general refuges, with the former being given much less money per bed space. This racism in funding is particularly disturbing in light of the fact that because of racism in the bureaucracies and systems outside the refuge, black refuges actually have to offer substantially more support to the women they accommodate. Because of the difficulty that black women have in getting their applications for housing and other support processed by statutory and legal organisations, many black women require the support of refuge workers accompanying them to the many statutory bodies they may have to deal with. In addition, black refuges also often incur additional expenses, such as the costs of providing translators for women who do not speak English, or sustaining women whose DHSS claims are encountering resistance. Black refuges may also sometimes get

281

more extremely brutalised women passed on to them. In one instance, a black resident at a general refuge with no black workers had observed an instance in which a woman of mixed black and white parentage, who was brought in with burns all over her body, was quickly transferred to a black refuge. This upset the black resident who described the woman as being frightened of black people, and white-identified, yet these particular white workers felt daunted and were therefore unable give their support to her.

Manifestations of racism in refuges

Racism within refuges can be expected to have a very different manifestation from racism in hierarchical organisations. Because refuges operate as collectives, there are no formal structural inequalities through which racism can manifest. Managers cannot, for example, persecute black workers by accusing them of being lazy or incompetent. The main divisions through which racism can acquire the power to damage the material interests of black women are those between workers and residents, or between workers and management. Since few women on management were interviewed, discussion here is restricted to the daily running of refuges, and only the manifestations of racism amongst workers and residents that emerged in interviews are discussed. Racism between workers, or between women in refuges manifests itself at the interpersonal level, since they do not formally exercise power over one another beyond that level. However, access to advice and support is to a large extent contingent upon good interpersonal relations, and power can be exercised through these.

Amongst residents for example, being new to the group, being introverted or lacking confidence is likely to make it difficult for that individual to stand up for themselves and bullying can (and on occasion does) occur. At this level, however, racism can be and often is, challenged by black women. Many however may well not find the emotional resources to do so, particularly if they are isolated as the only black in a refuge house. If the environment is not supportive of such challenges, then they are not likely to be effective, and may instead lead to the further marginalisation of the protesting party.

Similarly, black women can bully white women, especially if they are in the majority, or if they identify a racist attitude in a particular white woman. At the interpersonal level then, much depends on character and emotional state, as well as political consciousness and the situation of the women. More objectively, these dimensions are themselves influenced

282

by a number of factors, for example, how many black and white people are present, the culture of the refuge, and the extent of traumatisation that women have experienced before coming into the refuge.

The vast majority of the black women we spoke to had very positive things to say about refuges. None of them had anywhere else to go, and may well have faced destitution, even more serious injury or, in some cases may even have been killed by their partners if there had not been refuges for them to go into. Many had already been everywhere else: stayed with friends or relatives who eventually got tired of them or were also assaulted, and many had also experienced bed and breakfast accommodation. So for all of them, refuge provided desperately needed material support, and for most the emotional support epitomised in the concept of 'sisterhood' was also provided, either by other women or by refuge workers, or both.

For many, racism in the refuge was the least of their worries, unless it actually threatened their position in the refuge. This extremely serious experience appears to be rare, but in two cases — both African woman — not only did they experience ostracism by workers and other residents, they were also threatened with eviction. One of these two (who was given refuge outside London and was not therefore included in the data analysis for that reason) did not speak English, so that her difficulties were partly a result of language problems. The other felt that she was being punished for having succumbed to extended family pressure and returned to her husband once before. After that she was kept in the emergency room for several weeks and felt that both she and her young child were ostracised by the other women.

Many black women had no difficulty in asserting and standing up for themselves when white residents were deemed to be 'out of order'. This was particularly so in refuges with a higher proportion of black women, and at least one black worker with influence. Perhaps the most striking thing about the interview material is the number of black women who stay in refuges without feeling the alienation and isolation that characterise the emotional impact of racism. Not surprisingly the unhappiest accounts of coldness, isolation, and sometimes neglected needs for support came from black women who had stayed in predominantly white refuges, often as the only black person. Indeed, the chances of black women staying in such refuges for any length of time are slim: some contact the London Office and ask to move to another refuge as soon as space is available. It is worth pointing out here that during our fieldwork we did find black women to be somewhat concentrated in particular London refuges. Our suggestion that there may have been some kind of selective referral system operating to refer black women to refuges that have a good track record on race relations, was disputed by the regional office, who instead attributed this concentration to the location of those refuges in areas with sizeable black communities. It was also pointed out that with the serious shortfall of refuge space, women are allocated wherever there is space.

In many ways, the egalitarian nature of refuges reduces racism to the level of interpersonal conflicts. In refuges these are common, and regular house meetings are held to defuse the tensions of collective living. However, since getting support from workers in any area (eg housing advice, legal advice etc) also depends on interpersonal communication, racism at this level will result in black women not getting an equal service. Given the pressure that refuge workers are under at the present time, much of their energy is in fact spent struggling to keep refuges open and coping with the onslaught of changing legislation. This is bound to erode their energies and affect the amount of support they can offer all round, and particularly so where interpersonal relations are fraught or difficult due to racial difference.

By far the majority of complaints regarding racism centred around the ridiculous lengths of time that many black women are forced to spend in refuges. It is seldom realised that one temporary room may well become 'home' for two years or more. As was discussed in part II, however, the responsibility for this situation lies with the local authority housing departments, central government and women's lack of access to any other form of housing.

Black workers in mixed refuges

'In refuges, because its a very liberal environment, what you describe as racist behaviour of white women is often the absence of a feeling of kin, so that they're just not supportive to black women who are in the refuge. If you ask black women about it, they say, "Well, we had to ask her four times to see her", or whatever. Its just that kind of exclusion. Whereas they do have a feeling of kin with white women. I suppose the lack of that feeling is what alienates black women.' (black worker).

'The management are all white women' (black worker).

'You do have some women who would rather not have anything to do with you. When they come into the office they ignore you and they go straight for the white worker. You see it happen once and you think "well, I'll ignore that". But when you see it happening over and over, then you . . . well you can't really do anything about it.' (black worker).

'I'm married to a black man, so I get on with black people. But the black women come in here insisting on seeing Suzanne. If she's not in the office they go away and come back when she is. If they don't want my help . . . (shrugs)' (white worker).

Black refuge workers for the most part had good working relationships with their white counterparts. This was especially evident where black workers were in a majority, and where their co-workers had a high level of awareness and understanding. Black women who were in a minority, perhaps the only black worker in a refuge, experienced a greater lack of rapport with their co-workers, and some felt isolated. Some even felt guilty about mentioning this, and were worried about upsetting their white co-workers by drawing attention to their feelings. In some refuges where more than one black worker was employed, their work schedules did not overlap because of the felt need to have at least one black worker in the office to service the black women who preferred dealing with black workers. This meant that each effectively worked on her own with white co-workers, who would often giggle and joke together without being aware that they were excluding their black worker from the fun of collective work. In other words having one or two black workers in a given refuge does not necessarily solve the problem. Black workers are likely to have to face the extra demands of the black residents, both because they may prefer to relate to them, and/or because there are so many of them in a particular refuge.

Clear cut complaints of racism were rarely taken to management, but this could have been due to black women not pursuing incidents because they did not feel supported in doing so. This may also be a reflection of a generally liberal or laissez-faire attitude in refuges, which does not suddenly become a zealous attitude because of a racial incident.

The most clear indication that black workers collectively feel that racism is a problem in refuges came in the recent reconvening of the black women's group within WAFE, and their felt need for a black woman-only workshop at the national conference. This indicates that black women in Women's Aid still have difficulty in coming out and challenging racism openly. Given the amount of anger expressed in workers' accounts of racism in their own refuges, there is a great deal more work to be done in empowering and supporting black women in refuges to the point where it becomes more acceptable to discuss racism openly. Only this will ensure that incidents do not get swept under the carpet to fester and emerge angrily at some later date. Black and white women in mixed refuges need to be encouraged to talk about racism with each other. For this to happen, it may well be necessary as a first stage for black women to organise themselves separately, to work out for themselves the nature of things and to build their own confidence and awareness.

The evidence suggests that there are uneven levels of racial consciousness in WAFE. Many black women (and presumably white women as well) are not informed about the policy and therefore not able to make use of it or facilitate its implementation within their places of work.

Challenging racism from white residents
Workers have an obligation to challenge racism amongst residents and foster the spirit of sisterhood and a positive atmosphere in refuges. For the most part a good atmosphere did prevail in the refuges we visited. When it comes to challenging the racism of white residents towards black workers or black residents however, there was more evidence of a laissez-faire attitude than anything else. Women's tendency to avoid conflict can under these circumstance operate as a toleration of even quite overt racism. From black women's perspective this amounts to collusion with it, and indicates that they are unlikely to be supported in challenging it for themselves. In fact they are more likely to be seen as trouble-causing or as having chips on their shoulders by such easy-going white workers.

Interviews with white workers suggested that while few of them were likely to be actively or overtly racist, few would go out of their way to challenge racism from residents, or to support black women in doing so. For example, in one mixed refuge, a white resident took exception to the fact that only black women were being interviewed. Like the 'gutter press' which many women read, she was preoccupied with the spectre of black people getting something she wasn't and ran through both houses shouting and carrying on, trying to arouse other women to object, and to intimidate black women from being interviewed. The white worker I spoke to did not really know how to deal with this situation, let alone challenge this fairly typical display of racist sentiments. The black worker in the same refuge quite liked her co-workers and got on well with them individually, but felt excluded from the in-crowd that they became when there were several of them in the office. This would have had effects on her own ability to challenge racism from women in that house, since she could not be sure that she would be supported in doing so.

This reflects a lack of appropriate training. Most workers simply did not know that they had such an obligation, and had no idea how to go about fulfilling it. Skills they applied quite naturally in other forms of mediation appeared to freeze in the face of racism. In a liberal environment this is most likely to be a result of psychic defense mechanisms against arousing anxiety. White women experience a sense of collective guilt, which may manifest as anger or hostility to the victim of racism, or it may produce immobility so that the person does not act or intervene (see Sherwood 1980).

Some workers did complain that there were no, or not enough, black women on the management to give them any support. It emerged however, that there could be black women on the management without them necessarily operating in an anti-racist capacity. Similarly it emerged that there could be sympathetic white women who did or did not act in an anti-racist capacity. In other words it is not just the colour, but the also consciousness of the management members and workers that influences the race relations in the refuge.

This discussion of an ongoing struggle can perhaps best be ended by posing the question raised at the last WAFE conference: "Is anti-racism black women's work?" Opinion amongst black women was divided. Many argued that it was not and should not be, but felt that because racism disadvantaged black women the most, and white workers were not doing anything about it, the burden of anti-racist work remained firmly on the shoulders of black women. The expression 'who feels it knows it' captures the feeling, to which they would reluctantly add . . . 'and must fight it'.

Black women living in mixed refuges

'There was a programme on AIDS on the television, saying how it is supposed to have originated from Africa, and this woman was commenting about it . . . telling their children not to play with so-and-so. Yes, funny enough it was the white ones, you know.' (Joanna, Caribbean woman).

'The white worker is great, she gets on with everybody and she'll tell you exactly how she feels. The other one — the black worker pretends she understands, but she doesn't really. She doesn't really care, as far as I see it . . . I relate to white people anyway, better than I do to black people. That's because I was brought up with white people, and most of my friends are white people. I'll get on with anybody — colour don't even come into it, but the majority of my friends and the music I listen to and things like that are white . . . I don't eat yam and bananas, or ackee and salt fish.' (Elsie, woman of mixed Caribbean and white parentage).

'I wouldn't say the workers are racist, but the black worker will deal with all the black women, and the white worker is left to deal with all the white women, not through choice, but because all the black women go to the black worker. Its alright then — but if black women go to the black worker and white women the white, who do I go to? I made a big point of that. Maybe you should have a half-caste worker, you know, and I could go to her. I mean if you're going to segregate everybody, and they made a big issue out of that and said I shouldn't call myself "half-caste" because I was "mixed race". And I said "Well, that makes me like a tin of pedigree chum!"' (Elsie)

'Here, even though you are given sanctuary, there are so many rules and regulations — you're treated like a child. When you first come the help is there. For the first month or so the help is there, but you could have been suffering years of mental and physical violence, you know, and still feel funny inside. Maybe then you just need them there — perhaps to talk to, but I just feel my time is up now. I either get out or be thrown out . . . The workers are all new to it' (Corinna, African woman at new refuge)

'I thought refuges were for sanctuary, and this half-caste woman came in. She had been abused by her husband and her brother and they burnt her all over her body; she had fresh scars. She needed help, but instead of them trying to help sort her out, they just took her to a black refuge, and she was petrified of black people. They just took her to a black refuge rather than help to sort of give her trust. That upset me, and I just started seeing them in a different light from that day on . . .' (Corinna African woman, new mixed refuge)

'Its good in the sense that no men can come here, and that most of the women here have got the same problems and you can talk to them. But I'm not stable here. Its not a place you can really call your home and that. There's no privacy here. I mean I really think that because we've all got problems, we need more space. You've got people around you all the time telling you their problems' (Selena, Caribbean woman).

Certainly some of the black women interviewed did feel that they experienced racism in refuges. Others did not articulate their experience in that way, but did describe feeling alienated, left out and ignored. Some described how, in the absence of rapport, they found it that much harder to get the attention and support of refuge workers compared to the cosy warmth they observed between the workers and white women.

'I think a lot of women in these places go back to their husbands and to the same type of situation. I think if the housing situation was improved it would be different. The trauma of going through bed and breakfast for two years — its really bad. Older children can end up needing psychiatric treatment. Its very very serious. They should have a lot more support for the women. Its clearly a specialist job but there's not enough resources for them to have training.' (Charlotte, Caribbean woman).

'As far as these places go, this is one of the better ones. Relations in this house are quite good, but you do get people who are out of order, especially when you have to live in close with people' (Charlotte).

'The place is alright' (Roweena, Caribbean woman).

'The only refuge where I used to feel out of place was (name of refuge). There was not one black worker and not one black woman on the support group . . . there was only one girl who was staying there who was half-caste, and I was the only black woman there.' (Roweena)

Black British women were far more likely to describe their experienced alienation as being due to racism of white women than women who had less experience of white British society.

Women less familiar with British discourses on race, for example women who had lived in black communities with little exposure to white British people, tended to articulate their experience in cultural terms: mainly around food, language and hygiene. Examples include complaining about pork being cooked in the communal pans, lack of attention to hygiene by other women, English (white) women smoking and drinking, or allowing their children to go hungry so that others fed them out of their own scarce resources.

Some described witnessing white women bullying and stealing food from Asian women who, because they had not learned the ropes, did not at the time have the confidence to fight back or resist such treatment. White women therefore found it easier to intimidate them.

Fighting racism in mixed refuges: a workers' responsibility?

Refuge workers carry the main responsibility for the interpersonal manifestation of racism between residents. They therefore need to be skilled and empowered to take on this challenge. The workers we interviewed in WAFE refuges were aware of the anti-racist ethos of WAFE, but not all of them knew that there was a written anti-racist policy. This meant that they were therefore not making use of the policy to effect change, or to challenge racism when they identified it. Few had any anti-racist training, and of those who had, a minority felt that it was useful in their work. None had any training that specifically related to the work they were doing. In one refuge the four white workers had been brought to the stage of thinking that perhaps they ought to go for training because a black child-worker left her job, accusing them of racism. Few black women stayed at this refuge, and one that did during the course of the study also left, because she did not find the environment to be supportive or helpful. Incidentally, this particular refuge also had some of the best maintained facilities the researcher came across during the research, and a particularly good relationship with the local housing department which meant that they experienced little difficulty with getting their (nearly all white) residents rehoused.

As will be clear by now the main problem with written policies is that they may remain at the paper stage and not be developed into non-racist working practice, particularly if resources are not made available. As things stand, anti-racism in WAFE relies on the political will of individual workers and residents in the organisation.

Specialist refuges for black women

'WAFE recognises the need and supports the idea of establishing refuges for specific groups, where it will be particularly beneficial (ie where there are language or religious barriers)' WAFE written policy.

'The thing about having black this and black that and the other is that

I think it creates a lot of unnecessary ill-feeling among whites. I think that the only way for the white race to understand us is when they can work and live among us.'(black refuge worker).

'When women have suffered violence they are not in a strong state to be working on race relations' (black refuge worker).

'Some women are very particular about some things. Like Muslim women who don't eat pork. Sharing the same cooker and refrigerator and cooking is very stressful for them. It doesn't bother me really, so its different for me. But I think there is definitely a need [for refuges for black women], especially where there's a language problem' (Hamza, mixed refuge).

'We need black refuges because the amount of black women here is disproportionate to the amount of black women in the country.' (Charlotte).

Other black women complained that white-dominated refuges were 'too feminist' and did not understand the pressures on them from their families and communities, and therefore thought they were weak-willed when they were in fact being strategic and using the refuge to negotiate a better position for themselves in their familial relationships.

These examples indicate that there are mixed feelings in the refuge movement about specialist refuges for black women. This applies to white and black women; both present arguments on both sides of the fence. However, an Asian woman from a rural refuge who protested about the idea of separate refuges in the black woman's workshop at the 1988 Conference was loudly shouted down, which suggests that amongst black women at least there is more of a consensus in favour than against. It was also pointed out to her that she was behind the times, since black refuges have been in existence for a while, and that alone indicates that black women have felt the need to organise such provision in response. Furthermore, this initiative is correctly supported by current WAFE policy as was noted above.

The research findings indicate that the arguments made by both black and white women in the movement centre around particular notions of race, some of which this author would refer to as culturalised notions. This means that they hinge on conceptions of cultural difference (language, dress, culinary habits) rather than an understanding of racial inequality. The written policy on separate refuges accepts that they are necessary, but only on the ticket of culture. The culturalisation of race by local state structures can be challenged as a form of hegemony, which actually functions to suppress and deny other manifestations of racism. Indeed it appears that problems arising out of cultural differences are far more easily accepted and admitted than plain racism. This has particular consequences for the vast majority of black women who are quite familiar with white British culture and language, but still experience racism. It is not constructive therefore to dismiss complaints of racism as cultural misunderstandings.

In the refuge movement however there is a tendency towards mirroring the culturalisation of race that has been apparent in Labourite politics. The problem is that this culturalisation does not fundamentally challenge all the forms of racism that cannot be reduced to 'cultural difference'. This may explain the fact that Asian refuges have been resourced over and above refuges for other black women who are assumed to speak better English and have grown accustomed to English culinary habits.

Yet there are many women from other Third World contexts whose cultural needs are not provided for; for example the Chinese and African women in this study. Some black organisations have been content to collude in this culturalisation of racism in order to obtain resources on the ticket of culture, rather than to assert that they require resources because of racism in the wider society, thereby risk not getting any resources at all.

While it seems to be obvious that there is more to racism than cultural differences, there continues to be a lack of anti-racist initiatives that address this fact. Although this may often be the result of muddled thinking which conflates racism and culture, it must be challenged because it does have political consequences for the anti-racist struggle, as has been briefly indicated here. Nevertheless, a culturalised understanding of racism remains the dominant argument accepted by funding bodies, and thus limits the terrain on which black refuges (and other black organisations) can obtain resources. None appear to have obtained resources on the seemingly obvious basis that since racism in itself disadvantages black women, they need and have a right to extra support in their liaison with the wider society and all its organisations. The written policy of WAFE still falls short of this direct acknowledgement of the impact of societal racism on black women, regardless of culture. In other words the policy on separate refuges does not challenge the fact that while many black women may speak English and wear jeans they are not exempted from discrimination in housing, for example.

292

In the existing refuges for black women, the atmosphere is one liberated not only from sexism, but also from white racism. This has to be experienced to be appreciated. What it means is that black women are able to derive the valuable support and solidarity that white women perhaps take for granted in white-dominated refuges. The other side of the coin is that it also creates a space for prejudices between black women to emerge and be addressed, something which many black women have been so deprived of for so long that they have forgotten what it means. In view of the advantages, it is regrettable that not more are available, and that the few that are do not nearly meet (or attempt to meet) the needs of all the black women seeking to escape violence, who would prefer to be supported by other black people.

Most of the existing black refuges in London (five out of six) exclude women of Caribbean and African origin. Workers in the Asian refuges point out that they are understaffed and under-resourced, and that with numerous languages, religions and cultures and several nationalities to service, they have had to curtail their obligations. Whatever the reasons, as things stand black refuge provision so far only addresses the needs of women from South East Asia (mainly India, Pakistan, Bangladesh). Chinese and Philipino women, for example may be admitted, but are as likely to have language and food problems as they would in a mixed refuge.

It is important that the existence of refuges for South East Asian women is not used to segregate women who do not wish for or require that provision. Some Asian women interviewed expressed a preference for not going into an Asian refuge, because they felt that these were 'too traditional'. In contrast, there were older Asian women who occasionally found the workers in Asian refuges too young to understand, or too feministic, but would very likely have found it even more difficult in mixed or white-dominated refuges. Since there are growing numbers of second and third generation Asian women in Britain who may not want to go into Asian-only refuges, this too should be respected. Some are struggling to distance themselves from their particular community (perhaps because their husband may find them more easily in an Asian refuge), and this too should be appreciated.

Discussion: policy implementation in a non-hierarchical structure

This discussion raises general points about the problems of policy development and implementation in a national network of women's collectives. It also highlights what happens to political concerns and demands when they are processed through a large organisation, with the alternative structure that WAFE has, to emerge in written policy and organisational practices at local levels. It will be recalled that a similar perspective was adopted in discussion of Local Authority Housing departments in part II, but there we were looking at the processing of political demands into policy by traditional state structures. Here we are in a position to examine the extent to which the alternative structure and principles of Women's Aid, coupled with the more recently developed anti-racist policies, have enabled the movement to resist the natural tendency of organisations to reflect the dominant culture and reproduce existing social divisions in its practice.

In mixed refuges women from all walks of life find themselves living in close proximity to one another. Many black and white women will find themselves not just encountering the other casually, at their children's schools, in the local supermarkets or at work, but actually living together and sharing kitchens and bathrooms and on occasion bedrooms with one another. At one level, therefore, mixed refuges offer unique opportunities for black and white women to get to know each other and break down the alienated and stereotypical knowledge that they may well have acquired in the outside world. On the other hand, women who live in refuges enter with the broader society's prejudices and stereotypes. Black and white women have quite different types of knowledge about each other, and these are likely to reflect the dominant power relations of British society. As an older black woman from South Africa once pointed out to me, 'We know everything about them because we see all aspects of their lives, including their dirty washing, but they see only the little that they wish to see of us'. Clearly in this Western European social context, all is not equal prior to black and white women finding themselves living together in a refuge. One would expect a truly egalitarian context therefore to force white women to confront the various complexes they have in relation to black women.

The stressed and traumatised life situations they are in during their stay at a refuge are likely to have the effect of blocking attempts at forcing women to stop being racist. Even where racism is made an evictable offence (equal to violent assaults against other women in the refuge), white refuge workers are likely to be under pressure not to evict women they are supposed to be helping to sort out their lives. The commendable principle of providing a warm supportive environment for women to recover from the traumas of domestic violence, militates against coercive enforcement of any policy, including policies demanding non-toleration of racism. It would not be appropriate therefore, for anti-racist work in refuges to take on the disciplinary character available (but seldom implemented) for policy implementation in more hierarchical organisations, except in the most extreme and overt cases of race-hatred.

What we can hope for in a non-hierarchical and woman-centred organisation like WAFE, is the development of an organisational culture which does not tolerate or accept overt racism, and an organisational structure which disempowers racism, preventing it from being accompanied by any exercise of power which will disadvantage black women. Discriminatory behaviour can still occur, because power dynamics still operate in collectives, albeit in alternative ways. For example, a worker who accumulates particular knowledge of housing will be in a position to offer assistance that may affect the lives of residents in major ways. If she also finds it easier to relate to white women, this knowledge will be selectively available to those women. In other words, the absence of hierarchical power structures does not remove the exercise of power altogether. What it may well do is restrict the manifestations of that power inside the refuge to the interpersonal level. This can arguably be regarded as preferable to the more rigidly institutionalised and systematic racism that characterises traditional bureaucracies, but nevertheless it does not end racism, as the material above illustrated.

It will be clear from the preceding discussion of structure that the burden of anti-racist policy implementation is currently the responsibility of local refuges, through the workers and the management committee. While all WAFE member groups are expected to adhere to the written policy that exists, there are no centralised structures for enforcing implementation. Policy development occurs at all levels of the organisation, and the extent to which implementation is democratic depends largely on the consultation processes taking place through the structures outlined above. Written policies can be proposed and ratified at conferences and AGMs as well as through the regional meetings and the NCG.

Day to day administration of policy ultimately depends on the workers being aware of the policy, and developing practical rules of thumb or more formal guidelines on implementation. Local refuge management committees and workers therefore, also have an important policy development and implementation role to play in their particular refuges. Local developments can then be fed into the network for skill-sharing, and/or be taken up as national policies.

Recommendations

1. Increased support for refuges for black women.
2. Struggle to ensure that racism is accepted as a valid basis for specialist provision for black women.
3. For WAFE to devote extra energies to all aspects of the anti-racist struggle, as implied in their equal opportunities policy.
4. For all groups of black women to mobilise themselves and obtain resources for refuges.
5. For more refuges to follow the example of black refuges outside London and to establish refuges which take all black women, whatever their ethnic specificity. This would facilitate the refuge movement addressing racial inequality in the wider society more fully and directly.
6. For WAFE to find resources to ensure the development of an anti-racist training initiative that addresses the particular needs of the Federation nationally. This should target both black and white women, and provide for their different needs in respect of anti-racist work.
7. For WAFE to continue its commendable anti-racist recruitment strategies, the monitoring of these and annual reviews of their success.
8. For WAFE to develop its much needed outreach and childcare work so that it can better meet the needs of black and other isolated women.
9. For the WLM to develop housing strategies to meet the long-term housing needs of all groups of women, including women who have suffered violence. These should provide ways of tackling the problems that are being exacerbated by Thatcherite social policies.
10. For funding bodies to give concerted support to all aspects of refuge work.
11. For funders claiming to operate equal opportunities to resource refuges for black women locally, and the anti-racist struggle within WAFE as indicated above: through training and development work on the policy.

Notes

1. Chiswick Family Rescue was the first refuge in Britain and was started by Erin Pizzey and a group of women supported by the local women's centre. She later became obstructive to the refuge movement and is alleged to have actively undermined the attempts of other groups to secure funding for refuges. She also gained notoriety for propounding the pseudo-psychological notion that some women became chemically addicted to adrenaline, and so became 'prone to violence'. Current Chiswick policies are different, but they are unlikely to make themselves accountable to the Federation by affiliating, and continue to run on different lines. The researcher had the impression that they have a

more hierarchical managerial structure, for example.

2. Some of this debate is available in *Feminist Review* no.17 which was a special issue edited by a group of black women (Valerie Amos, Gail Lewis, Amina Mama and Pratibha Parmar) called on for that purpose. Subsequently there were a number of responses and rejoinders; see Barrett and MacIntosh's 'Ethnocentrism and Socialist Feminist Theory' FR 20, 1985, and the various replies to them by Caroline Ramazanoglu, Hamida Kazi, Sue Lees and Heidi Safia Mirza in FR 22, 1986. In 1989 the continuing white feminist reactions to black feminist criticism seem to have remained defensive rather than progressive (see eg Elizabeth Wilson in *Critical Social Policy* 1989).

3. It is this researcher's view that for training to be effective, it would have to be grounded in the nature of refuge work.

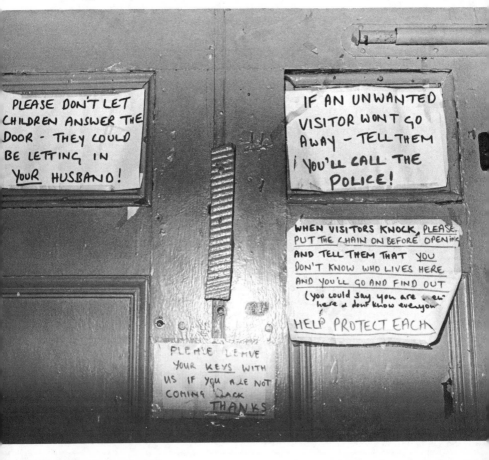

298

12. Conclusion

The nature of domestic violence against black women

The levels and forms of violence experienced by the women in this study were quite horrific. They were certainly as bad as the previously documented violence that white women experience. The emotional suffering that women in this study had been subjected to by the men they lived with or had relationships with was also alarming. The men who had abused them were from a range of social classes, cultural and religious backgrounds, and included both white and black men.

We saw that the privatised and hidden character of 'family life' operates to mask the everyday atrocities referred to as domestic violence in advanced capitalist contexts like Britain, and that violence is all the more hidden in black communities because of racism. The selective respect for individual privacy which allows for women to be maimed, tortured and sometimes killed by the men they live with must be condemned in any decent or humane society. Measures must be taken to stop woman abuse by demonstrating to the perpetrators that such behaviour is not acceptable. More immediately, strategies must be developed to ensure that women are not forced to tolerate violence in the home, and to support those who wish to leave. This support should deal with the social, emotional, economic and housing consequences of domestic violence that were evident from the international material (discussed in chapter 1) as well as in the lives of all the women who participated in this study.

In many countries of Africa, Asia and the Americas, domestic violence has to be understood in the context of the widespread structural violence produced by the extreme class, gender and racial inequalities that characterise life. Poverty, social disorganisation and political repression are just some of the factors which are likely to contribute to high levels of many different kinds of violence in many peripheral capitalist (neo-colonial) countries.

Apart from the material hardship that the majority of the people experience, there are also problems at the level of culture and consciousness as intellectuals like Fanon and Cabral long ago realised. Walter Rodney examined the ways in which Europe underdeveloped Africa economically, but studies of the cultural and psychological impact of imperialism demonstrate that it was not only economic systems that were underdeveloped during colonialism.

In some contexts violence is a manifestation of religious factionalism and ethnic chauvinism. Fanon also described the ways in which colonialism produced a reactive ossification and fixing of traditions, and a dependency on superstition and ritual, which he contrasted to the fluid and dynamic character of culture in less repressive circumstances (Fanon 1963). In other contexts, violence is the direct result of the promotion and arming of divisive forces. For example the apartheid regime in South Africa promotes banditry and terrorism in Mozambique and Angola (chapter 1). In short, populations and whole societies are kept in conditions that are inherently oppressive, violent and dehumanising, and this has consequences for all social behaviour, including relations across the divisions between the sexes.

Brutalised men are not suddenly humanised when they enter their homes to be with their families. Nor do men from the privileged classes and wealthy nations, in contexts where women are held in contempt, suddenly learn respect for women when they enter the private realm of the home. The fact that violence against women in the home appears to occur in all class, national, cultural and religious groups, supports the argument that it is intimately related to the more general oppression of women by men. We saw that religious and cultural orthodoxies are often invoked by men who attempt, expect or hope to coerce and oppress the women they live with or otherwise relate to. Both the Koran and the Bible contain passages which can be read as condoning physical chastisement of women by their husbands. Both also contain passages that can be read as condemning violence and brutality towards other human beings. The appropriation of religious and cultural doctrines by men to justify inflicting violence on women, is only possible because of the male dominance in the realms of religion and culture. Otherwise women could (and in some contexts are able to) equally invoke religion and culture against the beating of women by men.

Other institutionalised forms of violence like female circumcision, involve practices that are not advocated by any major religious doctrine. Rather it is a case of the society developing mutilatory practices for which justifications are then sought in religious doctrines, superstitions or traditional health beliefs. This view is supported by the fact that female genital mutilation occurs amongst Christians, Muslims and adherents to a range of African Religions alike, while on the other hand, not all members of any of these faiths feel obliged to engage in such mutilations.

Men often justify physical coercion on the basis that they are superior to women and as such have a right to enforce their own dominance. Similar views are used by oppressive political regimes: the Boers justify what they do to black people as the Nazis justified the gas chambers. The results of supremacist ideologies, whether across racial, class or gender boundaries are alarming. Women and progressive men alike must continue to challenge marital and other forms of violence against women, as unjustifiable manifestations of sexual inequality, and must fight to combat these in the interests of developing more just and humane societies.

The huge social and emotional pain caused by domestic violence, through its destructive impact on the lives of women and children has also been highlighted in this study. As if this were not devastating enough, we could also consider the costs incurred by the society through loss of productive time and capacities and resultant healthcare needs. Domestic violence, like the other forces which oppress and marginalise women cannot be afforded by underdeveloped and heavily indebted countries. It will however be tolerated by reactionary and regressive regimes that themselves rely on violence, and on the exploitation of social divisions and repression to retain, increase and exercise their own power. Violent oppression and coercion in the home, operates like other forms of social conflict to keep the people divided and at war with one another, and so more easily dominated.

In affluent Britain, many black and working class women are forced to tolerate violence by their unequal situation in the labour market and their restricted access to housing and other support. Institutionalised racism operates to deny black women the support that is available, making it significantly more harrowing for them to obtain decent incomes, accommodation and protection under the laws of the land. It is white racism, particularly the culture of racism in state bureaucracies and in the 'free' market, that ensures that black people, however many generations ago they settled here, remain concentrated in conditions of medieval squalor in the worst and most dangerous parts of the inner cities. These areas are often also heavily policed, but in coercive ways that militate against black women seeking or obtaining police protection from domestic violence.

Working class and unemployed black men, like black women without children are disproportionately represented amongst the growing homeless population, and have no statutory rights or access to public housing. They also have less access to the private sector because of their economic oppression, which is compounded by widespread racism by both private landlords and mortgage companies. As such black men are more likely to reach a situation in which they become desperate enough to contract 'cohabitations of convenience' with women who, for their part, do not have the heart to condemn them to the dangers of the heavily patrolled streets. The link between extreme oppression and fratricidal violence discussed above, is further supported by the evidence that women in this study gave concerning the circumstances of some, but not all, of the men who had abused them. Many (but again not all) also cited unemployment, economic and housing stress as factors exacerbating violence. Many of the abuses inflicted on black women by men in racist contexts can therefore be understood as a measure of the division and fragmentation of families and communities in racially oppressive contexts. At the same time it is clear that extreme oppression does not result in all men becoming violent towards the women with whom they live. On the other side of the coin it would be useful to identify any characteristics that may be associated with relationships that are able *not* to deteriorate into violence even in extremely oppressive circumstances.

The appropriation of state apparatuses and law enforcement agencies (police and immigration services in particular) by men, was also in evidence in some of the accounts that women gave of their experience. This supports the argument that physical violence is just one manifestation of abusive men exercising whatever power is available to them to coerce and terrorise the women with whom they live. In other words violence occurs alongside other forms of coercion and oppression. Men were not interviewed in this study, so it is not possible to comment on the emotional and relational dynamics accompanying their violence towards the woman in their lives, or what led them to use racist immigration laws against their partners.

Men's own experience of oppression is often invoked to explain the phenomenon, but is clearly not the only causal factor, since as we noted above, many oppressed men do not become abusive to the women in their lives. Furthermore, many powerful and privileged men also abuse and torture the women they have relationships with, often in even more premeditated and sadistic ways. It is also a gendered phenomenon, since violence is much more often inflicted on women by men and seldom the other way round, in the black communities as elsewhere.

The cultural content of the sexual and marital relationships that women in this study had been in (and in some cases were still in) varied between the different communities included in this study. The material and economic aspects of those relationships were very diverse, both within particular communities and across them. Some of the women were dependent wives who were obviously less empowered to challenge or resist violence, or to leave the violent man, particularly if they were from other countries. Others, in all three communities, had some economic autonomy, or held the tenancy on the home in which the abuse occurred (and so had more material power in their relationships) yet were still subjected to abuse and in many cases were driven out of their homes. It became clear that earning an income or holding the tenancy did not necessarily translate into autonomy or power in the women's relationships with men. What also became clear was that violence was even more likely to be hidden by professional or middle-class women who, as a result of their class privilege and professional autonomy, are accustomed to some sort of respect as individuals and are thus particularly ashamed of what they endure behind closed doors. This leads us to the conclusion that while it is important that women's economic oppression and limited access to housing be challenged, this is a minimum but not a sufficient condition for altering the unequal power relations between the sexes. Indeed it has become clear that changing the material inequalities must be part of a wider project to change the cultural, social and emotional inequalities that also characterise the relationships between the sexes within which such widespread torture and violence of women occurs.

The police state

The law in Britain has traditionally not protected women from abuse by their partners. In earlier historical periods, women had no civil status; wives were treated as chattels, whose husbands were entitled to abuse them as they saw fit. In this century women's equal right to protection from violent attacks, under the criminal law that makes it illegal for one person to inflict violence on another, has been stressed in the debates around the issue of domestic violence. Specific legislation to deal with domestic violence has also been developed. In practice however, it is clear that the law is not being adequately enforced by the police or in the law courts. Despite the widely publicised and acclaimed Force Order of 1987, women, and particularly black women, continue to be treated unsympathetically and even punitively by the police, and in the courts.

Black people in general have good reason to mistrust the law and its enforcing agents, in view of the evidence on police racism and attacks on black people. The particularly heavy-handed and coercive policing of the inner city areas where many black people live, has been implicated in causing the widespread street disturbances of the 1980s. The experience of the women in this study indicated that the police can and often do treat black men and women punitively when they are called to intervene in domestic violence. Their responses are sometimes helpful in ensuring that a woman gets to a safe place, but seldom concern enforcing the law, or legally prosecuting the woman's assailant. There were cases in which being called to the scene of domestic violence was used by the police as an excuse for assaulting a black man, and in one case, racially and sexually ridiculing and physically assaulting a black woman. Sometimes the whole affair is turned into an immigration investigation. Domestic violence in the black community continues to be a place were the law is not enforced by the police, and often not upheld by the courts.

Existing immigration laws must be condemned for their negative effects on black women's status in the home, as well as in the wider society. At present they undermine the rights of black women, as citizens and consumers, to the same standards of healthcare, education, welfare and housing that are available to white women. The imposition of a chattel status on women through the 'dependent wife' immigration status is unacceptable in the modern world. It means that women can be deported, perhaps away from their children, at the whim of an individual man, or simply for refusing to put up with violence and leaving a violent situation.

In the short term therefore we appeal to the Home Office to use their discretionary powers not to deport the women they know to be in this situation at the present time. More fundamentally the law should be revised to prevent this particular consequence and its disastrous effects on many women and children.

The recent increase in police powers cannot be defended as an appropriate response to the police reluctance to enforce the law in the case of domestic violence. Prior to the Police and Criminal Evidence Act of 1984, the police already had sufficient power to intervene in cases of domestic violence, but generally chose not to do so. The establishment of domestic violence response units, staffed by women police officers and resourced to do proper monitoring and follow-up work may be a good idea, but we were concerned to note that these are an initiative so far restricted to areas of high black concentration which are already heavily and oppressively policed. This raises the possibility that such units have a hidden agenda, concerned with convicting more black men, underpinning the publicly proclaimed agenda which stresses supporting and following up incidents in the interests of the women being subjected to violence. Training and other procedural developments (like the Force Order issued in 1987) must take on the fact that the race of both the assailants and the women they assault affect police responses in a number of negative ways. This raises the serious question of whether any amount of training can 'remove' the race hatred and misogyny that too often underlie police responses to domestic violence in the black communities.

All this evidence indicates the urgent need for appropriate legal support to be made available to black women, so that they are empowered to make use of the law in their own interests and as they see fit. This could include legal experts in all the relevant areas of law being employed in women's centres, black community centres and housing advice centres. These and other organisations should be equipped to furnish women with advice and information on how to contact lawyers who have specialised in this area, perhaps by holding well publicised advice sessions in local communities and developing a specialised referral system. Legal practitioners and law centres for their part should be encouraged and helped to develop expertise in these (less prestigious) areas of law, even if the financial rewards are not as high as in other areas.

Economic marginalisation and the welfare state

In societies in which women, and particularly black women, are denied equal access to employment, incomes, housing and a range of other things necessary for them to have a decent quality of life, the family is set up as a haven from the harsh realities of their social and economic inequality. Women are expected to be economically and social 'protected' by the men they live with. Yet statistical evidence indicates that it is inside the home that women are most likely to be attacked or killed, and that their most likely assailant is the very person who is expected to be their 'protector'. Once women have been assaulted in the home, their lives become haunted by fear, and when violence continues, many are forced to seek help outside their home and family, and sometimes outside their whole community. In Britain this often means running the gauntlet of the statutory services, and so confronting the realities of women's inequality under advanced capitalism. For black women the contempt that society has for single women and women-headed families in general, is compounded by race-hatred. As if this were not bad enough, there is also the general stigmatisation that people who have survived violent crimes and sexual assaults experience, and the specific ambivalence and mistrust that the public exhibits towards women who have been assaulted by their male partners.

The low incomes that are accessible to those black women who are able to work (because they are not mothers, or their children are at school, in state care, or cared for by other paid or unpaid women), do not allow many to enter the owner-occupying class. Black women, like working class white women therefore rely heavily on public housing. Many are locked into what has been described as the 'poverty trap' and are forced, by the lack of childcare support to live on welfare. Given the low wage levels and high unemployment of black men in London, black women are less likely than white women to be sheltered from economic realities by having a male provider.

The Welfare State often reacts to black women in severe need suspiciously and unsympathetically, if not punitively. The evidence of the women interviewed in this study showed the ways in which the welfare and the coercive state apparatuses come together, to have multiply oppressive and punitive effects on black women who have already been traumatised by domestic violence. We argued that what is needed is a quite different type of coming together; a supportive multi-agency response that responds to the needs and demands of the consumer rather than overwhelming, threatening and intimidating her.

Race, housing and domestic violence

The relationship between domestic violence and housing is particularly intimate. Housing stress is on the one hand deeply implicated as a factor generating and exacerbating violence in the family, while on the other hand, limited access to housing forces many women to remain in violent situations. Worse still are the housing consequences that women, who leave or escape from violent men, are forced to face. The suffering wreaked on woman-headed black families by the resulting long term homelessness is completely inexcusable. There are now approximately 30,000 families homeless in London, out of which a disproportionate number are black and/or women-headed households. The evidence here is that while most of these families live in conditions of Victorian squalor, black, single parent families are still subjected to racism on top of all this, both in the type of temporary accommodation they are forced to put up with and the time they have to wait before being rehoused. Finally the type of accommodation in which they are eventually rehoused is often of poorer quality than that allocated to their white counterparts. Racism appears to know no bottom line. Rather its impact increases down the scale so that black people at the very bottom are the most vulnerable and the most victimised of all.

Those local authorities that have attempted to develop policies based on need have in some areas developed strategies to prioritise women who have become homeless as a result of domestic violence. Lambeth is one such borough. Examining their policies in detail, there is some evidence to suggest that black women are rehoused more slowly than white women, and are expected to take poorer quality accommodation. This was also the impression of refuge workers in other Labour boroughs (Lewisham and Brent, for example) and draws attention to the fact that petty apartheid can be practised in relation to policies that have been developed out of feminist concerns, unless measures are simultaneously taken to address the race implications of these policies as, for example, the Women At Risk Team in Lambeth were attempting to do. Other local authorities, like Kensington and Chelsea, appear to be more concerned with minimising their statutory obligations to homeless families as far as possible, by fighting cases out in court if necessary. Here there were no race or gender equality initiatives, and the housing department had tried to use Women's Aid as a 'dumping ground' for all homeless women-headed households. Such extreme practices indicate the direction of things to come, since as a Conservative borough, RBKC is merely conforming to broader political trends and implementing the restructuring of the housing market in the name of 'market forces' and financial controls.

If the large state bureaucracies of local government and the welfare state are to continue to be dismantled and their powers and resources reduced in the ways we have drawn attention to, other agencies must be resourced and empowered to take on their obligations. Given the sensitive and highly specialised nature of working with black women who have experienced violence, resources should be made available to autonomous and voluntary agencies with established track records in this area. Women's refuges and black women's organisations are the best placed to alleviate the immediate problem of emergency provision for black women at the present time. Refuges must be resourced to do so, and not used as dumping grounds or forced to become long-stay hostels, left to correct all the wrongs of bad policies and cuts in funding, as appears to be occurring in some areas.

In the meantime, local authorities must be pressurised to make more accommodation available for women seeking rehousing, and not to operate petty apartheid within those housing quotas and policies that formally recognise the needs of women escaping violent men, so that black women too can be rehoused in decent accommodation In the longer term, housing associations and cooperatives must be strongly encouraged to take on these obligations. Better still, ways must be found to make them do so. Funding bodies like the London Borough Grants Scheme, and co-ordinating bodies like the Housing Corporation and the Federation of Black Housing Organisations have responsibilities in this area.

Independent strategies for challenging the abuse of black women

Many voluntary sector organisations and resource centres do not deal with the multiple problems faced by women who have been subjected to domestic violence. At best they may offer support in one area, for example housing, but not in the other areas. As such they too may end up referring women to a range of different other organisations instead of being able to assist them in sorting out their lives in the individually supportive but coordinated way that is necessary for women who are often having to deal with a range of legal, welfare and housing problems. Furthermore, women who have been subjected to violence may need social and emotional support from members of their own community, or particularly from women from the same community. This too should be made much more widely available across the voluntary sector.

Community organising

Our review of community and women's organisations indicated that few are in a position to offer any or all of the necessary support to abused women. This applies to black as well as white-dominated women's centres, few of whom are in any position to be able to offer support to black women who have been brutalised by the black or white men they have been in relationships with. Both black community and black women's organisations could play a valuable role in this area, but lack the resources, expertise and/or the will to provide the intimate and individual support that may be necessary. Others lack sufficient racial awareness and sensitivity to do so. The best that many can offer is a referral service, and only a few organisations (like the Southall Black Women's Centre, the

Chinese Information and Advice Centre and the Commission for Philipino Migrant Workers) attempt to offer more than this. African women in particular are likely to find that there is nowhere for them to get proper individual support. There are existing and established black women's organisations which serve the Caribbean, African and Asian communities, and these should be developed and resourced to offer a specialised service to minimize the problems that result from domestic violence. Community organisations should be equipped to do more outreach work on domestic violence, since it remains very much a hidden scourge in most black communities.

Both mixed and women's organisations should be encouraged and resourced to do work on domestic violence, and work that is not merely directed towards reconciliation of couples in the interests of 'the family' or 'the children', but work that prioritises the immediate interests of women and children over those of violent men. In the longer term, resources could be put towards addressing the deeper and even more difficult area of changing physically and sexually abusive men through therapy. Similarly it is in the longer term that the destructive relational patterns that prevail between men and the women they abuse can be addressed. In any case, therapeutic intervention may well have to be predicated on liberating couples from situations in which they are living together because they have been forced to by circumstances rather than because they have chosen to do so. For oppressed groups, therapy and counselling cannot undo or redress the injustices inflicted on them by continuing unemployment and under-employment, poverty, bad housing, police repression and racial attacks. Once these material conditions are changed, then therapy may prove effective, since only then will people be in a position to recover their dignity and respond positively to it. In the meantime, therapy can only concentrate on equipping oppressed people to channel the violence that oppression nourishes into different outlets (in this instance, away from the women they have relationships with). The mental health of black people has long fascinated the mental health industry, yet black people continue to be denied non-coercive and supportive mental healthcare, just as most are denied access to good education and the other means to self-actualisation and healthy personal development.

Black mental health organisations should be resourced to provide support for women who have been subjected to violence and feel that counselling or specialist therapy would help them come to terms with their experience. Therapy is unlikely to help women who perceive no option other than to continue to live in a violent or threatening situation, but it may help women to find the courage that it takes to leave violent situations, and it may assist in their recovery from the stress, trauma and emotional scarring left by domestic violence.

In short, therapy and counselling are not panaceas for oppressive and brutalising living conditions, or for sexual oppression and the use of physical coercion against women. It may help individual women find the emotional resources to leave, and to recover themselves, but in the long term the broader conditions of sexual inequality will have to be changed.

The refuge movement
In chapter 11 we drew attention to the unique role played by women's refuges in supporting women struggling with the grave consequences that domestic violence has on them and their children. The women's movement has yielded not only theory, but also practical action to support women seeking to leave violent men and establish lives free from this particularly destructive form of oppression. At the present time, the refuge movement is facing major challenges. It has historically been characterised by precarious funding. The funding was withdrawn from the national office of WAFE altogether for two years, and it is frequently withdrawn from local refuges. As a result, refuges close and new ones open continuously. Nonetheless, the movement as a whole has accumulated enormous experience and expertise during the 16 years of its existence.

At the present time, much energy is having to be devoted to investigating and coming to terms with the massive legislative changes which the present regime has passed, many of which have very negative implications for women, for women-headed families, and for black people, but particularly for black women. The gender and race implications of the Housing Acts, the Social Security Act; the war of attrition on local state apparatuses (eg the Greater London Council, the Inner London Education Authority), and the erosion of their resources (for example through ratecapping and the Local Government Finance Act), suggest that for black women fleeing violence, things are going to become harder than ever. Many of these women will be single parents, as well as being black and women, and will bear the brunt of societal racism and sexism, as well as the unsupportive attitude of their own communities. It is important that WAFE and the non-affiliated refuges are encouraged to take this fact on board and to continue to seek and develop ways of minimizing the destructive effects of Thatcherism on women who have been through

310

violence. Part of this work involves lobbying for amendments to particularly bad legislation, for which wider support is also necessary.

Involvement in this type of work places additional burdens on refuge workers, and should be independently resourced, locally and nationally, so as not to detract from the time and energies that they are supposed to be devoting to supporting women and managing and running safe houses. All legislative changes also mean that advice workers require further training, but staff levels and funding are already far from sufficient, and are particularly bad in the case of black refuges.

In a clear instance of overt racism, black refuges receive significantly less funding per bedspace than other refuges. This is something which funding bodies can find no justification for, given the evidence that black refuges, if anything, require extra resources to support women against racism and to be supportive to women from a range of diverse cultures, languages and values. These particular challenges are not made any easier in substandard and severely overcrowded conditions.

The problem of racism within the British women's movement in general, and within women's refuges in particular, and the anti-racist policies and practices initiated by the Women's Aid Federation, England (WAFE) were critically discussed. From that discussion we can conclude that women's refuges need to be resourced and encouraged to challenge racism within local refuges, and that this can be facilitated through specialised training which utilises the accumulated experience and practice of refuges, and particularly of black women working and living in them. In this way open discussion can be facilitated and women feeling oppressed or alienated by racism can be empowered to challenge incidents and events that would otherwise marginalise them from the resources of the collectives that make up refuges. The potential for genuinely challenging racism may be harder to unleash because of the decentralised and non-hierarchical structure of WAFE, but once set in motion, the process of changing consciousness and therefore practice, is likely to be more lasting than within traditional large bureaucracies. The growing numbers of black women living and working in refuges will be a major factor in facilitating the necessary change.

Summary of recommendations

Numerous possibilities for action exist to ameliorate the horrendous situation faced by black women who have been subjected to violence by their partners, exposed for the first time by this report. Here I shall outline some of those. We call upon the relevant agencies to initiate action immediately. Each day that passes exacts enormous human costs from women like (and including) those who participated in this study, many of whom are part of the growing long-term homeless population.

Central Government

1. Review and reform the law relating to domestic violence, and in particular its impact on women who are not living with their assailants, and women who do not wish to sue for financial recompense or for divorce.

2. The law making women who have been assaulted, compellable witnesses should be reconsidered in view of the punitive way it is already being used against women, since it is likely to further deter women, and especially black women from reporting violence.

3. The immigration laws which, as has been demonstrated, reduce women to the status of chattels by making their right to remain subject to the whims of men, should be reviewed and changed immediately.

4. The Government's legislation undermining the provision of affordable rented accommodation by the public sector should be reversed in the light of the appalling social consequences we are currently witnessing. These are having particularly detrimental effects on the housing rights of black people, women and single parent families. The impact of the resulting long-term homelessness on women and children who have already been

traumatised by the experience of violence cannot be countenanced by any society which considers itself to be civilised.

5. It is now long overdue for the Government to have heeded the recommendations of its own Select Committee on Violence in Marriage in 1975, and the Women's National Commission (1985) concerning the provision of refuges. There continues to be a serious shortfall, and funding is still grossly inadequate. Within the existing provision, only racism can explain how it is that black refuges are receiving less funding per bed space than other refuges. We therefore call on Central Government to fund, and encourage other bodies to fund, the development of Women's Aid. This should not only include money for more bedspaces, but also for the development of anti-racism within the refuge movement, the development of childcare provisions, outreach and campaign work, as well as funding for training to facilitate the development and sharing of management and other skills within refuges, and to improve the working conditions of refuge workers.

6. There is an urgent need for statutory bodies to develop multiagency responses that are co-ordinated in the interests of women, particularly black women, who are subjected to violence, and/or seeking to build lives for themselves free from violence or the threat of violence. The multiply coercive and punitive state responses by means of which we saw black women being further oppressed and brutalised must be stopped. Their impact can and should be immediately reduced by resourcing and developing proper community support, so that women's and community workers are available to liaise with the various statutory agencies (legal, housing, immigration, police and welfare organisations) on behalf of the woman concerned.

7. The Department of Health and the Environment should finance the training and development of the health services to raise consciousness and improve the responses of healthcare professionals to women, particularly black women, who have (or may have) been subjected to domestic violence.

8. Social services should conduct a comprehensive review of the responses of social services to women, especially black women, with whom they come into contact who have been subjected to violence. The present child-centred responses are not only inadequate and sometimes punitive,

but they are not always in the best interests of the child, particularly not where they involve removing black children from their mothers. Instead resources should be put into developing better practice, ie practice that is supportive to women who wish to leave violent men and establish independent lives for themselves and their children.

Housing

This report indicates the increasingly urgent need for safe and decent housing for black people, who are currently living under severe housing stress, which is a result of racism in housing, and is further exacerbated by widespread societal racism. Housing stress is seriously implicated in generating violence in the black communities, as well as in forcing women to tolerate life-threatening levels of abuse, which sometimes end in death.

1. Local authorities, housing associations and cooperatives and private sector housing organisations must be prevented from racist practice on the basis of the negative implications racist housing practice has for the whole society.

2. Public and private sector organisations involved in housing must also be prevented from discriminating against women and women-headed families, since these are in any case an increasing proportion of the population. Policies must be developed to improve women's independent access to all types of housing.

3. Local Authorities should have a London-wide policy on rehousing and housing women who have housing needs that result from relationship breakdown and/or domestic violence. The policy already drawn up by the Women and Housing Forum should be developed, on the basis of this research, to address the race implications of such policies and then implemented.

4. Local authority policies on relationship breakdown and domestic violence need to be subjected to a comprehensive review, and to be regularly monitored. Most obviously, there is a need for the race implications of such policies to be properly addressed, in the light of the findings of this report.

5. Housing associations and cooperatives must also be encouraged and

resourced to develop and implement policies which make specific provision for black people and women, but particularly for black women seeking to live in safe and decent homes, free from violence or the threat of violence. This group is currently being particularly discriminated against, and are, because of the circumstances exposed in this report, particularly vulnerable to racism.

6. Black housing organisations must be resourced and encouraged in their efforts to make decent and affordable accommodation available to black people. They should also prioritise the needs of women who are escaping violence, and particularly those who are not being accepted for rehousing by local authorities (these include women without children, women from the private sector, women whose assailants do not live with them, women who do not wish to take legal action against their assailant).

Policing

1. The policing of domestic violence in the black communities should be subjected to a comprehensive review. The impact of the Force Order of 1987, Domestic Violence Response Units and the extension of police powers under the Police and Criminal Evidence Act 1984 on the black community, and on black women in particular, should be the subject of such a review.

2. Police responses to domestic violence in the black communities as elsewhere, should centre around appropriate, effective and efficient enforcement of the law in relation to domestic violence. Responding to domestic violence should not be used to initiate immigration investigations, or as an excuse for assaulting black men or women in the ways that were found to be occurring during the course of this research.

3. Monitoring of police responses to domestic violence, particularly in the black communities should be undertaken by independent bodies, such as those that exist already (police units and voluntary sector monitoring groups). These should therefore be resourced and supported in their work on police responses to domestic violence in the black communities.

The community

1. Educational and campaigning work should be conducted to raise awareness on the nature of domestic violence and its negative consequences and to condemn all forms of woman-abuse, particularly in the various black communities where it is often hidden and excused on completely erroneous grounds. This report is one resource contributing to that work. Such work is best conducted by members of those communities.

2. Community organising on and around the issue should be resourced and encouraged by statutory and other funding bodies. Suggestions for such organising include:

a) The establishment of helplines and referral services on domestic violence that are sensitive to the various needs of women in the various black communities.

b) Resourcing and development of many more black women's centres and refuges for black women.

c) Resourcing and developing work on domestic violence within the existing black women's centres and refuges, since those that exist are at present too under-resourced to engage in the detailed and ongoing individual casework that is necessary.

d) Organisation to provide long term and permanent homes for black people to reduce the extreme and growing housing stress that black communities are being subjected to, with a view to creating a situation in which black women seeking to escape violence, need not be put through the additionally brutalising ordeal of long term homelessness, which is often made even worse by racism and race attacks.

e) Organisation to address the mental health-care needs of the black communities. Existing bodies dealing with black mental health-care are presently grossly inadequate, and should therefore be supported and resourced in their work, but in particular, to provide supportive counselling for black women who have been or are being subjected to violence by the men they are in relationships with. Black mental health-care professionals from the various communities are in the best position to undertake this work. Such counselling should focus on addressing the needs of women clients, and not on getting women to conform to any particular behavioural and familial norms, or to satisfy male interests.

317

Appendix: Deaths attributed to domestic violence

Below is a listing of black women who have died as a result of domestic violence between 1979 and 1989. It is not a comprehensive listing, due to lack of research time and resources. Rather it is a set of examples, presented here to highlight the destructive potential of continuing not to respond adequately to the problem of woman abuse. It is of course not only black women who are killed or driven to kill themselves as a result of torture and cruelty at the hands of loved ones. Official statistics show that women were more likely to be killed by their partner than by anyone else. Most victims are white women killed by white men. Official statistics on domestic murders and violence are not broken down by race, notably in stark contrast to other crime statistics. Even if they were, such figures would probably say more about the processes of crime reporting, detection and prosecution than about actual incidence of maiming and deaths of women by their partners in the various cultural and racial groups that make up the population of Britain. Worse still such statistics would be open to the same racist manipulation as existing race and crime statistics (such as those for 'mugging' — itself a racially defined crime category) have been. We exist in an environment in which senior police officers (and much of the public) declare their belief that black men, particularly of African-Caribbean origin, are 'inherently violent', with no fear of being challenged or disciplined. Remarks made by other senior police officers, and other supposedly responsible groups of professionals contacted in the course of this research, indicate that they also believe African-Caribbean men to be the main perpetrators of woman abuse.

MRS DHILLON and five children were killed by her husband in 1979. Her death, together with all her children was taken so calmly by the community that it shocked local black women, feeding into the developing awareness of women's oppression that led to the establishment of the Southall Black Women's Centre.

KRISHNA SHARMA, a young wife with two children was found dead in her home in Southall on 8 March 1984. No one has been charged or convicted in connection with her murder. The coroner's verdict of suicide outraged the local community, and precipitated demonstrations outside her husband, Chandra Mohan Sharma's family home. His relatives knocked down one protester and threatened another during the demonstration. The inquest was picketed by black women, who as it turned out, had correctly anticipated the outcome of no one being held or tried for her death. The clothes Krishna was wearing were torn, and her body was found to be marked with bruises from previous batterings. Her sister confirmed that Krishna had been subjected to violence throughout the eight years of her marriage, and had sought help from a number of sources. Most tragically of all, she had appealed to the police for help the very night before her body was discovered. They had advised her to take out a private prosecution against her husband, despite the fact that she was not confident in English.

In February 1985, 32 year old *AMARJEET THETHY* was strangled to death with a scarf by her husband Tarlochan, a crime the presiding judge described as the result of 'wicked and wrong-headed family loyalty'. Amarjeet had a five year old son. Her murder was said to have been provoked by Amarjeet failing to conform to 'traditional Sikh values' after an arranged marriage. When Tarlochan complained to his family, they plotted together to arrange the killing as if it had been committed by a burglar. Amarjeet's mother-in-law, Balbir, and two brothers-in-law, Paranjit and Palvinder, were convicted with Tarlochan for murder, and all given life sentences for their callous and premeditated killing of Amarjeet. A third brother who was alleged to have participated in the planning and covering up of the crime, Dr Sethi, was acquitted of murder and given 18 months for conspiring to obstruct the course of justice. A qualified dentist and doctor, Dr Sethi was also struck off the register, a decision which he planned to appeal against.

On 22 October 1985, *BALWANT KAUR PANESAR* was stabbed to death in a women's refuge in Brent, in front of her three daughters, all of whom were under the age of six. Another Asian woman who worked at the refuge was also injured as she tried to fight off the killers. Balwant's husband was thought to have been assisted by an accomplice, but only he was apprehended and convicted for the killing. Bhagwant Singh Panesar was sentenced to life imprisonment. Balwant's particularly horrible death (she was stabbed twice in the chest in her bedroom) provoked a wide-ranging campaign against woman abuse in the home. The campaign challenged the refusal of police to protect women whose lives are threatened by their partners. Like Krishna Sharma, Balwant Kaur had sought police protection. Only a few days before her death, the refuge had received a warning from acquaintances of Bhagwant Kaur, who had heard that he was searching for Balwant with the expressed intention of killing her. The court heard evidence from two men he had tried to recruit to assist him breaking in to the refuge for a fee of £3,000, an offer which they claim to have turned down when they saw him with a carving knife.

The women in the refuge were terrified by the threat and called the police, who merely sent one officer round to make 'routine enquiries' and did not give any further protection. The tragedy of the police non-response is that had they taken the women's plea for 24-hour protection seriously, Balwant's life might have been saved. Balwant was in hiding at the Brent Asian Women's Refuge, having left her violent husband after 10 years during which she was repeatedly abused. Balwant had taken out injunctions against her husband on at least two previous occasions, the second one with a power of arrest attached. This followed an incident in which Bhagwant Singh Panesar had attacked her with a screwdriver and kicked her in the stomach during a pregnancy. Her solicitor, Amrik Singh Gill described how he had made 18 telephone calls to agencies and charities, looking for somewhere for her to go. Despite the stipulations of the Housing (Homeless Persons) Act, Redbridge Council, like so many councils on too many occasions, refused to accommodate Balwant and her children. Instead instructing her to return home, since she had the 'protection' of a non-molestation order. When Mr Gill finally found that Brent Asian Refuge could offer her a place to stay, he gave her £25 and put her into a taxi with her daughters and the carrier bags of clothing they had escaped with. A social worker described Balwant in her struggle to establish a new life away from her sadistic husband thus:

'She was a wholesome person who lived for her children . . . she was a very capable woman whose confidence increased rapidly when she was in the refuge.'

This tragic case illustrates the possible consequences of the refusal of statutory agencies to take the pleas of black women seriously. Even the most meagre assistance that the police and local authorities are in fact statutorily obliged to provide, may prove to be life saving. Yet black women are too often denied the most basic protection, in the various ways that this report has documented.

On 3 May 1986, 34 year old *GURDIP KAUR SANDHU* was brutally attacked by her estranged husband, Gurbax Singh and his brother, Harbax Singh, in front of their 12 year old son, at their home in Caversham, Berkshire. They had been married since Gurdip was 17 years old, and she had been subjected to repeated violence for the next 17 years of her life. At the time of the attack they had separated, but Gurdip had also had to take out a legal injunction, which was supposed to prevent her husband from entering her home, because he had continued his violence and threats towards her. On the day in question, Gurbax and his twin brother Harbax came to the house. Gurdip was beaten unconscious, in the presence of her 12 year old son, carried away in a borrowed van and driven around town, before being dumped near the hospital. Some people passing by found her; she was admitted to the hospital and put on a life support machine. It took five days for her to die from a fractured larynx which was followed by heart and lung failure.

After her death, Gurdip became the subject of grave character assassination, and at the trial in January 1987, only Harbax Singh, Gurdip's brother-in-law was convicted, but for manslaughter rather than murder. Only then did the jury hear now, six years earlier, he had himself hired two men to try and kill his own wife, Surinder, for which he served a two-year sentence. Harbax had also been so violence that he had twice put his own wife in hospital and forced her to seek safety in a women's refuge. After she left him, Harbax abducted their son and a long court battle ensued until the Indian High Court reunited Surinder with her son. Surinder subsequently had to move to a secret address in Reading and was placed under police guard.

The murder charge against Gurdip's husband, Gurbax Singh was dropped before the trial when the Department of Public Prosecutions declared that there was 'insufficient evidence' to secure a conviction, so that he was not charged at all. Previously, while Gurdip was still on life support, a lesser charge of Grievous Bodily Harm against him had also been dropped. During Harbax Singh's trial it emerged that Gurdip's 12 year old son, a key witness to the events which led to his mother's death, had also been threatened with death.

Asian and women's organisations mounted a massive campaign for a retrial of Gurdip's husband when he walked free from the courtroom with no charges being pressed against him. As a spokesperson from the Asian Women's Network pointed out at the time:

> 'So many women, whatever their background, suffer violence — rape, murder, grievous bodily harm — in their own homes, only to hear, if they are still alive, their own characters torn apart in the courtroom, whilst their attackers receive minimal sentences due to "mitigating circumstances", such as being drunk, or "provocation". When will the judicial system recognise domestic violence as a serious crime?'

SURINDER PAL KAUR was only 19 years old when she was strangled by her husband and her body dumped under a pile of rubbish in a derelict garage near her home in Walsall. She was killed in 1986, after only three months in an arranged marriage. Her cold-blooded killing was allegedly the result of her attempt to talk to her husband, 20 year old Tarlochan Singh Bagri, about their poor sex-life. He denied murder.

AZRA DIN was also only 19 when she died at the hands of her husband, Parvez Aslam, a shopkeeper from Pakistan who had come to Britain to marry his British-born cousin. They settled with her family in Middlesborough, but when Aslam became violent towards Azra, he was thrown out. According to press reports in May 1986, he felt so 'dishonoured' by his rejection that he returned to Azra's family home to stab her to death with a knife in each hand. Azra was several months pregnant when she died from multiple stab wounds.

DENISE MONCRIEFFE, a 24 year old woman, was found dead in her Stoke Newington flat on Monday afternoon, 2 October 1988, by detectives. Denise had been brutally beaten, and suffered serious internal injuries after being repeatedly kicked and punched in her stomach. Her common-law partner, car mechanic John Smith, was charged with her murder and remanded in custody. Police interviewed over 50 neighbours in connection with the case, many of whom had heard her screams in the small hours of Monday morning, after she had returned from an evening with friends.

Bibliography

AAWORD (1983), *Seminar on Research on African Women: what type of methodology?*, Association of African Women for Research and Development, Dakar.

AAWORD (1983), *Statement on Genital Mutilation*, in M. Davies (ed).

ABDALLA, Raqiya Haji Dualeh (1982), *Sisters in Affliction: circumcision and infibulation of women in Africa*, Zed.

AFRICAN WOMAN (1988-1989), *African Woman: Quarterly Development Journal*, Issues 1-3, pub by African Woman, Wesley House, 4 Wild Court, London WC2B 5AU.

AHMED, S., CHEETAM, J., and SMALL, J. (eds) (1986), *Social Work with Black Children and Their Families*, Batsford Ltd, London UK.

AKANDE, J.O., (1979), *Law and the Status of Women in Nigeria*, UN.

ALCOLT, P. (1987), *Poverty and State Support*, Longman, UK.

AMADIUME, I. (1987), *Male Daughters, Female Husbands: gender and sex in an African society*, Zed.

AMOS, V., LEWIS, G., MAMA, A. and PARMAR, P. (eds) (1984), *Many Voices, One Chant: black feminist perspectives*, Feminist Review 17, London, UK.

AMOS, V. and PARMAR, P. (1984), 'Challenging Imperial Feminism' in *Feminist Review* 17, London, UK.

ARDILL, N. and CROSS, N. (1988), *Undocumented Lives: Britain's unauthorised migrant workers*, Runnymede Trust, UK.

ASHA, (1987), *Asian Women and Housing*, Shahida Omarsh, ASHA Asian Women's Aid Research Project, London, UK.

ASHA, (1985-6), *Annual Report*, ASHA, UK.

ASHA, (1986-7), *Annual Report*, ASHA, UK.

ASSOCIATION OF LONDON AUTHORITIES (1988), *Relationship Breakdown Policy and Procedure — Recommended Guidelines*, Report by London Housing Unit on Behalf of Women and Housing Forum,

18th April, London, UK.

ASSOCIATION OF METROPOLITAN AUTHORITIES (AMA), (1985), *Housing and Race: policy and practice in local authorities*, AMA, UK.

AMA (1987), *Greater London Housing Condition Survey*, London, UK.

ATKINS, S. and HOGGET, B. (1984), *Women and the Law*, Blackwell, UK.

AUGHTON, H. (1986), *Housing Finance: A basic guide*, Shelter, UK.

AUSTERBERRY, H. and WATSON, S. (1982), *Women's Hostels in London*, SHAC, UK.

AUSTERBERRY, H. and WATSON, S. (1983), *Women on the Margins*, City University Housing Research Group, London, UK.

BANTON, M.P. (1955), *The Coloured Quarter — Negro immigrants in an English city*, J. Cape.

BARRETT, M. (1980), *Women's Oppression Today*, Verso and NLB, UK.

BARRETT and MACINTOSH (1982), *The Anti-Social Family*, Verso and NLB, UK.

BELLO, E.G. (1985), *The Status of Women in Zimbabwe*, Harare, n.12-14.

BHATT, C. (1987), *Racial Violence and the Local State*, Foundation 2, LRHRU, London.

BINNEY, V., HARKELL, G. and NIXON, J. (1981), *Leaving Violent Men*, Women's Aid Federation, England, UK.

BOLTON, F.G. and BOLTON, S.R. (1987), *Working With Violent Families*, Sage.

BONNERJEA, L. (1987), *Homelessness in Brent*, Policy Studies Institute, UK.

BONNERJEA, L. (1987), *The Future of Public Sector Housing*, London School of Economics, UK.

BONNERJEA, L. and LAWTON, L. (1986), *Race and Housing in Brent: Summary*, Policy Studies Institute, UK.

BORKOWSKI, M., MURCH, M. and WALKER, V. (1982), *Marital Violence: the community response*, Tavistock, UK.

BRAILEY, M. (1986), *Women's Access to Council Housing*, Occasional Paper No.25, The Planning Exchange, 186 Bath Street, Glasgow G2 4HG, Scotland.

BRION, M. and TINKER, A. (1980), *Women in Housing: access and influence*, Housing Centre Trust, UK.

BRIXTON BLACK WOMEN'S GROUP (1979-1981), *Speak Out*, Issues 1-4, London, UK.

BRIXTON BLACK WOMEN'S GROUP (1981), 'The Brixton Uprising:

A Report', *Spare Rib* 107, June 1981, London UK.

BROWN, C. (1984), *Black and White in Britain*, Heinemann, UK.

BROWN, G. and HARRIS, T. (1970), *Social Origins of Depression*, Tavistock, UK.

BROWNMILLER, S. (1975), *Against Our Will*, Penguin, UK.

BRYAN, B., DADZIE, S. and SCAFE, S. (1985), *The Heart of the Race: black women's lives in Britain*, Virago, UK.

BURNEY, E. (1967), *Housing on Trial — a study of immigrants and local government*, IRR, Oxford, UK.

BUTTON, S. (1984), *A Study of Gender and Local Government Policy Formulation*, Women's Committees, SAUS, Bristol, UK.

CAMDEN TRAVELLERS SUPPORT GROUP (1989), *Anywhere But Here — travellers and homelessness in Camden*, LRHRU, UK.

CARLEN, P. (1976), *Magistrate's Justice*, Martin Robertson, London, UK.

CARLEN, P. (1985), *Women's Imprisonment: a study in social control*, RKP, UK.

CARLEN, P. *et al* (1985), *Criminal Women*, Polity Press, UK.

CASHMORE, E. and TROYNA, B. (1982), *Black Youth in Crisis*.

CHAR (1986), *Single Women and Homelessness*, Conference Report, 22 October, CHAR, UK.

CHAR (1988), *Single Women and Homelessness*, Conference Report, 22 October, CHAR, UK.

CHAR (1988), 'Single People Facing the Housing Crisis', Background Papers to Conference, 29 April, London, UK.

CHRISTIAN, L. (1983), *Policing By Coercion*, Greater London Council, Police Committee Support Unit, London.

CLAPHAM, D. and ENGLISH, J. (eds) (1987), *Public Housing: current trends and future developments*, Croom Helm, UK.

CLEVELAND REFUGE AND AID FOR WOMEN AND CHILDREN (1984), *Private Violence: Public Shame*, CRAWC/WAFE, PO Box 391, Bristol BS99 7WS, UK.

CONNORS, J. (1986), 'Violence Against Women', Paper submitted to Meeting of Commonwealth Law Ministers, Zimbabwe.

CONSERVATIVE RESEARCH DEPARTMENT (1988), *Reviving the Inner Cities*, Politics Today, 24 June, London, UK.

COOPER, S. (1985), *Public Housing and Private Property*.

COMMISSION FOR RACIAL EQUALITY (CRE), (1977), *Housing Need among Ethnic Minorities*, CRE, UK.

CRE (1984), *Race and Council Housing in Hackney*, CRE, UK.

CROLL, E. (1978), *Feminism and Socialism in China*, RKP, London, UK.

DAVIES, M. (ed) (1983), *Third World Second Sex: Women's struggles and national liberation*, Zed, UK.

DAVIES, M. (ed) (1987), *Third World Second Sex: Volume 2*, Zed, UK.

DAVIS, A.Y. (1981), *Women, Race and Class*, The Women's Press, London, UK.

DOBASH, R.E. and DOBASH *et al*, (1978), 'Wifebeating: the victim's speak, *Victimology* 2 (3-4).

DOBASH, R.E. and DOBASDH R. (1980), *Violence Against Wives*, London Open Books, UK.

DOE (1979), *National Dwelling and Housing Survey*, DOE, UK.

DOE (1982), *Priority Estates Project*, DOE, UK.

DONNISON, D. (1985), 'Why the Cohabitation Rule Makes Sense', in C. Ungerson (ed) *Women and Social Policy: A Reader*, Macmillan, UK.

DONNISON, D. and EVERSLEY, D. (eds) (1973), *London: urban patterns, problems and policies*, Heinemann, London, UK.

DONZELOT, J. (1979), *The Policing of Families: welfare versus the state*, Hutchinson, UK.

D'OREY, S. (1984), *Immigration Prisoners: a forgotten minority*, Runnymede Trust, London, UK.

DYOS, H.J. and WOLFF, M. (eds) (1973), *The Victorian City*, Vols 1-2, RKP, UK.

EALING, LONDON BOROUGH of (1988), *Ealing Borough Council's Response to the Government's Housing Proposals*, Ealing Housing.

EDWARDS, J. (1987), *Positive Discrimination, Social Justice and Social Policy*, Tavistock, UK.

EDWARDS, S. (1981), *Female Sexuality and the Law*, Martin Robertson, Oxford, UK.

EDWARDS, S. (1985), 'A Socio-legal evaluation of gender ideologies in domestic violence assault and spousal homicides, *Victimology*, 10(4): 186-205.

EDWARDS, S. (1986), 'Police attitudes and dispositions in domestic disputes: the London study', *Police Journal*.

EDWARDS, S. (1986), *The Police Response to Domestic Violence in London*, Polytechnic of Central London, UK.

EDWARDS, S. (ed) (1986), *Gender, Sex and the Law*, Croom Helm, UK.

EISEN, A. (1984), *Women and Revolution in Vietnam*, Zed.

ELLIS, P. (ed) (1986), *Women of the Caribbean*, Zed.

EL SADAAWI, N. (1980), *The Hidden Face of Eve: women in the Arab world*, Zed, UK.

EL DAREER, A. (1982), *Woman, Why Do You Weep? Circumcision and its consequences*, Zed, UK.

ENGELS, F. (1972), *The Origin of the Family, Private Property and the State*, Lawrence and Wishart, London, UK.

FANON, F. (1967), *The Wretched of the Earth*, Penguin, UK.

FARAGHER, T. (1985), *The Police Response to Violence Against Women in the Home*, in J. Pahl (ed).

FEMINIST ANTHOLOGY COLLECTIVE (eds) (1981), *No Turning Back: Writings from the Women's Liberation Movement 1975-80*, The Women's Press, UK.

FILSTEAD, W.J. (1970), *Qualitative Methodology: firsthand involvement in the social world*, Rand McNally College Press, Chicago, USA.

FIRESTONE, S. (1970), *The Dialectic of Sex: the case for feminist revolution*, Bantam Books, New York, USA.

FLETT, M. and PEAFORD, M. (1977), *The Effect of Slum Clearance on Multi-Occupation*, SSRC, Working Papers on Ethnic Rels, No.4.

FOUCAULT, M. (1977), *Discipline and Punish*, Peregrine Books, UK.

FREEMAN, M. (1987), *Dealing with Domestic Violence*, CCH Editions Ltd, Oxon, UK.

FRYER, P. (1984), *Staying Power: the history of black people in Britain*, Pluto, London, UK.

GEVINS, A. (1987), *Tackling Tradition: African women speak out against female circumcision* (Interviews with Assitan Diallo and Stella Graham), in M. Davies (ed).

GILROY, P. (1987), *There Ain't No Black in the Union Jack*, Hutchinson, UK.

GLASER, B.G. and STRAUSS, A.L. (1967), *The Discovery of Grounded Theory: strategies for qualitative research*, Aldine, Chicago, USA.

GLASS, R. (1960), *Newcomers*, Centre for Urban Studies, G. Allen and Unwin.

GLAZER, N. and YOUNG, K. (eds) (1983), *Ethnic Pluralism and Public Policies: achieving equality in the United States and Britain*, American Academy of Arts and Sciences/Commission for Racial Equality/Policy Studies Institute.

GLC (1986), *Housing Research and Policy Report No.3*, GLC, UK.

GLC (1985), *Relationship Breakdown and Local Authority Tenancies*, GLC, UK.

GLC, EMU (1985), *Planning for a Multi Racial London*, Report of Findings.

GLC (1983), *Survey of Local Authorities Policy and Practises*, GLC, UK.

GLENNING, C. and MILLAR, J. (eds) (1987), *Women and Poverty in Britain*, Wheatsheaf, UK.

GOODE, W.J. (1971), 'Force and Violence in the Family', *Marriage and Family* 33, 4:624-636.

GORDON, L. (1986), 'Silent Crimes Against Jamaican Women', in P. Ellis (ed).

GORDON, P. (1981), *Passport Raids and Checks*, Runnymede Trust, UK.

GORDON, P. (1986), *Racial Violence and Harassment*, Runnymede Trust, UK.

GORDON, P. and NEWNHAM, A. (1985), *Passport to Benefits? Racism in Social Security*, Runnymede Trust, UK.

GREATER LONDON COUNCIL (1985), *Relationship Breakdown and Local Authority Tenancies*, Report by Controller of Housing and Technical Services, GLC, London, UK.

GREATER LONDON COUNCIL (1986), *Women and Housing Policy: Reports Submitted to the GLC Housing and Women's Committees*, GLC Housing Research and Policy Report No.3, London, UK.

GREVE, J. *et al* (1971), *Homelessness in London*, Scottish Academic Press, UK.

GREWAL *et al* (1988), *Charting the Journey: writings by black and third world women* Sheba, UK.

GUTZMORE, C. (1978), 'Carnival, The State and the Black Masses in the United Kingdom', *The Black Liberator* 1, London, UK.

HAHN, C. (1986), Implementing Equality: Policies and Practices, Local Authority Housing and Racial Equality Working Party.

HALL, R. (1985), *Ask Any Woman*, Falling Wall Press, Bristol, UK.

HALL, S., CRITCHER, C., JEFFERSON, T., CLARKE, J. and ROBERTS, B. (1978), *Policing the Crisis; mugging the state and law and order*, Macmillan, UK.

HALL, S. (1988), *The Hard Road to Renewal: Thatcherism and the crisis of the left*, Verso, London, UK.

HAMBLETON, R. (1986), *Rethinking Policy Planning*, SAUS, University of Bristol, UK.

HANMER, J. and SAUNDERS, S. (1987), *Women, Violence and Crime Prevention*, University of Bradford, UK.

HENDERSON, J. and KARN, V. (1987), *Race, Class and State Housing: frequency and allocation of public housing in Britain*, Gower, UK.

HMSO (1965, 1972), *Report of the Committee on Housing in Greater London (Milner-Holland Report)*, HMSO Cmnd 2605, UK.

HMSO (1969), *Council Housing: Purposes, Procedures and Priorities (Cullingworth Report)*, Central Housing Adv Comm, HMSO.

HMSO (1975), *Report of the Select Committee on Violence in Marriage*, CMND 53311, London, UK.

HMSO (1981), *Security on Council Estates*, HMSO, UK.

HMSO (1983), *General Household Survey*, HMSO, UK.

HOLMANS, A.E. (1987), *Housing Policy in Britain: a history*, Croom Helm, UK.

HORLEY, S. (1988), *Love and Pain: a survival handbook for women*, Bedford Square Press, London, UK.

HUGHES, D. SNAITH, J. and FISHER, V. (1987), *Housing and Relationship Breakdown*, National Housing and Town Planning Council, UK.

HUNT, E.K. and SHERMAN, H.J. (1986), *Economics: an introduction to traditional and radical*, 5th Edition, Harper and Row, UK.

HYMAN, M. (1989), *Sites for Travellers*, LRHRU, UK.

IBRAHIM, A. (1978), *Family Law in Malaysia and Singapore*, Muslim Law, p.200-222.

INSTITUTE OF RACE RELATIONS (1987), *Policing Against Black People*, IRR, London, UK.

INSTITUTE OF HOUSING (1987), *The Key to Equality: the 1986 Women and Housing Survey*, Women and Housing Working Party, Institute of Housing, London.

JACKSON, P. and SMITH, S. (eds) (1981), *Social Interaction and Ethnic Segregation*, AP.

JACOBS, S. (1985), 'Race, Empire and the Welfare State: council housing and racism, *Critical Social Policy* 13, Summer 1985.

JENKINS, R. and SOLOMOS, J. (eds) (1987), *Racism and Equal Opportunity Policies in the 1980s*, Cambridge University Press, UK.

JENSON, R.H. (1978), 'Battered Women and the Law', *Victimology* 2 (3-4), pp.585-590.

JOHN, G. and HUMPHRIES, D. (1971), *Because They're Black*, Pelican.

JOHNSON, N. (1985), *Marital Violence*, RKP, UK.

JONES, C. (1978), 'The Caribbean Community in Britain', *The Black Liberator*, 1, London, UK.

JONKER, T. (1986), *Victims of Violence*, Fontana.

KAMUGISHA, S. (1986), *Violence Against Women* in P. Ellis (ed).

KANTER, H. *et al* (1987), *Sweeping Statements: writings from the Women's Liberation Movement 1981-83*, The Women's Press, UK.

KARN, V. (1969), *Property Values amongst Indians and Pakistanis in a*

Yorkshire Town, Race, Vol.X, 1969, pp.269-284.

KARN, V. (1976), *The Operation of the Housing Market in Immigrant Areas*, Final Report to SSRC (unpublished).

KARN, V. (1983), *Race and Housing in Britain: the role of the major institutions*, Heinemann.

KARN, V. and HENDERSON, J. (1984), *Race and the Allocation of Urban Resources: the case of public housing in Britain*, Urban Std.

KARN, V. and HENDERSON, J. (1987), *Race, Class and State Housing*, Gower Publishing Company, UK.

KELKAR, G. (1987), *Violence Against Women: an understanding of responsibility for their lives* in M. Davies (ed).

KOSO-THOMAS, O. (1987), *The Circumcision of Women: a strategy for eradication*, Zed, UK.

LADNER, J. (ed) (1973), *The Death of White Sociology*, Vintage Books, New York, USA.

LAMBERT, J. (1970), *Police, Crime and Race Relations*, Oxford University Press/IRR, UK.

LAMBETH, LONDON BOROUGH OF (1987), *Women in the DHPS Conference Papers*.

LAMBETH (1986), *Housing Needs Survey*.

LAMBETH (1987-88), *Housing, Police and Women's Rights Committee Reports*.

LANSLEY, S. (1979), *Housing and Public Policy*, Croom Helm, UK.

LAWRENCE, E. (1982), 'In the Abundance of Water the Fool is Thirsty: sociology and black pathology' pp.95-142 in *The Empire Strikes Back*, CCCS, Birmingham, UK.

LAWRENCE, E. and MAMA, A. (1988), 'Reproduction of Inequality in Housing', Public Lecture, Runnymede Trust, UK.

LE GRAND, J. and ROBINSON, R. (eds) (1984), *Privatisation and the Welfare State*, G. Allen and Unwin.

LEVISON, D. and ATKINS, J. (1987), *The Key to Equality: the 1986 Women and Housing Survey*, Institute of Housing, UK.

LOGAN, F. (1986), *Homelessness and Relationship Breakdown: how the law and housing policy affects women*, NCOPF, UK.

LONDON AGAINST RACISM IN HOUSING (1988), *Anti-Racism for the Private Rented Sector*, London, UK.

LONDON BOROUGH'S GRANTS COMMITTEE (LBGC) (1988), *Report of the Director, London Research Centre: estimating the level of need for family bedspaces in London*, 14 September, London, UK.

LBGC (1988), *Report of the Assistant Director, London Borough Grants*

Unit: *Women's Aid Refuges — Funding Arrangements*, 14 September, London.

LBGC (1988), *Report of the Director, London Borough Grants Unit: Women's Aid Organisations — Funding Arrangements*, 12 October, London, UK.

LONDON HOUSING UNIT (1988), *Just Homes? The equal opportunities implications of the Housing Bill*, London Housing Unit, UK.

LONDON RACE AND HOUSING RESEARCH UNIT (LRHRU) (1986), *Race and Housing: developing a research strategy for London*, LRHRU, UK.

LRHRU (1989), *Anywhere But Here: Travellers and homelessness in Camden*, Camden Travellers Support Group/LRHRU.

LRHRU (1989), *Black Women's Housing Needs*, Black Women in Housing Group/LRHRU.

LRHRU (1989), *Migrant Workers Project*, LRHRU/Kensington and Chelsea Anti-Racist Housing Action Group.

LONDON STRATEGIC POLICY UNIT (1986), *Police Responses to Domestic Violence*, Police Monitoring and Research Group Briefing No.1, LSPU, UK.

LONDON STRATEGIC POLICY UNIT (1987), *Tenancy Implications for Women of Relationship Breakdowns — A Review of Borough Practice*, LSPU, UK.

LONDON STRATEGIC POLICY UNIT (1988), *Race and Gender Monitoring of the Public Sector Housing Service*, Women's Equality Group/LSPU, London, UK.

LUTHRA, M. (1982), *Black Minorities and Housing in Ealing: comparative study of Asian, West Indian and native communities.*

MAGAIA, L. (1987), *Dumba Nenque, Run For Your Life: peasant tales of tragedy in Mozambique*, Trenton: Africa World Press, USA.

MAMA, A. (1984), 'Black Women and the British Economic Crisis', *Feminist Review*, 17, UK.

MAMA, A. (1987), 'Race and Subjectivity: a study of black women', Unpublished Ph.D Thesis, University of London.

MAMA, A. (1988), 'Race and Research Processes', *Foundation*, Summer 1989, UK.

MAMA, A. (1989), 'Black Women and Domestic Violence: race, gender and state responses', *Feminist Review* 23, UK.

MAMA, A. (1989), 'Imperialism, Patriarchy and Domestic Violence: towards an international perspective', unpublished lecture delivered at the Institute of Social Studies, The Hague, Netherlands.

MAMA, A., MARS, M. and STEVENS, P. (1986), *Breaking the Silence:*

Women's Imprisonment, Women's Equality Group/London Strategic Policy Unit.

MANUSHI (1983), 'Indian Women Speak Out Against Dowry', extracts republished in M. Davies (ed).

MARCOVITCH, A. (1976), 'Refuges for Battered Women', *Social Work Today* 7 (2), pp.34-5.

MASSELL, G.J. (1968), *Law as an Instrument of Revolutionary Change in a Traditional Milieu: the case of Soviet Central Asia.*

McNICHOLAS, A. (1986), *Going it Alone: your rights and relationship breakdown: a guide for unmarried women*, SHAC, UK.

McGUIRE, S. (1988), '"Sorry Love" — violence against women in the home and the state response', *Critical Social Policy* 23, autumn, Longman, UK.

MERCER, K. and JULIEN, I. (1988), 'Race, Sexual Politics and Masculinity: A Dossier' in R. Chapman and J. Rutherford, *Male Order: unwrapping masculinity*, Lawrence and Wishart, London, UK.

MERRETT, S. (1979), *State Housing in Britain*, RKP, UK.

MIES, M. (1986), *Patriarchy and Accumulation on a World Scale: Women in the International Division of Labour*, Zed, UK.

MILL, J.S. [1869] (1986), *The Subjection of Women*, Prometheus Books, USA.

MIND (1987), *A Place of Safety*, MIND, UK.

MULLARD, C. (1973), *Black Britain*, G. Allen and Unwin.

MULLINGS, B. (1989), *Race and Housing Investment*, London Race and Housing Research Unit, UK.

NAIROBI LAW MONTHLY (1988), *Violence Against Wives and the Law*, Nairobi, Kenya.

NINER, P. and KARN, V. (1986), *Housing Allocations: achieving racial equality — a West Midlands case study*, Runnymede, UK.

NORTHERN NIGERIAN CRIMINAL CODE, Section 55 (i) (d), Nigeria.

ORGANISATION OF ANGOLAN WOMEN (1984), *Angolan Women Building the Future*, Zed, UK.

ORGANISATION OF WOMEN OF AFRICAN AND ASIAN DESCENT (OWAAD) (1979), *Black Women in Britain Speak Out*, papers from the First National Black Women's Conference, 18 March 1979, Abeng Centre, Brixton, London, UK.

OUTWRITE WOMEN'S NEWSPAPER (-1988).

OWAAD (1979-1980), *FOWAAD!*, Newsletter of OWAAD, Issues 1-5.

OSPINA, S. (1987), *Housing Ourselves*, Hilary Shipman, London, UK.

PAHL, J. (1982), 'Police Response to Battered Women', *Journal of Social Welfare Law* 337.

PAHL, J. (ed) (1985), *Private Violence and Public Policy*, RKP, UK.

PARKER, J. and DUGMORE, K. (1976), 'Race Allocation of Public Housing: a GLC survey', *New Community*, CRE, UK.

PARKER, J. and DUGMORE, K. (1976), *Colour and the Allocation of GLC Housing*, GLC Research Report 21, UK.

PATTERSON, S. (1965), *Dark Strangers*, Penguin, UK.

PEACH, C. (1968), *West Indian Migration to Britain: A Social Geography*, Institute of Race Relations/Oxford University Press.

PEACH, C. (ed) (1975), *Urban Social Segregation*, Longman.

PHILIPS, D. (1986), *What Price Equality*, GLC, UK.

PHIZACKLEA, A. (ed) (1983), *One Way Ticket: Migration and Female Labour*, RKP, UK.

PIZZEY, E. (1979), *Scream Quietly or the Neighbours Will Hear*, Penguin Harmondsworth, UK.

PRYCE, K. (1979), *Endless Pressure: a study of West Indian lifestyles in Bristol*, Penguin, UK.

POLYTECHNIC OF SOUTH BANK (1984), *A Safe Place to Live? Safety for women on Southwark's housing estates*, Research and Development Group, London Borough of Southwark, UK.

POLICY STUDIES INSTITUTE (1985), *Ethnic Minorities in Public Housing in Islington*, Policy Studies Institute, UK.

RACE TODAY (RT) (1974), 'Bengali Squats in the East End', September issue, London, UK.

RT (1975), 'Terror in the East End', May issue, London, UK.

RT (1975), 'East End Housing Campaign', December issue, London, UK.

RT (1976), 'No Retreat from the East End', June issue, London, UK.

RT (1978), 'East End Housing Struggle', July/August, London, UK.

RAO, N. (1989), *Black Women in Housing*, Black Women and Housing Group, London, UK.

RAQUISA, T. (1987), 'Prostitution: A Philipine Experience' in M. Davies (ed).

RATCLIFFE, P. (1986), *Race and Housing in Britain: a bibliography —* 2nd edition, Centre for Research in Ethnic Relations, UK.

REASON, P. and ROWAN, J. (1981), *Human Enquiry: a sourcebook of new paradigm research*, J. Wiley and Sons, UK.

RHODES, D. and McNEILL, S. (eds) (1985), *Women Against Violence Against Women*, Onlywomen Press, London, UK.

ROACH FAMILY SUPPORT COMMITTEE (1989), *Policing in*

Hackney 1945-1986): an enquiry commissioned by RFSC, Kanci Press.

ROBERTS, H. (ed) (1981), *Doing Feminist Research*, RKP, UK.

ROSE, H. (1968), *The Housing Problem*, Heinemann, UK.

ROSE, E.J.B. et al (1969), *Colour and Citizenship: a report on British race relations*, Institute of Race Relations/Oxford University Press, UK.

ROWLAND, J. (1985), *Rape: the ultimate violation*, Pluto Press, UK.

RBKC (1981), *Census of Population — Area Profiles*, RBKC, London, UK.

ROYAL BOROUGH OF KENSINGTON AND CHELSEA (1988), *Policy Regarding Domestic Violence*, RBKC, London, UK.

RBKC Health and Housing Committee Reports (1987-1988).

RBKC Tenants Handbook, London, UK.

RBKC (1988), *Living in the Royal Borough: Housing Needs Survey*, RBKC, London, UK.

RUNNYMEDE TRUST (1975), *Race and Council Housing in London*, Runnymede Trust, UK.

RUSSELL, M. (1989), *Taking Stock: Survey into Refuge Provision in London*, Survey commissioned by Women's Equality Group/London Strategic Policy Unit.

SANGHATANA, S.S. (1983), *War Against Rape: a report from Karimnagar* in M. Davies (ed).

SCARMAN, LORD (1981), *The Brixton Disorders 10-12 April 1981*, Cmnd 8427, HMSO, UK.

SHAC (1985), *A Woman's Place: your rights and relationship breakdown — a guide for married women*, SHAC, London, UK.

SHAC (1986), *Going it alone: your rights and relationship breakdown — a guide for unmarried women*, SHAC, London, UK.

SHELTER (1987), *Briefing: The Impact on Women of National Housing Policy since 1979 and Prospects for the Future*, Shelter, London, UK.

SHEPPARD, F.H.W. (ed) (1973), *Survey of London*, Vol.XXXVII, N. Kensington, GLC, UK.

SIMPSON, A. (1981), *Stacking the Decks — A Study of Race, Inequality and Council Housing in Nottingham*, NDCRC, UK.

SKROBANEK, S (1987), 'Strategies Against Prostitution in Thailand', in M. Davies (ed).

SMART, C. (1976), *Women, Crime and Criminology: A Feminist Critique*, RKP, UK.

SMART, B. and SMART, C. (1978), *Women, Sexuality and Social Control*, RKP, London, UK.

SMITH, D. (1977), *Racial Disadvantage in Britain*, Penguin,

336

Harmondsworth, UK.

SMITH, S.J. and MERCER, J. (1987), *New Perspectives on Race and Housing in Britain — Studies in Housing 2*, Centre for Housing Research.

SMITH, D. and WHALLEY, A. (1975), *Racial Minorities and Public Housing*, PEP, UK.

SONDHI, R. (1987), *Divided Families: British immigration control in the Indian subcontinent*, Runnymede Trust, London, UK.

STAPLES, R. (1982), *Black Masculinity: the black male's role in American society*, Black Scholar Press, USA.

STEADY, F.C. (ed) (1981), *The Black Women Cross-Culturally*, Schenkman, Cambridge, Massachusetts, USA.

STEDMAN-JONES, G. (1971), *Outcast London: a study in the relationship between classes in Victorian society*, Clarendon Press.

STONE, E. (ed) (1981), *Women and the Cuban Revolution*, Pathfinder, New York, USA.

THIAM, A. (1986), *Black Sisters Speak Out — Feminism and Oppression in Black Africa*, Pluto Press, UK.

TINKLER, A. and LITTLEWOOD, J. (1981), *Families in Flats*, HMSO, UK.

UNGERSON, I. (ed) (1985), *Women and Social Policy: a reader*, Macmillan.

UNICEF (1989), *Children in the Frontline States*, UNICEF, UK.

UNITED NATIONS (1987), *Report of the Expert Group Meeting on Violence in the Family with Special Emphasis on Women*.

URDANG, S. (1979), 'Fighting Two Colonialisms: Women in Guinea-Bissau', Monthly Review Press (p.2-9).

VISRAM, R. (1986), *Ayahs, Lascars and Princes*, Pluto, UK.

WAMALWA, B.N. (1987), 'Violence Against Wives and the Law in Kenya', paper presented at the Regional Meeting Africa and the Middle East on Law and Shelter by the International Federation of Women Lawyers, Nairobi, Kenya.

WATES, N. (1976), *The Battle for Tolmers Square*, RKP, UK.

WATSON, S. (1987), 'Ideas of the Family in the Development of Housing Forms', in M. Loney *et al* (eds), *The State or the Market?*, Sage, UK.

WATSON, S. and AUSTERBERRY, H. (1986), *Housing and Homelessness — A Feminist Perspective*, RKP, UK.

WELSH WOMEN'S AID (1986), *The Answer is Maybe . . . And That's Final!*, Welsh Women's Aid, Incentive House, Adam Street, Cardiff.

WILSON, E. (1983), *What's To Be Done About Violence Against Women? Crisis in the Eighties*, Penguin, UK.

WITHERSPOON, S. (1985), *A Woman's Place: your rights and relationship breakdown: a guide for married women*, SHAC, UK.

WOMEN IN NIGERIA (1985), *The WIN Document— Conditions of Women in Nigeria and Policy Recommendations to 2000AD*, WIN, PO Box 253, Samaru, Zaria, Nigeria.

WOMEN IN NIGERIA (1985), *Women in Nigeria Today*, Zed, UK.

WOMEN'S AID FEDERATION ENGLAND (1988), *You Can't Beat A Woman: Women and Children in Refuges*, WAFE, PO Box 391, Bristol, UK.

WOMEN'S INFORMATION CENTRE (1987), 'Shelter for Battered Women in Thailand' in M. Davies (ed).

WOMEN'S CO-ORDINATION UNIT (1986), *Domestic Violence — you don't have to put up with it.*

WOMEN'S NATIONAL COMMISSION (1984), *Violence Against Women: Report of an ad hoc Working Group*, Cabinet Office, London, UK.

YLLO, K. and BOGRAD, M. (1988), *Feminist Perspective on Wife Abuse*, Sage.

YOUNG, J.D. (1976), 'Wife-Beating in Britain 1850-1914: a socio-historical analysis', Paper presented to the American Sociological Association Convention, NY City, USA.

ZIMBABWE WOMEN'S ACTION GROUP with GAIDZWANA, R. (1987), 'Operation Clean-Up' in M. Davies (ed).

ZARETSKY, E. (1976), *Capitalism, the Family and Personal Life*, Pluto Press, UK.

Index

The abbreviations LBL for London Borough of Lambeth, and RBKC for Royal Borough of Kensington and Chelsea, are used throughout this index.

treatment in case of relationship breakdown, RBKC 226
with violent fathers 94, 97, 98-9
in violent situations 170
China, women in 17
Chinese Information and Advice Centre (CIAC) 263, 309
Chinese interviewees 40
Chinese refuge 281
Chinese women 17
in refuges 281, 293
Chiswick Family Rescue 233, 276, 296 (n.1)
Christian religion and marriage 148-9
Circumcision, female 9-10, 300-1
see also Mutilation
Citizen's Advice Bureaux, RBKC 264
Civil law 146-7
and black women 158-62
case studies 160-1
Class *see* Social class
Closed communities in Britain 24
Co-wives *see* Polygamy
Cochrane, Kelso 209
Cohabitation, influence on rights 122, 232
and the law 142, 146
and tenancy 125, 202
and violence 41
Cohabitations of convenience 118
Colonialism, and violence 20-1, 299-300
and women 23
Commission for Philipino Migrant Workers (CPMW) 263, 309
Common lodging houses 188
Commonwealth, complex law situation 141-4, 145, 146
Commonwealth Immigrants Act 1961 195
Communist states *see* Socialist states
Community, recommendations relating to 321
Community organising, for black woman abuse 308-10
Community organisations 33, 261-8
Community policing 240, 241

Community relations, black/police 167-8, 214
Community Relations Advisor's Office 264
Computer database for research data 34, 35
Conferences for women, LBL 249
Conjugal rights 152, 153, 157-8
Consumer group, black women as 136 (n.1)
Controls over women, India 5-6
see also Mutilation; Patriarchy
Corporatisation 135
Council housing *see* Housing, Public
Counselling, needed for couples 309-10
on rape 158
see also Legal counselling
Court battles, RBKC 215-17
Crimes, and Victim Support, RBKC 266
Crimes Against Women Officer 246, 249
Criminal law 144-6, 154-8
Criminal Law Revision Committee 157
Criminal prosecutions 143
Criminals, female 166
Cross-referral between agencies 91-2, 134
Cruelty, types of 40-1
Cuban women 14, 17-18
Cullingworth Committee 1969 195
Cultural background, and research 30
Cultural differences, and race 291-3
Cultural oppression 112-14, 302
Culture: aspect of violence 4
use by males 112
Custody 161
Customary law 141, 142

Decade for women 1975-85, UN 3, 16, 143
Delhi 7
Department of the Environment working party 204
Deportation, of black men 116
British policy 177-9

Federation of Black Housing
Organisations 308
Federation of Cuban Women (FMC)
18
Female circumcision 9-10, 300-1
Female criminals 166
Feminism *see also* Woman's liberation
Feminist praxis, accounting for social
divisions 4, 272-3
Feminist theory 3-5
Fertility control, India 6
Filipina *see* Philipinas
Force Order 1987 165, 183, 303-4, 305
Foucault, Michel 149
FOWAAD 36 (n.2), 45, 262
Free market ethos 136 (n.1)
see also Thatcherite Britain
Freedom Party 263
Funding, Citizens' Advice Bureaux
264
victim support 266
WAFE 271-2
women's centres 267
Funding required, for refuges 310,
311
by voluntary organisations 307
for WAFE 310

Gay relationships 231
Gender, and housing policy 116,
185-96, 214-15
and the law 166
General practitioners, unhelpfulness
172
Genital mutilation *see* Circumcision,
female; Mutilation, genital
Genocide in Africa 12
Ghanaians, treatment of 30
Gifford enquiry 168
Gishiri cutting, Nigeria 10
Government, housing policy criticised
247
recommendations to 317-19
Governments in Africa tolerant of
abuse 13
Grassroots Bookshop 263
Greater London Council, abolition
262, 310

survey 1983 202
Greater London Council Women's
Committee 166
Greater London Mobility Scheme
(GLMS) 219
Greenwich refuge 281
Groce, Mrs Cherry 166, 169, 240-1
Guardianship of Minors Act 1971 158
Guinea-Bissau, women's
organisations 13

Hammel, Mrs 215-216, 235 (n.13)
Harassment, clauses 228-9
domestic violence as 228
in RBKC 207, 208, 209, 216
see also Police harassment; Sexual
harassment
Haringey London Borough 201
Haringey refuge 291
Harris, Betty, quoted 150
Headstart 263
Health and welfare services, needed
for black people 22, 23
Higgs, Mary 191-2
Historical aspects of wife abuse 147-52
Home Office, and deportation 304
funding for Victim Support 266
Homeless, classes in danger 302
in RKBC 208
women treated as intentionally
such 225
Homeless Persons Act 122, 202
Homeless Persons Units (HPU) 103,
105, 113
LBL 250, 251-2
RBKC 219, 220, 222, 223-5, 227,
230, 233, 265
Homelessness, of black men 118-19
extent in London 306
Lambeth Borough 238-40, 243
male and female 48
priorities in RBKC 217
Homosexual prostitution 8
Hoogsraten, Baron 208
Horn of Africa, mutilation in 9
Hostels 128, 129, 131
for black women, LBL 266
for black people in LBL 240

343

Privacy of family, upheld 152
Private prosecutions, police
recommendation 155
Private rented sector housing, LBL
241
RBKC 208, 212-13
Private sector housing, black women
in 132-4
Professionalism of black people in
housing departments 197
Professionals, use of their material
29-30
Professionals, black, condoning
violence 87
Prosecution 144
compulsion on woman to
prosecute 183
Prostitution, African 11, 23
and colonialism 20
Cuban 18
and housing 189-90
in Philippines 8
in Thailand 7-8
Protection, lack of 170-2
Protestantism and women 148-9
Provocation by wife 153
Public funds clause in immigration
status 114-15
Public services, coerciveness 134-5
Punishment 147-50
Purdah 23

Questionnaires 34

Race, aspect of violence 4
conditions in Britain 21
and public housing 185-96
WAFE policies 278-80
and women's movement 272-5
Race and ethnicity, ethnic origins,
table 43
birthplace table 44
of interviewees 43-4
Race relations, Britain 5
Kenya 11
LBL 238-41
and research 30, 31
RBKC 208-35

Race Relations Acts 23, 154, 195
Race Today Collective 240
Race Unit, Housing Department,
LBL 246
Rachmanism 194, 208, 209, 234 (n.2)
Racial discrimination in housing 105-
6
Racial origin, and use of social
workers 93, 100
Racial violence 170-1
Racism, in Britain, institutionalized
21, 301
as cause of black violence to
women 174
and culture 291-2
and housing policy 105-6, 129,
195-6, 247-8
in LBL 238-9, 247-8, 251
of police etc 163, 165
in refuge residents 286-90, 294-5
in refuge workers 284-6
in refuges generally 282-93
in RBKC 207, 209
between wars 193-4
in women's movement 311
see also Anti-racism
Rape, in Africa 11
in the Americas 14
in marriage 157-8
Rape, mass 6
Rastafarians 85
Ratecapping 310
Reception centres 129
Referral from organisations to refuges
262-3, 308
Reform Act 1832 150
Refugees to Britain 24
Refuge movement 310-11
Refuges 30, 31, 269-72, 280-97
aid in research 32, 33
Asian only 253, 266, 293
bed spaces in London 101
funding of black refuges 311
and housing departments 102-3,
219, 252, 253-4
ignorance of 102
importance 261
increase in numbers 200-1

Sharia law, marriages under 142
Sheltered accommodation *see* Refuges
Short stay accommodation *see*
  Hostels; Temporary
  accommodation
Sierra Leone, mutilation in 10
Singapore militancy 7
Single mothers 199
Single-parent families 245-6, 306
Single Parents project 267
Single women, special problems of
  rehousing 104
  and WAFE 278
  without dependants, LBL 249-50
'Sink' estates 199
Sistren 15
Slavery, abolition 150
Slaves, women, Americas 14
Slums 188, 194, 195
  LBL 238-9
  RBKC 208-9
Social class, Caribbean 15-16
  and violence 3, 46
  and woman's liberation 272-4
Social policy research 27
Social problems and violence against
  women 20-1
Social Security Act 310
Social services, contact of sample,
  table 94
  relations with housing
    departments 94-7
  and research 30
  role 93-100
Social workers, interviews, research
  method 31
  lack of powers 93
Socialism and feminism 272-3
Socialist states and women 17-18
South Africa, abuse 12-13
  police 145
  violence 300
South East Asians, militancy 7
  and refuges 293
  domestic violence 43
South London Women's Centre 267
Southall Black Sisters 84, 268 (n.1)

Southall Black Women's Centre 45,
  308
Southall Monitoring Group 167
Southwark London Borough 104, 201
Southwark ASHA 281
Southwark Women's Aid 276
Soviet Union, women in 17
Special Needs Officer, RBKC 216
Squatting, blacks in Lambeth 240
Statistical Society 188
Status, as citizens 44
  immigrants 114, 115, 177-9
Statutory agencies, black women's
  experience of 91-134
  black women in private sector
    132-4
  black women in temporary
    accommodation 128-32
  corporatisation and coercion 91-
    100
  exploiting isolation 114-16
  experience of housing debts 100-12
  impact of tenancy status 116-27
  power in relationships 112-14
Submissiveness, expected by males
  47, 114
  Filipinas 8
  India etc 7
  Linked to protection 6
Subordination *see* Control
Subservience *see* Submissiveness
Sudan, mutilation in 9
Supplementary benefit, LBL 244
Support, family, lack of 85-6
Survey of black women and
  institutions 30
Suttee 5

Temporary accommodation 103, 128-
  32
  in LBL 250, 253
  in RBKC 220-1, 224, 225, 233
  statistical indicators 128
  see also Hostels
Tenancies, given up by women,
  RBKC 225
Tenancy status 117-27
  changes 119

War in Africa 18
Wardens of hostels 129
Welfare state 305-6
 see also Statutory agencies
West Indian women 14-16
Westway Housing Advice Centre 208
White men, violence to black women
 21
 violent to white women 25
White women, in refuges 286-9
 subject to violence 25
Wife battering 11, 15, 41
Williams, Mrs Linda 169
Witch hunts in Europe 7
Wives, history 147-52
 sale of 150
Wollstonecraft, Mary 149
Woman abuse, in Britain 19-25
 current British law 152-3
 and the law 141-64
 in London 39-89
 by police 166
 a private matter 84
 and temporary accommodation
  RBKC 221-2
 see also Violence to women
Womanpower 274
Women, as heads of families 306
 see also Single-parent families
 housing policy: gender
  implications 185-6
 and public housing 197-201
 inferiority alleged 147-52
 as labourers in Americas 14
 mutilating women 10
 non-collaboration 180-1
 research on 27-8
 as strong castrating figures 88
 supporting women 278-9
 violent to women 4
 after World War I 193
Women and Housing Forum 203
Women at Risk Group, LBL 237,
 246, 249, 250, 252, 254-5, 307
Women criminals 166
Women in Nigeria (WIN) 11
Women in the Directorate of Housing

and Property Services Conference
 1987 (DHPS) 249-50
Women's Aid, case study 98
 groups 276-8
 increase in referrals 101
 network, sources for interviewees
  40
 and RBKC 219, 265, 307
Women's Aid Federation England
 (WAFE) 269, 271, 272, 294,310,
 311
 organisation of 275-8
 and race 278-80, 290, 291, 294-5,
  296
 structure 276-8
Women's centres 267
Women's Equality Group, London
 Strategic Policy Unit 202, 281
Women's hostels see Hostels
Women's Information Centre (WIC),
 Thailand 7-8
Women's Liberation movement 199-
 201
 and black women 272-5
 socialist countries 272-5
 and WAFE 278
Women's movement, growth 269-72
 and race 272-5
 response 269-97
Women's organisations, Jamaica 15
 and research 33
 role 92-3
 Trinidad 15
Women's refuges see Refuges
Women's Unit, LBL Housing
 Department 246
Workhouses 190
World Conference, Nairobi 1985 16

Yan Daukar Amariya 11

Zimbabwe, abuse in 12

Compiled by J.D. Lee.

352